Making Room For You

Mary Ann Clarke

Copyright © 2017, 2019 by: Mary Ann F Clarke Scott

KDP Print ISBN 978-1-988743-29-5

Other Print ISBN 978-1-988743-07-3

eBook ISBN 978-1-988743-08-0

This book was previously published under the title Disruption by Design by M. A. Clarke Scott

ALL RIGHTS RESERVED. No part of this publication may be reproduced, distributed, or transmitted in any form or by any means, including photocopying, recording, or other electronic or mechanical methods, without the prior permission of the publisher.

This is a work of fiction. Any resemblance of characters to actual persons, living or dead, is purely coincidental. MaryAnn Clarke Scott holds exclusive rights to this work. Unauthorized duplication is prohibited.

Cover design: Brian Foot

Want to read the First Book in the Having it All Series?
Buy on Amazon B082HMCLDM

Want to connect with me?
maryann (at) maryannclarkescott.com
maryannclarkescott (dot) com

If you enjoy reading this book, please rate it and leave a review on Amazon or wherever you purchased the book. Your opinion can make or break an author's success, and it means the world to me.

MAKING ROOM FOR YOU

HAVING IT ALL: BOOK 2

MARYANN CLARKE

Praise for Making Room For You

"These two people are brought together and it is like lightening striking when they meet as the chemistry between them is powerful. Will Alexa change her mind about love? To find out you are going to need to purchase a copy of this beautifully written book... DEFINITELY RECOMMENDED."
Amazon & Goodreads reviewer

"I loved this book!! My absolute favourite part was definitely the ending of the story. I cannot recommend this book more! If I could give it more than five stars I would."
Amazon reviewer

"A really well written, enjoyable book with an interesting story and lovely characters, Bruce & Alexa, who have great chemistry and interaction that pulls you in and keeps you engrossed...I would recommend it to anyone."
Amazon reviewer

To all the women in Architecture, whose passion and commitment to form and function outweigh all the obstacles in their path. May you have all that you need, including a champion to lift you higher.

CHAPTER 1

Alexa's eyes danced lovingly over the harmonious lines of the Arts Centre in the digital rendering hanging on Krystof's office wall. Her heart swelled with pride at its elegance and beauty, and her pulse raced in anticipation of Krys's imminent arrival. The committee simply had to select it, and then, if all went well, she'd be appointed the project architect to see her own design through to realization.

"It's brilliant. Your best work. You know it'll win," Peter said from over her shoulder.

She turned to offer her friend a grateful smile. The buzz *had* been encouraging. Today the Coal Harbour Civic Society would award the new Albion and Beatrice Rose Arts Centre contract. She was convinced Vision Architecture would win, and at last she would get to be project architect on the development of her deepest desire. Her castle-in-the-air would become a genuine, bricks-and-mortar monument in the city. And she would be a star. "Let's hope I actually get the chance to see it through, Pete." Then she'd finally get recognition for her talent and hard work. When others saw and acknowledged her work, then she'd know she'd achieved success. And the only way she knew how to do that was with her name: Alexa Jenner.

"Don't fret, honey. Krys has to give you the job. It's your concept. He's knows you're the only one who can execute it properly."

"Thanks, Pete," Alexa whispered, and gave him a quick hug. "You're a contender too, you know."

"Hardly. But I'll be happy to work on it with you."

"You two make me sick." Nathan's superior lazy voice cut in as he sauntered in through the office door late for work, even today, and as unconcerned as ever. "Not only is that patently untrue, but the odds are Krystof will assign me as project architect. You know he wants to. The Roses know me, after all."

Tension fluttered behind her ribs. Alexa knew that was true, at least technically. It shouldn't matter. There was no place for nepotism with this project.

"That's not how you get ahead in this business, Nathan. You've got three years less work experience than Alexa. You couldn't even manage the Arts Centre if it fell on you."

"We'll see," Nathan replied with a smirk and swivelled, plopping down into a chair. His usual chair, the one he always seemed to be in when he and Krystof were joking around, instead of at his desk working like everyone else.

Arrogant prick, Pete mouthed to her behind Nathan's back. His eyes fluttered and rolled to the ceiling in characteristically melodramatic fashion and Alexa suppressed a smile.

"First we have to win the contract, people," Alexa said.

The three colleagues and rivals all turned toward the door as a ripple of awareness fluttered through the office like a Pacific Northwest gust through the downtown core, telegraphing the boss's arrival. Outside in the studio, people tensed, sat up, inhaled. Alexa's pulse skipped a beat.

She had been an architect long enough to know that the glamorous image of architecture portrayed in books and movies was only partly true. It was true enough for a very small number of lucky individuals. The chosen few. Like Krystof Konstantin. In this business, a lot of talented people toiled away in obscurity their entire careers. That wasn't enough for her. Architecture was a business in which stardom was determined as much by politics, charisma, connections. And commitment. She didn't have the benefit of Nathan's connections. People who didn't know her well thought she was hard, driven, even humourless. That stung. They didn't understand her at all. She'd sacrificed too much to give up now. She had a plan. This high profile project was an important step. A recognizable name. One day soon, she'd own her own studio with the freedom and autonomy that brought. She could feel adrenalin shudder through her body in anticipation.

"Peter," Krystof said as he entered in his quiet, rasping tenor with an exotic hint of his native Polish accent. "Alexa. Nate. Sit down, please."

She looked up as he spoke her name, Her face impassive hiding her stuttering heartbeat. She had to let things unfold naturally.

No one knew Krystof had as good as promised her this role. No one knew of their understanding. No one, not even Peter, knew of their relationship.

They sat in a row facing his desk. Krystof stood behind it, his back to them, staring out over the city view. His neatly manicured, elegant hands were clasped loosely at his back forming a 'V', his sapphire ring gleaming in the sunlight. Alexa could picture them sketching, inspired fluid lines flowing from the nib of his fountain pen. Krys's perfectly groomed salt-and-pepper hair gleamed, and she dropped her eyes. She looked at the others instead of staring at Krystof's trim body in his slim custom Gucci suit. It wouldn't do to get caught ogling the boss's ass, tight as it was. She sighed, feeling a tingle of heat flood through her, not sure if it was the excitement of his pending announcement that caused her flux, or the remembrance of his expert kisses and embraces.

A part of her mind shied away from the truth of her affair with Krystof, but she knew in her heart that if she got this project, it would be because of hard work, sacrifice and merit, not because she also happened to have a relationship with the boss. That was another thing altogether. No one worked harder or was more committed than she was. And she had talent too. Plenty of it.

Peter shifted his weight from one side to the other, uncrossing and crossing his legs. Nathan leaned back, stroking his pretentious little moustache, unable to hide his eagerness, despite his entitlement and expectation of success. He hardly needed to shave at all, but that didn't stop him from pretending to be mister haute couture, with his slicked back hair and trendy almost-beard.

Alexa tried to stay calm, but her nervous energy couldn't be contained, either. Her own foot jiggled uncontrollably.

Krystof turned and braced his manicured fingers on the polished hardwood desktop, immaculate and clear of clutter as usual, and leaned forward slightly, his graphic Dior tie swinging out gently like a clock's pendulum. Tic-toc. She glanced at his lean handsome face at the exact moment his lips parted in teasing grin.

She recognized a predatory gleam of amusement and sexual energy in his pale silvery eyes. He loved this opportunity to perform, to hold an audience in his grip. To say he was vain was an understatement, but he was awfully good to look at.

They had both long ago mastered their emotions and their body language in the office. His family, her career, both their reputations depended upon discretion. Office romances were problematic, that much they acknowledged.

Finally he spoke, his voice as seductive as a wisp of opium smoke, slipping across one's senses. Hypnotic. No wonder he was such a successful architect. That, and being brilliant.

"I want to commend all of you on your very hard work on this proposal." He sat down, spine straight and clasped his fingers in front of his chest. "Also, I wish to congratulate you on a well done job. You have reason to be proud, especially Jenner for her brilliant concept, as we know. I have good news." He flashed his best Hollywood smile as he looked at each of them in turn, Alexa lastly and very briefly. "We have been awarded the contract for the new Rose Centre for the Arts."

She followed suit when Peter and Nathan shot their fists into the air with hoots and shouts of triumph. News travelled quickly through the thin office partitions. As their colleagues interpreted the news of their collective success from their own cheer, the walls muffled a thundering reply of shouts and applause.

Krystof smiled indulgently and continued. "This is a big one, even for a firm the size of Vision. At least two of you will continue working on this project to completion."

Alexa sensed rather than saw Pete and Nathan nod, each holding his breath.

"Unfortunately, I can name only one of you as Project Architect. But, as you know, I value each of you the same, and it will be a difficult…" He waved a expressive hand through the air, "…and somewhat arbitrary decision. You are each worthy and capable."

Silence. That wasn't true and they all knew it. Alexa caught a smug expression on Nathan's face from the corner of her eye. He was so sure of himself, but he would be sadly disappointed. It would feel good to wipe that cocky look off his face.

"But!" Krystof's white smile was broad and sunny. "We will not think of that today. I will decide in next week. Today is a day of celebration for all."

So. No decision today. They let out their held breaths as one, and began to rise. She wouldn't mind facing down the envious stares of her peers when she was chosen. At least Pete would congratulate her, and mean it. But from Nathan, she dreaded the suppressed animosity. He was such an ass.

She turned to Peter, who embraced her. "Congratulations, Alexa. You did it."

She had. "We did this together," she said, leaning into him with a satisfied grin.

"Oh please. Are you girls done hugging so we can get back to work?" Nathan opened the door and stepped out murmuring, "Who do you think you are Jenner, a star-chitect?"

Ever loyal, Peter elbowed past him, head shaking, and returned to his desk without acknowledging Nathan's snark.

"She's got some serious design chops, Nate, and you know it," Krystof said. "You could learn a thing or two from Alexa if you got out of your own way, boy." At Nathan's petulant look, Krystof sent him a meaningful glance.

"Go to work. Try to get something done, and later we'll all have a drink together."

Alexa lagged, affecting indifference, but moved towards the door without looking back.

"Jenner. Just a moment. May I have a word with you?"

She stopped and turned, feigning mild surprise. "Sure, Krystof. I was going to ask you about that change order on the Surrey research lab, anyway."

"Yes, about that... Close the door, please."

She did.

His hands gripped her hips silently from behind, and pulled her into the hard ridge of his groin, his face nuzzling her shoulder, his hot breath on her hair. She turned in his arms, and he pulled her close so she could inhale the scent of his warm body and expensive cologne. More hot flashes.

"Oh, Krys. I'm so happy. This is a... such a coup for us." She kept her voice low, just above a murmur, despite wanting to squeal.

Between clenched teeth, on his breath, he whispered, "This is your triumph. Your vision and your energy, Jenner. You're the reason we won this job." He squeezed her butt and pulled her more tightly against his erection, the rasp of his face against her neck.

She stifled the urge to make mewling, falsely humble denials. It *was* her and she knew it. That proposal and those presentations contained a piece of her soul. "Why are you stalling with the assignment?"

"I want everyone to be able to celebrate the win before having to let anyone down with mundane project management decisions. The whole team worked on it together. I don't want any sophomoric jealousy to spoil the day."

Alexa conceded, he had a point. That was one of the reasons he was such a good leader. He really understood people.

"*And* I want to have a private celebration with *you*, my dear," he whispered, his voice hoarse with need as his mouth closed in on hers. "Give me that sexy mouth of yours." He covered her mouth with his own, his tongue probing urgently, possessively, sending a coil of heat spiralling through her core. But this was not the time or place.

"Easy, Krys, you'll wrinkle my shirt. Not in the office." What was up with him? He was usually more discrete. She squirmed and pushed gently at his chest as he resisted, then stepped away, whispering, "I want it settled so we can start work."

He straightened up, stepped back with a frustrated sigh. Then he flashed her a charming leer. "You're so sexy when you're working. Your brain makes me hard as a rock. I love you bossy. It makes me want to distract you."

She dipped her head and smiled up at him. "If you do I'll make you very sorry, in more ways than one." He could tease, but she wouldn't be distracted. She'd work harder than ever to convince him to give her this project.

He laughed. "I can't wait. When can we meet?" His silver eyes darkened under the square shelf of his brow.

She shrugged. "That depends on you."

A shadow passed across his eyes and he turned back to his desk. "It's true. Biljiana wants me around to help with the kid."

"What's he doing now?"

"Jaroslaw's fifteenth birthday is this weekend. I have to be there." His voice was soft, apologetic. "But tonight?"

She nodded. She was glad he made himself available for his son, even though he always complained about spending time with his ex-wife. "I'll see you later." She shrugged, opening the door. Not a proper date. They could perhaps slip away from the work crowd for a brief interlude.

Krystof's voice rose and carried out the door with her. "Don't be afraid to put your foot down, Jenner." His smile patronized as he followed her to the door, standing there. "You need to be tough with these guys or they'll push you around." For appearances sake, he always gave her a gentle rebuke.

It was kind of ridiculous, given her reputation at construction sites. She shook her head, smiling a little at the ruse. As if she'd ever had trouble dealing with contractors. They shook in their steel-toed workboots when they saw her coming, all five foot feisty two of her. Krystof liked to play off her petite size, coaching her to be tougher. But he knew exactly how tough she could be, on the job and after hours. Tough was how he liked her.

When she got back to her desk, the message light was blinking. She picked up the receiver and pushed the button.

"*Alex! It's me.*"

Kate! And she sounded frantic.

"*Markus and I are on our way downtown. Meet us at the food fair in the mall for lunch. I have to tell you something important!*"

What could be so urgent?

The morning sun refracted into a startling starburst through the dark branches of the fir and hemlock trees that capped the ridge of Eagle Point to the east. The sun was still too low to shine its weak light on his *Belle-Etoile*, docked under the morning shadow of the ridge.

Bruce Koczynski stopped on the tarmac, mopping the water that dripped from his freshly washed hair onto his brow and bare shoulders. The cool sea air lifted moisture from his bare skin, tingling, raising goose bumps. He gazed across the forest of masts swaying gently at their moorings, and his soul sung. He gazed at the glittering jewels of bright white light dancing on the surface of the rippled water, and his heart soared like the seagulls drifting overhead. He gazed at his beloved sailboat, his freedom, his home. At least for now.

He would never tire of this view.

Tien and Juan could keep their fancy corporate offices with corner views of sprawling parking lots in Silicon Valley. Bruce missed his friends and ex-business partners, of course, but he wouldn't miss the amorphous years of back-breaking, eye-crossing drudgery cooped up in a stuffy, windowless room. He wouldn't miss breathing the stale off-gases of yesterday's pizza, Red Bull and beer. He wouldn't miss the accumulated body odours of a bunch of overgrown adolescents who never went home to bathe.

And he didn't need any more money, thank you very much. He had his millions and now he was living the life of his choosing. A life free of responsibilities and encumbrances.

No, he would never tire of this view. A grumbling voice drew his attention from the water.

"Goddam kids! Why don't you carry your own shit?"

Bruce turned toward the exasperated exclamation, his neck tensing in reflex at the echo of his bullying father's strident voice. A man about his own age wrestled with a wheelbarrow filled to the gunwales with gear, half of it tumbling onto the pavement as he struggled to open the security gate leading down to the dock.

Bruce loped forward. "Hey man. Let me give you a hand." He leaned on the gate, holding it open with his back, the cold steel grid pressing into his bare skin. While the guy wrestled with a heavy, lopsided duffle bag that threatened to topple to the ground, Bruce bent and retrieved a few of the objects that had already fallen, including a grimy threadbare stuffed cat with a missing ear.

A family man. Bruce gut twisted. He may be Bruce's age, but he carried himself like an old man, browbeaten. Broken. Almost the way Bruce had felt at the end, before they'd sold the company. All worn out.

"Thanks," he said as Bruce straightened up, handing him his stray items. His smile was ready enough, but Bruce saw the lines of exhaustion and stress around his eyes.

Bruce grinned. "No problem. Take it easy, dude."

The guy trundled his load down the ramp, lurching with the effort. Despite the early hour, his blue t-shirt was darkened with patches of sweat.

Bruce followed him down the dock as he approached a forty-two foot Catalina with the name *Sea-Renity* painted on her hull– that was so obviously *not* the case. She was really more of a floating RV than a serious sailing vessel, and the guy wouldn't be finding any serenity there. The deck was crowded with small bodies, water toys, colourful bags, plastic crates. It was a miracle the tub was still afloat under all that family crap.

He shook his head. Bruce preferred his Spartan subsistence aboard his thirty-seven foot racing X-yacht. *Belle Etoile.* His one true love.

"Dad-deee!" shrieked a tiny voice as a small red-haired girl hurled herself at her father, nearly toppling him off the dock into the chuck.

"Neil? Did you unload the cooler?" murmured a distracted woman, her head popping up through the hatch, pokes of auburn hair straying from its long faded braid, a small infant strapped to her torso like koala to a tree. "I've got to get that stuff put away before it gets warm. And Cicely needs her milk." The wife's head swivelled toward Bruce as he sauntered past, a wistful admiration in her eyes. The harried mother yearning for escape. The dad looked desperate.

"Gimme a goddam chance, Sarah," he muttered under his breath.

Bruce's throat threatened to close up, and he forced air through his nostrils, pushing the sensation away. Not exactly a picture of marital bliss, as if there were such a thing.

He tossed Sarah a sexy wink and a charming smile. Let her believe she was attractive and desirable. Her jaw dropped, she blinked, and then she lit up with a bright, bashful smile. He recognized the girl under the burden. It was always nice to be noticed and admired by the ladies, even if they were overwrought mamas.

"Neil? Did you hear me?"

A beleaguered sigh issued from the guy as he parked the wheelbarrow and unloaded it onto the deck of the boat. "No-oo. Not yet."

"Aayeea Mateeeeee!" An older, freckled boy leaped from the foredeck into the cockpit and climbed up onto the gunwale again, swinging on the lifeline. "Can I drive, Dad? Can I?"

"Get down off of there."

"But Daaaad. You promised!"

"Not now." Neil stepped over the gunwale and, unexpectedly, leaned in to kiss his beleaguered but now smiling wife. With a broad grin, he cast his gaze at the colourful disorder around him. "Ready, gang?"

Poor bugger. No one thinking clearly about their future could possibly want a wife and three kids. No privacy. No peace. No solitude. It was exactly the chaotic mix of mayhem and misery he remembered from his own childhood. Minus the mother. Bruce ignored the tightness in his chest and walked on, paying no heed to the cheer that rose up from Neil's menagerie.

Bruce laughed off the family drama and carried on down the dock.

Nothing could disturb his sense of peace and contentment on this most perfect of days.

His friend Simon, with two kids already, was an intelligent guy. Bruce'd always looked up to him, envied him even. Ever since college, Simon seemed to have the edge. He was the one who was better at everything, the first to do everything, including getting married and having a family. But that went pretty sour the first time around, and Simon had a rough go of it for a while, raising Maddie on his own. Which only proved that having a family was a huge mistake. You couldn't expect both parents to stick around for the duration. And if you couldn't be there for your kids when they needed you, you shouldn't have them at all.

He was glad Simon was now married to Kate, though. What a transformation. Finally he could be happy with someone who loved him and appreciated him. He deserved that more than anyone. Bruce guessed it was to be expected that they would have kids together.

But, as much as he admired his friend, Bruce preferred his peaceful solitude. He had it good. After dodging decisions and shirking responsibilities since he'd sold the software company last year, Bruce finally had it all figured out. He'd bought his beautiful sailboat, *Belle Etoile*. He'd found the perfect little investment property to renovate. And he was going to have the summer of his dreams.

He was living an uncomplicated bachelor's life aboard the boat, and would turn that tumbledown shack into a sexy bachelor pad and a tidy profit. It would be fun. Excellent fun.

He'd lost his direction the past few years, working too hard and playing too hard, and then woke up one day and realized he wasn't having fun and he didn't much like himself, either. Selling the company was part one. Deciding to buy the house and work on it gave him something to focus on, a project with tasks and a goal, something to add structure and discipline to his new life as well as make him feel productive. He was counting on it to pull himself out of the hole he'd dug himself into.

It was easy to make money when you had money. And he was looking forward to doing much of the work himself. Despite his father's opinion of him, he wasn't a soft, klutzy computer geek that didn't know one end of a hammer from the other. After growing up the underdog and perpetual novice in a family of tradesmen and handymen, Bruce was anxious to put his renovation skills to the test. He'd always enjoyed working with his hands, but his craftsman's approach had never met with anything but criticism and scorn. For once in his life, *he'd* be in charge of a job and would do it his way, testing and honing his skills as he went. And if that didn't go well, he had the money to hire the help he needed.

Movement up ahead caught his eye. The old guy was up and about, sitting in his fishing boat three bays over, sorting and untangling his gear. It stupefied Bruce how much time the old guy could spend mucking with his fishing gear. But then, unlike family-dude Neil, he had plenty of time on his hands. Just like Bruce, he was alone. Peaceful and alone.

Bruce raised a hand in salute, and…what was his name? Oh, right, Jørgen. From Norway. Jørgen waved back with a nod of his speckled balding pate. He was a nice guy.

Jorgen's melodic voice rose up over the sounds of rigging pinging in the breeze. "Do you still want to go out fishing with me, son?"

"Sure do, Jørgen," Bruce replied. "When?"

Jørgen glanced up at the sky. "Tomorrow."

"You bet." Bruce smiled and dropped down into his own cockpit, ducking into the cabin. It was roomy for one. What did a guy need, after all, besides a sleeping bag, a bit of granola and some beer, and a good book for the evenings? He missed having a television, since his was in storage, but there was always somewhere you could go to catch a game and a little company.

It would be great when he finally moved into his new place, though, even if it would be for only a year. Meantime, he would have a little fun with his summer project.

His cell phone rang, and he rummaged for it under last night's discarded clothing. "Yeah. Bruce here."

"Bruce. It's Simon."

"Sharpy! What's up?" Speak of the devil.

"I have a favour to ask. Have you got some time today?"

Bruce consulted his watch. "I'm heading up to the house in a while. Meeting a guy up there. Have lunch with me. You want to bring the burgers and I'll pick up some beer?"

"Okay. See you in about an hour."

"You remember the address? Seaview Place, you'll see my truck."

"Right."

Bruce pocketed his phone, wondering what could be important

enough to drag Simon out of the office and across the bridge mid-day. He had time to pick up a cold six-pack from the pub and deal with the hauler before Simon showed up. He hadn't had breakfast, but what the hell. Burgers and beer for breakfast were okay with him. After all, he was used to cold pizza and Red Bull.

CHAPTER 2

The food fair was quickly filling up for the lunch hour rush, the din of voices increasing even as Alexa walked in. She scanned the busy room for their golden heads, found them, and made her way over.

"Hey, you." Kate and Markus sat together in a booth in the middle of the food fair.

"Hey. Hi Marky." Alexa bent to kiss Kate, and then nuzzle the towheaded toddler, who squirmed around on the bench like a perpetual motion machine. "So what's up? It sounded urgent."

"I'll tell you in a sec. Can you grab some food? I'm starving."

"Awick," Markus said, his arms upthrust, smiling at her with his mouth full of adorable baby teeth, half chewed French fry filling his round, rosy cheeks. He looked so much like Kate it made Alexa's heart squeeze with affection.

She lifted him and gave him a tight hug, pressing her face into his angel hair and deeply inhaling his baby scent. He felt so good in her arms, the softness and heft of him.

Kate broke into her reverie. "Earth to Alex. You okay?"

"Hmm?" Alexa opened her eyes. "Yeah. He reminds me so much of Owen at this age."

"How old is he now?"

"He'll be twenty-two next month. I was fifteen when he was born." Alexa had helped raise them all. But of the six of them, her youngest brother had seemed the most like her own, and her pulse still beat a little harder at the memory of him. "Mom was so overwhelmed with working two jobs, Owen was all mine. He was almost Markus's age when I left for college. It broke my heart to leave him."

"It's a wonder you got through high school with all the extra work. How's he doing now?"

"Okay, I guess. A bit muddled. He's at college on the island, doing alright."

"And the others?"

Alexa mentally reviewed the daily status reports on all her siblings. "Rhys and Dylan, the eldest, have settled down, the rest are... you know. As well as you can expect kids for in their twenties. Finding themselves." She laughed.

"Can you get me some sushi, please? The cooked stuff? Markus will eat while we wait for you."

Alexa went to get the sushi. The line up was still short enough, but she had a few moments to ponder the woozy feeling she always got after a hit of Markus. Her biological clock had settled down. But no matter how much she denied it, her gut clenched with regret at the realization that she'd never have kids of her own. It had been easier before her best friend started pushing them out. She thrust the feelings away. After years of taking care of a houseful of brothers and sisters, she should have had her fill, yet she loved them. But, she'd made that choice and wouldn't go back on it. Her career was her life; she wasn't willing to compromise. She grabbed Cali rolls, tuna sushi, and two large green teas for Kate and herself, and returned to the table, where Markus was managing to get ketchup all over Kate's jacket sleeves with his flailing hands. She nodded to herself. Focus on the negatives.

"Here. Marky. Come and sit with Auntie Alex so Mommy can eat, okay?"

"Otay."

He wiggled down and she lifted him past her into the end of the booth, where he could squirm and wiggle, but not escape. She laughed and kissed his soft, sweet blond head while he continued to macerate chicken fingers and fries. "He still smells so good," she said.

"Not always." Kate made a face. "He had a bath this morning."

Alexa deftly intercepted Markus's grasping hands and lifted her hot tea out of his reach, while Kate gobbled her sushi like a prisoner of war. How quickly one forgot the speed and determination of a three-year-old exploring his world. "Sit still and eat nicely and Auntie Alex will buy you a treat later, okay?"

"Don't bribe him, Alex," Kate complained through a mouthful of sushi. She pulled a small wooden dump truck out of her bag and set it on the table in front of his food. His hand immediately darted out and grabbed it.

"Why not? It works, doesn't it? The way I figure it, anything goes at this age, as long as you survive."

Kate snickered, almost choking on her food. "You crack me up." She snorted, her eyes watering. "Shoot, I got wasabi up my nose."

Alexa laughed, waiting and sipping her tea while Kate finished eating. Markus, thankfully, was a slow and methodical eater, and would obligingly take a half hour to chew a few mouthfuls of chicken.

"While you're eating... I have good news. Almost. It's not official yet, but the firm has been awarded that contract I was telling you about, for the big Arts Centre downtown. My design won it for us, and Krys should be appointing me as the project architect, next week probably."

Kate's smile was a little thin. "You sound very sure about that. I hope he doesn't disappoint you."

"Of course, I'm sure. He's pretty much promised it to me from the beginning."

"I hope so, for your sake."

Alexa sighed and eyeballed her friend over her glasses. "I know you don't trust him. But this is professional. I earned this, Kate."

She nodded. "That, I know. And then some. But you've also complicated things."

Kate had never approved of Alexa's personal relationship with Krystof. Okay. Yes, though separated, technically he was still married when they first got involved four years ago. But, he was divorced now. Alexa leaned in, whispering. "Krys would never give me the job just because of our relationship, Kate. I'm the best man for the job."

Kate lifted an eyebrow. "Man?"

Alexa flicked a hand, frowning. "You know what I mean."

Kate dabbed her mouth with a napkin and pressed her lips into a twisted line. Alexa drew a deep breath, preparing for another lecture. "I will never understand how you can be involved with your boss. You can do better, Alex."

"Do better how? We're perfectly compatible. He's a remarkable man.

He's smart, talented and attractive. I even envy him a little. He's exactly the kind of architect I aspire to be one day."

"So you've said."

Do we have to do this again? Alexa leaned in closer and met her friend's eyes straight on. "We admire each *other*, Kate. It's cool. We only keep it on the sly to avoid making people uncomfortable."

"I don't know, Alex. There's something wrong with a guy who sleeps with employees."

Alexa laughed. "I know. It sounds morally reprehensible. But it's not like that. I'm not only an employee. I'm a colleague."

"What about his ex-wife?"

"I didn't cause that mess. That was between him and Biljiana. And she's no saint. The only reason he still has to deal with her is because she owns half the firm."

"Well, regardless of what you see in him, what about you?" Kate's earnest, glassy stare communicated the subtext—*what about your heart? You'll get it broken and I'm worried for you.* "I just don't get the feeling you're in love."

Alexa leaned back and sighed. "It's not like you and Simon, if that's what you mean. What we have is more… about mutual admiration and respect. We have a meeting of minds."

Kate's lips puckered into a moue of disapproval. "More than your minds are meeting."

Alexa shrugged. "It's stimulating for sure. You can't understand. I'm different than you. My needs are different." Kate, with her perfect, doting, romantic husband, would never understand. For Alexa, having a partner who understood and appreciated her one-hundred-per-cent focus on her career was about as perfect a setup as she could imagine. "No one understands the way I feel about architecture like Krys does. Our relationship is an expression of our mutual passion for our art. We're kindred spirits. Intellectual equals. Krystof supports and values me as an architect, Katie. He will never be a burden to me, or hold me back."

"Hmph. *Methinks she doth protest too much.* Will you get married eventually?"

Alexa shrugged, shoving aside her frequent fantasy about the two of them, architecture's power couple, married, co-owners of the best firm in town, in the spotlight. "It's too soon after the divorce. I wouldn't want to pressure him. It's not important."

"What about your own kids?"

"Ah. I don't think so. He's not interested in going down that road again."

At Kate's scowl, Alexa said, "I'm fine! I'm perfectly content."

Kate blew out a sigh. "Well no matter what happens you know I'll support you. I'll always be here for you."

"I appreciate that, Katie," she said as Markus slid off his seat and crawled under the table to return to his mother's side. She picked up a piece of sushi and aimed it at her mouth. "So, what's the problem you mentioned on the phone?"

Kate's demeanour fell. "Agh. It's a big one."

"What is it?"

"Simon's dad's taken ill," Kate said, but her expression said much more.

Alexa squinted at her, chewing her sushi, nodding for the rest.

Kate grimaced, then blew out a big gust of air. Her glassy eyes foreshadowed something grim. "They're overseas travelling, again. And they're stuck in Bangkok."

"Oh, damn." Alexa put down her sushi. "So... what does–"

Kate shrugged. "Simon has to go deal with it. His mom can't manage. They need help with doctors and insurance, and have to make arrangements to get him home. He's apparently very weak. Simon's leaving tomorrow."

"So, that means you're on your own with the kids. Will your Mom come and help?"

"No. She can't leave my dad. He still can't manage after his stroke."

Alexa's breath rushed out while her stomach clenched. Was Kate going to ask her for her help? The timing couldn't be worse. She swallowed. "Do you need–?"

Kate's eyes flew open. "No! Oh, I would never do that to you right now. No, Simon's talking to Bruce today. I'll be fine. And he'll check in with me to make sure I don't need anything. Help out a bit."

Alexa released the breath she was holding. Bruce. He was Simon's oldest and closest friend, but he was also the last person on earth you would trust with your precious children. He was like a child himself. Sexy as hell, but not father material. "Well, better him than nobody, I guess."

Kate's laughter wavered with an undercurrent of uncertainty. "Honestly, Alex. He's not that bad. You seem to bring out the worst in him."

"Jeez, Kate. Well, how long will Simon be away?"

"I don't know. A week? Two?"

"What about that course you were supposed to teach at the Justice Institute?"

Kate shook her head sadly. "Nope. I had to bail."

"Aw, Katie. You were really looking forward to getting back into working. Weren't you?"

Kate's eyes slid to the side, and she bit her lip. "Yeah… well. Maybe not right now. There's one other thing I haven't told you." She pushed her hair behind her ear.

Alexa leaned in, frowning.

"I'm pregnant again." Kate grimaced.

"What!"

"I'm just over seventeen weeks. We've been keeping it secret until we knew everything was okay."

"And now this. When will you have another chance to kick start your career?"

"I will." Kate shrugged, deflating. "It's okay. There'll be other opportunities to get back into practicing. When the kids are older."

"So, what are you going to do until then? Be a stay-at-home mom?" Alexa knew that Kate knew how Alexa felt about *that*. She wouldn't do it herself, and she wouldn't wish it on her worst enemy, never mind her best friend.

"Awick!" declared Markus, banging his dump truck on the table. "Vroom!" Right into the ketchup.

Kate yanked out wet wipes and quickly sanitized the toy, pulling the remains of Markus's lunch out of reach.

"Well. If you need me, you know you can call."

Kate nodded. "I know. I'll try not to."

Bruce spied the dump truck before he pulled up outside of his house. He'd bought the place a month ago and the front yard was piled high with junk he'd pulled out: old appliances, skanky carpets, moth-eaten draperies and the weird and worthless kind of garbage that people left behind. An old widow had lived alone in the house until she died.

Bruce waved to the guys loading the junk from the pile onto a big beat up truck, and stood watching.

"Morning!" He waved.

The house needed major work, but its redeeming feature lay beyond the old cracked terrace. The water. The view from the marina was spectacular, but it had nothing on this. Standing on the crest of the ridge where his house perched, he could see through the trees, down into the marina, the yacht club and the sparkling water. Right across to Bowen Island and the straight. Not only would it be fun to renovate, but it was a damn good investment.

When the guys were finished loading, he thanked them and cut them a cheque and they drove off. Then it was quiet, peaceful. He stood, soaking up the serene atmosphere, waiting for Simon.

It wasn't a large house, but it would be plenty big enough for him, even big enough for a family like Simon's. He pictured Simon's kids running down the hall, playing in the sunken living room. Someone – not him – puttering about in the new kitchen. He'd maybe retreat to his den to watch a game or read, the sounds of family life muffled in the distance. Families had a certain comforting appeal, if you were the type. Bruce shrugged. He wasn't the type.

Simon, on the other hand, needed that sort of thing; he was sensitive and wanted to feel like he belonged somewhere. Unlike Bruce, Simon always needed a woman in his life. Bruce liked to get laid as much as the next guy, but he could do without the complication of actual relationships with women. They got in his way, made demands and freaked out over everything he liked to do. And they invariably clung or left when you least expected it.

Eventually, when he moved on, the house would sell at a pretty profit. Meanwhile, it would be for him. Maybe he would get a dog. Until now he'd never had time or space. A nice golden retriever to keep him company and walk on the beach. A sailing dog that liked the water as much as Bruce did. Someone to talk to that wouldn't talk back.

Movement caught his eye, and he glanced over to his neighbour's yard. Dragging a curly hose, a tall blond woman watered purple flowers in containers on her deck. She wore oh-so-short shorts, and a tight white t-shirt. He tried not to stare, but then she turned away and bent over to tend a pot, and he couldn't help himself. He'd noticed her before a few times. She stood up and turned to face him, smiling and waving. "Hi!" It was almost as if she'd done it on purpose. As if that were necessary. She was exactly what he liked, long-legged and curvy.

He waved back. "Hi, yourself." He wondered if she was married. He'd seen evidence of kids, but no one else around. Not that he was planning on it, but if he ever did decide to settle down with a woman, she would be something like that, soft, feminine and maternal. Someone to keep the home fires burning.

"Are you moving in?" Her voice was high-pitched and didn't carry well.

"Eventually." He waved an arm at the obvious destruction and mess around him. "Hopefully by the end of summer."

"I'm Gillian. Welcome to the neighbourhood. Come by and say a proper hello sometime."

He nodded and waved again. He might do that. She seemed pretty open to... whatever. That might be nice.

"Koczynski?" Simon's voice drifted around from the street. Bruce hadn't heard his car pull up.

"Sharpy! Here!" he shouted, and Simon appeared, picking his way across the uneven ground and broken sidewalk pavers in his shiny lawyer's shoes, holding a greasy takeout bag away from his grey summer suit.

"Amazing! Look at the view."

"Am I gonna make another mill on this, or what, eh?" Bruce smiled. "Want a quick tour before we eat?"

"Of course." Simon followed him through the old sliding glass door into a long narrow room with a sloped timbered ceiling and a smooth concrete fireplace on the end wall. The living room had windows all along one side under a deep overhang.

Bruce led him through the rabbit's warren of tiny rooms off of narrow corridors. An unconventional layout, the house was broken up into a central area comprising interconnecting open spaces. The kitchen was tucked into one corner, half a level up from the living room. A pod of small rooms stretched off to each side.

"The plumbing and wiring are shit." Bruce explained how he planned to rip it all out and build a sleek new kitchen with state-of-the-art appliances.

"And that's for what, exactly?"

"Ve-ry funny." Bruce glared at him. "I can cook. Or, well, I can learn, anyway. Can't eat hamburgers every day."

"I'll believe it when I see it," replied Simon, following him into the bedroom wing.

"Well, it's not for me anyway," mumbled Bruce.

Simon was a uniquely talented and ambitious cook. Most of Bruce's holidays were spent stuffing his face on Simon's pan-Asian buffet dinners, or his famous lasagna, or waffles and strawberries. Bruce admired Simon's talent, but he wasn't jealous. He had never taken an interest in cooking. TV dinners and take out had always been more than adequate. Ha! Well… adequate, as long as Simon and Kate had him over for home-cooked meals once in a while. But then, if he applied himself, he could add that to his roster of skills. Why the hell not? He liked being a self-sufficient Renaissance man. It would be handy. Maybe he'd invite his new neighbour over for dinner. Yeah. Dinner and desert.

"These bedrooms are half the normal size," Bruce said, leading the way down a narrow corridor. "I'm planning to take a sledge hammer to the walls and opening it right up."

"Don't bring down the roof," cautioned Simon. "Did you consult an engineer or a contractor, at least?"

Bruce pushed aside a niggling irritation at his friend's condescension. A reminder of his family. Why did no one believe him capable of doing shit? He wasn't a child. "Nah. I can handle it. It's a wood house. What can go wrong?"

"It's a good thing you're loaded, buddy." Simon laughed and shook his head. He was pensive as they came back out through the central rooms. "You know, Kate's friend Alexa is an architect. She was a big help to Kate when she renovated her old loft in Yaletown."

"That stick?" Every time he'd seen Kate's best friend, she'd found a way to pick a fight, despite his best efforts to charm her. "That girl takes herself way too seriously. Why would I ask her opinion? She's such a bossy know-it-all, she'd as likely shove it down my throat."

"Hmm." Simon strolled back outside and carefully sat down on the jagged edge of the patio, overlooking the marina below. There was rubble laying about, after Bruce had removed the remainder of the falling-down railing. The concrete deck stopped abruptly and the wild, overgrown yard tumbled steeply down to the edge of the forest below. "That reminds me why I wanted to talk to you."

Bruce plopped down next to him and opened two bottles of beer, handing one to Simon, and accepting the bag of food in return. He tried to suppress the rolling feeling in his gut. For several minutes they snarfed their burgers in companionable silence, but Bruce's appetite was off.

Choking down a bite, Bruce finally asked, "And why's that?"

"Well." Simon chewed and swallowed, taking a slug of beer. "I'm glad you're finally settling down a bit. Selling the company was the right thing for you. And I'm relieved you decided to stay here."

"Gee, thanks Pop." Bruce glanced at his friend. "What would I do in California anyway? This is my home."

"Well, I'm happy for you. You've got financial independence and you're living the idyllic bachelor's life. You've got your boat, and a new home. It's great. You could really put down roots here. It would be good for you."

Well, it wouldn't really be his home, though he'd enjoy it before he flipped it, but Simon wouldn't understand that. Simon was a lawyer, not a big risk-taker. Bruce detected a note of implied criticism, though, in Simon's well-meant words. Whatever he came to talk about, he hadn't gotten there yet. This was his way. Bruce waited for him to build his case.

"I have to confess," Simon said, "I've been worried about you this past year. You seemed a bit aimless. Living fast and loose, drinking too much…"

Here it comes. His face heated with embarrassment. Nothing got past Simon after all, it seemed. Bruce glanced down and tugged on the front of his ratty Canucks t-shirt. "I've cleaned up the past few months."

"I noticed. And I'm relieved. I like this version of you better. I don't feel as though I have to pull my punches."

Whoah.

Simon gestured vaguely to the forest and the sea. "You were hanging with the wrong crowd, and it… it stressed me a bit. I didn't know what you were going to do with yourself."

Bruce swallowed. He didn't used to keep secrets from his friend. But he was still embarrassed at how low he'd fallen. He could still remember the shame he felt when he'd woken up one morning back in February with two naked strangers in his bed, and no recollection of who they were, or where he'd hooked up with them. Pathetic! What had begun as a celebration of his freedom and unexpected wealth had quickly spiralled into a colossal wallow. He'd been so out of it. So out of control. No idea where he'd been or how he'd got home. And it had been his wake up call. Time to get his shit together. Time to make a change.

Bruce flashed him a tight grin. "It's because you married Kate and left me all by my lonesome." He turned away and took a long pull on his beer, washing down the bile that rose in his throat. His joke fell flat, far too close to the truth.

Simon obligingly forced a laugh.

Bruce had not been happy with his work near the end. The acquisition had come along at precisely the right time. For him, at least.

Simon sobered and said, "Like I was ever good company for you, taking care of Maddie by myself, dealing with her mother, afraid I was going to lose my little girl."

Some women weren't cut out for motherhood. Like his, he supposed. "Thank God Rachel moved to Toronto. She giving you any shit?"

"No. She's happy to be relieved of the burden. Everything's good. *Very* good." He smiled like a Cheshire cat, and Bruce couldn't help but mirror his silly grin.

Bruce could see how happy Simon was with his new life, his new family. He positively glowed with it. "It's because you're getting it regular, dude."

Simon laughed, but a pink flush rose to his ears. "Ha. What about you, buddy? It seems like your nesting instinct has kicked in. Now you've got your dream house, you need a wife, too. Someone to keep you on the straight and narrow."

Bruce's stomach dropped. "Ack! Like hell. No way. This baby's purely an investment in my future. Family's your thing, Sharpy. Not mine."

Simon gave him the stink-eye and shook his head, and Bruce refused to ponder what his friend was thinking. Simon knew him better than anyone—maybe even better than he knew himself. They sat, eating their burgers and fries and drinking their beer, their eyes resting gently on the panorama.

"So. About that." Simon wiped his mouth.

Here it comes at last.

"I need you to play daddy for a while."

Bruce's heart slammed against his rib cage. "What?"

"I have to go away for a couple of weeks."

Bruce frowned. "Are you taking Maddie out of school early?" Please say yes.

Simon's mouth thinned and he turned to look at his friend. His nostrils flared slightly. "No. I have to leave them and go alone. To Bangkok. My parents are there, and my dad's fallen ill."

"Oh, shit. He's okay? Not… dying or anything?"

"No. God forbid. But they can't deal with it. Mom's beside herself. She can't handle the stress, and make arrangements."

He had an ominous feeling. Was Simon asking him to take care of the kids? Bruce was horrified. A wave of nausea rose up his gullet. "Surely you have better prospects, someone better suited. How about Kate's parents?" His voice squeaked.

Simon shook his head. "Her dad's still recovering from last year's stroke."

"What's Will up to? Can't he help?"

"No. He's already gone up North to plant trees for the summer…" Simon inhaled and shook his head.

Bruce cast his mind around for other options, then jabbed a finger at Simon's chest. "Aha! Casey and Michelle would be thrilled to help out."

Simon shook his head slowly.

"What?"

"You know Michelle nearly died last year. She had that bout of meningitis and pneumonia. She was in a coma for a while, and it was a miracle she survived. And now their little boy Jackson had another surgery on his wandering eye."

"Jesus. Is there anyone you know who's not having a life crisis?"

Their eyes locked.

"Me. Right." He scowled. Bruce was cornered.

Simon's expression was plaintive. He wouldn't beg, but neither could Bruce deny his best friend help if he needed it. They'd had each other's back since the early days. "You, my independently wealthy friend, are the only one with free days. It would mean a *lot* to me if you would watch out for Kate and the kids while I'm gone."

"Oh! *Kate* and the kids." He let out his breath. That was different. "Of course. You can count on me." Bruce couldn't let him down.

Simon nodded. "You should know something else."

Bruce held his breath. What more could there be?

"We haven't told anyone. But Kate's expecting again."

His heart thudded. Another kid? He drew a deep breath. "Congratulations, Sharpy."

Simon beamed, obviously thrilled. He turned toward Bruce and met his gaze, intense. "I know I shouldn't worry. But it kills me to leave her. I don't want her to get over-tired or stressed. She needs help with the kids."

"I understand."

"Maddie's in school for another couple of weeks. Someone has to watch Markus all day, take him to the park and stuff, and pick up Maddie from school. It would be great if Kate didn't have to do all that running around." Simon lifted his brows.

Bruce was silent, trying to visualize his days gobbled up chasing Markus around a playground, feeling an impending sense of panic and doom.

"You know I'd never say no, Sharpy. I mean, I love Maddie and Markus, *but*...I've got zero kid experience. You know that. What...what if I do something wrong?"

"Come on. You're great with the kids. And Kate'll be here. You're just backup and relief pitcher. I'm confident or I wouldn't ask. Anyway, I trust you. You've always been there for me. You're my best friend. Who else am I going to ask to take care of my family?"

What could Bruce say to that? He nodded and smiled. "Alright." He cast his gaze across the patio to take in his semi-demolished house. He whimpered.

Simon laughed. "It's only two, maybe two and a half weeks, buddy, and–" Simon's cell phone rang, and he reached into his pocket, glancing at it. "–sec. Hi, honey." Bruce waited, his eyes roaming over the familiar face of his best friend. "Not bad. Mmmhmm. Yes, okay. That'll help. Okay, see you later. Love you." He turned back to Bruce. "Kate." A smile flickered on his face.

"Yeah. I figured." No one else made Simon glow like a beacon.

"So. Good news." Simon's brows rose, and he smiled.

"You found someone else?" Bruce asked, only half joking.

"No." Simon laughed. "Kate heard back from this day care she likes, and they found a spot for Markus, but only in the mornings. It'll lighten the load for both you and Kate. She can rest and you can do your house stuff until you have to pick him up."

"Great! When do you leave?" How long did he have to get his own life in order before he had to be responsible for three others?

"Tomorrow."

"Okay, then."

CHAPTER 3

Alexa sat beside Kate on the edge of her bed, her arm around the hunched form of her friend.

"I would die if anything happened to Simon. I have to be there."

"Don't say another word. I know you have to go," Alexa said. The timing couldn't be worse. But somehow she'd figure it out. She'd done it before. She'd managed to graduate from high school and get into university while helping to raise six kids. This would be a piece of cake.

Kate's eyes filled with tears again. "I do."

"I can do it." It was insane. "How long?"

Kate's mouth thinned. "Two-and-a-half weeks."

"And there's nobody else that can do it?"

"Not... exactly." Kate explained how her own parents were unable, and that Simon's brother Will was away all summer.

"So that leaves me," Alex said.

"And, because you're at the office all day..." she hesitated, hiding behind her cup of tea. "And I know you can't *not* do that. We need someone else to fill in."

"Yeah...?" Alexa prompted.

"Bruce will have to do it," Kate said.

"What? You must be out of your mind!"

Kate visibly deflated. "I knew you'd hate the idea. But he's great with the kids, he really is. They adore him. And he's the only person that's flexible enough to fill in the gaps while you're at the office." She shrugged. "He's already been helping me. And you know you'll need back up. I trust Bruce completely."

"I can't imagine why. That player? How can he take care of the kids? He can't even take care of himself. He's like a big teenager. He won't be any help at all." As soon as the rant had left her lips, Alex wished she could take it back. That was no way to convince Kate to leave her kids and go rescue Simon.

"Someone has to be available and run the whole show while you're working. I already feel terrible that I'm forcing you into this. This isn't a good time for you with the big project and all. You know I wouldn't if–"

"I know, Kate. It's okay. Don't worry about the kids, or me and Bruce - just go get your man and bring him home."

"To be fair, you underestimate him. He's a terrific guy and incredibly smart and talented. Resourceful. He knows how to do everything–"

"Except dress like an adult and behave civilly to women. Well. I'll be damned if I'll feed him and do his laundry," she murmured with a smirk intended to soften her outburst with humour.

They all knew what Bruce was like, didn't they? Ever since Alexa had met him again four years ago, she'd done her best to avoid him as much as humanly possible. He got under her skin like a thorn, a sharp prick and then hours of itching and irritation that made her grouchy as a bear.

She made it a habit never to be in his company that long. But what was the point of arguing? As annoying as he was, they had to make it work. They had to, for Kate.

"Bruce and I will be fine. It'll give us a chance to get to know each other better. We'll work it out." Lord help her, she didn't know how.

The doorbell rang.

"He's here."

~

His first couple of days as Kate's helper had gone smoothly, and he'd begun to feel complacent that she wouldn't demand too much of him, after all. On the third evening, however, after he'd already crossed the bridge and settled into his boat, he gotten her frantic call to come back immediately. Naturally concerned, he hopped in his truck and raced over. Little did he know that this visit would turn his life, his very world view, upside down.

Ever since they'd met and become fast friends in high school, Bruce had always treated Simon's place like a second home. In fact, it was the closest thing to a real home that Bruce had had since– well, since his Mom had left in the third grade. Simon's parents had been kind to him. It had always been a safe haven from the perpetual state of chaos and persecution that he suffered growing up among his three boisterous older brothers and under the bullying dictatorship of his own father.

Some of his best meals had been shared with Simon and his brother Will as they watched games together. Starting in university, Simon had also hosted their occasional poker nights. Now that Kate was in the picture, and since Markus had been born, Simon's house had taken on a feminine vibe, an atmosphere of domestic harmony and comfort, a qualitative difference from his first less-than-perfect marriage. Something that Bruce found vaguely disquieting, if oddly compelling. It smelled too sweet. And it seemed the last place on earth you'd set up a poker table. He always looked forward to coming, and just as eagerly longed to escape back to his floating bachelor pad.

He both longed for and feared the sense of safety, stability and belonging that it represented. But the price was too high. You just couldn't trust relationships to last, and it hurt too much when you counted on someone to be there for you always, and then they left.

Bruce had stayed for dinner the day Simon had flown to Thailand, and been happy to head home afterwards. Tonight, the moment he arrived, he knew something was wrong.

Kate met him at the door and pulled him into Simon's den. Bruce leaned in, kissing her cheek. "Evening, Beautiful."

She gestured to a chair and sat down. Then she just stared at him. Her eyes were red and puffy.

Oh, dear God. His gut clenched. "What is it?"

"Simon's been in an accident."

Bruce couldn't breath. He was horrified. He was a afraid to ask. "What happened?"

"He was running around trying to make arrangements for his parents, distracted I guess, jet-lagged. He was hit by a motorcyclist."

He waited, his heart in his throat.

Kate shook her head. "He's okay, I guess. Bruised up. But his leg is fractured. So now he's in hospital, too. But they took him to a different hospital than where his Dad is, so it's impossible. Everything's in chaos. He can't do what he went there to do. He's trying to arrange his father's health care and insurance as well as his own, and keep his mother calm, all from a hospital bed. Travel home at the moment is impossible. None of them can manage. I have to go to him. I need you to take care of the kids."

"What? By myself?" Of course he'd do it if he had to, but... "Wouldn't the kids be better off with a professional? You can hire nannies for temporary gigs, can't you?"

Kate's eyes darkened. "I couldn't do that to Maddie. After all she's been through with her mother. Simon's never left her before, and her first experience with a nanny when she was a baby was... not good."

Bruce remembered. Simon had had some horrific experiences with nannies and sitters when he'd been a single dad, and Rachel was notorious for disappointing Maddie by cancelling last minute. "Don't you have girlfriends? Surely a woman would be a better choice. The kids would–"

She nodded. "Alexa's here, too."

"What... Alex... You're not... That harpy?" He bit back more vitriol. He should know better than to bad-mouth Kate's best friend.

"You don't know the first thing about her."

"I know she's never had the time of day for me. How's this going to work?"

"I know you and Alexa don't have a great history, but... you two got off on the wrong foot years ago. You have to get to know her better."

"Ri-i-ight." Bruce nodded sceptically. He never knew whether he wanted to screw her senseless or punch her lights out, she drove him so nuts.

"Alexa is terrific. She's a smart, caring, funny woman and my oldest, dearest friend. You'll make a great team."

Strange, somehow that had escaped Bruce's notice. The terrific, caring, funny part. Okay, he'd admit she was smart. Too smart. But caring? funny? Nope. She was humourless and abrasive. She was so serious about her career she didn't have time for fun and leisure. Almost a caricature. She was attractive, he'd give her that, in a skinny, dark, exotic sort of way, though not *his* type. Not attractive enough to brave the prickly gauntlet of her personality. They never seemed to be able to get along without bickering. "You expect me to..."

"Cooperate. She has to work full time. What choice do any of us have, Bruce?"

Bruce wanted to run. He knew she needed his help. His, and obviously Alexa's. There was no way out of this. "Of course I'll do it. But you're worried about something?"

"Yes, frankly, I'm concerned that you two *are* going to fight like cats and dogs."

"Calm down, Kate. I promised Simon I'd take care of you and help you. I didn't know it would be like this, but it'll be fine. We'll cooperate. Of course we will." Bruce wasn't sure how, but he'd find a way.

"You need to get along, that's all. Listen and be respectful. Don't be a macho jerk."

"I'm not the one who picks fights with her, you know." Okay, maybe he was somewhat responsible for giving her a certain less-than-favourable impression of who he was. And trying to get a rise out of her. It was so easy to provoke her.

"I really mean it."

"Hmph. Do you remember the time we first met up again, four Christmases ago? She nearly tore me to shreds." Bruce's voice rose an octave remembering. He felt the hair on his arms rise, tingling, and remembered the ache in his groin from their momentary encounter in the darkened hallway.

"You kissed her!"

Bruce grimaced. "There was mistletoe."

Kate rolled his eyes. "That's what I mean. She's not the kind of... tart you're used to dealing with, that's all."

"You can say that again."

"Bruce." Kate shook her head, scowling. "I want your word. Be respectful. Play nice."

"I promise..." Bruce made a pleading gesture with his hands out. "I'll...er, I'll do my best to get along, I'll even learn to like her. Okay?" Even if he had to stop poking fun at her. It might even be boring. He took Kate's hands in his and squeezed them. "And I promise you, Kate, the kids will be perfectly okay. You and Simon don't have to worry about a thing."

Kate stood up. "I knew I could count on you, Bruce." She wrapped her arms around him and held on tight. He returned the hug, but then she clung, and he felt her body temperature rise, felt her shoulders tremble, before he heard her sniffle.

"Hey, hey." He rubbed her back gently.

"I'm so worried about him. I never should have let him go alone."

"He'll be okay. He's a tough guy. Remember he's got a ton of experience travelling around Asia. I'm sure a broken leg won't slow him down."

She lifted her head and glared at him.

"Okay, obviously it will slow him down. I mean, he can cope. He's Sharpy. He can do anything. Right?"

She sniffed again and nodded. "I know. But what if something even more serious had happened over there? I can't bear to think–" Her face buckled.

"Well. It didn't." He set her away from him and looked around for a tissue or something. Finding nothing, he pulled up the tail of his shirt and wiped her cheeks with it. "Look this is a logistical nightmare. And that's why you have to go. But nobody's dying here, Kate. Everything's going to be alright. Okay?"

"Okay."

∼

When they entered the hall, Alexa stood there with both Maddie and Markus in their pyjamas, looking scrubbed and combed, with their cheeks glowing pink.

"Koczynski."

"Right." Well, it took two to tango, but he would do his best to lead this dance, and choose his steps carefully. What choice did he have, after all?

"I'll take them upstairs," Alexa said.

Kate's smile was indulgent as she picked up her son. "Say goodnight to Uncle Bruce, Markus."

From her arms, Markus stared at him for a minute, but with a little jiggle from Kate, he finally said, "Night, Boos."

They sure were cute kids. Three-year-old Markus was the spitting image of Kate, with her fine, smooth golden hair. Except he had Simon's blue eyes.

"G'night, little buddy," Bruce said, grinning. "Gimme five." He presented his palm to Markus, who giggled and slapped at it wildly.

"Ouch!" A sharp pain shot through his shinbone. "What the…?" He looked down at Maddie. She'd kicked him viciously with her bony little foot. Simon's seven-year-old daughter Maddie looked more like her mother Rachel, with her thick brown curls and catty green eyes.

"What's up, Scallywag?" He scrubbed the top of her head. "Am I ignoring you?"

She stood with her arms folded, glaring up at him.

"Maddie! Apologize right now," Kate said, frowning.

Madison responded immediately, if half-heartedly, chuffing the carpet with her bare foot. "Thor-ry."

He wasn't convinced. He could see an evil smirk pulling at her lips. Maddie apparently took after her bitchy mother in more ways than one. He pulled a funny face at her, trying to elicit a smile. It'd actually be fun to spend more time with the kids.

"Maddie isn't thrilled with the arrangements," Kate explained as they moved away. "It's not you, though. It's the fact that Simon had to go away in the first place. She has a bit of separation anxiety. He's never left her before, so she's actually furious at *me*. But she's taking it out on you."

Oh, great. Bruce squinted back at Maddie and said in a syrupy voice, "Good night, Madison."

"'Night," she snarled, and stomped upstairs to bed.

Alexa followed her upstairs. "I'll be right down."

"She seems okay with Alexa," Bruce said.

"Yes. They're used to Alex. She babysits pretty regularly."

Bruce was surprised to learn that.

Kate led the way to the dining room, where a casual dinner was laid out on the table. "Help yourself to a beer, Bruce, and some lasagna and salad. I'm just going up to kiss the kids goodnight."

He did, and returned to the dining room, studying the food she set out. When Alexa returned, he ignored her but watched her through his peripheral vision. She sat down at the table, skulking behind a half-empty glass of red wine, like a mean little leprechaun ready to pounce. She scowled at him.

"Hey, partner." He grinned at her. "Looks like we're working together."

"Koczynski." Her husky voice was flat. She glared at him over the dark rims of her angular eyeglasses, obviously no more thrilled at the arrangement than he was.

He offered her a brilliant smile. "None other. How're you doing, Al?" He sauntered around the table, flopped into the chair next to her.

He still wondered if it was possible to melt through the ice with sufficient charm. Kate had no idea what she was asking him to do. He threw an arm across the back of her chair and leaned in to kiss her on the cheek.

"Don't get any ideas, Koczynski." She turned her head away, and his face landed in her silky dark hair. It smelled of the tropics. Spicy and sweet. Almost like that cologne he used to wear– what was it called? She may not be his type, but she was like a burr in his hide, small, prickly and stubborn, hard to ignore. She was caramel-coloured with a petite, boyish figure. Kind of cute though. Even though she was the only woman he'd ever met who was persistently immune to his charms. Until she opened her mouth.

That mouth twisted in scorn and she shoved him away, looking like she might hit him with something. Instead, she plucked his arm off and handed it back like it was a rotting log full of maggots. "Do you mind?"

He smiled and shook his head, feeling the first rebellious stirrings from his body. There was something about her throaty voice that seemed to yank his chain.

He took a long draft on his beer, leaning back. "Aah." A small belch escaped. "Pardon."

Alexa shook her head, looking bored with his antics, and slightly annoyed. "So. I'm surprised you agreed to this little arrangement, Koz. You don't strike me as the domestic sort."

You're one to talk. A bark of laughter escaped before he could prevent it. "Like we have any choice."

"What are you laughing at?"

He opted not to reply, instead smiling and taking another sip of beer. She reminded him of Cruella De Ville—hard and mean-spirited. All she was missing was a shock of white in her dark hair and a long cigarette holder. Oh, and a coat made of puppies.

"Nothing at all," he replied, sniggering, then sobered. "You're looking well." She did, too. Her dark hair shone, strands of it somehow sticking out artfully. It managed to look both precise and post-coital at the same time. Everything about her was a carefully considered design statement. It suited her. He flicked the end of her scarf. "Love this, Al. Great colour on you. Matches your eyes." He leaned in closer and flared his nostrils and let his gaze slide over her slender limbs.

Those eyes were narrowed at him now, her suspicions aroused.

There was a vaguely exotic quality about her eyes. They were a strange greyish-green, like a stormy sea, and tilted up at the corners. It might be appealing, if she would smile once in a while. He saw a twinkle of amusement in her eyes, though. Maybe he was getting somewhere.

"That's Alexa to you, Koczynski." She pursed her full lips and eyed his torso.

He sat up taller. "Like what you see?" Raising his arm to flex his bicep, he flickered his eyebrows at her. "I've been working out more."

She let out a gust of air, rolling her eyes. "Nice shirt," she deadpanned. "Not wasting all your time at clubs and parties? I heard–"

He gave her a hard look, his teeth set. "Actually, it's not having to work eighteen hour days that's made the biggest difference." He smiled broadly. "And you could call me Bruce."

She ignored him. "Oh, right. I'd forgotten you were one of the idle rich these days."

His eye twitched with tension, and he forced himself to relax. He tilted the beer bottle back, taking a long drink. "What kind of name is Alexa, anyway? Italian or Egyptian or something?" He'd always wondered if she was mixed race.

Again she ignored his question. No wonder she got under his skin. She retaliated with, "What's with the long hair and Hawaiian shirt? Auditioning for a Hawaii Five-O remake?"

Bruce shrugged, combing a hand through his shoulder length hair. It wasn't that long. "I see you can't keep your eyes off of me tonight, Al." He felt a warm stirring in his trousers. Even though she was trying to goad him, the sound of her sexy voice always had this regrettable effect.

"Hah! In your dreams, Hefner."

He grinned. Feisty little thing. He'd forgotten how she oiled his gears. Her voice was velvety soft and deep, like a spell that spoke directly to his blood, causing it to surge out of control. A Siren's song. He took a page from Odysseus and filed those thoughts away. Far away.

"So. How's this going at work, Ms. Architect?" he asked, with another generous smile.

She sighed. "You're such an ass, Koczynski."

It was sheer torture, being physically attracted to someone you wanted to throttle. She was like a baby panther. Cuddly cute until the claws and teeth came out. *Oh*, that helped. His inconvenient boner eased off a little. That was another good reason to avoid contact with her.

Alexa continued to peer at him with obvious disdain.

"Seriously, tell me about your name—" but she didn't have a chance to reply.

Kate entered the room, flustered, her hair in disarray. Both Bruce and Alexa sat up taller, pasting friendly smiles on their faces. It wouldn't do to advertise their ongoing war of wills to their worried friend. In that respect they seemed to be on the same page. "Well they're down. I guess we'll see tomorrow how they react when I leave."

"Tomorrow?" Bruce said. So soon?

She nodded. "Help yourself to food, you guys." She filled a plate and set it down, pushing at it with a fork, taking tiny nibbles, distracted.

"So, not much time to prepare, but Kate's made a few notes for us," Alexa said, shoving a stack of crinkled papers toward him.

He took them and scanned them. The handwriting was almost illegible. The words seemed almost randomly arranged, as though Kate had jotted down fragments of ideas as they came to her. Not surprising, he supposed. Frowning, he looked up and met Alexa's gaze with a silent question. Was this supposed to make sense? She peered steadily at him, as though trying to convey something telepathically. Again he perused their so-called "instructions." He let out a soundless whistle, smiled again and nodded. "This looks great. We won't have any trouble at all, Kate. Nothing for you to worry about."

Possibly for the first time in history, he earned a smile from Alexa Jenner. What do you know? He did the right thing. He offered a half smile in return.

After a few minutes, Kate picked up an envelope and said, "I got a flight out tomorrow afternoon. You'll pick up Markus from day care, Bruce, at twelve-thirty. Then give him a snack, some exercise, and a nap. Then you pick up Maddie at school at 2:30. She'll need a snack and some down time too. I know it sounds rigid, but trust me, that will make it easier on everyone. I have it all written down there."

Bruce nodded. "I can handle that."

"Don't worry, Katie, it'll be fine." said Alex, her voice soothing and calm. It was almost enough to calm the frenzy of panic rising in his own gullet. But not quite.

Bruce shot a glance her way. He hoped she was as chill about this as she seemed.

Kate continued. "The next part, I'm not so sure about. Alexa, you'll get them ready for bed... you'll have to stay at the house, I guess," Kate said. "Besides, someone has to take care of the kitties, too."

Alexa nodded. "Anything special there? I know Lucy needs her shots." Alexa adjusted her glasses to scan Kate's list.

"Right. Once a day, evenings are fine," Kate said. "And Oscar's no trouble. He's so old, he sleeps all the time."

The subject in question coiled around Bruce's ankles. He looked down. *Fuck, that mangy old cat better not keel over on my shift.*

Kate let out a big breath. "So, Alexa, your mornings will be a bit wild. You'll have to get them up, fed, dressed, and drop Maddie at school for 8:45. Then Markus right afterwards."

Bruce watched Alexa process this information, her eyes cast down at the list, her brow furrowed. "So I won't be able to start my work day until almost nine-thirty," Alexa said, her brow drawing down, her exquisite wide lips pursed.

Bruce studied the long dark lashes grazing her smooth tan cheeks.

She sighed. "With the new Arts Centre project starting, I'll have a team expecting answers from me first thing." She turned to him. "It would be better for me if you could come by here at about seven-thirty, and then drop the kids off."

He froze as her words sunk in. "Do what?"

"Come early and take the kids to school?" She dipped her chin and peered at him over the frames of her glasses, creating the illusion that he was being scolded by a sexy little librarian.

Hell no! He cleared his throat. "It's quite a ways for me to get over here from West Van." His smile felt tight. He could imagine the hours it would take him coming over the bridge four times a day. He'd go nuts. "Morning rush hour traffic on the bridge can be brutal. I couldn't guarantee getting here on time."

Alexa slumped in her chair. "Oh. I see."

The clash of cutlery against Kate's plate jarred his nerve endings as she dropped a knife. He glanced at her, taking in her pinched expression, and remembered his vow to Simon. She offered him a watery smile.

He raised his hands, palm out and responded *sotto voce*. "But don't worry, Kate. Maybe we can take turns or something. Al and I will iron out the details. It'll be fine." He met Alexa's steely eye. "Right, Al?"

"Okay, alright." Alexa nibbled her nail. "I'll have to work longer in the evenings, I guess."

He squinted. Both ends of this stick were getting shorter by the minute.

Kate nodded. "Well, the issue is dinner. I'm sure you'll be home early enough to do the bedtime routine most days, but if they don't eat at a reasonable time, you'll be really sorry. They become unmanageable. It snowballs. If there's one lesson I've learned–"

"I know all about that," Alexa smirked. "A houseful of over-hungry kids is insanity."

How would she know? "What time do they eat?" Bruce asked, frowning.

Kate said, "I'd say, six would be the latest."

"Some days, maybe, I could be off work by five thirty and get here. That makes for a very short work day. I'll draw up a work schedule so you know when you have to cover for me."

"Well, I can feed them dinner," Bruce said. He'd have meals delivered from that gourmet place. "That's easy." Why that earned him a skeptical glance from both women he didn't know. He was resourceful. They'd see.

"Well don't worry too much, Bruce. Alexa is an incredible superwoman with house and family things."

His head jerked up. "How's that?" It certainly wasn't how he saw her. She was all about her career. He couldn't even visualize her in a kitchen. A bedroom, yes, but…

"Don't you know she practically raised her six younger brothers and sisters while graduating from high school? This woman can do anything!" Kate gushed.

Six? He narrowed his eyes at Alexa, blinking. No, he didn't know that. He tried to picture the shrew caring for six younger siblings and failed. That was a story he'd like to hear. The image didn't fit. "You might have to give me some lessons, then, Al." He shrugged, imagining some up-close one-on-one time in the kitchen, and his body heated. He took a deep breath and let it out through his open mouth. He shut his eyes. *Forget that.*

"I hope I don't have to teach you everything," she said, smirking while she leaned back and crossed her arms. "But I have my doubts."

"Whoah. You underestimate me, sweetheart." Bruce looked for support at Kate. "I have skills, too—"

"He certainly does, Alex. That's why Simon asked Bruce to help me in the first place. He's fantastic with the kids, you should see them together. They absolutely love spending time with him. Nobody does fun and games like Bruce."

"Fun and games," Alexa repeated, straight-faced. Her eyes slid over to Bruce. "That'll come in handy." Her mouth twitched.

He gave her a half smile, cocking one brow. "You have no idea." He'd like to have some fun with her. If only she were capable of letting loose for once. Or maybe not.

Alexa eyed him with flat, grey-green eyes that managed to communicate her lack of faith in him without a word. Somehow, he felt eight years old again.

He had promised to be nice, *cooperate*. He took a deep breath. "Right. We'll make a plan. "Alexa and I make a great team. She's gonna help me with cooking lessons, and I'm gonna help her plan fun and games."

She nodded, her eyes narrowing.

"Okay, then." Kate stood up, taking her mostly untouched plate to the kitchen. "I'd better pack," she said absently. "I'm exhausted already and I need a good sleep tonight." She turned back. "There's something I'm forgetting…"

Alexa got up and took the plate from her hands. "Let me clean up here. You go to bed. We'll see ourselves out."

Bruce rose too. He couldn't sit while she worked. "I'll give you a hand." He picked up some dishes and took them into the kitchen, then caught her smirking at him, a twinkle in her green eyes. "What?"

"This should be interesting."

"Well good night. I'll see you both tomorrow."

"You bet, Kate." He went to her and took her upper arms in his hands, meeting her gaze. She seemed frail. He wondered what it would be like to find out your one true love was injured half way across the world. "Don't even think about us. We're in control here. You just take care of yourself and bring Simon and his folks home safely." He leaned in to kiss her forehead.

She nodded and slipped away.

A moment of tense silence followed. They stood until they heard her bedroom door close. Alexa's long slow exhale was audible.

Bruce raised his eyebrows at her. "Well?" he finally said, throwing down the gauntlet. Enough pretence—they needed to have this out.

"I get the impression you're not happy about doing this," she said.

"Not at all. I adore Maddie and Markus. We're gonna have a blast," he drawled, leaning towards her ear. His nostrils filled with her sweet, spicy scent, and he leaned back, regretting their proximity, and exhaled slowly.

Her darkened expression said he'd scored a point. "You can get out of the mundane shit like shopping and housework because you're Mister Fun and Games. I have a very demanding job and a huge project starting up, so you're going to have to pull your weight around here and then some, Hefner."

She couldn't be serious. "I don't see a problem. I'll spend my mornings renovating my house and head over here for the afternoons. Easy-peasy."

"I know you. You'll try to weasel out of chores." Alexa said. "It will take a little more time management. I have good software for that. We'll make up a spreadsheet, and divide up the responsibilities to make sure everything is covered. I'll have to plan ahead as much as possible and keep you posted on my workdays so you'll know what to expect from day to day."

"Spreadsheets." She was nuts. She was trying to take control of his whole bloody life. He rolled his shoulders and rubbed the back of his neck with a hand, trying to loosen a knot of tension. Next she'd be giving him minute-by-minute instructions.

"You'll have to find time for shopping and chores."

The air in the room grew thin. Did he just get stuck with shopping *and* cooking? He'd have to hire an army of help. "Don't you trust me, Al?"

"No." She blinked. "We're both making personal sacrifices for our friends. You'll have to do your share, Koczynski. Get over it."

"How can we possibly fail?" He offered her a wide smile. "You have project management software. Right, Al?"

She took off her glasses and shoved them into her hair so she could rub her eyes.

"Why are you worried about me, anyway? Sounds like you're the one that's got time management issues. It'll be fine. I can catch up on my construction work on the weekends." Bruce grinned at Alexa, and she stared back.

"Unfortunately, I work most weekends." She pressed her lips together, nodding. "You'll have to stay with the kids during the days and some evenings, too."

"You're not going to dump extra work on me so you can slip a few drinks with co-workers into your week."

Then a slow, inscrutable smile spread across her face, and her voice dropped down a notch, sultry with a hard edge, like the cruel caress of a sharp blade. "Not that it's any of your business, but if I'm working after hours, I'm actually working."

Damn it, that voice! If he ignored her words, it almost sounded like an invitation. For someone else. Not for him. "You mean you have no social life? *Quel surprise!*"

She made a sound, a cross between a scream and a roar, but she kept her mouth clamped tight, so it seemed to bleed out of her ears. God, she was a tiger. Her smoky eyes burned with a fiery light that made him wonder what she would be like in between the sheets. "My personal life has nothing to do with this negotiation. I have responsibilities at work. Period."

Jeezus, she was tense. It's probably because she worked so much she never got any sex at all. Someone should redirect that ferocious energy into bed, and then give her a darn good reason to relax. Not him though. His erection twitched again. Not helpful. It made him so mad he could spit. *Claws and teeth. Claws and teeth.* He sucked a breath slowly in through his clenched teeth and forced a smile.

The stick! "I have to meet tradesmen at my house sometimes. It sounds like you're trying to offload all the work to me."

"Hardly. I'm going to be living here. We'll have to put it on the schedule."

"Right. I guess we will," he replied, grinning past gritted teeth. Despite his promise to Kate, Bruce laughed, because he knew it would annoy her. "I mean what does a thirty-something professional workaholic know about child care anyhow? I'm trying to be helpful, here. I know it'll be a hardship for a career woman such as yourself, honey, but I guess you'll have to pull up your garters and cope with your share of this childcare deal."

"Please don't call me honey." Her shoulders slumped. "I know more than I ever wanted to about childcare and homemaking, thank you very much."

Alexa sliced her hand across her other palm. "All I want is to split this up evenly and disrupt my life as little as possible. If we project manage our schedule and list of duties, we should be fine. I'll put Kate's list in my software and then you can add your constraints. If I can manage the design and construction of an entire civic building, I can handle a couple of weeks co-parenting with you."

Bruce sighed. They were never going to be able to coexist in peace. That much was clear. "Fine. That suits me perfectly."

She crossed her arms. "We'll share the work fair and square, *including* weekends. You do your half and I'll do mine. But let me make myself perfectly clear. I don't care what you think of me, Koczynski. But please *try* not to make this situation any worse. Do your part and stay out of my way."

He nodded. She so totally didn't understand him. He'd do anything for Simon and Kate their kids. "It might be best if we try to stay away from each other as much as possible."

They glared at each other.

"So. We have a deal?" Alexa thrust out her hand like a knife.

He gripped her small, strong hand firmly in his own and squeezed, perhaps a little tighter than he should have. "Deal."

CHAPTER 4

Two days later, on the last day of May, Alexa stood with Kate and the children in the front hall of the house as Bruce loaded Kate's luggage into the car. The plan was that she would stay with the kids while Bruce drove Kate to the airport, but she had her doubts.

"I'll take the SUV," said Bruce to Kate, as he wheeled a suitcase onto the porch. "Since it's got the child seats, I'll be driving it the most, I guess."

Alexa gazed after him out the open door. *He's got no idea.* She caught Kate's eye, smiling.

"And there's room for all the gear," Kate said.

"Gear?" said Bruce, hefting the bags into the open back of the SUV, the muscles in his arms bulging. What a sexy brute.

Alexa looked away. She didn't care that he was the most dangerously attractive man she'd ever met, even more sexy now that he'd tidied up his curly rocker hair to a respectable length. He was nothing but trouble. He was as annoying as he ever was, though she was resigned to put up with him for the next two weeks or so. She wouldn't be able to manage without his help, nor he without hers, and they both knew it.

"Well, there's the jog stroller. You might want to use that sometimes." Kate smiled at him. "And there's lots of room for groceries."

Bruce met her eye, scowling. "Ha. Ha."

Alexa muffled her laughter as they walked out to the car. Boy did Koz have a lesson coming.

The good-byes were not going well. Markus clung to Alexa, whimpering persistently, confused about what was happening. Maddie lunged at Kate. She lifted her up, and she wrapped her skinny legs around her and buried her face in her neck. "I miss Daddy."

Alexa's throat squeezed in sympathy, and her eyes burned. This was rough.

"You be a good girl, Maddie. I'll bring Daddy back as soon as he can travel and we sort out Grandma and Grandpa, okay. You'll be fine with Auntie Alex and Bruce." Kate tried to sooth her, stroking her hair and her back over and over, but her face was tight.

"I won't. I won't be fine. I want to come with you. I want to see Daddy."

Maddie and Simon were very close, Alexa reflected. All those years, before Kate, they had only each other. And they'd never been apart until last week. Her heart thumped, thinking about the special bond between father and daughter, and how frightened she must be to learn her Dad was hurt in a far away place. Kate loosened her grip and let her slide down.

Bruce coughed and bent to lift a carry-on bag that sat by the door. He stood up, his wild curls backlit by the porch-light like a lion's mane. "We'd better get a move on." His eyes were suspiciously glassy.

Alexa stepped up to Kate so she could kiss Markus good-bye. He threw himself at her, howling "Mamaaaa!" forcing Kate to grab him.

"Come on, baby. Let Mommy go."

He cried ever louder, refusing to release her, and a tug-of-war ensued. Markus was winning. Alexa's gut twisted with anxiety. Not an auspicious beginning to her tenure. They'd never make it to the airport at this rate.

"How about a movie, kids?" she tried. No response. Okay, that wasn't going to work.

Bruce looked at her, his eyes widening. "How would you kids like to drive Mommy to the airport?"

Maddie turned a tear-streaked face toward him, sniffed and nodded pathetically. "Can we, Kate?" Her voice croaked through her tears.

Kate sighed. "Very well. Let's get going. Grab their jackets," she said, still holding onto Markus.

Oh, great. Alexa could imagine Bruce alone at the airport with two traumatized kids. "I guess I'm coming too."

Bruce peered at her with eyes narrowed. "It's okay. I'll bring the kids right back," he said. "We'll be fine. Right, Scallywag?"

Maddie glared at him, her green eyes owlish and wet.

Alexa could picture the two hysterical children and him, alone in the car. He'd probably bail on the whole venture, and leave her stranded for the duration. "I'm coming."

The forty minute drive to the airport was uneventful. Kate sat in the back between the kids, who whimpered quietly, continuing to cling. Alexa sat up front, next to Bruce, who drove in silence, his knuckles white on the wheel. Conversation was scant, and tended to be between Kate and Alexa, and entail last minute details and reminders.

Finally, they were checked in and heading to the departure gate. When they reached security, Alexa wrapped her arms around Kate for a good-bye hug and kissed her cheek. "Be careful. Take care of yourself too, okay?" Alexa pried Markus off of Kate, not taking no for an answer this time. He was more pliable now, exhausted from his crying. She held his soft heavy body tightly against hers, reassuring both of them, despite the twist of anxiety in her gut. They'd get through this. Somehow.

Bruce tried to take Maddie's hand, to gently tug her away from Kate's side. She yanked her hands away more than once, until Kate finally insisted. At last, Kate walked away. Maddie stood sullenly by Bruce's side, his hand on her shoulder, watching Kate go, fresh tears trailing down her cheeks. Alexa's throat tightened in sympathy, and tears welled in her own eyes. They stood until Kate stopped to glance back one last time before rounding the corner, out of sight.

"Come on, Scallywag," Bruce croaked, not without sympathy in his voice. He hoisted her up.

Maybe he was fighting back tears too. Then she realized who she was talking about. Not the most sensitive of guys. Stupid. "Let's get you home, kids."

Maddie turned on Bruce suddenly, punching and kicking. "I hate you, I hate you. Leave me alone!" and turned to Alexa, flinging her arms around her neck, knocking her glasses askew.

Alexa was overwhelmed, nearly knocked off her feet with Markus's weight in her arms. She looked at Bruce with wild eyes, and he had no choice but to take Markus from her so she could comfort Maddie. She crouched down to hug her. Koczynski might be able to lift a seven-year-old but she could not.

"Let's go, Marky." He shifted the little boy to his other arm, grunting under the weight, and then lifted him up onto his shoulders. "How 'bout a ride?"

Markus squealed with surprise, momentarily forgetting his grief. Good move. Then Bruce said, "How about some ice cream to cheer everybody up? What do you say, Scallywag?"

Alexa eyed him gratefully. Maybe the guy had some instinct for this after all.

It turned out they couldn't find ice cream at the airport, and had to drive back to town, debating possible locations all the way.

"There's a little Italian place on Denman," suggested Bruce.

"I want pas-moni," insisted Markus.

"It's spuh-moni, Marky," corrected Maddie. "And you don't really like it. You only like the name. He won't eat it. He just likes to say it."

"We don't need to go downtown. There's a Baskin Robins near my condo. It's on the way back to the house."

"Sure," Bruce agreed. "What's your favourite flavour, Scallywag?"

No answer.

"Don't be a sourpuss, Mads. Bruce asked you a question."

"Strawberry."

"I'm more of a chocolate girl, myself," said Alexa, pushing up her glasses.

She caught the flash of Bruce's dark eyes and the quirk of his lips as he glanced her way.

"You've got a problem with chocolate?"

"Not at all. I like chocolate." He let his eyes roam down her body and up again. "I like caramel even better."

She felt herself blush. Was he suggesting she was caramel? "What's your favourite *ice cream*?"

"I'm partial to lemon sorbet, actually."

She chortled. Now, that was a surprise. It was something she'd expect Krystof to say.

"What?"

"Nothing," she replied, laughing under her breath. "I took you for a tin roof sundae kind of guy."

"You mean I lack maturity, subtlety and sophistication?"

She declined to answer, watching the street go by. That's exactly what she'd meant, and it irked her that he saw through her so easily. She even wondered if he'd said lemon sorbet just to mess with her head.

As they drove down Broadway, they noticed a familiar red sign. "How about DQ instead? Plain ol' vanilla for everyone. Would you guys like a Dilly Bar?"

Everyone agreed, so he pulled into the parking lot and they went in.

"Markus should have a kids dipped cone, instead," said Alexa. "The Dilly Bars are too big. He'll be sick."

"Nah," Bruce grinned. "Let him have what everyone else is having, Al. He doesn't need to be made to feel small."

"He is small," she insisted. "He doesn't care. And wipe that stupid grin off your face please." Damn him, why was he so good-looking? Every time their eyes met, she felt naked, and had to pull her gaze away.

"Don't worry about it," Bruce answered as he pulled out his wallet to pay.

"So far, so good," said Alexa when they sat down with their ice cream, and the kids seemed happier. She eyed him. "Admit it, we came here because you didn't want to have to order lemon sorbet, because you secretly like tin roof sundae."

He eyed her, his expression amused and shook his head. "You are so weird. Cute, but weird," he said, biting into his ice cream bar with a grin. "I actually like everything lemon, because it reminds me of my Mom."

She looked at him. That sounded like the truth.

They finished their ice creams, Markus eating so slowly that his melted all the way down his shirt and arms to his elbows. "Can you wash him up in the men's room?" asked Alexa.

He looked at her like she was crazy. "No."

"You'd better get used to it. You'll have to take him to the bathroom all the time when I'm at work."

"Not today," he said, gathering up their garbage. "You're here."

She scowled at him. "I'll do it. But you'd better get your head around taking him to the bathroom. You realize he needs help with the potty. When he deigns to use it, that is."

He made a face, half incredulous, half horrified. "You mean, he still wears diapers?"

"Pull ups," she smiled knowingly, taking Markus by the arm and leading him away. Lemon sorbet or not, it was going to be amusing watching Koczynski learn a lesson or two about adulting.

"Same thing, right? Isn't it? Isn't it the same..." his voice faded as they walked away. She laughed. This might turn out to be fun. Good sport, watching Bruce come unhinged under the pressures of daily childcare.

When she and Markus emerged from the washroom, Bruce and Maddie were waiting by the door. They got back into the SUV and pulled out of the parking lot, heading back to the house. Not three minutes passed before Markus spoke.

"I sick."

"What?" said Bruce, glancing over his shoulder. "What'd he say?"

"He said he feels sick," said Maddie.

"Does your tummy hurt, Markus?" asked Alexa. "I told you the Dilly Bar was too big for him, but you wouldn't listen. Stubborn man."

"He didn't have to eat it all," Bruce replied.

"Shows what you know about kids," she said.

"I know about kids. I was a kid once, too, you know."

"You still are one," said Alexa, laughing.

"I sick," said Markus again. "I–" and let loose a huge belch.

"He's going to puke," announced Maddie.

"What?"

"Vomit," clarified Alexa, snickering uncontrollably. Ha! Vindication. This would teach him a lesson. "You'd better pull over."

~

"I heard her! Jesus H Christ!" shouted Bruce. "Just a minute. Hold on Markus, there's no place to–" he checked traffic wildly, twisting his head this way and that. Then he cranked the wheel and turned into a side road, stopping the SUV with a lurch and ramming it into park. Leaping out, he yanked open the back door, released Markus from his restraining belt, and lifted him out just in time for Markus to let loose the contents of his stomach on the front of Bruce's shirt. "Faaaa–!" he stopped himself in time, holding Markus at arm's length. Setting the boy on the ground he turned to her with a look of utter horror on his face. "God damn it! What the hell are you laughing at!?"

Alexa was speechless with mirth. The look on his face! She'd never forget it. She opened her door and rounded the vehicle to take charge of Markus. She pulled wet wipes out of the bag and cleaned him up, watching Bruce storm and sputter beside her.

"I can't friggin' believe it!" He shuddered and stripped off his shirt holding it out towards her between pinched fingers, providing her an unobstructed view of his sun-kissed cut pecs and rippling six-pack abs. Her eyes locked onto Bruce's naked skin like a heat-seeking missile. She was undone. This was Bruce? The player she loved to hate?

She forced a laugh, lifting Markus into the back of the SUV to keep him off the road. "What do you want me to do about it?" Oh. My. God. She was flustered. He said he'd been working out, but... well! She'd never been this up-close-and-personal with such a buff male torso. Her gaze flicked again and again to his golden biceps, abs, pecs, pointlessly trying to decide which part was the most delicious. It knocked the wind right out of her.

If only she could feel this kind of heat with someone she could trust and respect, who trusted and respected her. Wouldn't that be something?

"Jeez, Al. Help a guy out already, will you?"

It took her a stunned moment to answer. "Here." She handed him a plastic shopping bag from the back of the car, trying not to laugh, while unsure whether she wanted to run away screaming or plaster herself to his body. On the other hand, gorgeous as he was, he smelled pretty bad and looked sweetly pathetic. She handed him a few wet wipes as well.

He stuffed the filthy shirt in the bag and tucked it in the car.

"How do you like your Dilly Bars now, Koczynski?"

"Okay. You were right. I guess I got what I deserve." He looked sheepish.

I was right? Did she hear right?

"But how was I to know he couldn't eat it? I remember eating a ton of ice cream as a kid."

"I knew. I–"

"Told me so." He stepped up close to her. Too close. "You did. So what you're saying is, I should listen to you?"

"It's a start," she said, trying not to smile, her gaze darting to him, away, to, away. Her face felt hot. Uh. Was this the cause of the classic fluttering eyelashes of storybook flirtation? Some combination of his sexy naked skin and endearing humility was making her very hot and bothered. Her heart pounded with the thrill of it. She stepped back, turning her face away. "You smell."

He shook his head and bent to Markus, who was now giggling with Maddie over the mishap. "You okay, little buddy? Not sick anymore?"

Markus giggled harder and fell over backwards.

He lifted Markus to return him to his car seat. "I'm sorry I let you get sick, Marky. I should have stuck with Plan A and taken you all to the Italian gelato place. At least there you get a tiny bowl."

"It's okay, Uncle Bruce," Alexa said, buckling herself in the stinking car, snickering "We'll go for lemon sorbet next time." And she had to grant him this, they'd all forgotten why there were they in the first place.

CHAPTER 5

Bruce pulled the SUV into the pre-school parking lot to pick up Markus the following afternoon. Alexa had kept her criticism light-hearted, but he knew he'd screwed up. If he hadn't noticed the fact she could hardly hold a straight face he might not have seen through her stern scolding. Maybe he'd never given her a reason to believe he was anything but a fool. Well, he'd learned his lesson. There were so many details to parenting that he hadn't a clue about. He knew that. He'd also noticed, with some satisfaction, her wide eyes glued to his chest when he'd stripped off his shirt. He smiled, remembering. So she wasn't entirely immune to his charms, after all.

He strode to the door of the school, making his way through the milling parents who were waiting to pick up their kids, or already had them in hand. Some were heading to their cars, others to the playground beside the building.

Once inside, he stood, bewildered, gazing around at the brightly-coloured, half-scale space, willing his mind to order what it saw into a recognizable pattern. Little blue boxes lined the walls, a rainbow-hued cornucopia of objects tumbling out onto the floor. Bodies, large and small, sliding around each other and mewling like demented cats. The noise level was numbing. Finally, he saw that the boxes were cubbies for personal gear, the objects were jackets and lunch kits and shoes, and the parents were trying to gather their children and belongings, but not without a significant amount of social chatter going on over the heads of their small charges.

"Excuse me," someone said, pushing by, dragging a youngster in a yellow hoody.

"Are you lost?" said another, but passed on by without waiting for an answer.

He searched the mayhem for something that resembled Markus. There were plenty of small bodies, blond, brown, dark and red-haired. Where was Markus? His eyes almost crossed in confusion.

At last he realized that there were a number of children still within the classroom on the other side of a half open Dutch door, where he had come with Kate to meet the pre-school teacher the previous week. Peering inside, he recognized Markus, and went through.

Yes, there he was. He waded into the room, even more colourful and cluttered than the corridor. He hardly recognized it as the same quiet, organized space he'd visited before. "Hey. Markus, buddy," Bruce said, swooping down to pick Markus up, tossing him into the air and catching him.

Markus's reaction was not what he expected. He let out a terrified scream at the top of his surprisingly powerful lungs, squirming and kicking like a salmon yanked from the sea.

Bruce recoiled, his heart whupping his ribcage like a fist.

"Sir! Please put that child down. Sir!" barked an unfamiliar stout woman, lurching toward him with the speed and force of a steamboat. This was not the teacher he'd been introduced to.

Bruce turned toward her. "Pardon?"

"Put. Him. Down." She wasn't shouting, but her tone of voice was terrifying, bringing back memories of every stern teacher, every scolding he'd ever received from his father. He froze.

Setting Markus down on the floor, Bruce grinned at the woman, his habitual response to sooth attackers. "Hey, there. How you doing?" He stared at Markus, who was now clinging to the woman's leg. *What the hell?* Wasn't today Markus's first day in this place? How could he feel safer with this strange, frightening woman than with him, Bruce, who had been there the day he was born? "Marky? It's me, buddy."

More high-pitched screaming, muffled by the fact that his face was buried in her skirt.

"Who are you? What are you doing here?" demanded the woman.

He took a calming breath to slow his heart, and reminded himself that he was in the right, and Markus was just a toddler. With moods. He leaned in and offered his hand, laying on the charm. "I'm Bruce Koczynski, and I'm here to pick up Markus Sharpe, obviously."

She cast a gimballed eye toward the keening Markus at her knee. "Not so obviously."

Bruce hid his confusion behind a wall of bravado. "You must know the reason he's in day care is that his mother had to leave town suddenly. She brought me in last week, and I met another teacher... Debbie something. It's all been arranged."

"Mamaaaa," cried Markus.

"I'm aware of the arrangements. But never having met you, how can I be sure who you are?" she said.

"Who else would want somebody else's three year old kid?" he asked in wonder.

She pursed her lips and raised her eyebrows in reply, her eyes icy cold. Well. It wasn't such a stupid question.

"Okay, alright. Jeez." He pulled his wallet out of his jeans and opened it, flipping to his driver's license and showing it to her. "Would you check your information please? Because I'm going to be here every day for the next two weeks or so. And I'd like–" but she had sailed away, Markus trailing her like an oil slick in her wake.

At a desk in the corner, she stared at her computer screen, clicking her mouse again and again, frowning. "Mr. Koczynski?" She mangled it, like most people did.

"Koczynski. Just call me Bruce."

She scowled at him, but her wrath had softened to a mix of skepticism and apology.

He pushed his wallet toward her again, and she glanced at it, nodding. "Does Markus know you at all?"

Bruce smiled incredulously, shaking his head. "Of course. He's known me all his life. He's freaked out about being here, and his parents leaving, I guess."

At these words, Markus resumed his whimpering.

"Give me a minute with him. He'll be alright." Bruce squatted down and tried to meet Markus's eye. "Hey, hey little buddy." He reached out a hand, without touching him. "Don't you want to go home, Marky?"

Markus stared at him with huge, swimming eyes. "Mommy?"

Bruce smiled softly. "Mommy's gone on a trip to get Daddy, buddy.

You remember? The airport yesterday? The ice cream?" He smiled hopefully.

Markus processed, his brows twisting. "I sick."

Bruce nodded. "All over my shirt, dude."

Markus giggled. "Funny."

"Hilarious. I'm really hoping you don't do it again. My shoes still smell really awful."

Markus let him take his little hand. "Hee-wawus."

They smiled at each other.

Bruce looked up, meeting the teacher's eyes. She nodded and pushed a clipboard toward him, with a form for him to sign, even though he was convinced it was the same one he'd signed last week.

"How was he today? Did he enjoy himself?"

She screwed up her face. "Eventually. He was a bit reluctant to let Miss... er, Miss..." She glanced again at her computer screen.

"Um. Jenner," Bruce offered. So he gave Alexa a hard time, too.

"Yes. We got off to a rather difficult start this morning, but..." she looked down at Markus. "We're okay now, aren't we Markus. You had fun with us, didn't you?"

Markus shrugged. He looked earnestly at Bruce. "Mommy home?"

Bruce then knew the strange and unfamiliar sensation of trying to smile and frown at once, moderating bad news with good intentions. It hurt his face, and also his heart, somehow, looking into Markus's tortured little countenance. "No, buddy. Mommy just left. It'll be a while yet."

Markus's face scrunched up.

Shit, no. No more screaming. "Hey. There's this terrific park I drove past today. It had a great set of swings, and a big climbing fort, like a... like a sailing ship. You want to come with me and check it out?"

Markus nodded, and Bruce let out a tense, shallow breath in relief, flashing a smile up at the teacher. It worked.

"Okay, then. Let's go." He stood up. "I'm sorry. I didn't get your name."

"Darlene. Darlene Swinton."

"Well, I guess we'll see you tomorrow, Ms. Swinton."

Bruce's spirits were buoyed as they left the pre-school. They may have gotten off to a rocky start, but everything was going to be fine. Everyone was overreacting. The trick to this was a little common sense, and most importantly, staying calm. Fortunately, he had indeed noticed a good-looking playground on his way to the daycare, and drove directly there.

Markus was pleased enough, racing across the mulch ground to climb up the structure. Bruce caught up with him and stood, watching Markus's fearless ascent, smiling. Kids weren't that complicated. You had to put yourself in their shoes.

"Boos!"

He stepped up to the ladder Markus was suspended from. "Whassup, l'il buddy?"

"Hep me up," Markus insisted.

Bruce placed his palm on Markus's little padded backside and guided him to the top of the ladder, standing back to watch him crawl around up there on the quarter-deck, the captain of a ship, gripping the rudder wheel in earnest, gazing off at the horizon. Kids wanted to have a little adventure, have some fun, and at the same time feel safe. Feel like they had a safe harbour to sail home to when the adventure was all done.

Bruce laughed. "Can you see the pirates over there?"

"Whe-yo?" said Markus, his brow beetling.

Bruce turned and pointed at the street beyond the playground. "Can't you see them?"

Markus clung to the side railing. "Boos?"

"Aye, matey."

"Boos?"

Bruce looked up. "What is it Markus?"

"I sca-wed."

Bruce grinned. "There's not really pirates, Markus. I'm pretending."

"Come down now!" Markus's panic built.

Bruce sighed. "Okay, come on down."

Markus inched to the top of the ladder, gripping the railing tightly in his pudgy little hands. "I sca-wed."

"Come on, I'll catch you."

"Too high," Markus said, gazing down at Bruce, a little hummock rising on his forehead.

What the hell now? He scanned the structure, looking for easier ways for Markus to descend. He eyed a bright yellow, spiral slide on the other side. "Hey, Markus. Do you want to slide down?"

Markus looked hopeful.

"Come over to the slide, and I'll catch you at the bottom. Come on."

Markus inched over to the slide, looking longingly down its curving length.

"Come on down now, buddy."

Markus sat down, his little sneakers sticking over the ledge of the slide, and rocked forward and backward, forward and backward.

"What now, Markus?"

"Too high." His face crumpled up, and he cried. "Come down nowwwwww."

Bruce pinched his finger and thumb to the bridge of his nose, sighing, and scrubbed his face with his hand. "Do you need help, Markus?"

"Dowwwwwn!" Markus wailed.

Bruce realized he would have to climb up there and get Markus down. Somehow, he never imagined himself crawling around on a play structure as part of this job, or ever again, for that matter. He took a deep breath and climbed up the ladder, hoping it was designed with his weight in mind. "Hold on, buddy. I'm coming up to get you."

Markus clung to him the moment he got near, practically climbing up into his arms like a chimpanzee. The space up there was cramped, not being designed to accommodate full-grown men, never mind one the size of Bruce. He crouched and twisted his body through the space, and back down the narrow ladder to the solid earth. Markus hung on tightly to his neck, burying his hot, wet face in Bruce's shirt, whimpering and gasping for air as they walked back to the car.

"No py-wits, Boos. Mark don't like py-wits."

"Okay, buddy. No more pirates."

All seemed well, and Bruce decided it was time to move on.

"What now, Markus?" he asked, not sure how to calm the child. "Is it time to go and get Maddie at school?"

"Mmm-mad-*hic*-y," gulped Markus in reply.

That seemed to be a good omen, so he opened the SUV and attempted to pop Markus in his car seat. Markus clung to him, refusing to let go or be strapped down. The harder Bruce tried, the harder Markus resisted, making his little body rigid, and screaming in protest.

"Hey, Markus. What is it now? You want to get Maddie, don't you?" But nothing he said made a difference, and the battle continued. Bruce kept a smile on his face, and tried teasing, tickling and cajoling, but his patience was disintegrating until finally he had to use brute force to drag the strap across Markus's squirming body and lock it into place. Markus continued to scream and kick as Bruce got in the car, and drove towards Maddie's school. He rolled his shoulders to loosen them, swearing under his breath. He was sweating. Jeezus! Who knew a little kid could put up such a powerful fight?

Thwack! Something hit Bruce in the back of the head.

"Hey!" What the hell? He looked down at the object that bounced onto the floor at his feet. Some sort of stuffed duck, as far as he could tell. "Very funny, Markus," he scowled into the rear view mirror. "Settle down now."

Thwack!

Ow! A small board book bounced off his ear into his lap. That time it hurt. "Not funny, Markus! Stop that!"

He glanced into the rear view mirror just in time to catch Markus with a sippy-cup in his fist, poised overhead. "*Don't* you dare. That's enough of that."

Markus glared back, pure hatred burning in his little icy blue eyes. Their gaze locked for a fateful moment, and Markus tossed the cup, fortunately missing Bruce's head this time, and simultaneously letting out a furious battle cry that continued unabated for several blocks.

Damn, he missed the turn.

Bruce glowered as he drove along, grinding his teeth, astonished that Kate and Simon could tolerate this existence, held hostage by this miniature savage beast. The screaming finally ceased, but its echo bounced around in Bruce's throbbing head. He stopped at a red light, and glanced into the mirror again, only to see that Markus was sound asleep, his body lolled over to one side like a rag doll, his mouth hanging open, and a string of drool stretching down to his lap.

Shit! Bruce smacked himself on the forehead. That's all it was. The kid was exhausted. Suddenly Bruce remembered his instructions to give him a nap after pre-school. It never occurred to him that the kid's stamina was so limited. He was like a puppy, hyperactive one moment and unconscious the next. A painful lesson.

He needed to be more organized next time.

When he stopped to pick up Maddie, he pulled the somnambulant Markus from the SUV and carried him in. Markus didn't wake, but wrapped his hot plump arms around Bruce's neck, his solid weight heavy, moist and pliant.

He assumed that the worst was over, Maddie being a somewhat rational seven-year old. Instead a sullen, red-eyed, dirt-streaked ragamuffin sat on the floor inside the classroom, clutching her knees. "Hey, Scallywag. What's up?"

The teacher approached him warily. "Mr. Koczynski?"

"Yes." He smiled, relieved at least to be acknowledged as the legitimate guardian this time.

She shook her head. "Miss Carol Shapiro, Madison's teacher?"

"Yeah, I remem–"

"Can I speak to you for a moment?" Miss Shapiro was a tall, big-boned woman, her hair a dark Brillo pad with the light from the window behind her silhouetting the coils that had gone astray during the school day.

Bruce's eyes swept over her pleasant curves, and the rather attractive collar bones peeking above the neckline of her blouse. The hair though!

He glanced down at the unresponsive Madison, and turned back to the teacher. "Sure."

She led him over to her desk. "Please have a seat."

He looked around. Miniature chairs were mostly pushed in under small desks, higgledy-piggledy. He opted to lean instead against one of the desks, shifting the slumbering Markus to his other arm. "What is it?"

She spoke in hushed undertones. "Madison didn't have a very good day today. I gather she's worried about her father, who has never left her before?"

"Uh. Yeah. That's right. He was a single dad until he married Kate. And she's just left as well."

"Well. How familiar is Madison with you?"

"I've known her father for years. I've been around since she was born," Bruce answered. "Why?"

"But how much time have you spent with Madison? She was very low today, and had a bit of a kerfuffle in the playground this afternoon. When I asked her about it, she admitted she was worried about her father."

Why was she giving him the third degree? What did she expect?

He nodded. "Well. I suppose she is. They're very close." Bruce remembered how upset she was yesterday afternoon. It'd brought a tear to his eye, and he'd nearly lost it. Simon's departure must have been even harder on her. He knew what it felt like to be abandoned.

Bruce remembered being pretty close to his mom, before she took off. He'd been only a little older than Maddie was now, and had been devastated. Shocked. Numb. After all these years, he still didn't quite believe or understand it. His heart squeezed in sympathy, and his breathing became shallow and constricted. Poor Madison. A kid can't know it's only a holiday. She feels cut loose! That he could relate to.

Afterwards, his Dad refused to coddle him, opting instead to toughen him up, he said. His older brothers had been recruited to the cause, and each did their part to 'turn him into a man.' He'd had no choice but to get over it and get on with his life. Mom wasn't coming back, after all. Although it took him a while to understand that.

Miss Shapiro's voice jolted him back to the present. "Madison said she thought her father didn't love her, or he wouldn't have left her with you and your wife.

Wife?

She said something about..." Miss Shapiro hesitated. "I hate to be rude, but she said you... she implied there were...I mean, I felt there were trust issues. Have you taken care of her before?"

Bruce bristled, pushing his shoulders back, and jutting his chin forward. "Of course I have. We both have." He and his *wife*! Ha! He indicated Markus with a tilt of his chin. "But her parents wouldn't have entrusted us with their children if they didn't trust—"

"It's not that. Please don't misunderstand me, Mr. Koczynski."

This Miss and Mister stuff was making him feel like an imposter. He squirmed. There wasn't a single instance in his entire life that required that degree of formality.

She continued. "I really noticed the difference in Maddie today. She was sullen and low energy. Not her usual cheerful self. I wanted you to know, that's all." She tilted her head to one side, her expression conciliatory, but Bruce couldn't help but feel the implied criticism. What should he be doing that he wasn't doing? What chance had he to do anything yet?

"Look, Miss... I'm sorry, can I call you Carol?"

She blinked at him, uncomprehending, her eyes glassy as an owl's. He gathered that it was not done.

He shook his head. "Never mind, I... anyway. Madison will be fine. We haven't had much time to get used to each other yet. It's not surprising that she needs a little reassurance. This is a big change for her."

"Yes. Of course."

"We'll be fine. Trust me. We... she needs a little time. She'll be fine. I'll talk to her about it."

"Alright, well I'm glad you know what you're doing, Mr. Kocz–"

"Bruce. Please." He smiled. He wished he did know what he was doing, but at least he could empathize.

She blinked at him again, and shook her head in a little tremor. "We'll see you tomorrow, Mr. Koczynski. I'm sure it'll be a better day."

He nodded, frowning. "Right. Sure." Bruce moved to the door and helped the sulking Madison to her feet. He scowled after her as she shuffled out the door. She needed reassurance, that's all. Maybe he could help her to feel that everything would be alright, even with Simon away. After all, he knew exactly how she felt. Although in her case, he knew her parents were coming back. He ought to be able to figure out what she needed to be okay. He pulled her toward him with a hand on her bony shoulder and gave it a squeeze and a rub. "Let's go home, squirt."

∽

Alexa genuinely didn't notice Krystof enter the office until he breezed by her desk and offered a haughty cursory greeting to several of her colleagues sitting in the same aisle of the studio. She was so preoccupied with the kids, and of their inauspicious kickoff the previous afternoon, she'd failed to hear him come in.

She looked up abruptly and caught his eye just as he turned away, cruising into his private office and closing the door.

The trill of her phone startled her, and she jumped, assuming it was Krys.

"Yup."

"It's Toby Millar, from Thunderbird, Alexa. Are you in?" inquired Leslie, at the front desk.

She sighed. "Yes. I'll take it, thanks Les."

Click.

"Alexa Jenner."

"Good afternoon, Alexa. Toby here. We've got the feedback from the elders you were looking for. It would be worthwhile your driving out here to hear what they have to say first hand."

She flipped a page and scanned her appointment calendar for the following two days. "That would be great Toby. I could come out tomorrow afternoon. I'd like to bring Stephanie along. I'd like to introduce her to you."

"Good. See you then." He rang off.

Excellent. Alexa had been wanting an opportunity to introduce her to the clients since Stephanie had started working on the project. She was doing a great job, and she could handle more responsibility. If only Alexa could get her to carry the bulk of the project. Alexa could be available to oversee and troubleshoot, and sign off on the drawings. It would buy Alexa more time for other things, like the Arts Centre... and the kids.

She sat, tapping her pen on the desktop, pondering Koczynski's role over the next couple of weeks, in relation to her own. She removed her glasses and rubbed the corners of her eyes. His inexperience and devil-may-care attitude could make the whole ordeal much more challenging for her. Not to mention being around him every day was already confusing her. He was so off limits and she needed to get her hormones under control.

She supposed she hadn't seen him since he'd sold his company. Kate always said how hard he worked, though Alexa had never seen him do anything but lounge around on the sofa watching hockey games. His formerly "needs a haircut" dark curls now caressed his neck in sexy, cover-model waves. A huge improvement, but confusing as hell. And he was so fit! She didn't know. She found his physical proximity, his overt masculinity disturbing. She found her own visceral response to him disturbing. The fact that she often couldn't control the direction of her hungry gaze was particularly disturbing.

He'd always been a tall, handsome hunk, though she'd told herself he wasn't her type. But she'd managed to keep her distance from him before. Except that Christmas he'd stolen a kiss under the mistletoe. He'd been drunk, but she hadn't been and she *still* remembered chemistry off the charts.

Now she couldn't seem to drag her mind away from the memory, she chastised herself, focusing on her screen. The one thing, aside from his hotness and her reaction to him, that needled her brain, was how good-natured he was. Though entirely different from Krystof in every way, he was confident, funny, cheerful under duress, and never arrogant. It took a pretty wonderful guy to get puked on without losing his shit. She wasn't sure she could've done that with half the grace.

Her phone trilled again, the internal intercom. She pushed the hands-free button. "Yup."

"Jenner. A moment, please." It was Krystof this time, summoning her in his usual loud, cursory manner, when others could overhear. "Bring the school file." There was no point responding. He'd hung up.

She sighed and stood up.

Entering his office she closed the door. His silver eyes grazed her body like a hungry lion, and she found herself wishing he would look in her eyes and smile and talk to her about work, the way he used to do. When *did* he stop doing that?

"Lock the door."

She quietly turned the latch.

Krystof slid out from behind his desk and coiled his arms around her.

"I thought you wanted to discuss the Thunderbird First Nations school project," she said, leaning away slightly, smirking at him sardonically.

"I want to discuss this weekend, darling Sasha." His mouth claimed hers. His kiss was hot and demanding.

She noticed the familiar silky, melting feelings his practiced kisses and embraces engendered, but pulled back. She hated when he called her that. "Don't mess me, Krys. I can't go back out there wrinkled and flushed." He never seemed to remember. Or care. Lately he was impatient and glib with her.

He said, "Where have you been? I want you to be mine. I'm tired of sneaking around."

"You know it has to be this way, for now," she replied. Besides, she didn't belong to anybody. Although there was a way to make it official and public. But she'd have to be a partner or it wouldn't work.

He pouted. "I'll be away until Sunday. Maybe in the afternoon we could–"

"Oh. No. I'm taking care of my friend's kids for a couple of weeks, staying at their house. That's why I haven't been around. I won't have free evenings or weekends. It depends…" on the deadbeat. The hunky deadbeat.

"I hate this babysitting you're doing. I want to see *more* of you, before Jerry comes to stay with me for the summer. Not less."

She laughed. Typical. "So it's okay for you to have kids but not me? Try to understand, Krys. I have to do it for my friend."

"You are cruel. My heart is breaking." He turned away, in genuine or mock dejection, and looked back at her over his shoulder. "I love you, you know."

She nodded. "I know."

Krystof didn't appear to hear her, and went behind his desk to sit down, his eyes already scanning the papers in front of him.

"Listen, Krystof. About this project. Why don't you give it to Stephanie outright. She's been doing the work anyway. I'll introduce her and make the transition smooth." Alexa laid the file on his desk, and stepped toward the door. "Her father's Metis, did you know? So she's sensitive to the issues. She can handle it, and she's been working really hard. And she's almost registered now. She deserves a break. It would free me up to work on the Arts Centre. I'd like to have more time to dedicate to that, and the team will need me."

"Sure, sure. We can do that. This is the big one for you, Jenner. You deserve a break too."

Yes, I do. She was satisfied. He wouldn't object if she gave Stephanie the leading role on the school. It was a sweet project, but her focus was elsewhere. With that in hand she could leave the office a bit early to be with the kids this evening.

~

She pulled into the driveway at five-fifteen, already feeling the pressure of having to leave the office early. Damn it! How was she going to sustain the energy for this and keep up with her work?

Alexa put on a smile as she entered. "I was able to leave early today. I wanted to–" but before she had a chance to explain how she wanted to spend an evening with the kids, Markus came shrieking into the living room. He wore no pants. Bruce came right behind him, a diaper in hand. He looked up.

"Thank God. You're here," he said as she walked in the door. She couldn't believe her eyes. It looked as if a bomb had landed. There were discarded clothes and bags and mess everywhere. The living room cushions were strewn all over the floor. Maddie, her hair in tangles, her face streaked with dirt, sat on the sofa holding Lucy in her arms. Her bare feet dark with ground-in mud.

"I am so in over my head here, it's not even funny. You might want to turn around now and walk out while you have a chance. Save yourself!" he said, cheerful despite the mayhem, but she saw the utter exhaustion in his face. He stopped in front of her, letting Markus carry on, disappearing down the hall back into the kitchen. How many laps had they made before she interrupted the chase? She looked up, taking in Bruce's own state of disarray.

"Is that poo on your shirt?"

Grimacing, he looked down, yanking his shirt out, trying to see what she saw. "Ugh. Probably. He had a whopper of a full diaper when we finally got home, which he wouldn't let me take off, and I still haven't managed to get a clean one on him." Bruce turned and set the clean diaper down on the hall table next to her purse. "Oh, shit! Dinner!" He turned and sprinted to the kitchen.

She shook her head, following him, surveying the scene again, trying to understand what was really happening. There was a green plastic cup and a pool of milk on the floor next to the table. Bruce was banging a smoking pot into the sink and swearing. Dinner, or whatever that was, was apparently burnt. He lifted his gaze to hers with a stunned expression and raked a hand through his hair, causing curls to stick up like devil's horns.

She sighed. "Markus! Come here, please."

His little face, smeared with something black all around his mouth and chin, appeared around the corner. His hands too, were black. His filthy face was streaked with tears.

"Why are you running away, sweetie? Don't you want clean pants?"

He cried, "Awick," and then wailed, stumbling toward her.

She peered closely at him, bending to take his arm.

He was sticky and stunk like a cesspool. "Nooooo!"

"Why not?"

He started to howl again.

"Lord above. I need to change my clothes. Bring him upstairs. Maddie you come too." She raced upstairs to get out of her good work clothes and into sweatpants and a t-shirt and met them coming up the stairs. "How did this happen?"

Bruce stood in the hall, Markus in his arms. "How did what happen?"

She gestured around them. "Mess. Filth. Chaos."

He blinked. "This isn't normal?"

"No. This isn't normal, Koczynski." She rolled her eyes. "Give him to me." She reached for Markus but he clung to Bruce. When Alexa peeled him off, he whimpered. Her nose recoiled, and her nearly empty stomach bucked. She held Markus at arm's length and gave Bruce a sharp look. "What the hell? Didn't you change him all day? He reeks and he's got diaper rash."

Bruce shrugged and said, "Too busy having fun."

"How could you all get so dirty in one afternoon?"

"Park, playground, beach, mall."

"Didn't you– oh, never mind." Bruce had evidently not taken a moment to wash them, or even wipe their faces. She led them all into the bathroom and started to fill the tub. "What happened to the two of you? You both look like Pigpen. Maddie put Lucy down."

"Luthy's going to die!" Maddie whined, tears in her eyes, but complied.

Alexa stripped all their clothes off and dumped them in a pile. "No, she's not. What's the matter?"

"She hasn't had her shot."

Alexa, squatting by the tub, sloshing suds into the water, looked up at Bruce. He grinned and shrugged. "I am so mad at you. Go clean up downstairs. Please."

"What's for dinner, Auntie Alex?" demanded Maddie crossly. "I'm hungry."

"Didn't you have a snack after school?" asked Alexa.

Maddie shrugged, and Markus snivelled and whimpered. "I hungwy too."

"Are you telling me Bruce didn't give you a snack?"

Another shrug from Maddie. "Sort of."

Alexa inclined her head and stared at Maddie over the rims of her glasses. "What?"

"Chipth and a cookie," said Maddie.

Markus lifted his head long enough to say, "An' wik-wish!"

Alexa was incredulous. "Liquorice?"

"I *hate* liquorice!" said Maddie.

"Marky like it," said Markus. That explained the black smears around his mouth, on his shirt, and under his fingernails.

Alexa swore under her breath and went to set Markus into the tub.

"Ew, grossth. I won't bath with him. Daddy wouldn't make me." Maddie hung back. She stood, her bony arms crossed, glaring.

"Come on Mads, help me out here. I'll wipe his bottom before he gets in. Just do it. You a have to watch him while I make dinner, so you can eat sooner. You might as well get clean and soap him up while you're at it."

Maddie oversaw Alexa cleaning up Markus, curling up her nose. Alexa had to wipe him four times. When he met with Maddie's approval, Alexa set him into the bubble bath. "Get in Madison. Watch Markus and help him wash, please."

Alexa eyed them, and offered a thumbs-up. "S'good?"

"Th'okay," said Maddie, donning a snorkel mask and sinking under the suds.

"Okay, just get clean and into your pyjamas and by the time you're ready I'll have some mac 'n cheese and peas ready. Okay?"

Maddie sneered. "Kate feeds us dinner first and then we bath before bed."

"I hungry now!" whined Markus.

"Well I haven't got anything for you to eat yet, and Bruce burnt whatever he was making, so tonight we'll do it backwards."

Exasperated, furious with Bruce, she scooped up the dirty clothes and dropped them into the hamper, then she dashed down the stairs.

∽

Bruce stood in the living room, his arms full of clothes and bags when Alexa came downstairs. "You're amazing," he said. "You've only been here half an hour and you've already got everything under control."

Arms crossed, she tilted her head and met his gaze. She obviously was trying not to laugh, and failing. "You really are something, you know?"

He laughed. "I know. I know."

He followed her to the kitchen, in awe of her fierce efficiency. She cleaned up the spilled milk, tossed all the dirty dishes into the dishwasher, put a pot of water on to boil, all by the time he found somewhere to set down the clothes in his arms.

"Don't put those there. Take them to the laundry room for heaven's sake."

Bewildered, he picked up his pile.

"If you want to survive this, Koczynski, you're going to have to acquire some skills. And learn to strategize. First of all, don't handle anything twice. Put it where it needs to go the first time, otherwise things pile up."

"Yeah. I got that." He carried his bundle to the laundry room and dumped it in a hamper. Then figured he might as well learn from the master. He moved it into the washing machine, added a few things that were nearby and set it going.

Back in the kitchen, Alexa had cleaned all the surfaces and set the table. She was tossing pasta in the water and had a second pot cooking. He peeked in. Green stuff. "You are a miracle of domestic efficiency. I never knew."

She huffed. "Yeah, well. This was exactly what I feared. Your so-called help means twice the work for me."

"And yet..." He grinned at her, his brows raised question.

"Yes. I know. I can't do it without you, either."

"I'm sorry, Al. I'll get better."

She nodded, draining the noodles and adding cheese, stirring. "I'd book time off work. But I just can't. This is a critical time for me. This high profile Arts Centre project is too important. I have to commit the time... I'll never make partner if..." She sighed again.

A piercing squeal interrupted her, and she dropped her wooden spoon into the pot and raced upstairs calling, "Markus? What's wrong?"

Bruce stirred the mac and cheese, took it off the heat –he'd already burned his first efforts tonight– and followed her upstairs in time to witness even the amazing Alexa losing it.

"She hit meeee!" screeched Markus, splashing a huge wave of water over Maddie's scowling head, most of it slopping over the rim.

"He hit me first."

"She dwown me," wailed Markus, desperate to be vindicated.

"I was only washing him. He's thplashing too much," said Maddie, standing up in the tub, sheets of water and suds streaming down her scrawny, smooth limbs, her arms akimbo. "And then he thlipped so I grabbed his arm."

Water was everywhere, pooled on the floor. The bath mat was sodden. Clouds of bubbles clung to the tiled wall, slowly slipping down. Cripes, they'd only been gone ten minutes.

Maddie climbed out of the tub, into the waiting towel that Alexa held up. Markus continued to scream and splash.

"Stop that, Markus!"

Splat! A glob of soapy wetness landed on Alexa's glasses. She swore under her breath, sighed, looked up. His gaze followed hers. More clumps of suds hung from the ceiling, dripping off like stalactites.

Bruce stepped in and bent to lift Markus up out of the water, holding him up, dripping.

Alexa grabbed another towel, wiped off her face and wrapped it around him. "Okay, you. Enough bath time." She took him from Bruce to set him on the floor, rubbing him vigorously dry.

"Ow! Ow!" He continued to cry in a half-hearted way, as though he hadn't the energy for a full effort.

She slowed her movements, turning him around to look at his backside, showing it to Bruce. "Look," she said, meeting his gaze. His poor little bottom was red with diaper rash. "This is what happens if he spends too long in a soggy diaper, and doesn't get properly wiped."

Bruce offered an apologetic smile, properly chastised. "I am sorry. Why does he still wear diapers, anyway?"

As she smeared diaper cream on Markus's rash, he peed on his towel and she just about lost it. "Aargh! That's why, Koczynski!"

Bruce grabbed Markus and stepped right over Alexa and Maddie. He wiped Markus clean, dried him and squatted down to pull a clean pair of pull ups onto him. "There. Safe at last."

He sat, cross-legged with a drooping Markus between his knees as he towelled his pale hair. Alexa, who had Maddie likewise in her lap sat opposite. She let out a deep sigh, and met his gaze. "Is this day almost over?"

He looked at her with sympathy. She held her wet glasses in her hand, and there was a coil of suds sticking up on the side of her head, and another on the side of her face. Despite the almost wild glaze he saw there, her green eyes sparkled with humour.

He sniggered. Sure she'd be furious, but she just looked so darned cute. For the first time ever, she was loose and while not exactly relaxed, she was easy in her body. Not so stiff and dignified and scowling at him. She looked touchable. He reached over and wiped the suds from her cheek with his thumb. He shook his head, grinning. "Oh, Al."

Her lovely lush mouth was pursed in disapproval, yet quivered with suppressed laughter. He chuckled. She snorted, and soon they were all laughing hysterically, even the kids, who didn't know what they were laughing about.

CHAPTER 6

It's a darn good thing she was used to the chaos of a houseful of younger children. But she sure didn't need the added stress right now.

"Pyjamas now. Go, Maddie. I'll dress Markus. Dinner is ready."

Maddie stomped off to her room, tugging a brush through her wet, tangled locks, still grumbling.

"I'll take him," Bruce said, and carried a squirming and whining Markus to his room to dress him. "Come on you."

"I'm still mad at you," Alexa said as she turned and jogged down the stairs.

Shit! The mac and cheese was dry and crusted to the bottom of the pot. She warmed it, added a little more milk, and dished it out with the shrivelled peas. Bruce came down with the kids and sat them down at the table.

She poured herself a glass of wine. *I need something stronger than this.* She pondering various forms of torture she might inflict on Koczynski, as she sat, twirling her glass. Although he *was* sticking with her, and despite being clueless, seemed open to learning from his mistakes. She'd give him that much. Also, he was endearingly sexy, sitting there trying to get an exhausted Markus to eat.

"*Zoom, zoom.* Here comes the airplane," Bruce tried, swooping the spoon of macaroni through the air before zooming in for a landing. He didn't even get a giggle out of him. "Come on Marky, open up the hangar."

She scrolled through her phone messages. A text from Megan. What was up with her? Every week she had some complaint, mainly about their sister Bronwen.

Maddie sat shovelling food into her mouth, sullen and desultory, but clearly famished.

"Peas, too," Alexa said.

"Daddy doesn't make me—"

"Well your Dad's not here and I'm in charge now, so you're going to eat vegetables every day." Bruce shot a glance her way. That was a bit harsh. It wasn't Maddie's fault. She softened her tone. "They're good for you, Mads." The truth was Alexa would be lucky to get veggies on the table every day.

Markus wiggled and thrashed about, then grabbed his spoon, glared at Bruce, and threw it on the floor with a clang.

"Hey!"

"He did it on purpothe," said Maddie, helpfully, a sardonic gleam in her dark eyes as she pushed macerated macaroni through the gap in her front teeth.

Bruce nodded and sighed. "You're tired. I'll help you, buddy." He took a clean spoon from the drawer and pulled a chair up beside him, scooping up some macaroni. "Here you go."

He clamped his mouth shut and turned his face away.

"Come on Marky. I know you're hungry."

He shook his head fiercely, his little pale brow beetling. "Don't wannit!" He swept an arm across the tabletop, sending the bowl crashing to the floor. *Thuk-klang, rat-tat-tat-tat, sploosh.* Mac 'n cheese and peas flew everywhere, sticking to the edge of the cupboard, rolling off into distant corners. Oscar, who'd been angling for food, shot out of the kitchen.

"Sonuva—!" Bruce shot to his feet. "Markus!"

She winced. Alexa's heart sank like the Titanic. "Well, I can't make anything else. It's too late."

Her phone pinged and she picked it up.

"It's a message from Kate."

Hey Alex! I made it. What an interminable flight. 14 hours! And then I found Simon and just slept. More news later. Love to the kiddos.

Alex noticed unread texts from Owen, and Megan again, and sighed. They'd have to wait.

"Mommy sends you her love, guys."

"Mamaaa." Markus wailed. He cried pitifully, runny snot dripping from his nose. "Want Mama."

"He's just not going to eat," Bruce said, shaking his head and lifting Markus up.

Alexa closed her eyes. *Give me strength.* She gritted her teeth and stood, ignoring the mess on the floor. "I'll warm a cup of milk and he can take it to bed." She put it in a sippy-cup and held it to his mouth. He obligingly gripped it in his little fist and sucked on it. She let out a breath. "Off to bed, you. Tomorrow we'll do better."

Alexa left the mess and escorted Maddie to her room, while Bruce tucked in Markus. Alexa peeked in to see him lying beside Markus, who lay still, sucking noisily on his warm milk, his eyes already closed. He'd be asleep in nano-seconds. Bruce's eyes were drooping too, as he softly stroked Markus's hair. It had been a long day for both of them. But tough as it was, she had to admit, it was easier with two.

Alexa returned to Madison. "Bedtime."

Madison scowled, heading for her room. "I want a thtory."

"Aw, Mads. It's too late. We're both tired."

Madison pointed to the clock by her bed. "It's only theven."

Alexa gazed at it in disbelief. How could it be only seven? It felt like eleven. "Okay. Teeth first." She rifled through a stack of books on a shelf by the bed while she waited. When Madison returned, she inspected her teeth and nodded. "Good enough. Climb in."

She tucked Maddie in bed and perched on its edge, book in hand. Lucy jumped up on the bed and curled up next to Maddie's legs

"Not that one," protested Maddie.

"Why not? *Paper Bag Princess* is a classic."

"Thnow White is classical."

"I won't read that drivel."

"Thnow White!" Maddie grabbed it off the shelf and shoved it at Alexa.

They faced off, Alexa scowling at Maddie, Maddie's shaded green eyes glaring back.

"Daddy–"

"Alright! But we'll do it my way." Alexa opened the book and read, but she didn't get far before she couldn't stand the stereotypical brainwashing bunkum. "This poor old woman is awfully shallow. She must have been raised in a time when girls were taught they had to be beautiful to be valuable." She met Maddie's eye. "We know that's a lie, don't we Mads."

Maddie stared stonily.

Right, just read. When she got to the part where the huntsman had taken Snow White to the forest to kill her, at the behest of the jealous step-mother queen, instead of the huntsman taking pity on her, she said, "He wasn't a very bright fellow, so Snow White tricked him into letting her go free, by promising him a great reward when she returned home and became queen."

"That's not right."

"Sure it is." Alexa continued. When she got to the part about the seven dwarves in their cottage, she said, "She found the little cottage a terrible mess, with dirty pots in the sink, macaroni and cheese on the floor, and dirty socks all over. There was nothing to eat, so she lay down on one of the little beds and fell asleep, exhausted from her day of hiking through the forest."

"That thounds like Goldilocks. And the dwarfs were very tidy," complained Madison.

"That's utter nonsense," countered Alexa. "Seven little guys living alone in a hut in the woods? Get serious! It'd be like seven Markuses."

Maddie giggled. "Grossth!" She was smiling for the first time today, and Alexa grinned at her goofy-looking missing front teeth.

"Anyway, when she woke up, there they were: seven short, hairy, stinky, hungry little men, with big noses and beady little eyes. They gazed at her, amazed, and asked her where she came from. She explained about her jealous, vain step-mother, and her plan to get even one day. The dwarf named Cranky said she could stay with them for a while, as long as she cleaned house, did laundry, cooked meals and washed dishes for them. Snow White said, 'Get serious! You little pigs! Clean up your own mess.'"

"Auntie Al!" Maddie snorted.

"Instead, she talked them into to giving her a share in their diamond mine, and promised them double their profits if they let her be project manager."

Maddie rolled her eyes back and threw her head on the pillow, squeaking with laughter.

"So, Snow White told... *Dim* to stay at home and do the housework, while she led the other six dwarfs to mine for diamonds. She organized them, and made the whole operation more efficient, so they extracted piles and piles of diamonds. More than they had in ten years. But while they were working, the wicked queen disguised herself as an old peddler woman and brought her poisoned apples to the cottage in the forest. At the same time, a handsome prince was traveling through the woods, and stopped at the cottage to ask for food and shelter. Dim invited him in, but said that dinner would not be ready for hours. When the queen came by, the prince paid for the apples, which was generous of him, but foolish, and both he and Dim ate them and fell to the floor dead." Alexa dramatized this last bit, falling sideways onto Maddie's bed, clasping her throat. "Gak!"

Maddie sat up abruptly. "No, Auntie Alex. The prince can't die!"

Alexa peered at Maddie with a stern expression on her face, suppressing her desire to smile. "Why not? The Brothers Grimm made Snow White die."

"Yes, but–"

"*Shh*. Don't interrupt now. So, when Snow White and the six dwarfs came home from the mine with their truckload of diamond ore, they found Dim and the strange guy lying unconscious, the cottage as big a mess as when they left. 'He'th very handthom,' said Timid, shyly, poking the prince with his toe. 'He is rather good looking, though a bit of a pretty boy,' said Snow White, eyeing the prince's pink tights and sparkly golden tunic." Alexa made stupid faces for each of the speaking parts, and acted out their parts.

Maddie hooted and snorted, her giggling non-stop now.

"Shh. You'll wake Markus," continued Alexa. "Then Barfy cried, 'Oh Quack! Can you save them?' Quack ran for his doctor's bag, and took their vitals, saying, 'They're not really dead, but only poisoned by a magic apple, that is stuck in their throats.' 'Maybe they only need a good night's sleep,' suggested Slug sleepily. 'Maybe they can be revived with a little shot of whisky,' suggested Tipsy tipsily. 'Well, let's let them sleep it off,' decided Snow White. 'Move Dim to his bed. This fellow can sleep on the sofa, I guess.' As the other dwarfs were dragging them to their beds, the apples came loose and fell from their throats. The prince awoke, coughing, and gazed up at Snow White. 'You are the most beautiful maiden I have ever seen. Forsake me not!'

"Oohhh," sighed Maddie.

Alexa shook her head. "Snow White rolled her eyes at him, and thought perhaps he could be reformed. She said, 'If you are willing to work for your living in our diamond mine, we will keep you around.' The end." Alexa pushed her glasses onto her head and smiled at Maddie."

"What happened to the wicked thtep-mother?"

Alexa pursed her lips. "Well. Very sad that. She grew old and lonely, gazing at her wrinkly face in the magic mirror, and finally realized that beauty is only skin deep, and she had wasted her life worrying about it, when she could have been doing something really useful. So she moved to Florida and joined the senior ultimate frisbee team. Snow White and the seven dwarfs moved to the castle, and lived happily ever after."

"Tha's good," murmured Maddie, her eyes heavy with sleep. "Auntie Al?"

"MmHmm?"

"I misth Daddy." Her voice trembled. "Is he going to be okay?"

Alexa bent to kiss her cheek and tucked the blankets around her chin.

"I know, honey. He'll be back, good as new. I promise."

"What about the prince…?"

"Never mind him, honey. Princesses rock all by themselves."

"But I want to keep him."

Alexa chuckled to herself. "Alright, honey. You can keep him."

∽

Bruce worked on his house the next morning. Though he had yet to knock out any walls, he'd picked up a stack of wood studs and some other materials at the building supply, and carried them into the house from his truck. He contemplated the previous day, unable to avoid the realization that he'd brought on much of last night's challenges himself.

He didn't feel guilty exactly. Except about the diaper thing. He really did feel badly about that. Poor Markus. He'd been pretty creative all afternoon keeping the kids active and entertained. So he overlooked a few details. So what? How was he to know any of that? It did make him feel a little bit foolish, however, which he hated. He'd always been on the receiving end of criticism and lectures and condescension growing up with, essentially, four big, gruff macho men who couldn't deal with the fact that Bruce was different. And though she'd been laughing, Alexa thought he was an idiot, too. He'd always managed to keep a smile on his face, and tell himself he was okay. He didn't want to be like his brothers or his father, anyway.

A stud slipped off the stack, tumbling to the sidewalk. It bruised Bruce's arm on the way down, bouncing over his work boot. "Damn!" He kicked it aside. Then the whole load shifted in his grip, and Bruce threw it down with a growl, like an oversized game of pick-up-sticks. "Fucking, fuckity-fuck!" He expelled a gust of air, frustrated with his clumsiness. He could feel the scornful eyes of his father, hear his brothers laughing in his head, nit-picking, cutting him down.

Shut up! I can do this. He didn't need anyone's permission or approval to renovate this house on his own. This was for him and him alone. He may not be in the contracting business like the rest of the men in his family, but he wasn't the soft, mouse-pushing, computer geek they saw him as either. Well, maybe he *was* a mouse-pushing computer geek, but he was a damned successful one and he didn't need to prove himself to anyone. Least of all her.

But he did, for some reason, want to deserve Alexa's approval and respect.

His cell phone rang in his pocket as he hefted the stack of studs back onto his shoulder. He steered his lumber through the vaulted living area and climbed the four stairs to the upper level, where he planned to knock out and reframe some walls to enlarge the master bedroom, and set down the stack of lumber. Straightening, he checked his cell phone. *Hmph.* It wasn't Alexa, who he was half expecting to call and lecture him; it was actually Derek, his older brother. Odd, he hadn't heard from him in ages, even though he only lived a couple of hours away.

Bruce wandered back down to the living room, perched on a window ledge and dialled, his gaze pulled out over Georgia Strait tracing the outline of the islands, blue on blue. The sky up here was clear, but there was a pinkish haze hovering over the city today. Some kind of temperature inversion.

"Hey," he said, when his brother picked up. "You called."

"Yeah. How ya doin' little brother?"

"I'm... good." Bruce hated to whine to his brother about his problems. It was hard enough getting any respect on a good day.

"You on the boat today?"

"Nah, up at the house, trying to get a head start on some demolition. I bought some studs, and I'm trying to decide which walls to pull out."

"You need a hand?"

"Thanks, no. I've got it covered." That's all he needed. "I'm in no hurry, and, you know. I kind of want to do it myself."

"Sure." Derek paused, and Bruce waited to hear why he'd called.

When he said nothing, Bruce said, "Hey, can I ask your opinion about something?"

"Yeah?"

"Well, it's Simon and Kate... his second wife, you know..."

Derek grunted.

"They're overseas in Asia for couple of weeks and I got stuck taking care of their kids..."

A beat of silence. "You've got to be kidding."

Bruce paused a moment before answering. "Uh, nope. Not kidding actually. Anyway, a bit of advice?" Derek had two kids, after all.

"Shoot." He could hear Derek choking back suppressed laughter.

"Well, what I... Shut up!"

Derek released a great belly laugh. His voice came out in a squeak. "Sorry. Can't help it," he gasped. "You. Babysitting!" more guffaws.

Bruce gritted his teeth, waiting for the flood of shame, the gush of inadequacy, to flow through him. Why did Derek –any of his family, for that matter– feel entitled to cut him down at every opportunity? What did they know about him and what he'd accomplished in his life? Obviously building a successful business and making a few million bucks wasn't enough to change their opinion of him. Why shouldn't he be babysitting? He was as capable as anyone else. When Derek had calmed down, Bruce said, "Of course, I don't have much experience, but–"

"Like, try *none*. You've never been alone with mine!"

Bruce, exasperated with the same old bullshit, pictured his macho big brother sitting in a lawn chair with a beer while his wife ran around after their two kids, doing all the work herself. "And you have?"

A pause.

Aha. Gotcha.

"Well, of course Cheryl does the lion's share, but obviously I've been alone with my kids, stupid." His gruff tone indicated a measure of irritation.

"Ok, know-it-all, you can answer my questions then." He peeled a bit of old paint off the window frame with his fingernail.

"Maybe."

"It's about meals, and naps, and diapers and washing, and... stuff like that."

"Uh. You mean, basic childcare?"

"Shit, Derek. It's philosophical. What I mean is, as long as they're safe, how important is all that stuff? Obviously you have to feed them. But isn't it good for them to get a little dirty, and tired, and to wait for a meal until you're ready?"

"How old are these kids?"

"Seven and three."

"Hmm. That young, eh?"

Bruce brooded for a moment. He wasn't getting anywhere. He should have known better than to ask Derek. Bruce was certain he did as little as he could get away with. "But, seriously..."

"Hey." Derek laughed again. "You're asking the wrong guy, brother. You want me to put Cheryl on? That's her department."

"No! God, no. I was looking for a guy's perspective. Alexa's already made it clear I screwed up."

"*Alex-a?*"

"Kate's friend. We're sharing... duties."

"Aaah. Babysitting, not body fluids."

Bruce's breath caught, a wave of gooseflesh making him shudder. "Oh, God, no."

"A dog, eh?"

A nail in the windowsill was cutting into his ass. Bruce shifted his weight to the other cheek, his view rotating to the wooded side of his property, the panorama of Eagle Harbour and Bowen Island framed between giant Douglas firs beyond the cracked patio. "No. Not at all. Only not... uh, my uh, usual type. She's a bit... abrasive. And uptight."

He pulled the hammer out of his tool belt with his left hand and idly tapped in the offending nailhead. It bent over.

"So that's what this is about. She's been giving you shit, and you want to show her up."

The muscles on the back of Bruce's neck flexed, and his jaw involuntarily jut forward. His brow furrowed as he pondered Derek's suggestion and he silently snuffed air through his nose, like the blow of a horse, dismissing the notion as nonsense. Of course he'd like her respect, but... "Naw. It's not about her. I want to do the right thing here, with Simon's kids. He's trusting me with this job. It shouldn't be a big deal. I just wanted a few pointers about the kids."

"Like, whether it's okay to make them suffer a little?"

"Toughen them up a little. Builds character, huh?"

Derek inhaled loudly, and Bruce could picture him leaning back. "That's what the old man used to say."

"Makes them more independent?"

"Don't want your kids to be sissies, hanging on your shirttails, making a nuisance of themselves."

The too-familiar words caused Bruce's chest to tighten, pressing in on his heart like a vice-grip. "Well, right. That's what I meant. We weren't pampered and doted on." Or hugged or kissed or indulged or listened to. He levered at the bent nail, trying to get the claw under the crooked head without success.

"Exactly," said Derek. "And you're like him."

Indignation inflated his chest. The urge to punch something surged through him, and he whacked the hammer against the nail once, hard, smashing it flat into the frame. "What? I am not! I'm–"

"And look how great we turned out! We had a terrific childhood. Tons of fun. Practically free of parental policing."

–*nothing* like Dad. "Ri-ight." For you and Mike and Luke, maybe. His own position was rather different as the lonely little boy with a runaway mother, a tough-love father, forever at the mercy of his scheming and bullying older brothers. Basically, alone.

Well, he'd learned to survive, and he thrived. But he'd rather do anything than inflict that kind of pain on Simon's kids, even if it was only for two or three weeks. No, he wouldn't repeat his father's mistakes. He'd do this his own way.

"Well. Never mind, I just–"

"Hey, I'm in no position to tell you what to do. But that reminds me why I called."

"That is?"

"It's Mom."

Bruce's heart lurched, and he quickly brought his thundering pulse under control and calmly said, "Oh? She okay?"

"Oh, yeah. She's fine. But she's been on my case to call you."

His heart squeezed, slow and tight, thickening his throat. Bruce set the hammer down and shifted the phone to his other ear. "She call you very often, then?"

"All the time. Look, she's in town right now. With that weird boyfriend of hers, the old hippy, Lawrence, to shop and they stopped in to see the kids."

Hippy boyfriend?

"She's been begging me to ask you to come by. Keeps asking why you won't talk to her. Gets all teary."

Teary? Over him? "She didn't call *me*."

"Get real, little brother. She's afraid to call you herself. You've been blowing her off for years, and whenever you get caught in the same room, you're cold as a salmon from the freezer and you rush off on some feeble excuse."

Bruce's stomach clenched, and his skin prickled with a cold sweat. "That's bullshit!" Same old fight or flight. Who got a fight or flight response to their own mother? "I can't help it if I'm busy when she–"

"Sure you are. Busy, busy Bruce. Just like Dad. Even on Christmas day, birthdays." Derek's voice was so dry his words peeled off like the paint on Bruce's walls. "Anyway, she's frantic. Desperately wants to see you before she dies of old age or something. She's got some heart condition–"

"What heart condition?"

"Ah... angina, or something. Anyway, how about dinner this week, while they're here in town?"

Bruce froze. "This week? Um, no. I've got the kids, eh."

"You've also got Alexa, right?"

"Yeah. No. Couldn't do that. Not right now."

"That's what I told her you'd say. She said to tell you to come for a visit this summer. Take your boat over."

"You've been there." It wasn't a question. He wasn't jealous. He could see his mother if he wanted to. It had been several years now, since she'd got back in touch with them. Well, with the older boys. She'd never actually called Bruce. Or... well if she'd tried he didn't know about it.

"Yeah, we've been. The kids love it there. She's got chickens, ducks and goats." Derek laughed. "Maybe she can answer your parenting questions."

"Right. Well..." Bruce cleared his throat. That must have been a joke.

"The island is nice this time of year. Peaceful."

His mother had been passing messages like this through his brothers for years, off and on. Until recently, he was always, conveniently, too busy with work to worry about it. Why was he even considering it now? Why didn't he believe she really wanted to see him? "I'm really trying to make progress on the house. And I'll be tied up with these kids 'til the end of June, so..."

"I thought you said you're not in a hurry. Anyway, take them with you." Derek stopped talking. Bruce could hear his steady breathing. He continued. "She'd really appreciate it and the kids'll like the goats, eh? Think it over. Get her off my case, anyway."

"Yeah. Yeah, I'll see." Bruce stood up, his butt thoroughly numb, and glowered out the window. He should probably remove two or three of those trees, to open up the view to the west. "So, about the kids... You suppose..."

"Let Alexa worry about that stuff. She's the one with female instincts."

"Yeah, maybe, but she's..."

"What?"

"Nothing. Never mind." Not really the nurturing type. Or so he'd assumed. In any case, she wasn't the one with the problem.

He hung up the call, swore at the top of his lungs, and kicked the wall stud. It fucking hurt. He grabbed his hammer, wound up and flung it down the hill into the back yard like a boomerang.

"Fuck!" That was an expensive hammer. What an idiot. He raked a hand through his hair and blew air out of his cheeks, letting the tension roll away. Every damned time. A soft breeze rustled the tree branches, and the song of rigging tinkling drifted up from the marina, soothing him. *Let it go. You're okay, Dude.*

Afterwards, he found himself stewing over Derek's offhand comment that he was like Dad. He'd nearly spit. As a kid, he'd sworn, if he was ever a father, he'd be sure not to be like Dad. Well, it wasn't likely he'd ever have his own kids, but for these three weeks, he could do right by Simon's, and avoid that unforgivable crime.

Bruce remembered when Simon's first wife Rachel got pregnant. She wanted to get rid of it, and Simon begged her not to. Literally begged. Once Maddie was born, as soon as she could, Rachel walked away, back to her career, her high life, her lovers. Simon struggled on his own as a new father, determined to make up for Rachel's lack. He was the most loving, most nurturing, most devoted father Bruce could ever imagine. Nothing like Bruce's own. Why would Bruce look any farther than Simon for a better role model?

Simon would never do anything to let Bruce down. When they were young, in high school, college and after, they'd always covered for each other. Countless times, Simon had rescued Bruce from the edge of perdition, cleaned up the mess, fed him and then covered his tracks. He owed him.

Bruce was determined to repay that debt. He was determined to make Simon proud of him. Bruce could never let Simon down. He was determined to be proud of himself, too. And if, along the way, he won that damned hostile woman's respect, that would be alright, too. He was mighty tired of Alexa treating him like some half-witted juvenile delinquent. She might even discover that he was an appealing man worthy of her feminine attentions. That sounded like a challenge. He smiled to himself.

CHAPTER 7

On Monday, Bruce was ready. He'd already located and made arrangements for delivery of groceries and prepared meals to the house. One less job to do. An hour before he was due to pick Markus up at pre-school, he drove into the city and stopped at a supermarket. Cruising the aisles, his sight was trained on portable, kid-friendly food, and he was shocked and amazed to find the shelves were full of options designed especially for his predicament. Not that he ever did much grocery shopping, but these were things he'd never noticed before.

He stocked up on string cheese and dried fruit chunks, little cracker sandwiches filled with peanut butter and tiny juice boxes. Some of this stuff must be in the pantry at the house. He hadn't been at the house long enough to check, and would do so later. Yesterday he'd gone about it all wrong, so he'd prepare himself today. Passing the produce section, he realized that bananas and apples were Mother Nature's way of addressing the same problem, and grabbed enough to last for the week. He could use a quick snack himself from time to time, and fruit seemed a healthier choice than his previous habit of eating nacho chips.

Back at the car, it occurred to him that having a small cooler would be practical, and he drove over to Canadian Tire to pick one up. Once there, he discovered coolers you could plug into the cigarette lighter in the car to keep them cold all day. He could make good use of it to keep a few brewskis cold up at the house. Better and better. By the time he arrived at the preschool, he was feeling pretty confident. He knew this wouldn't be so very difficult once he set his mind to it. He'd simply never applied himself before.

Arriving a few minutes before dismissal, Bruce stood in the corridor with the other parents picking up their children. Most were already engaged in conversations and took no notice of him. He stood by the door and peered through the half-light at the children, ostensibly picking up and putting away their toys under the direction of the teacher, although it bore a distinct resemblance to herding cats. Bruce followed Markus's progress, hoping to catch his eye and give him a smile.

"Are you new at the school?" A female voice came over his shoulder.

He turned toward it, and found an attractive brunette smiling at him. Her direct gaze, and her toothy smile, however, were vaguely threatening. "Yes," he replied.

Her eyes widened even further, as though awaiting more information. His smile faltered, and he raised his eyebrows in question. As far as he was concerned, the ball was in her court.

"I'm Fran. That's my daughter Estelle, there, with the french braids," she said, pointing through the window at a miniature of herself in purple tights.

Bruce blinked, nodded and smiled again. "I'm here to get Markus. The little blond boy." He pointed at him through the window as Markus turned and noticed him. Markus scowled and turned away.

"Oh? He must take after your wife, hmm?" said Fran, her eyes sweeping over his arms and chest.

"I'm not married," said Bruce. "And I'm not his father."

"Oh! You're a... manny?"

He chuckled. He actually enjoyed messing with people's expectations. Let her figure it out herself, since she was so curious. He'd always hated gatekeepers and busybodies. They always seemed to him faintly sinister. He preferred to mind his own business.

A bell rang in the distance. Doors opened, and children spilled out into the corridor. Ms. Swinton opened the Dutch door, and the parents in the hallway flooded in, zeroing in on one child or another. Bruce stepped through the door, but hung back by the wall, observing the chaos. He could see Markus hesitate also, on the opposite side of the classroom, dragging a listless hand through a raised tray of sand populated by plastic dinosaurs, his gaze casting around. Bruce crossed his arms over his chest and leaned back against the wall, waiting to see what he would do.

After a few minutes, it was clear that Markus was confused and undecided. He expected Bruce to make the first move. Bruce didn't want to alienate the poor kid, but another minute or two of doubt would probably strengthen his position. Finally, he swooped in and grabbed Markus under the arms, tossing him into the air and catching him. "Hey, Markus, buddy!"

"Eeee!" squealed Markus. "Boos!"

Bruce set him down. "Get your things. Let's go."

Markus waddled over to the cubbies, and grabbed ineffectually at a hoody snagged on a small hook. Bruce retrieved it for him, and crouched to put it on. He whispered into Markus's ear, "How are your pants, my friend?"

"Mizwinton made me go potty," he replied, in a rather loud stage whisper.

"Excellent." As they followed the others out the school doors, Bruce noticed that many parents let their kids play right there at the school playground before heading to their cars. "Want to play here a bit?"

"'Kay!" hollered Markus and ran off to join his classmates.

Bruce watched to see if he had any particular friend, but then noticed that they didn't really seem to interact. They did things in small groups, without talking or looking at each other. He frowned.

"It's called parallel play, at this age," said Fran, sauntering over to his side.

He eyed her critically. How'd she know what he was thinking?

"In another year, they'll form real friendships." She smiled. "I gather you're new at this."

"His parents are away."

She nodded, her curiosity finally satisfied. "I see." She stuck out her hand. "I'm Fran."

"So you said." Bruce flashed her a half-smile and took her hand. "Bruce."

"Nice to meet you, Bruce."

They stood making small talk for another few minutes, until Markus dashed over, breathless. "Boos, Boos!"

Bruce lifted him up. "Hey, dude. Ready to go?"

"Wik-wish?"

"No way, man. That was a bad idea."

Markus frowned. "I like wik-wish."

"Me too. But wait 'til you see what I got! It's the cat's meow." He turned and strode toward the car and, noticing Fran smile and wave, raised a hand in farewell. "See you tomorrow, Fran."

The snacks he bought were a hit with Markus, almost as much as the mini fridge humming in the back of the SUV. He strapped Markus in with fistfuls of food and drove off.

Twenty minutes later, Markus's appetite slaked, Bruce pulled into a parking stall near the Rowing Club at the entrance to Stanley Park. He hauled the jog stroller out of the SUV and strapped Markus into it. As he was locking the car, Markus piped up. "Miwk!"

Bruce paused. "Oh, yeah?" That seemed to be a sign that Markus was ready for a snooze. Maybe... He got the sippy-cup of milk out of the lunch pack and handed it to Markus, and then pushed off toward the seawall walk. It seemed as good a place as any to spend the afternoon. At least Bruce wouldn't be losing his mind, standing at the edge of a playground.

Markus was restless at first, squirming and talking a blue streak. He pointed out various sights along the path. Bruce kept up an entertaining banter, and then noticed that Markus's end of the conversation had dropped off. He paused and peered around the canopy, and sure enough, Markus was sound asleep. His sippy-cup dangled from his pudgy little hand. Smiling to himself, he pulled out his cell phone, and continued walking the seawall, checking for messages, and making a couple of calls to tradesmen that he was interviewing. There was this one stonemason he was keen to engage. He was reportedly very talented, if difficult to pin down. He was learning this was true of most guys in the trades.

It was a pleasant spring day, the sun shining enthusiastically, and it was getting truly warm, even though it was only early June. Tulips and daffodils bloomed in beds, and flowering rhododendrons lined the path. They passed a wide cross-section of park users. Young lovers on roller blades grasped each other's jacket sleeves. Groups of middle-aged folks engaged in loud and animated debates in tongues he couldn't decipher. Japanese tourists pointed and snapped pictures of themselves against the flowers and the sea.

One incredibly hot chick in lycra sprinted by on her toes like a graceful gazelle, pushing a jog stroller with a huge, fat girl strapped into it. The girl looked plenty old enough to be walking, close to Madison's age. The woman was as thin and flawless as a model, her blond hair tied back in a bouncing pony tail, her skin perfectly golden, her lips glossy pink. She reminded Bruce uncomfortably of Simon's first wife Rachel, Maddie's mother, who now lived in Toronto. It struck him that the woman was so caught up in her own fitness and beauty that she hadn't even noticed that her baby had outgrown the routine and could use a little exercise herself.

In time, Bruce noticed others with jog strollers and got the idea that this interlude with Markus could actually be put to good use. With all his added responsibilities, it would get more difficult for him to get to the gym to continue with his new workout regimen. But if he could fit in a good hour long run each afternoon, while Markus slept, and that seemed to be going smashingly well, then he could kill two birds with one stone. He could even make it all the way around the seawall walk, instead of having to double back as he had today. It was a foolproof system. Excellent.

Finally he packed a drowsy Markus back into the SUV, folded up the stroller and stashed it in the back, and drove off to pick up Maddie from school. Yes, he was very pleased with his new plan. He would come dressed for running, and after a little exercise, a hearty snack and a cup of milk and fresh air to knock Markus out, Bruce would be free to run a good ten kilometres before he had to get Maddie, and Markus would be in excellent shape.

Arriving at Maddie's school, Bruce found that most of the children had already been whisked away. A few parents hovered around chatting while their kids played ball or climbed on the play structure. He couldn't spot Maddie so he headed for the classroom, Markus in hand. She was there, standing by her desk, pulling out some books and stuffing them into her backpack.

"Hi-ya, Scallywag," he said, entering.

She turned to glare at him through narrowed eyes. Uh-oh. Now what?

As he walked toward her, she suddenly turned and screamed at full volume, "Get away from me! Don't touch me!"

He stopped on the spot. "Wha–?"

The teacher moved quickly toward them. "What is it Madison?"

Madison broke down into theatrical tears, gasping and sobbing, clearly fake to Bruce's eye, but convincing enough to concern the teacher. Madison clutched at her. "Don't thend me with him, Miss Shapiro, pleeeaase!"

Oh, Good grief.

Miss Shapiro looked sharply up at Bruce, and down again at Maddie. "What's wrong, dear? What are you afraid of? You can tell me."

"He's a baaad maaan!" Maddie howled. "He... he touched me!" She turned malicious green witch's eyes on Bruce. "He hurt me," she hissed in Miss Shapiro's ear.

The hair on Bruce's neck stirred with tension. *What the hell?* "Hey! Hey!" He poked at Maddie's shoulder with his forefinger and grinned at her. "Madison? That's not funny. What kind of scam is this?"

Madison responded by screeching in terror and burying her face in Miss Shapiro's skirt, cowering behind her for protection.

Markus, who'd been standing at Bruce's knee observing all this in stunned silence, cried and whimpered. "Maddie? Maddie?"

Bruce's heart slammed, and a cold sweat broke out all over his body. How could this be happening? He met the teacher's eye, intending to convey his incredulity at Maddie's fantastic performance, but was met with Miss Shapiro's skeptical, judgmental glare. He glanced over his shoulder, looking in desperation for support from some quarter, but was met by open-mouthed stares from the few parents who stood in the doorway and corridor beyond. He couldn't believe it. He'd been branded some kind of perverted pedophile by a vindictive child, and nobody would support him.

His face flooded with heat, and his very embarrassment made him angry. He'd done nothing wrong. He was falsely accused. What was wrong with these people?

Panting, he jerked forward and grabbed Madison by her arms, hauling her up onto a chair so he could look her in the eye. "Madison! Enough of this game. This is no joke!"

"Mr. Koczynski, please," said Miss Shapiro. He didn't like the tone of her voice. There was a hint of condescension in it, as though he ought to lie down and surrender. "Take your hands off of her."

He gripped Madison's shoulders and shook her slightly. "Madison! Stop this." He stared directly into her eyes, that sparkled dark green like a devil, and he knew what pure malevolence looked like. He was shaking all over, his body flushed with heat, and he laughed, high-pitched, on the edge of hysteria, out of control. His usual playful coping mechanism seemed to be broken. He lowered his voice in a threatening hiss. "What's this about, Madison? Do you think your dad will magically come home? Is that it? Because you're wrong, kiddo."

"Boos, Boos. Stop yewwing!" whined Markus, tugging on Bruce's pants leg.

Suddenly Bruce's arms were grabbed from behind. "Hey!" Miss Shapiro was tugging on him, and someone had run in from the corridor to help. Between them, they pinned his arms behind him and pulled him backwards, tearing his arms away from Maddie's shoulders. "Let me..." He tripped on a chair leg and stumbled to the floor, hitting hard, pain radiating through his hip. "What the hell?"

"Mr. Koczynski. Please control your temper. You can't be manhandling children here in the school." Her voice rose to a high pitch. She blushed and added. "Or anywhere!"

He shrugged free of their grasp, his anger mounting. "Let go of me. I'm no pervert." He leapt to his feet, facing off against Miss Shapiro and a youngish man in a red tie, probably another teacher. The younger, smaller man cowered under Bruce's glare and stepped back. He turned on Miss Shapiro, his vision blurring with unshed tears. "These kids are my responsibility. I love them like their mine. I'd never do anything to hurt them. And under the circumstances I'd appreciate a little support dealing with the situation. I don't need to be assaulted and accused of creepy crimes." He shrugged his shirt back into place, feeling his neck and face flush hot with anger and humiliation. Turning, he caught a twinkle of mischief in Madison's eye, and a twist of humour on her lips. He felt a vein in his temple thrum with blood. He turned on her, pointing an accusing finger in her face.

"You think this is funny, miss? Do you? All you're going to do is get everyone in a lot of trouble, including yourself, and make a huge mess of things. Do you want Alexa to have to leave work and come to your rescue? Is that it? She'll come, alright, but she won't be happy. And then she'll have to go back to work. What then?"

Madison had the decency to be silent, her eyes downcast, her smile forgotten. Perhaps she expected him to cower with his tail between his legs. Or more likely, she hadn't considered the consequences of her brilliant scheme at all. He certainly remembered what it was like to act out in fury against everyone and everything after Mom left. There was no rhyme or reason to it. Just a wild expression of pain.

In a moment of inspiration, Bruce thought of something even worse than his own undesirable guardianship. "We'll have to hire a nanny, that's what. I can afford one, you know. Is that what you want? You want to hang out with a stranger for the next two weeks?"

Markus cried in earnest.

"Because that's exactly what you're going to get." Bruce pointed down at Markus. "Markus won't like that. Do you think Kate would want that? Do you believe I won't do it?"

Maddie froze, staring at him with huge, shocked glassy green eyes, and he could read the dawning realization in her face.

God! She'd made him into an angry man, just like his father. Talk about manifest destiny. How the hell had this happened? He stood waiting, his arms limp at his sides.

Madison's eyes welled with tears.

Bruce raked a hand through his hair in frustration. He frowned at her. "Maddie? This is your idea. You have to clear it up. Please apologize to Miss Shapiro for scaring her."

Madison tugged her frightened gaze onto her teacher, her little mouth pinched into a tight knot.

"Maddie? Is this true? Have you told a fib?"

Bruce snorted and ground the heels of his hands into his eyes. That was the understatement of the century.

Madison bit her trembling lip, her eyes downcast. She mumbled something unintelligible.

"Maddie? I can't hear you."

"I'm thorry, Miss Shapiro. I... I didn't mean to hurt anybody. I want my Daddy to come back." Great alligator tears coursed down her cheeks. Bruce felt sorry for her. He could readily empathize with her feelings of abandonment.

"I understand, Madison. You've done a very naughty thing, but I believe it was unintentional," said her teacher.

Bruce caught the eye of the teacher, hanging back, wringing his hands.

"Sorry, man."

Bruce waved him away. "Forget about it."

"Take Markus to the corridor, Madison. I want a word with your teacher," said Bruce in a stern voice. Christ! This parenting was one harrowing job.

Maddie inched forward and took Markus by the hand, leading the snivelling toddler out the door after the man in the red tie. Bruce's gaze followed them, and caught the snapping heads of several parents, suddenly engaged in earnest conversation as though oblivious to the whole scene. Not bloody likely! He was sure they'd be whispering for weeks.

"Shit!" was all he could come out with once the kids were gone, and he'd met the teacher's eye. Brilliant.

She seemed implacable, and shook her head. "It'll be alright, Mr. Koczynski. I see you're not accustomed to the vivid imagination of children."

"What. This is normal? You can't tell me this is normal!"

She waffled. "Well... no, not exactly this–"

"Was she weird today?"

Miss Shapiro's face pinched in like she'd sucked a lemon. "She's been very withdrawn, which is not at all like her. She's a very lively, happy girl, normally."

"Hmm."

"There was a point at which I was quite concerned. It looked like she was having some kind of seizure."

"What?" Now what? He was going to die of heart failure. "Why didn't you call me?"

"Well. I nearly did. She sat in one place, unmoving, and unresponsive, for quite a long time. Maybe half an hour. I thought perhaps she was having an epileptic fit."

"Epilepsy!" Bruce couldn't help it. He screwed up his face in disbelief, then barked with laughter. That would be too much. "Hah! She was probably cooking up this scheme all day."

Miss Shapiro rocked her head back and forth, undecided. "I don't know what to suggest, Mr. Koczynski. You'll have to do something to put her at ease. We can't have outbreaks like this. It's upsetting for everyone."

He bugged his eyes at her. "You can say that again." He'd never survive another one himself. Hopefully Maddie's bag of tricks was empty.

"Oh, and Mr. Koczynski?"

He turned back.

"If I might make a suggestion... you might want to watch your language around the kids."

Once he had both kids in the car, he turned to her. He didn't know what to say. Sure, she was upset, but she was old enough to understand she couldn't get away with maneuvers like that. He was torn between comforting her and punishing her. What would his father have done? Told him to buck up and be a man, probably. What would Simon do? Take her in his arms and hold her tight, most likely. "Well? What have you got to say for yourself? You can't seriously expect to get away with that." Shit, he sounded like some kind of cartoon parent. He didn't even believe himself. He was so out of his league. How the hell did his father manage to stay so uninvolved in his life? He must have been a cold bastard. But then, Bruce already knew that.

Instead of the chagrin or remorse he expected, Maddie screeched at him. "You can't tell me what to do! You're not my dad. You're nobody's dad. What do you know anyway? You're stupid and I hate you. I hate you!"

He winced and then sighed. "Come here, Scallywag. It's okay. I'm not mad at you." He opened his arms and waited. She hesitated, shrinking back, eyeing him suspiciously, her face working through a host of emotions. Then she broke down into hysterical tears that continued all the way home, while Bruce clenched his teeth and swore he would stay one step ahead of them from now on.

~

"Have you got a minute?"

Alexa glanced up from her notes for the luncheon meeting with the Roses to find Stephanie standing with a sheaf of papers clutched in her hand. "Sure. What's up?"

"I was rereading the statement of intent from the Squamish band, and... well, I may be reading between the lines, but I sense some conflict between the goals of the chief, and what the elders are looking for. It could get messy if we don't clear it up before we invest any more time on concept design."

"Oh, yes? Well, that's why we have a face-to-face scheduled with the elders. I was hoping to get them to open up a bit and talk turkey. It takes a bit of finesse to get past the stoicism, you know?"

"I do know. I reworked the program, and looked again at the site, so I have a few fresh ideas in case our original scheme gets trashed by one party or another."

Alexa smiled, pushing up her glasses. This was why she wanted Stephanie on this job. She understood the delicate politics better than anyone. "I have every intention of bringing you with me to meet the elders." Alexa stood up, her expression somber. "I've spoken to Krystof about you."

Stephanie's dark eyes widened. Her full lips pressed together in expectation. "Yes?"

Alexa beamed at her. "He's open to the idea of you running the whole thing, Steph. Let's see how the clients react to you tomorrow. I'd be very happy if you could take it and run with it." While I focus on the Arts Centre.

Stephanie's face lit up like the sun, her smile broad and white, accentuating her prominent cheekbones. "Solo?"

Alexa nodded. "I'll confirm the meeting. Let's see those new ideas of yours."

Stephanie pulled up a chair and they went over her sketches for the use of the site, some changes reflecting traditional buildings and ritual sites that were no longer used, but still significant in the minds of the elders.

"I like this one. You're working with the tree metaphor, and it has a strong silhouette." Alexa was impressed with Stephanie's insight and sensitivity, and her design sense was sharp too. She was good, and she deserved to get ahead. It was hard enough for women to compete in this profession. If she could help a colleague get her due, she would do what she could. "Show me the–"

"*Hel*-lo, ladies."

Stephanie flinched, and Alexa's eyes slid up over the rims of her glasses, taking in the plaid shirt, bright blue blazer, elaborate beard and man-bun of her arch-enemy, Nathan. She straightened, and raised a brow. "*What* are you wearing?"

His smile fell a notch. "What do you mean?"

She rolled her eyes, laughing inwardly. She had to be careful not to ridicule him too openly, because he had zero sense of humour, and was likely to throw a temper tantrum. He was really rocking the hipster Urban Lumberjack look today, complete with suspenders. It would be ironic, if he had an ounce of self-awareness. But then this business was full of eccentrics with their heads in the clouds. "You are a walking cliché, Nathan. For God's sake. Do you have to be such a slave to fashion trends? You're supposed to be a designer"

Stephanie's shoulders shook with a suppressed giggle.

His sandy brows rumpled together, and his lips thinned to a

straight line beneath flared nostrils, his moustache flaring like wings, as he smoothed the front of his pouffy scarf. Prissy bastard. "For your information, I'm dressed for our lunch with the Roses and Weinstein." He leaned toward her. "I want to form a good picture in their minds when Krystof introduces me as Project Architect. You haven't forgotten, have you?" His gaze scanned up and down Alexa's dove grey suit jacket. There was a slight sneer on his face.

She sent him a bland smile, rolling her eyes. God, she hated him, the smarmy, underhanded snake. Where he got the notion that he would be project architect she didn't know. Krystof would never have said so, surely. "Why would I have forgotten lunch with our most important clients, Nathan?"

"Oh, I don't know," he said airily, tossing an elegant hand. "I saw you two girls gabbing and I figured it slipped your little mind." He sniggered, turned and strode away with a swagger. Alexa met Stephanie's eyes, her brows twisted, and they shared a silent grin. Even Pete, who could get away with it, didn't mince as well as Nathan, unless he was hamming it up. Or in drag. But that was only at parties, not at the office. When it came to catty behaviour, Nathan took the prize. How ironic that sexism in the workplace had come to this.

She shook her head and turned back to Stephanie's sketches. "Where were we?"

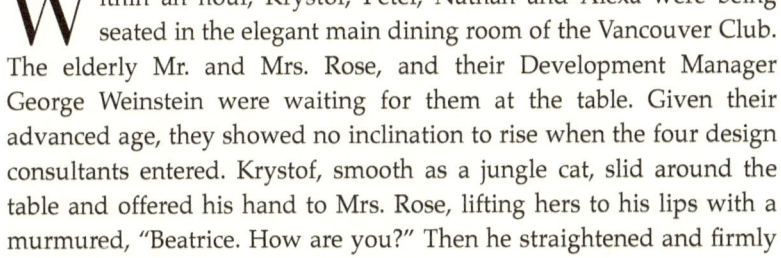

Within an hour, Krystof, Peter, Nathan and Alexa were being seated in the elegant main dining room of the Vancouver Club. The elderly Mr. and Mrs. Rose, and their Development Manager George Weinstein were waiting for them at the table. Given their advanced age, they showed no inclination to rise when the four design consultants entered. Krystof, smooth as a jungle cat, slid around the table and offered his hand to Mrs. Rose, lifting hers to his lips with a murmured, "Beatrice. How are you?" Then he straightened and firmly shook hands with Mr. Rose and the stout Mr. Weinstein in his brown suit.

Alexa made her way confidently to Weinstein and shook his hand in greeting. "George." She hovered near Krystof waiting to be introduced to the Rose's.

Although Alexa had met Weinstein on a couple of occasions, and of course been part of the team that presented the proposal to him and his selection committee, she had not yet met the elderly couple who had donated the bulk of the funds for the new Arts Centre. Her pulse raced. At last she was playing with the big boys and girls. It was thrilling. Contacts like this would make her career. She could do anything, go anywhere, on the strength of this experience. Moreover, being associated with a high profile public building like this would significantly ratchet up her status as a professional. And for her, personally, it was exciting to play a crucial role in creating a building that would be used and appreciated by the citizens of Vancouver for decades to come. Her contribution to the fabric of the community would be truly meaningful.

The Roses were British expats of a certain generation that moved in the highest echelons of society. Beatrice Rose was an exquisite socialite, even at her advanced age, which was surely well into her eighties. She wore her white hair in a cropped and curled bob that was better suited to a woman twenty years her junior, but not a hair was out of place. Her large gold jewelry perfectly accented her neatly tailored ivory suit. Despite the perfect grooming, her eyes were warm and inviting, and Alexa made a point of meeting them, and smiling. Albion Rose, beside her, was a tall, gaunt, man whose rod-straight bearing spoke to his role as a naval officer, right down to his dark blue, double breasted jacket with shining brass buttons. His moustached thin mouth turned sharply down at the corners, carving deep lines between the flaps of skin that now formed the bookends of his jowls.

Krystof stepped to one side and swept one graceful hand out in an arc to indicate his underlings. "George, you're already familiar with everyone."

Weinstein mumbled a greeting, nodding generally at all of them together.

"Let me introduce my team to you, Beatrice and Albion." Krystof placed a hand on Peter's shoulder, as he stood closest and said, "Meet the talented young people responsible for the proposal that you chose. Peter Zilco here, the lady to my right is Alexa Jenner, and–"

Nathan stepped forward, making a point of obscuring her view of their hosts, elbowing Alexa aside. "Mr. Rose. How are you, sir?"

Mr. Rose's face lit up. "Nathan, my boy! Of course, of course. I was hoping to see you today. My you've grown into a fine young man." They shook hands enthusiastically.

Alexa shot a glance at Peter, who responded with a grimace.

"Mrs. Rose," Nathan stepped closer and bent to kiss her cheek.

She smiled up at him. "Hello, Nathan, dear. How's your grandmother?"

"She's very well, thank you. They'll be home from Florida soon."

"Oh, lovely. We'll have to get together. I heard a rumour that you're getting married, young man. Is it true?"

Nathan lifted his chin and grinned. "Well... I am engaged, yes."

"Good for you, boy," Mr. Rose said. "Good to hear you'll be settling down and starting your own family."

Krystof cleared his throat while Alexa and Peter exchanged another appalled look.

As Nathan stepped back at last, opening a view to Alexa. Mr. Rose appeared surprised as his watery eyes flashed on her, his sagging face suddenly flushed with a rosy hue. He attempted to stand, though he fumbled, and required the steadying hand of Weinstein and the fluttering attentions of his wife before he gained his footing.

"Mr. Rose, Mrs. Rose." Alexa said, offering him her outstretched hand for shaking. "A huge pleasure to meet you both at long last. I've so enjoyed taking this project from concept to contract, and I'm really looking forward to hearing your views as we take it to the next stage."

"Miss... Jenner," he said, a tremor of feeble uncertainty in his ancient voice as he hesitated and then took her hand. His pale eyes darted to Krystof, and then to Weinstein, and finally to his wife.

Alexa's brow tightened a little. The old guy seemed momentarily flustered.

She released his hand and bent toward the seated woman. "Mrs. Rose. It's a wonderful thing that you're doing for the community. This will be a lasting legacy to your vision and generosity."

Beatrice Rose's grip was bony and firm. "My dear, Miss Jenner. Lovely to find a young woman here to keep me company. Please sit by me." She patted the chair.

Alexa hesitated. She had been angling for the seat next to Weinstein, but Nathan already had his hand on it. She glanced at Krystof, who gave a minute shrug and a nod of approval, so she moved around the table to take the seat next to the old woman. Beatrice Rose was a force of nature, having a long and illustrious career of charitable work in the city, and was known everywhere. This was a women Alexa wanted on her side, even though George Weinstein was likely the man who would manage the project day to day, and strongly influence decisions.

Once they had drinks and meals ordered, general chatter gave way to more serious conversation about the project itself. Alexa strained to follow the quiet discussion Krystof was having with Weinstein and Rose opposite, while trying to keep up with Mrs. Rose on her left, who insisted on asking her a string of personal questions unrelated to the project. Nathan was leaning toward the men, his ears pricked, completely ignoring her and poor Peter, who was sandwiched between, looking left out and bored.

Once the waiters had placed salads in front of them, conversation resumed.

"How long have you worked for Krystof, dear?" enquired Mrs. Rose.

"Almost five years now," she replied, striving to be polite while bending her ear for pertinent conversation across the large round table.

"He's a charming man, is he not?"

Alexa looked up, casting a fleeting glance across the table at Krys. "I suppose so, yes. I know his clients find him so. But I admire him more for his talent and knowledge than his charm, per se." She smiled at the older woman.

"Oh, yes? And, tell me, Miss Jenner. What is your job description, exactly? Are you a..." she waved a veined and bejewelled hand in a circle, "...personal assistant to Krystof, then?"

Alexa's fork hung midair, her smile frozen on her face. She peered into Mrs. Rose's eyes to determine if she was serious. "I'm an architect, Mrs. Rose." A bit of escarole hung suspended on her fork. She noticed that the curly edges were brown and set it down at the edge of her plate.

Mrs. Rose's face registered her surprise and confusion. "Are you, really? Well that's wonderful. It never ceases to amaze me what young girls are doing these days."

Girls! She pressed her point, loud enough that the others couldn't help but overhear. "Didn't Mr. Weinstein mention that I presented the design proposal to the selection committee? I thought you and Mr. Rose knew I'd be leading this project."

Alexa lifted her wine glass and took a sip, her teeth clenched tightly, and her heart squeezing in her chest. How could a woman so involved in the community be so clueless? A tight lump formed in her gut, and she set down her fork, suddenly uninterested in her lunch.

Mrs. Rose turned to her husband and laid a hand lightly upon his arm, interrupting his conversation with Krystof and Nathan. "Did you know that Miss Jenner is an architect, too, Albion dear?" What a shame. Alexa had the impression she was more involved. Now they were both sidelined.

He smiled at her, blinking rapidly. "Naturally I did, dear." His chilly, piercing gaze slid over to assess Alexa. His neck flushed a dull red above his tight collar, and he raised his glass of scotch. "I'm delighted to have Miss Jenner as part of the design team." He turned toward Weinstein, Krystof and Nathan. "My wife is forever telling me that the ladies retiring rooms in these sorts of facilities are always sorely lacking in space and amenities. I'm confident ours will be uniquely well-designed, with the addition of Miss Jenner's expert, feminine perspective." He took a slug of his drink.

"I'll be sure to give the ladies *retiring* rooms as much of my attention as every other corner of the Arts Centre, Mr. Rose," Alexa said through clenched teeth, her head heating with rage and shame. She visualized herself tossing her glass of cold water in the old prick's face.

It was Krystof's turn to flush a deep lobster red. His head looked like it might explode. Peter's mouth hung open in shock, and Nathan, the snake, grinned into his drink. Krystof cleared his throat. "Actually, Albion," Krystof said, "Alexa's talents are quite remarkable. She's a fully qualified architect. It was her concept that we chose to develop–"

"Indeed, indeed," blustered Mr. Rose, leaning back in his chair. "There doesn't seem to be anything these young women can't do." His rolling laugh was deep and condescending as he met the eyes of the other men at the table, avoiding her own, and putting an end to the thread. "Tell me your honest opinion of the parking situation, Krystof. You too, boys. Foster over at City Hall was of the opinion we were going to run into trouble with the local merchants' lobby group, and you know full well we can't afford to screw this up."

Nathan was only too willing to jump in with detailed numbers about the parking garage, holding Mr. Rose's attention and preventing her from pursuing her position.

She sensed Krys's embarrassment and annoyance, but unwillingness to contradict his important client. Alexa's face heated and prickled with anger and humiliation. The old bastard. How dare he?

Her eyes fixed on Krystof's face, urging him to persist in defending her credentials and her contribution. He had to push forward the idea that she would be in charge of the project. But he sat back, allowing the old man to direct the conversation. A conversation that soon faded in Alexa's ears. She caught Krys's and Pete's and even Nathan's darting glances from time to time, as if they were wondering if she had spontaneously combusted. Instead, she sat there in a hot pool of humiliation, like the idiot she was.

∼

Alexa turned the key in her apartment door and strode in, Krystof on her heels. She tossed down her coat and bag and stood, rooted, in the centre of her dim, dusty living room. She hadn't been here in days, and it seemed foreign and uninviting compared to Kate and Simon's warm, cluttered house. He stood behind her, and she braced herself for his groping.

"Sasha, my love. I know that was horrible for you. I'm sorry."

She turned to him. He was trying to soothe her with his annoying pet name. Perhaps he was more sympathetic than he seemed at lunch. But he made no attempt to touch her. They had concluded their business and driven here separately, as previously arranged, so she'd had no opportunity to debrief with him over the nightmare at lunch. She stared at him, imagining her gaze as bleak as it felt. She felt dead inside. Was she a naive idealist, or had she just been cruelly betrayed by her friend, lover and mentor?

He scowled. "You are not angry?"

"Of course I'm angry!" Suddenly her pent up rage and frustration burst out, thrown at Krys like a slap, even though she knew it was Rose who deserved her wrath. "We should be past this kind of thing, Krys. How could this be happening now, after all the hard work and success?" She strode across her living room and back, her fury fuelling her agitated movement. "I've paid my dues. Haven't I? Why didn't the old son of a bitch know about me? Didn't Weinstein mention even once that there was a woman leading the team? Did you never have an opportunity to mention me? I was utterly humiliated."

"I was as shocked as you, darling. I had no idea he would feel this way. You know, his wife–"

"I know! Exactly. I'd heard such great things about her philanthropic work. But she was no help at all! How could he be such a dinosaur, Krys?" She struggled to stop the hot tears from erupting, but they would not be stopped. It felt like her heart was being ripped from her bleeding chest. A sob escaped and her shoulders shook, and at last Krys took her arms in his long-fingered hands and pulled her to his chest. "I've worked so hard. My whole life... struggling to overcome this very thing. Always... battling to be taken seriously. I can't believe..." The gut-wrenching sobs won out, and, after pulling his handkerchief out and handing it to her, encouraged her to bury her face in the crook of his shoulder with a gentle hand on the back of her head, stroking and stroking.

Alexa hated to show her weakness to Krystof. She was acting like a girl. She wished she had Kate to talk to. Kate would know what to do, what to say to comfort her. But Kate was thousands of miles away, across the Pacific Ocean dealing with a nightmare of her own. And Krys was trying to be kind, even though he couldn't possibly understand how she felt at this moment.

He hummed softly into her hair. "It is not fair, Sasha. In my home country, you would not be having a problem. At least that's one good outcome of communism. Everyone with equal training was treated as equal. Female architects from Poland are strong and talented and smart, like you, but do not have such social obstacles to overcome."

"If that's true why didn't you defend me, Krys? How could you sit there and allow him to shut me out?"

"That was not the time or place, Alexa. We must not offend them. I will straighten out the situation. I promise." He stroked her chin with his soft knuckles.

They continued to stand for several long minutes, until her tears dried, and her quaking ceased. Then he silently guided her to her bedroom, and gently, slowly unbuttoned and slipped off her blouse, removed her slacks, unclipped her bra and slipped it from her shoulders. She stood, passive and detached, allowing him to bare her skin and gaze at her nakedness. Finally he bent and slid her panties down her legs, until they pooled around her ankles on the floor, a halo of black on the taupe carpet. She looked down, and stepped out of them, and then he lifted her and lay her on her bed, her head against the large pillow shams stacked against the headboard.

Then while she watched him disinterestedly, he leisurely, fastidiously undressed himself, hanging his jacket and shirt on a hanger, and shaking out and draping his trousers neatly over the back of a chair. When he was completely nude, he stood a moment, allowing her to take in his lean, tanned limbs, the curls of greying dark hair upon his chest. The fine hair continued in a pencil thin line across his lean, flat stomach to his groin, pointing to the gleaming erection that stood proudly there, pink and blue tinged. He directed his cool gaze at her, the corners of his thin lips curled up slightly, and raised his hands, palm up, as if offering himself for her inspection. Usually she found him quite beautiful. Today she was oddly unmoved. Not surprisingly, she wasn't in the mood for sex, but she could always trust Krystof's sensitivity and skill to remedy that.

As he approached, kneeling on the bed and crawling toward her unhurriedly, he purred in his scratchy deep voice, "Where is my feisty tiger? Shall I lick your wounds for you, darling pussycat? Let me sooth your injuries, poor thing."

Alexa could not make herself move, could not rouse herself to react or respond, so she continued to lie there, inert, while he arched over her and covered her body with gentle kisses. He stroked his long-fingered, soft hands over her body, tracing every curve and line on the left and the right, as though drawing her with a pencil, admiring her proportions and her symmetry, as he had always done. He licked and sucked and nibbled as promised, pulling at her erect nipples, methodically covering every inch of her with his tender care and attention, until finally she thawed, and then heated, and then trembled and tensed. Perhaps this was the release she needed.

"Krys..." she murmured, feeling comforted by his familiar caresses.

He grabbed her thighs and pulled her down off the pillows, and with his knees pushed her legs farther apart, until she lay flat and spread-eagled upon the bed, the whole time his cool, silver eyes boring into hers, raking over her body. He lowered, himself between her knees, and pressed his smooth face toward her feminine core, breathing hot moist air over her, heating her further, making her close her eyes and quiver in anticipation. His mouth covered her, and his hot wet tongue darted over her folds and between them, licking, and then sucking her most sensitive place, until she was quaking with desire. At last he rose up, deftly slid on a condom and pressed his stiff throbbing cock into her, sliding deeper, planting himself firmly and completely inside of her. They were silent, and she opened her eyes and watched him withdraw and thrust, withdraw and thrust again, methodically, carefully, building the heat and tension between and within them, until she could feel his control giving way. He juddered and lunged deep, collapsing onto her, jerking and quivering in his ultimate release with a quiet moan and a sigh.

They lay there, Krys heavy and damp with perspiration on top of her, for several long minutes. When he finally slipped out and rolled off of her, she moved away and stood up. "I have to pee," she whispered in apology, and walked to the bathroom. Closing the door, she leaned back against the vanity and stared at her naked slender tan body in the full-length mirror. Then she stared into the empty blackness of her own dark, dilated eyes, and slid a hand down her belly to her private core, dipping her fingertips into the slick wetness that Krystof had left behind. It didn't take much, just the right delicate pressure, a minute vibration, and she closed her eyes, threw her head back and went over the edge of the abyss alone, floating on her release at last.

CHAPTER 8

At the Aquatic Centre, Bruce realized, suddenly, what the family changing room was for. He led Markus in by the hand, taking the tiny, shuffling steps he was becoming accustomed to. Changing in front of all the other naked, adult men– something Bruce, with three older brothers in an all male household had never flinched at– now seemed somehow disturbing, with Markus beside him.

He was relieved to find generously sized change rooms with sturdy benches and hooks, and helped Markus squirm into his little swim trunks. There was a package of *swim* diapers in the bag. Seriously?

"Swim diapers? Sounds uncomfortable. Tell you what, Markus. You let me know if you gotta go, alright? And if you accidentally piss in the pool, well, you won't be the first. The filters'll take care of it, okay?"

"Otay."

He led Markus out to the pool deck.

A sensory onslaught awaited them.

The large, cavernous space echoed with the barking shouts and squeals of children playing in the water. The sounds of splashing formed a constant atmospheric backdrop. Bruce's nostrils filled with the pungent smell of chlorine, and he plunged into humidity, warmth and sublime comfort. He'd spent a lot of time at the pool as a youngster, initially with his mother, before she left, and later in swim lessons and on the swim team. He'd excelled at swimming. Water, for him, was home.

"Hey, Marky. Let's gooooo!" He seized Markus around the middle and lifted him up, swooping down into the shallow toddler zone, skimming him along the surface. Markus screeched with fear and delight, and Bruce set him down to get his bearings.

Markus was comfortable with the water, and took to it like a tadpole, wiggling around and jumping. He dived after a number of colourful floating toys, and when a skimboard came free, Bruce grabbed it and pulled it out to deeper water with Markus clinging for life, a smile wreathing his chubby cheeks. The warm water of the kids' pool enveloped Bruce's submerged limbs and he smiled too. He and Markus were kindred spirits, and he delighted in the communion of shared joy as they paddled out deeper where Bruce no longer had to bend over.

Bruce pulled and pushed Markus to and fro for quite a while, Markus demanding, "More, Boos, more," and "Again, Boos!" until he seemed to be getting worn out. Bruce lifted Markus bodily on top of the skim board, and showed him how to paddle himself around. He was thrilled. He took off, splashing and paddling around in a little circle.

Bruce lay back, relaxed, floating on his back for a moment, gazing half-seeing at the steel trusses far above, bridging the broad open space, the reverberating sounds muted in his submerged ears. He was glad Markus enjoyed swimming. It pleased him that he'd remembered to bring him.

He remembered his times at the swimming pool with his mother, especially. That was the birth of his love affair with water. His whole being suffused in calm and well-being. Those were some of his favourite memories, when she took him off to do something special, one-on-one, because he was younger than his brothers by several years. He was often excluded from his their games and sports because he was small, so Mom would invent a game or activity especially for them. Something exclusive. Memories of those times alone with her, he cherished.

Even at the age of six or seven, he'd been overwhelmed by the houseful of noisy older boys. Overwhelmed by the loud and demanding voice of their father. As, he now suspected, his mother had been too.

He really didn't know, he realized, what had happened. It seemed to him she'd often been sad and overwhelmed, somehow apart from everything that was going on in their home– a gaunt, shadowy figure that faded into the wallpaper –unless they were out together. Maybe that's why she took him off alone. Maybe it was her way of escaping from that same oppressive environment that made him feel small and defeated. He wondered...

The sudden shout, and piercing whistle brought him upright out of his reverie with a heart-pounding jolt. A general hubbub rose up around him, a tsunami of bodies converging toward him. When he got his bearings, he realized that they weren't coming toward him, but rather racing to get out of the pool.

"*Everyone please evacuate the pool. The pool will re-open in one hour.*"

The lifeguard was holding Markus.

His chest squeezed so tight he could draw no breath. He lunged forward in the water, lost his balance and steadied himself. "Markus!" What the hell was going on? "Hey! That's my kid," he shouted to the guy hauling Markus out of the pool. He ignored Bruce. Bruce pursued him through waist high water that felt heavier than wet cement, and hauled himself out of the pool. "Hey!" When they were standing at last on the pool deck, the guy turned to Bruce, a deep frown etching his face.

"He yours?"

"Yeah," answered Bruce, breathless, reaching out for Markus. "What the–"

"Well, you're one helluva dad. The kid's not wearing a swim diaper. He left a floater in the pool." He handed Markus over to Bruce, who hoisted him up in his arms, cradling him.

Markus buried his face in Bruce's wet, naked shoulder, sputtering and whimpering.

"He's okay, but..." Lifeguard shook his head, scowling.

Bruce's face heated, his body tensing defensively. "A floater?"

The lifeguard turned and pointed to the water where they'd just been. Sure enough, there was a floater. A brown lump bobbed in the water, now entirely vacant. Swimmers stood around on the deck, whispering, and more than a few shot glares his way.

"Is that–?" Shit? A guffaw of laughter bubbled up, but one look at the expression on the lifeguard's face was all he needed to push that baby down. What an idiot, he was. He dutifully frowned instead. "From Markus?" Bruce tipped Markus over to peek inside his shorts.

"Yes. It is. You're lucky it's an intact log or we'd have to shock the pool and close for twenty-four hours. Thanks for ruining everyone's swim, dude. It's jerks like you that keep me earning my salary," he muttered, turned and walked away, leaving Bruce chagrinned and flustered.

Bruce pulled Markus away to look at him. "Are you okay, buddy? You were going to tell me if you had to go."

Markus just blinked at him, apparently still disoriented and upset at being hauled out by a stranger. A stew of pool water and snot ran down his face, mingling with his tears. Jesus. He'd only zoned out for a couple of minutes. This parenting thing was unrelenting.

He wiped Markus's face with his hand. "I'm so sorry, buddy. Ready to go?"

"Swim, s'more," gurgled Markus.

"Pool's closed now, my little friend." Bruce wasn't sure he'd ever have the nerve to show his face here again. He grinned at Markus. "We had fun, though, hey? We'll come another day." And we'll be using one of those special swim diapers next time.

He took his time shuffling off to the change rooms, certain they would not have any friends waiting for them there.

～

They were barely showered and changed, when Bruce's cell phone rang.

"Mr. Koczynski?" asked an unfamiliar male voice.

"Yes?"

"This is Ted Glenn, Building Inspector for the Municipality of West Vancouver."

Bruce's heart lurched. Uh-oh. What the hell? "Yes? How can I help you?"

"Are you the owner of 7632 Seaview Place?"

"Ye-e-es," Bruce answered. This couldn't be good.

"Mr. Koczynski, it has come to my attention that you may be engaged in an illegal demolition project, or perhaps a renovation project. I'd like to meet you at the property immediately to make an inspection and report. I'm in the neighbourhood this afternoon, if you're available."

Bruce drew in a sudden breath; it stuck in his throat. "Ah. Well," he glanced at his phone to check the time. "I have to pick up a… a chi… er, my daughter from school in half an hour, Mr. Glenn. But I could meet you there by three-thirty. Would that work for you?"

"Yes. Fine." He sounded annoyed. "I'll meet you at the property at three-thirty." He rang off.

Officious bastard. Christ, he had to hurry. He didn't want the guy poking around before he got there himself, drawing his own conclusions. Damn! "Gotta hurry, Marky. Change of plans. We'll go for our run tomorrow. Let's go get Maddie, hey?" And then what?

He threw their stuff in the bag and grabbed Markus, racing out to the SUV. On the way to Maddie's school, he dialled Alexa's number. It rang and rang, but all he got was her voice mail. He hung up without leaving a message. Where the hell was she? He'd have to head over to her office and drop off the kids there.

This was a disaster of huge proportions. He'd really hoped to clean up the general demolition mess before anyone noticed. Afterwards, he could putter in the interior of his house and no one would know. It wasn't as though he was doing any major alterations, after all. Stopping now to get a building permit in place could ruin his plans to make the place livable by the Fall. He couldn't possibly handle this with the kids underfoot. He parked illegally close to the door of Maddie's school, grabbed Markus and raced in to get her, praying there would be no tricks today.

Twenty-five minutes later, he pulled up to the curb outside Vision Architecture's office on West Eighth Avenue. He was barely going to have enough time to get across the bridge and to his house before the damned inspector showed up. With Markus hooked under his arm and Maddie in tow, he speed dialled Alexa again as they entered the building, hoping she could come out to meet him. It rang and rang.

Answer, damn it!

"Alexa Jenner."

"It's about time. Shit, I need you."

"I beg your pardon?"

"You know what I mean. I need your... help. Can you come to the lobby?"

"Lobby? I'm in a meeting. Who is this?"

"Damn it, it's me, Bruce," he shouted. She knew damned well it was him.

"What do you want, Koczynski?"

"I have to meet someone at my house ASAP. It's urgent. I have to drop the kids off with you. I'm at your office."

She snorted. "I'd really love to help you." Her voice dripped with sarcasm. Sure, she'd love to help him. "But I'm in Squamish at the moment."

He heard the laughter in her voice, and his heart plummeted.

"Squamish?" Goddam it. Now what? She'd have to pass right by his neighbourhood on the way home. "Okay, that's fine. Listen, if I give you my address, can you swing by my house and pick up the kids? As soon as you can get there would be fine."

"Would it?" She was silent. "It so happens I'm not finished my workday, and I also travelled up here with a colleague. I can hardly drag her along to save your ass, Koz."

Bruce drew in a tight breath. He clenched his teeth. "I'm begging for help here!" he ground out. "It's the building inspector. I need to focus. Come on! I'll owe you."

"Well." He heard her laugh, a bright, hoarse, sexy sound that grated on his nerves. *Come on! Stop toying with me.*

He cleared his throat, swallowed, and lowered his voice. "I can't watch the kids. It's not safe there. There's a drop-off... and demolition. Please."

"I knew this would happen! I'm in a bad mood, Koz, and I'd like nothing better than to inconvenience you, but alright. Since you asked so nicely. But not likely before four. You'll have to manage until then."

"Four!"

"That's the best I can do. Take it or leave it."

"Okay! Four."

"And I will demand compensation," she laughed again.

He gave her the address and some general directions and hung up.

"Ahem. Are you lost, sir?" Bruce looked up to find the receptionist blinking at him.

"Uh. I– er... um." He swallowed, suddenly aware of how crazy he must appear flying into a business with two kids, hollering into his phone.

"I was going to drop the kids off, but... she's not here so... uh. No. Thanks."

A lean young man with glasses passed by just then, and turned to face them. "Oh, hey! Are you Bruce? These must be the darlings!" He came over and bent to tweak their cheeks. "Hello Maddie. My name's

Peter. I'm a friend of Alexa's." He leaned closer and continued in a falsetto voice. "And you must be Markus. Hello you Cutie Pie." Peter caressed Markus's damp messy hair with the palm of his hand. "Aren't you the most gorgeous thing?"

Bruce leaned away. "Yeah. Uh... hi, Peter?"

"Did you stop by for a visit? That's so sweet. But Alex isn't here right now. She's–"

"She's in Squamish with Stephanie. Who's this?" A thin, handsome older metro-sexual had stopped behind Peter, his lip curling in distaste at the scene. His well cut, fashionable suit and perfect grooming reeked of vanity and arrogance. He carried himself and his beautiful clothes with an unfettered confidence and sense of entitlement, and he scowled and glared at Bruce and the kids like they were some kind of accident that was polluting his front porch. He looked like he owned the place. Maybe he did. Bruce instantly disliked him, and consequently ignored him completely.

"She just told me." Bruce stuck his hand out, waving his cell phone. "Nice to meet you Pete, but, we've gotta run."

"Sure," Peter said with a puzzled expression as Bruce backed out of the door and ran back to the car, the kids in tow.

∼

"Now listen, you two," said Bruce as he pulled the SUV up outside his house. "This isn't an ordinary house. There's broken stuff. It's dangerous. And there's no railing, so you can fall down the mountain. You'll have to sit here in the car until Alexa gets here."

"No!" shouted Markus.

"No way!" agreed Maddie. "Why should we sit here?"

Bruce sighed. "You've got games and stuff."

"No."

He glared at them, trying to figure out how to contain them and keep them safe. He needed to go through the house alone, and the inspector would arrive before Alexa did. "Sit here for two minutes while I talk to the neighbour. Maybe she can watch you for a bit."

Markus let out a howl of protest, into which Bruce shouted, "Chill! She's got kids! It'll be fun." Markus stopped.

"Okay? Sit tight." Bruce leapt from the SUV and locked the door with the key remote as he loped over to Gillian's place, praying she'd be there. Lucky for him, she answered on the second knock. "Boy, am I glad to see you."

She smiled, a suggestive smile, and said, "Well, I'm glad to see you too." She let her gaze drop down to his bare legs, and slide slowly back up his body. Then she raised her delicate brows and stepped back into the house, inviting him in with her body language.

"Erm." Wrong idea, babe. Bruce let his eyes dance over her curves. Or maybe just wrong timing. Who knew you could use kids as a pick up line? He almost laughed. He glanced through the open doorway, flashing a smile. "Are your kids home?"

She made a complicated, blinking, eye-rolling expression. "You're in an awfully big hurry, aren't you?"

He liked her soft, sexy femininity. She was affectionate and nurturing with the kids, but in a lazy way, as though it came easily to her. If he ever decided to settle down, not that he did, Gillian was probably the perfect woman for him not to want. Someone who would make life easy, and not make demands. She certainly seemed open to a little liaison, but he got the sense he'd have to work for it, charm her a little. He wasn't quite sure dating a single mother was a good idea, though. But then, fantasies notwithstanding, he really was never in it for the long haul, so as long as he made that clear...

He scowled, shaking off the entire pointless tangent. "I have a favour to ask, Gillian. I've got kids in the car, and I need to meet with the building inspector in a few minutes. Could you watch them for... about forty-five minutes, until my... em, their, uh, aunt arrives to pick them up?"

"Kids?" Gillian was still processing his request. "You've got kids?"

"Yes and no. I mean, I do at the moment. I'll explain later, I promise, but can I bring them over now?" He remembered Alexa's reaction to his near-begging on the phone. "Please. I'll make it up to you. Maybe dinner sometime?"

Her eyes lit up, even as she pouted, her fine brows knitting, as though she didn't quite recognize his offer as the bribe that it was. "Alright. Uh, how many kids?"

"Two. Seven and three," he said over his shoulder as he hiked back toward the SUV. Not that he'd mind taking Gillian on a date. It's only that he wasn't sure–

When he opened the sliding side door, the car was empty. "God–

dammit!" He raced into his house, certain he'd find them on the precipice of death. "Maddie! Markus!"

He scanned the big room and raced down first one corridor and then the other, peeking into each room in turn. No kids. "Damn!" He raced outside to the patio, his heart pounding for the second time today, and stopped in his tracks, rocking on his heels. They sat side by side, holding hands, on the edge of the patio where he and their father had eaten lunch. He let out his breath in relief. Jesus, he wasn't going to survive another two weeks of this!

Saving his scolding for later, Bruce settled the kids at Gillian's and was finally free to prepare for his encounter with the inspector. Gillian's two kids, Matthew, about six and a little girl of four, were the perfect playmates for Maddie and Markus, and they were all happily sharing toys when he left. He was confident that they would be both safe enough and well-entertained, despite Gillian's casual, distracted air. Maybe with practice he too would relax into the job.

∽

He'd only walked through the house, straightening things and mentally preparing his arguments when he heard a car pull up outside. He strode out with an air of confidence to greet Mr. Glenn from City Hall.

Ted Glenn was a man of few words and fewer social graces, a man who evidently took his job and himself very seriously, judging by the starched shirt and clipboard. After a curt greeting, he sniffed and moved into the house, his thin face pinched and his darting, shrewd grey eyes missing nothing. Bruce could only trail along behind him in an attempt to buffer his impressions. He knew he was in trouble. The man moved silently from room to room, making copious notes on his clip-board and snapping photos with a small automatic camera he kept tucked in his shirt breast pocket. He wore a turquoise windbreaker over it, and each time he reached behind the front lapel to access his camera, Bruce flinched, as though the man would pull a gun.

Finally he stopped in the middle of the living room and turned to Bruce. "So what exactly were your plans here, Mr. Koczynski?"

Were. Bruce did not like the sound of that. He pasted a conciliatory smile on his face and tried for his most charming, relaxed tone. "Nothing much, really. I know it looks like a big mess at the moment, but basically I pulled out the old carpets and drapes and appliances. Everything was dirty and dilapidated. All I want are fresh new finishes. Paint, flooring, fixtures. Give the old place a new life, you know?"

Ted Glenn eyed Bruce from under loose, hooded eyelids, his eyes icy and unsympathetic. "Tell me about your kitchen."

Bruce cast his gaze over the gutted hole near the wall where he'd torn out cabinets and counters, as well as appliances. Old wires hung out of gaping holes he'd gouged in the walls, like long, decapitated snakes. "Well, yes. The old kitchen wasn't safe. It's best to replace everything, and I thought shift it over a bit–" he gestured to the centre of the upper level, trying to make it seem as small a change as possible.

Ted Glenn sighed. "You do realize building an entirely new kitchen, which it's clear to me you now have no choice but doing, requires building and plumbing permits, Mr. Koczynski."

Bruce peered at him, his face immobile, but he could feel a hot flush creeping up his neck, into his ears. "Uh. Well, no. I didn't, obviously. The improvements I have planned are very minor, really. And that was a very spontaneous… decision."

The inspector strode to the gutted kitchen and picked up the end of a trailing wire. "This live?"

Bruce's eyes bugged. "Course not!"

Glenn nodded. "Strikes me that this wiring is pretty old. Not up to current code standards."

"Yes!" Bruce agreed. "Probably dangerous, as well as inadequate for a modern house."

"So you're going to replace it all?"

A trap closed in. "Perhaps?"

Glenn's nostrils flared. "You do realize, Mr. Koczynski, that new wiring, installed by a qualified electrician, will of course require an Electrical Permit?"

"Erm…" He knew he'd been optimistic, avoiding City Hall. Perhaps he'd been optimistic, but the scope of work had sort of crept as he'd got in here and started ripping it apart. But this was ridiculous. Glenn was making him look like an idiot, or a very sleazy guy, neither of which was very flattering.

"Show me the bathrooms please."

"Huh? It's not really… working."

The inspector glared at him. "I saw some chipped porcelain in the front yard. That from here? You throw away some old plumbing fixtures?"

Oh, right. It was clear to Bruce where this was going now. He wasn't going to pull the wool over this guy's eyes. He took a deep breath. "Yes. A couple."

Bruce swallowed and led the way to the master bath. It was an empty room with chopped off PVC and old copper pipes jutting from the walls, scraps of tile on the floor.

Mr. Glenn sniffed. "So. All new appliances and, dare I say, water and septic lines. Have you seen any No-Corrode drain pipe in the yard?"

"I don't know." No idea what he was talking about now.

"Other bathroom the same?"

How did the guy even know there was another bathroom? Bruce sighed. "Yup." It was a lost cause. By the time he found someone to throw some drawings together and got his permits, it would be the end of July. He'd never get the place livable by September, or even October. When it got wet and cold enough he really wouldn't enjoy living on the boat anymore. He'd have to go to the trouble of renting an interim place.

Glenn moved through the remainder of the house, poking his head into closets and holes, turning up his nose at rotten wood window frames and water stains on the walls. Then he ventured outside onto the patio overlooking the marina below. Bruce followed.

"You'll need a railing here, Mr. Koczynski," he said, peering over the edge.

"Of course."

"We'll want to see an engineering stamp on that."

"Yes. Of course." Was there a hoop left he wouldn't have to jump through?

"You must not proceed with demolition work until you have at least the demolition permit in place. If you submit drawings promptly, you could have that permit in place within a week."

A week? Bruce glared at him, feeling dead inside. This was a complete shutdown. He'd make no further progress now, until he answered this man's demands. The smile he dredged up and pasted on his face was the hardest thing he'd ever done, but he knew it would do him no good to make an enemy of this guy. "Right. I'll take care of it, Ted. Don't worry about a thing." He shook the inspector's hand, and forced a laugh to go with it. He was used to soothing and calming antagonistic opponents. Humour almost always worked. That had been the best strategy in dealing with his unruly, malicious older brothers.

"I have some papers to fill out. Please don't leave until I can give you a copy," said Glenn, heading for his car.

Bruce turned to watch him, his heart a lump of lead in his shoes, feeling as discouraged about his fabulous summer project as he could feel.

Just then, a familiar car pulled up. It was Alexa's Saab, the one he'd seen parked in the driveway at Simon and Kate's house when he'd dropped the kids off. He strode over to it as Alexa stepped out, dressed as ever in a striking black and brown pantsuit and polished shoes.

"Where's the Audi?"

She peered at him over the top of her glasses, her eyes drifting up and down, and he cringed inwardly, regretting his meagre running attire, self conscious of his bare legs and shoulders. She smirked and shook her head. "Why would I drive Kate's car to work?"

"So, no car seats?"

She twisted up her face in scorn.

He shrugged, smiling. "Okay, no problem. I'll move them over from the SUV." As he approached her, another young woman stepped out of the car, taller than Alexa, but equally dark-haired. She gave him a broad white smile when she saw him, the kind he was used to eliciting from women that weren't Alexa.

"Hi." Her eyes darted over his body, and colour rose to her face. She, unlike Alexa, apparently liked what she saw.

She was cute, with freckles on her small broad nose. Probably no more than twenty-five, though. But it was flattering to be admired again. He gave her his flashiest smile. "Hello. I'm Bruce. Thanks for accommodating my emergency this afternoon." He offered her his hand, and she shook it, blushing and grinning, her eyes jumping up and down.

"Where are the kids?" Alexa moved toward the house, peering through the windows. Her movements were quick and jerky. She seemed especially short-tempered. The young woman wandered off, into the house.

"Next door, with the neighbour."

She stopped in her tracks and spun around, her eyes flashing. "You had someone to watch them and yet you disrupted my meeting and made me detour here and drag Stephanie out?" Her voice was like steel, hard and sharp, climbing up in pitch as her words marched out.

He pulled back, cringing inwardly, offering her a conciliatory smile. "I didn't know that when I called. It was a last minute thing, because the guy was coming, and..." he waved a hand in the direction of Gillian's house, "...anyway they can't stay there long. It's an imposition."

The look Alexa gave him made it clear Gillian wasn't the only one being imposed upon.

"Come on, Al. I can't help this. Everyone assumes I have no responsibilities during the day, but..." he gestured at Ted Glenn's car.

She nodded curtly. "Get them."

He raised a finger. "Give me another couple of minutes, please. I'll move the kids' seats over to your car. The inspector is still here, and I can't leave in case he wants–"

"Alexa, come over here! This place is amazing," the assistant, or whatever she was, called to Alexa from inside the house.

"Stephanie?" Alexa glanced toward the house, then turned back to Bruce with a pointed finger. "A few minutes. That's all. We have to get back to the office for a meeting."

Bruce shot a furtive glance at Ted Glenn, sitting in his car with the door ajar, writing his report. Bruce followed Alexa into the house.

Both women were standing below the entry and kitchen level, in front of the living room fireplace. Stephanie spun and swept an open palm around the room, like Ginger Rogers on stage. "See what I mean? If this isn't an early Ron Thom, I'll be a monkey's uncle. Look at those huge overhanging roofs. The glazing. And this fireplace!"

Alexa nodded and squinted, peering around at the house. "You might have something, Steph."

"What's a Runtum?" he asked.

Alexa ignored him, climbed the four steps to the top level, turned and stalked down the narrow corridor, disappearing into the master bedroom at the end. Stephanie trailed after her. He could hear the excited escalating tones of their muffled discussion.

Bruce stood on the spot, baffled. "Architects," he mumbled, shaking his head.

"Well, that's it for now, Mr. Koczynski," came Glenn's voice from the open doorway, papers in hand.

Bruce flinched and turned toward him.

He handed a pink copy to Bruce, and he took it, peering suspiciously down at the man's neat, tightly spaced, slanted handwriting. He'd had a lot to say, but what caught Bruce's eye was the stamp at the bottom. *NO PERMITS. STOP WORK.*

Fuck.

Alexa strode toward them down the hall, Stephanie behind her. "What do you know about this house, Koczynski?" she demanded. "Oh, hi Ted, how are you?"

Glenn glanced up, puzzled. "Ms. Jenner?"

Bruce blinked. They knew each other?

Alexa was staring at him, her grey-green eyes stormy, waiting for an answer.

He shrugged. "Some old lady lived here alone. For years, I guess. She died."

"Do you know the family name?"

He was baffled. "Um. Might be on the… why? What does it matter?"

"She might have been the original owner, that's all. That'd be why it was never catalogued. I'm almost certain this is a Ron Thom. Do you have any idea what a valuable resource you're sitting on here? Who have you got working on it?"

"Erm. No one yet. I've got some framers lined up, for the…" he caught Ted Glenn's eye. "… nothing much. I had a couple of students helping with the demo…"

"Demo?" she screeched. "What have you done? What have you torn out?"

He waved an arm. "Just the kitchen, really. And the railing around the patio, it was falling–"

"Quite a lot, actually, but nothing fatal," drawled Glenn. "Yet. Do I hear you correctly, Ms. Jenner? This is a Ron Thom designed house?"

She nodded. "You'll have to check the records, Ted, but I'm pretty sure. It has all his trademarks. If it weren't quite so old, I'd say it could be a later knock off, but you can clearly see from the details that it dates from the early sixties. It's a little rough, as though he was working things out, experimenting."

"Who the hell is Ron Thom?" Bruce voice sounded hysterical to his own ears. Something was happening here, out of his control, and he liked it not one bit.

Alexa flinched. She turned to him and her smoky green eyes wide, whooshing figurative steam from her nose like a dragon. "Oh, no one important." Her voice oozed sarcasm. "Only one of Vancouver's most celebrated architects, famous for his West Coast houses. Formative of the regional style."

"Very interesting. This could be an important heritage resource, then."

"What?" Bruce said. "This pile of shit? You've got to be kidding."

Alexa made a face at him –a warning– *shut it, stupid.*

Ted Glenn cleared his throat. "No, I'm not *kidding*, Mr. Koczynski. In fact this is a far greater infringement of municipal bylaws than I originally suspected. You must not touch another thing until this issue is properly investigated. You've already done enough damage before your architect could advise you."

"My architect?"

Alexa scoffed. "You haven't even consulted an architect, have you?"

"My architect!" He flashed a smile and hooked an arm around her shoulders.

"You mean you haven't been retained, Ms. Jenner?" said Glenn.

She shrugged his arm off. "Me? I should say not! I would never have let this happen, Ted."

Bruce's usual calm control was slipping. He was desperate. His pulse raced. This situation was too bizarre. His hands clenched into useless fists, only drawing attention to his powerlessness, futility, and frustration. "Come on, Al. Help a friend out here."

"I'm sorry." Glenn hesitated, scowled, pursed his lips. "Then *why* are you here?"

Bruce glanced at Alexa and they both turned to Ted Glenn. Some things were beyond explanation.

The kids! He'd completely forgotten them in the momentary implosion of his entire goddamned life. Bruce turned his wary gaze to Alexa. "They'll be okay for a while yet? I hope." She nodded, and he calmed a little.

He shrugged at the inspector. "It's personal."

"You won't be free to do as you please with this house, in any case, Mr. Koczynski. It's very likely a B-list heritage resource. Maybe even an A. It's best you *do* have someone like Ms. Jenner to advise you."

"Well, I can tell you, it won't be me."

"I'll do it," offered Stephanie, who had been standing slack-jawed, listening.

"I don't... I hadn't planned..." Bruce sputtered.

"You can say that again!" Alexa said, shaking her head. She huffed a laugh. "You are such a joke."

Bruce bristled, glaring at her. *I am not a joke. I got blindsided here.* There she went, berating and insulting him, again! And this time in front of the inspector. He set his jaw, standing a little straighter. He'd show her. What had he done to deserve to have this... this arrogant, know-it-all shrew inflicted on him? Why did she have to treat him like an idiot child? Every time they were in the same room, he ended up humiliated and frustrated as hell. Those fiery green-grey eyes flashing, and that velvety, raspy voice reminded him of an alley cat riling for a scrap. Well he was more than willing to engaging in battle, and, damn it, God was cruel– he had another boner.

CHAPTER 9

"You are such a lucky bugger! Naive, but lucky. This is like digging a well and discovering oil!" Alexa's heart raced with excitement, and her voice rose with passion. A well-designed building always charged her up. And this was such a find. She would love to work on it herself, to direct an inspired restoration but of course he wouldn't agree. And anyway, she didn't have time for pet projects right now.

In contrast, he seemed to believe it was rather *un*lucky. He had deflated, was pouting and scowling like a little boy with a broken toy. "More like poverty than riches," he grumbled. "I'd have never bought it if I knew. I figured I'd make a tidy profit one day. Now I'll be squandering my fortune preserving a decrepit old relic."

Ted Glenn had finally left, and Alexa had suggested that Stephanie take her car back to the office alone and give Krystof her apologies for missing the strategy meeting. "I don't need it. I'll pick it up another day, and I don't want to keep you." It would be easier if Bruce, Alexa and the kids, drove together in the SUV to Kate and Simon's and saved the hassle of moving the car seats over and back.

He was still pouting and glaring at her when they were alone in the house. "Do you have any idea what you've cost me today?"

It was hard to feel too sorry for him. She shrugged. "I didn't cost you anything. And you have plenty of money. So you keep telling me."

"That's not the point!" he bit back.

Grumpy as a bear, his usual calm control and lazy charm had

slipped. He had an dark edge, and seemed suddenly very manly. It was a little scary. And kind of sexy. "How is it my fault?"

"You've taken my already considerable problems and made them a thousand times worse!" He paced and flung his bare, muscled arms around. Then stopped abruptly in front of her, his arms fisted on his hips, biceps twitching.

Her heart fluttered and her breath quickened in response. His t-shirt was damp with perspiration, and she was suddenly aware of his long, bare muscled legs. Alexa tilted her head and regarded him serenely, curious about the warm stirrings his tantrum kindled. Maybe it was because he was serious for once, his fake veneer of charm forgotten.

"I'm trying –was trying– to finish this reno by October, so I can move in before the rains start. I'm living on my boat, for Chris'sake, and this was supposed to be my summer project. For fun! You've totally messed that up now! It could take weeks to get the permits. Or more! Godknows what I'm going to have to do now that you've spilled the beans about this architect guy."

Spilled the beans? That woke her up. "You mean you knew it was a Ron Thom?"

"Of course not! I didn't even know what that was. I just want to get on with it. I was planning to do most of the work myself. Now my summer's wasted."

"Well. Not wasted." She smiled, casting him an oblique glance. "You have more time to take care of the kids, now." At least he wasn't intentionally dishonest. That was a relief. Not that she cared. Of course she didn't.

He let out a rude sound, a stifled scream. "Right! After I find someone to do the drawings, and apply for the permits, and Godknows what else they're going to make me do now."

"It won't be a big deal. You have to convince them that you understand, that you're going to do it right. That you're not going to spoil this fabulous treasure. Someone could do the drawings for you in a few days."

"The least you could do is help me out," he spat. "Treasure. You architects! Your head's in the clouds. This place is a dump. Anybody can see that. The only thing it's got going for it is the view. Have you even looked at it?"

What? How could he fail to understand the profound beauty? Was he blind? "Have *you*? Looked, really looked, at this place?"

"Of course I've looked. All I've seen is rotten window frames, cracked tiles, drapes and carpets that reek of cigarette smoke and cat piss, and tiny cramped bedrooms you can't even turn around in!"

"No, nonono," she moaned. "You're missing the point."

He scowled.

There had to be a way to…

"Come!"

She took off down the hall, leading the way into the master bedroom at the corner of the house. Surely she could make him see.

He followed. As soon as he passed the doorframe, she grabbed his arm and dragged him over to the back wall, waving her hand at it. His arm was large and firmly muscled, but she tried to ignore it.

He raised his eyebrows. "Yeah?"

"Tell me where you'd put your bed."

"There's no bloody choice, is there? It has to go there." He pointed at it. It was the only solid wall in the room. Clever boy.

She gazed at the wall, at him, out the window. "Right. Right. Come here and sit down." She dragged him by the arm again, trying to ignore how big and hard it felt in her hand, spun him around so their backs were to the wall, and slid down onto the dirty subfloor. He sank down beside her, legs straight out. "Now look."

He looked.

She imagined them sitting side by side on a queen size bed. There was no more than three feet from the "bed" to the window wall on two sides. She could feel the moist heat of his bare leg against her thin dress trousers. His strong legs, covered with fine damp dark curling hairs, drew her unwilling gaze.

"So?"

"So? So?! What do you see?"

He looked, finally, out the windows, because there was nothing else to look at. "Trees."

She didn't reply. Just sat beside him, his warm arm pressed against her, staring out the window at the forest that bound his property on this side, urging him to understand. *Come on. Come on.*

He looked. She followed his gaze out, into the forest, under the canopy of the evergreen trees, out to glimpses of silvery water and shadowed blue islands in the strait beyond. He was right about the view from this house. It was spectacular. Obviously the great designer had agreed.

She sensed his heart rate slow, and his breathing calm. He sat for several minutes in contemplative silence, and she waited, inhaling his scent of male sweat and soap faintly tinged with chlorine.

"Well?"

He jolted at her voice, turning his head slowly toward her. His gaze was soft, his espresso brown eyes warm and unmasked. He seemed almost surprised to see her, as though he had forgotten she was there.

She was afraid to disturb his peace. "Where did you go?" Her voice was tender, barely more than a whisper, reaching out to him, secretive and intimate, like a caress.

He shuddered.

"Uh. Out." His eyes darted back to the view. "Out there."

"Uh huh." She smiled to encourage him, and his gaze snapped back to her face, and fixed there, pinning her own, fascinated.

His gaze dropped to her mouth, he licked his lips, and her breath caught. Was he going to kiss her?

Against all reason and good sense, she almost hoped so. Heat radiated off of him and her blood heated in response. He leaned closer, flaring his nostrils, inhaling deeply. She could smell him too, his masculine scent rich and dizzying. Oh, damn, this was not good. She blinked twice, snapping herself out of it.

"So? Do you get it now?"

He tore his eyes away from her mouth, and looked outside again.

"I get being here, on this land."

"That's what this house is about. This is not a common house. It's not a box on a lane in which to keep your stuff. It's about being nestled here on this land."

He turned his head to peer at her again, solemn and intense. The sexual intensity had diminished, but the connection between them remained, like the mellow aftertaste of a sip of fine brandy.

She needed to explain. She wanted him to understand. "This room, this house, is like a little shelter in the woods, an eagle's nest, with a breathtaking view of the whole world." She drew pictures in the air with her hands, cupping them together, spreading them apart. "But not from a place of dominance, like a castle or a fort. We're here, outside, a part of the natural landscape. We're inside, but we're outside. This little room encloses us, but we're not here, we're there. Do you get it?"

His brows and lips twitched in a tiny momentary frown and he nodded.

"So it's not a tiny room. It's a cozy alcove in the grand space that's out there."

"Yes!" He got it.

She beamed at him. "The play between in and out, closed and open, small and infinite."

He screwed up his face, puzzled, processing. "I..."

She leapt up, brushing dust and debris from her pants with a satisfied flourish. "Let's go get the kids. It's time for dinner."

Alexa followed Bruce to the neighbour's house feeling a warm camaraderie and lightness of being she hadn't felt before, certainly not with Bruce Koczynski. It was unexpected. There were deep undercurrents to him that she hadn't glimpsed before. *I've been too hard on him. I ought to lighten up a little.* It would make getting along for the next two weeks easier, at least, even if they never became true friends.

"Gillian?" Bruce pushed open the door, which stood ajar when they arrived. They could hear the squeals of the children playing somewhere in the house, but couldn't see her. "Gillian!"

Still no answer. He took two more tentative steps into the hallway, while Alexa hovered in the doorway behind him. "Where are they?" she asked.

"Dunno." He stepped into the kitchen, looked around, shrugged.

She could smell something good baking in the oven. Chicken maybe.

"Madison! Markus!" Bruce called.

"Hi. Are you staying for dinner?" A soft, feminine voice replied.

Bruce turned to the sleepy voice. A tall, shapely blonde had approached from the hallway, wispy strands escaping from her ponytail, her face creased, leaning on the wall. She wore a wrinkled, oversized t-shirt, and was bare-legged, with legs that went on for miles. So this was Gillian? Alexa stepped back.

"Did I... wake you?"

She shrugged. "I had a little nap."

"Where are the kids?" He turned his head, cocking an ear for the sound of their voices. "I called but..."

She laughed, a seductive tinkle. "They're in the playroom downstairs. Don't worry. I lock the door. They don't even know, and they can't wander off."

"Huh." Bruce raised a brow and scanned her body, obviously liking what he saw.

Alexa frowned. Interesting approach. The stupid bimbo. What if they needed help?

Gillian sidled up to Bruce, lifted a lazy hand and laid it gently on his bare arm. Alexa's stomach tightened uncomfortably, and bile rose in her throat. Now she understood. She felt like a voyeur. She took another step back into the shadows of the entry porch.

"So? Can you stay for dinner? I have a casserole in the oven." Gillian's voice was liquid and inviting, and Alexa wondered what, if he stayed, they'd be having for dessert. He glanced over at Alexa, and their eyes locked. He looked a little shell-shocked, a bit embarrassed. She couldn't help shooting him a questioning glance, and had to drop her gaze.

"Er. No, sorry. Can't stay. I have… " He gestured toward Alexa. "We have to get going. I'm sorry that took so long. Things got a little complicated."

Gillian sharply turned to Alexa, her face crumpling, then hardening. "Oh? Hi. You're the… um, the aunt? I expected someone older."

Alexa scowled. She shot a look at Bruce. What had he said to Gillian? He seemed out of his element, but Alexa didn't know if it was because Gillian was coming on so strong, or because Alexa was watching.

He turned his shoulder to Gillian and met Alexa's gaze, rolled his eyes, shrugged in answer, and she stifled a laugh.

"I see," said Gillian, her face falling into a little peevish frown. What did she think? That they'd had a tumble among the rubble next door?

Bruce looked back at Gillian, chagrined. "I mean, you know, things with the building inspector got a bit ugly. He's shut me down."

"Oh, that's too bad. So you won't be around?"

"Not as much. I can't work on it, but I'll be here." He was quick to correct her. Wouldn't want to burn that bridge, would he? What a player. "I have to do plans, get permits, stuff like that."

"Oh." Her voice was small, coy, inviting. "So I'll be seeing you, then."

His smile then was warm and friendly, sexy and responsive, the good old charming Bruce Alexa'd always known. "Thanks a lot for helping out today, Gillian. I was in a real pinch. Maybe we could do the dinner this weekend. Can you get a sitter?" His voice was low and suggestive.

Her eyes brightened. "Sure." She glanced in Alexa's direction and said to Bruce, "Can you?"

But Alexa had stepped back around the corner, out of sight. She could still hear their voices, but she wanted to disappear, curious to know what would happen.

"Yeah, yeah. No problem."

"So, Maddie and Markus. They... yours?"

Alexa heard him laugh and explain the situation to Gillian.

"I see."

"Well, we'd better get going," said Bruce. "Can we get those kids released from prison?"

Alexa heard Gillian's footsteps descend the stairs. Seconds later, the four kids were charging up the stairs like a pack of dogs, howling and squealing.

"Boos!" hollered Markus.

Bruce thanked Gillian again, and emerged from the doorway with Markus and Madison.

Alexa waited by the SUV. Bruce held Markus in his arms, wrapped around him like a monkey in a tree.

"Auntie Alex!" shouted Maddie, wide-eyed, running to Alexa. "What're you doing here?" Alexa bent and hugged her.

Once everyone was strapped into the SUV, and they were headed home on the highway, the kids nodded off.

She didn't know why, but she was suddenly irritable. She shifted on her seat, crossing and uncrossing her legs, twisting to gaze out the side window at the city and ocean view from the highway, glancing back at Bruce. An awkwardness descended after their exchange in the bedroom. Was that moment of connection all in her imagination? She was a fool to think that he looked at her that way, anyway, that he would be interested in her, that he wanted to kiss her. He knew she wasn't like the women he normally hooked up with. Like Gillian. It took a more mature, intellectual sort of man to appreciate what Alexa had to offer. She knew she wasn't attractive to most men in *that* way. And that was okay with her. She'd fought her whole life for respect, fought *not* to be seen as a sex object, so this was to be expected, right? It's what she preferred.

It was clear what he liked in a woman, and it was exactly what she would have expected –that sexy blonde bombshell. His tastes were unsophisticated and stereotypical. If they weren't already humping like teenagers, it was clear they soon would be. Well, Gillian was welcome to him. They deserved each other.

Maybe she had imagined the spark between Bruce and herself earlier. Had she really got through to him? Hadn't he responded on some emotional, even spiritual level? Probably he would never understand the nuanced beauty of his house, or care about the kinds of ideas that moved her to tears. It was completely wasted on him. What a shame.

Well, he was Bruce Koczynski. What did she expect? She swallowed, blinked, stiffening her spine. It didn't matter.

Alexa turned to him, a sudden surge of irritation sharpened her tongue. "I can't believe you started demolition without permits. Without even checking the files. That's a significant architectural resource. And you didn't even know." She laughed, but it sounded too harsh in her own ears. "How dumb can you be? What is it with you? You remind me exactly of my little brother Jack - so incredibly reckless."

He kept his eyes on the road, and she could hear his regular slow breathing, see his chest rise and fall in the dim cab.

"An oversight," he mumbled, giving a snort of disbelief as he glanced her way.

"Yeah, I'll say. More like total freaking willful blindness."

"Alright already!" he barked, and she jumped back, her pulse rattling in her throat at the sudden rebuke, and she blinked and stared at him while he continued. "Lighten up, eh? Have a little pity on me. I've got enough problems without you harping at me for the next two weeks, Al."

He was right. Her attack was unjustified. Her reaction to seeing him with Gillian was irrational. *You're an idiot, Alexa.* She snickered at her own stupidity as she stared at the side of his head in the dim light, trying to figure out what had happened to her good sense and judgment. "I'm sorry. You're right. That was unkind."

"I just thought I could handle a few minor renos without anyone noticing. I'm not evil."

What did she care? She wasn't attracted to him anyway. *Liar!* Perhaps it was the proximity, and the fact that the kids were keeping her from seeing Krystof regularly. She was craving male attention. Touch.

"You know..." Alexa warmed her voice, trying to ease the thickening silence between them. She could detach from her body's needs and focus her mind on what was important, and it most certainly wasn't that buxom bit of fluff next door. "The reason I find your disdain so annoying is because design matters to me a great deal. If you paid attention to *anything* besides sports and poker and beer and *sex*, you'd understand."

He snorted. "You're pushing your luck, Al."

"No, listen, Koczynski. You're sitting on a cultural landmark of great significance, a carefully crafted artifact, exemplifying the inspired work of a visionary artist who helped to establish our very..." she hesitated, searching for words, warming to her subject, "...the fabric of our cultural identity, here on the West Coast, in the modern era. These ideas were formative to an entire movement that influenced design right up to today. There are many faces to modernism, and this particular regional expression so embodies the world view, the social and geographic context, the lifestyle and the self image of the West Coast, that it's helped to define us as a people."

Bruce shot her an incredulous, amused glance, shaking his head. His face was screwed up, in confusion or disdain, she didn't know. The late afternoon sun shone sharply across them, burnishing the side of his rugged cheek with warm golden light, glinting off the stubble of hair that showed along his jawbone where a muscle twitched. "You call that falling down wreck carefully crafted?"

"Did you hear a thing I said?"

"I'll tell you about craftsmanship, Ms. Smarty-Pants." He pointed a finger at her, driving his point home. "Craftsmanship is what I was planning to do this summer, with my hands and my heart and my eyes and the materials I choose." He thumped his fist against his chest, and inexplicably, Tarzan came to mind, and she wondered what Bruce would look like in a loincloth. Pretty damned hot, that's what. She shook the image off with a laugh when he continued talking.

"These ideas you're blathering on about are all abstract mumbo-jumbo. That's not real. That's not what matters, in a house, or anything." He thumped the steering wheel with the heel of his hand. "Do you think anyone but you and your fellow architects give a rat's ass about that stuff?" He snorted again. "Well, let me tell you. They don't."

Was she really having this debate with Bruce Koczynski? A man she believed incapable of these intense opinions and complex ideas? She didn't even know he had the vocabulary. It was utterly disorienting.

"What are you *laughing* at? I'm being serious, here."

He chuckled too, and she felt another bubble of laughter rising up. Was she actually debating architecture with this man? And enjoying it?

"I know you are," she shook her head again. Was this actually happening? "...but you've completely misunderstood me." Perhaps intentionally. Trust him to twist what she'd said. For a moment she feared he was just toying with her, and she felt disadvantaged. She was losing the bearings of her own argument. "You're so wrong, Koczynski. You don't realize how important these things are. Even when people aren't conscious of them, they are aware. The rightness of things seeps into their perception at some cellular level. There's a kind of cosmic rightness to good design that you can sense, even without the training and the language of big-A architecture. They are *not* abstract."

"Sure they are! Most people judge a space by how well it serves them. Their lifestyle. Their activities. Even their self-image. And they care about design only to the extent that..." He held up one one finger, "...a, things work the way they're supposed to and b..." He held up two fingers, "...they're pleasant to use. It's about the experience, the process. It may be aesthetic, but it's not intellectual. People like you who get caught up in the status of things... those are just words... words you use to justify your own existence. 'Big-A' architecture, as you call it, manifests the worst vices of mankind: greed, materialism, ego. At best, it's only material stuff that distracts people from what's really important in life."

Alexa drew in a shocked breath. A squeak escaped her lips. She caught herself and glanced over her shoulder at the kids. They were, she could see, still conked out from their impromptu play date, mouths slack. Thank God, because this discussion had gotten way out of hand.

"You know what your problem is? You take yourself too seriously. Life's about the process, the experience, the road traveled."

She stared at him, "Pish. You're way off base. I'm not talking about status or ego. Good design is for everyone. You're politicizing something you know nothing about." She paused. She was impressed with his original ideas, but he was still missing out on an important concept.

"Why have you never expressed an articulate opinion about any of this before?"

He shrugged. "You never asked."

"Hmph." Peering through the front windshield as they dropped down Taylor Way and swung onto the Lions Gate Bridge, she continued. "I don't know where your ideas are coming from, but you must see that it's not all about what you experience or feel. That's such a superficial assessment. Things have an inherent value. There is some fundamental structural meaning underlying every object in our world, whether natural or man-made. Some things, when they are created with care, and often even when we do it unconsciously, embody meanings and messages that are archetypal and expressive of our very existence as human beings!" She gasped for breath. "You know what your problem is? You don't take yourself... or anything... seriously enough!"

After five kilometres of intense hi-brow debate, it was an absurd claim. She stared at him, and as they slowed and stalled in rush hour traffic on the bridge, he turned to stare back. Their gazes met, sparkling with humour and mutual admiration, and she recognized a kindred spirit - intellectually sharp –how could he be otherwise and be Simon Sharpe's best friend all these years– principled, caring, funny, and frighteningly, distractingly attractive. Boy was she in trouble.

As rays of sun raked across the windshield, temporarily blinding them, he pulled a pair of dark sunglasses from the visor overhead and slipped them on, obscuring his intense gaze and effectively ending their debate.

∼

Bruce woke the children and helped get them and the day's gear inside once they'd gotten back to the house. He was too stunned to speak, and clearly Alexa was too, so dealing with the groggy kids was a relief as it gave them both something to do, and relieved the tension of arguing with each other half the way home, and then sitting in silence for the other half.

After begging her to come to his house to pick up the kids and bail him out of his emergency meeting with the building inspector, Bruce felt he owed her something. He might have felt obliged to stick around and help her with the evening routine of dinner and bedtime. But now

... now that she'd aggravated his troubles with City Hall, got all huffy after picking the kids up from Gillian's, insulted his intelligence in innumerable ways, and generally exasperated him with her woo-woo ideas, he wasn't sure who owed who what. Or was that 'whom'?

Despite his indecision, he stayed to unpack the bags, took Markus's swimsuit, towel and soiled clothing to the laundry hamper, and noticed it was full. He might as well toss it in the machine and run a wash while he was here. He wasn't sure he was doing these things to avoid her criticism or gain her favour, or just because it needed doing and he wanted to. Lucy, Simon's little black cat, followed him into the laundry room and rubbed against his shins. He bent down to pet her and scratch her head, and she looked up at him expectantly with her soulful green eyes.

He sighed, not sure what he'd expected this experience to entail. He shouldn't really be surprised that he couldn't foresee its precise form.

Then he took the lunch and snack bags to the kitchen and unpacked them, tidying up, putting stuff in the dishwasher while Alexa took the kids upstairs to get them bathed. He wanted to mention that Markus was clean, since they'd been swimming and showered afterwards, but couldn't bring himself to break the radio silence. She'd figure it out.

He missed the strange gentle moment of intimacy he'd shared with Alexa this afternoon, an almost painful physical awareness of each other– he was sure it was mutual– if only for that brief moment. There had been that odd interlude in his bedroom. The silence. The peace. The way she'd spoken to him in her velvet voice, like a mesmerist, and slowed his heart rate, calming him, almost putting him in a trance. Before everything went sideways. He sighed.

Since he was in the kitchen, he decided tonight, hellish as their afternoon was, was a perfect time to pull out one of the prepared meals he'd ordered from the gourmet place and heat it up in the oven. Lucy appeared again and let out a pitiful, almost silent little croak.

"I suppose you need to eat, eh?" He went to the fridge to look for cat food and dished some out for her as well as Oscar, setting it down. Adorably, she rubbed him once more before starting her meal. He sighed.

By the time Alexa and the kids came downstairs, scrubbed and in pyjamas, the food was ready. So he dished it out and carried cutlery to the table. There was enough, so he served himself as well, and brought all the plates to the table while Alexa poured the kids' milk, responding to their babble and answering their questions in a subdued way. He couldn't bring himself to participate, and though Maddie squinted at him curiously, Alexa avoided looking at him at all.

Before she sat down to eat, she went to the fridge and pulled out a small black case, unzipped it and pulled out a small vial and a tiny syringe. Expertly tilting the jar, she filled the syringe and prepared it. He realized she'd been doing this every night, and he didn't even know how. Surreptitiously, he watched what she did, in case he had to do it. He wanted to ask the dosage of insulin, but couldn't bring himself to break the silence. Alexa picked up Lucy, nestling her in her lap, and squatted low to the floor to expertly administer the shot to the skin on the cat's back. She rubbed it gently for a moment before setting her down and washing her hands at the sink. Then she joined them at the table. Her food was probably half cold already, but she ate without complaint.

They ate in near silence. Fortunately the kids were weary from their day, and hungry. Everyone seemed to like the food. A feather in his cap. Alexa didn't question it's source, and he didn't volunteer the explanation. She got up to clear away the plates when the phone rang. They all jumped.

Alexa picked it up. "Hello?" They all stared at her. The phone at the house rarely rang. "Simon!"

Bruce's gut twisted. Tonight of all nights. He glanced up and briefly caught Alexa's eye, and she widened her eyes and shrugged, but lowered her gaze immediately. It was the first she'd acknowledged his existence since the drive.

"Daddy!" Maddie squealed and leapt from her chair, jumping up and down and grabbing at Alexa. "Let me talk. Let me talk."

"Just a sec, Maddie. We're going to... hold on. Okay Simon. Five minutes." And she abruptly hung up.

"Nooooo! Daddeeee," Maddie whined.

"It's okay. He's calling back, but on the computer. To save money. Let's set it up."

Bruce lifted Markus from the table and they all scrambled into Simon's den. Alexa booted up the desktop computer and clicked on Google Hangouts. Bruce dragged another chair over to the desk while the application got going, and he settled Markus on his lap. Within a very few minutes they were connecting, the four of them squashed close together staring at Simon and Kate's grinning faces on the pixelated jiggedy screen.

"Hi sweeties! Hello my darlings. Oh, look at you!" Simon and Kate gushed at the same time.

"Daddy! Daddy!" Maddie squealed. "I miss you."

I do too. I could use your advice right about now, man.

"Mommy," Markus wailed, reaching out pudgy hand to touch the face of his mother on the screen, leaving a streak of grease.

"We're so glad you're all there. What great timing," Kate said.

"Yeah, it's not often that we're both here for dinner," Alexa replied.

"You all had dinner… together?" Simon asked, sounding puzzled.

"Sure," Bruce replied glibly. "Why not? I made dinner tonight while Al did the baths and stuff. We're an efficient team."

After a half beat of silence, the conversation resumed, the questions flying back and forth.

"Are you in a cast, Simon?" Bruce asked, and they were rewarded with a display of his blue walking cast as he lifted his leg up for the camera.

"It's not too bad. I'm semi-mobile now, which means Kate and I can see a few things, and get out for meals with my Mom."

Simon gave a brief summary of their activities so far, and Kate highlighted the sights they'd seen in Bangkok and environs on a driving tour they were able to arrange one day. They let the kids talk to their parents, and listened to anecdotes about the Grand Palace and Wat Arun.

Bruce kept a grin plastered to his face, but he studied Simon's face intently. There were definite signs of strain, which he was sad to see.

"How's your Dad doing, Simon?" Bruce asked.

"Good. He's stable," Simon said. "There was a pile of paperwork and discussions with hospital officials. It's all very bureaucratic and tedious. But now we're just hanging around until he's a little stronger so we can arrange travel home."

"How are you feeling, Kate?" Alexa asked.

Her answer, though smiling, was non-committal.

Frowning, Alexa asked, "What's wrong?"

"Nothing. But I'm finding the pace quite gruelling. I've been on my feet a lot. I'm not used to it. With the jet lag, and the pregnancy, it's been a bit much."

"She's exhausted," Simon said. "So we've done minimal sightseeing. But it's tedious sitting around either at the hospital or the hotel."

"Any idea when you'll be able to fly back?" Alexa asked.

Simon sobered. "It's hard to say. They'll discharge Dad soon, but then we have to decide if he can fly. We were talking…" he glanced at Kate. "With everything, we thought it might do us all good to spend a few days at the resort in Phuket before the big flight. We'll see."

Sharing details of their own trials and tribulations seemed pointless. There was no way he'd be burdening Simon with his troubles. And despite the trying day, Bruce had an odd sensation that they'd crossed some sort of watershed. They'd get through this somehow.

"Well, let us know, but relax and try to enjoy being there, despite all the hassles. And don't worry about a single thing. We've got everything here totally under control," Bruce said. "Right, Al? Hey, Scallywag. Lean in and give your Dad a big smooch." She did so, and generated the laughter Bruce had hoped it would. He then lifted Markus up to do the same.

"Aw, baby. I miss you so much. We love you both," Kate said, her eyes glistening.

Bruce's throat tightened. A quick glance at Alexa revealed that she was about to lose it too.

It was time to end this love-fest before all six of them were bawling. A few minutes later, after a million good-byes and promises to talk again in a few days, they signed off. Bruce said his goodnights to the kids and slipped out the door.

On the long dark quiet drive back over the bridge to the marina, he had plenty more time to think. What a day! But however challenging it had been, the thing that left the deepest impression on him was the magical effect Alexa's dreamy green eyes, and sultry voice had on him when it dropped in register as she spoke of the ideas that mattered to her, almost like pillow talk. Like a drug, it wove its tendrils around his brain and had the same effect the view from his house did – leaving him with simultaneous feelings of intense exhilaration and utter calm and safety.

~

Some days were harder than others. Alexa removed her glasses and set them down on top of her drawing table, leaned into her hands and rubbed her eyes, mascara be damned.

I wish I'd had a chance to talk to Kate alone last night. She glanced at her phone to check the time and did a quick calculation. No point trying to call Kate's cell phone. It would be the middle of the night. Alexa was miserable, but a call like that would stop Kate's heart, assuming some disaster had befallen the children. She could pour out her woes in an email, but it was obvious to Alexa that Kate didn't need any more worries to add to her load. The combination of traveling, pregnancy and the stress of dealing with everyone's ill health in an unfamiliar foreign location seemed to be taking its toll on her stamina.

She sighed.

I'm on my own.

But what else is new? Alexa had always had to make it on her own. Her needy family, while supportive in their way, invariably misunderstood what she was about. Her career. Independence. Accomplishment. They got all that, but they didn't know what it cost her.

Alexa's mother had encouraged her from a young age to be independent and look out for herself, to pursue her dreams and talents, and to fight for what she wanted. She could hear her tired voice like it was right beside her, she'd heard it so often. *Don't get sucked into the dream of romance and family - there is no happily ever after.*

That was her mother's message. Above all, Alexa wasn't to compromise her goals and dreams for anyone, like she had done. She was all too aware of the sacrifices Alexa had already made by helping to raise her brothers and sisters.

Mom wouldn't understand what Alexa was doing now. She'd be appalled at the situation she'd got herself into, and at the worst possible time for her career. But anyway, it wasn't taking care of Maddie and Markus that she found challenging at the moment. It was him.

And so, to get what Alexa wanted, she'd had no choice but to make it on her own, and give up what others had, whatever the price. And she had. She was getting there, anyway. *Look at me. I'm a senior associate in a large, prominent architectural firm. I'm well-known and respected by clients, peers, officials. My projects have won awards. Even the critics are kind to me.*

But still. She wasn't done yet. She wanted to be her own boss. She wanted to be in charge. She wanted to call the shots, and she was willing and able to both deal with the flack and take the bows, given the opportunity. That was the problem.

She wanted the Arts Centre.

That would lift her to the top. And then, if Krystof didn't want a partner, she'd find someone who did. There would be offers. Or if she had the money, she'd open her own firm. Maybe that would be best anyway. Krystof was starting to grate on her. What had always seemed an unquestioned authority lately felt more like arrogance. Was it her imagination or had he been colder than usual? Maybe it was just the constant contrast with Bruce, with whom she'd been spending so much time, with his joking, flirtatious, playful manner, and explicit physicality.

Design development had begun in earnest on the Arts Centre project, despite the fact that Krystof had delayed a formal announcement of team leader. What was he waiting for? She and Peter and Nathan had been working together in the meantime, because the work had to go on. No one had questioned her authority when she'd divided up and assigned the tasks. Not even Nathan had grumbled, just sat contentedly at his desk crunching numbers, code checking, calculating floor areas and parking requirements. Something about that irked her. Why wasn't he complaining?

And Krystof seemed to be avoiding her. Maybe it was her imagination. Or perhaps it was that she'd been so extra busy with the kids. She and Krys hadn't been alone together since the afternoon of the disastrous lunch with the Roses. Alone-alone. As in intimate. She could feel her sexual frustration building day by day, despite how unsatisfactory their last encounter had been. More than usual, even.

And yet.

And yet she hesitated to set something up. Why? Was she avoiding him? It's true she didn't feel the usual pull of sexual attraction she was used to feeling around him. Was she afraid he'd say something about the Arts Centre project that she wouldn't like?

But that was nonsense. She sat up. Put her glasses squarely back on her nose. Sniffed. She needed to talk to him. She needed to get him to formally announce her role as project architect once and for all. He'd stalled too long.

Her stomach knotted. She bit her lip. Something held her back.

Bloody politics! She wished she could go directly to the clients and make her arguments, but it was Krystof's firm, and Krystof was partner-in-charge. It wasn't done. It wasn't that Krystof wouldn't lobby for her with the Roses. He wanted to give her the job. He was a charmer. A diplomat. He'd find a way. Wouldn't he?

It occurred to her how different he was from Bruce. As different as two men could be. She admired Krystof's sophisticated urbane masculinity. His cool, professional bearing. His strategic intellect. But he was hard to read. She wanted him to fight for her. But so far, he'd displayed no passion for the subject. And he likely wouldn't. Just brooding, strategizing, she supposed.

Bruce, on the other hand, was easy to read. Simple. She was critical of his childishness, but he was also so open and honest. It charmed her, how concerned he was to be taken seriously. He's so earnest, so incredibly bad at hiding his insecurities with a veneer of boyish charm. Determined to be liked and admired. Afraid to be criticized. Convinced he was fooling people. Not so simple.

And yet criticize was all she ever did. Find fault.

Feeling a wave of remorse, she determined to be nicer. Kinder. She would make an effort.

Alexa actually felt sympathy for Bruce. No matter how valuable a design resource a heritage building was, it *was* always a pain in the butt for the owner who had to deal with the hassles and pay the bills. She couldn't help liking him. Yesterday, when they had a quiet moment to talk about the house, he showed some potential. He was more sensitive than she'd given him credit for, open-minded and willing to learn. Then he'd gone and blown it by flirting shamelessly with that bimbo next door. Her fists clenched at the memory. It made her so angry she couldn't stand to look at him anymore. He'd disappointed her somehow. When they finally got in the car she picked a fight with him to let off steam, and he'd surprised her by holding his own in a totally unanticipated debate. He'd let her know he was playing with her, though his arguments seemed sincere, nevertheless making her feel like the fool she was.

What a surprise to find he held such ardent opinions. Despite his harshly spoken words in the car last night, she'd been impressed by his deep reflection, his thoughtful, articulate views. And by the passionate feelings that fuelled them. Not at all what she'd expected from Bruce. He believed he was arguing with her, but she'd agreed with everything he said. He didn't understand what she was talking about, and how their ideas fit together. Not yet. She'd find a way to help him with his house. Then he would see.

She contrasted Bruce's honesty and passion with Krys's aloof mien and his smooth control, which made it impossible to know what he was really feeling. She'd always found that polish reassuring, but for some reason now it was disconcerting. Hard trust. *I wonder what he really wants, and where his loyalties lay?*

Well, enough sitting and waiting. I'm going to find out.

She got up and strode to his door, knocking sharply.

"Enter."

She went in.

"Ah. It's you, Jenner. Close the—"

She closed the door without waiting for him to finish.

"Sasha." His smile was broad and welcoming.

She folded her arms across her chest. Maybe the difference between Krys and Bruce was that she hadn't yet seen through Krys's veneer of charm. Or hadn't wanted to. Maybe all men were basically the same, underneath the crap.

Krys leaned away, narrowing his eyes. "Or is it Jenner today?"

She sighed. "I need to talk to you, Krys."

His smile fled the room, and he sat down behind his desk without approaching her. "Sit."

She remained standing. "Everything's moving forward with the project– code, FSR, parking, program. We're going over it all now. Our earlier analysis seems to be holding true."

"Any upsets?"

"*I'm* upset."

"Still? Aren't you over the lunch meeting?" He looked away, shuffling a stack of file folders to the side of his desk.

"I'll get over it when the Roses accept me as Project Architect and it's made official in the Journal. And I get some respect from them. What have you done about it?"

He waved an elegant hand. "There's no hurry."

"Krystof! The team needs clarity. I need to know."

He covered his mouth and chin with one hand, scrubbing it in circles, tugging down. He looked up, meeting her gaze with his cool, silver eyes, his brow pulled low. He sighed.

"I am working on sweet-talking the client, Jenner. It's taking some effort. You must be patient."

She harrumphed and plopped down into the chair opposite him, feeling all the hot air, all the anger seep out of her. Her eyes burned, and she pressed her mouth together, trying to prevent its trembling. "You know how important this is to me." Her voice was soft, girlish. She tried to stop it. She didn't want to be weak, to whine, to cry, to plead. She wanted to be like him. Cool. Strong. Dominant. She sat up straighter and pulled her shoulders back, meeting his eyes. "Krys?"

He leaned back, his arms on the arms of his desk chair. His rings, one on each hand, caught her attention. Two bands, one gold family crest, with its gleaming sapphire, the other silver and simple. Two commitments: Family and Architecture. No conflict there. Life was so uncomplicated for men.

"Give me time. I can't force it on them. You will learn one day. The client is never wrong, Jenner. You should know that. Architects have enough difficulty maintaining credibility."

"But you Krys, they love you."

He pulled his eyes away, rummaging in his desk drawer for something. "You can never be too sure of yourself in this business. I'm working on it. Trust me."

She fingered her own silver pinky ring, pushing it around with her thumb. Alexa wondered if she could trust him to advocate for her. Perhaps he was more concerned for his own hide and comfort than for hers. It was time for her to reconsider her goals and plans for her own future.

CHAPTER 10

Bruce grabbed the looped handle on the back of Markus' lifejacket and hauled him up onto the deck of *Belle Etoile* like a six-pack. "Careful climbing up, Maddie. Hold the stanchion, not the lifeline." Bruce touched the vertical support to show her what he meant.

"'Kay." Maddie pulled herself up. She was all elbows and knees. Bruce wondered if she was eating enough. Although she seemed happier, she was still lacklustre and mopey about Simon's absence, especially in the wake of the video call.

"Okay, sit down and listen." He handed each of them a box of grape juice from his backpack. "Rule one. No running or jumping on the boat. Rule two. No running on the dock. Got it?"

"Yup," replied Maddie, already crushing the life out of her empty juice box, her tongue protruding through the gap where her front teeth should be.

"Markus?"

Markus's tongue poked out from between his determined lips, as he mashed unsuccessfully with his straw on the juice box.

Bruce grunted. "Hand that over." He took Markus's juice from him and shoved the straw in. "You want a banana?" He pulled them out of his bag and handed them over, opening Markus's first.

Bruce's gaze was carried upward. It was an exquisite day. The sky a clear happy blue, not a cloud in sight. The sun just warm enough, the breeze perfectly cool and sensual. He breathed in the clean, bracing sea air and absorbed the gentle cacophony of sounds and sights the marina offered. Ahh. It was too perfect a day to stay away from his boat. Bringing the kids down here was a great idea.

"So, if you two behave yourselves, maybe next weekend we can go out for a little sail. What do you say?"

"Thailing?" Maddie said, suddenly alert. "On your boat?"

Markus blinked at him. "Boat wide!"

"That's right. But today's a test. If you–"

"Brrruce!" came a shout from down the dock.

Bruce's head shot up.

"Over here, son. It's me, Jørgen." Who else? A soft chuckle followed his words on the sea breeze that drifted across the cockpit.

Bruce gazed across the intervening slips to see Jørgen standing on his bow, waving with his crooked, arthritic hand. He waved and hailed him back. "Hello, Jørgen!"

"Brrring your little guests for a visit over here."

Bruce considered. Why not? "Okay. We'll be there." He waved again.

"Rule three." He made sure both kids were paying attention. "Do exactly what I tell you. Disobey me at your peril. Got it?"

Maddie gave him the evil eye, but nodded solemnly.

Markus stared at him wide-eyed.

"Rule four. Don't disappear. Stay where I can see you. At. All. Times."

They nodded.

He stood up, hopped down to the dock, and reached up first for Maddie then Markus. "And rule five. When visiting someone's boat, be on your best manners. Otherwise the captain is at his liberty to toss you overboard. Got it?"

"That's not true." Maddie giggled and stood on the dock with her arms akimbo, blocking his way.

He gently shoved her along, and set Markus down behind her. "It is true. The captain is the boss." He was about to mention gang planks and pirates, but considering Markus's sensitivities, changed his mind.

He led the way to Jorgen's boat, three slips along, and found him standing in his cockpit wrestling with some fishing gear.

After brief introductions, Jørgen said, "Do you want to fish?"

"Fish!" said Markus with obvious enthusiasm.

Maddie gazed up at him, her eyes bright.

"Here, help me," said Jørgen, handing Bruce a small, older dinged up rod. Its line and tackle were tangled with those of another that lay on the lazarette. Jørgen disentangled the last few bits of line and lure, and picked up the second rod to hand over. "This one will do for the lad."

Bruce assessed the two old rods as he handed them over. They were on par in vintage and quality with the stuff he and his older brothers had fished with way back when. The ferrules were slightly rusted, and the cork handles chewed and chipped.

"I've got a bucket of worrrms," said Jørgen, smiling and bending low to show them an old green coffee tin full of dark brown loam. Naturally they both leaned in, fascinated by his offering.

In minutes, both hooks were baited, and Jørgen directed the children to the main dock and pointed into the dark water with a practiced eye.

"See those wee dark shapes shifting here and there. If you're verry patient, you can catch the fry, and put them in this bucket here." He bent and scooped some seawater into an old ice cream bucket and set it on the dock beside them. With a patient and experienced hand, he got both kids set up, their weighted lines dangling into the still reflective water of the marina. "Don't pull out too much line. It's not veery deep here, and you'll catch the bottom. And be quiet as can be so as not to scare the feeshes."

The kids were instantly absorbed in their task, staring expectantly at their lines disappearing into the water, whispering and pointing when they saw their potential prey swim by.

Climbing back aboard his boat with a grunt and a sigh, he disappeared into his cabin and returned with two cold bottles of beer, handing one to Bruce.

"Teell me about these two," he said, taking a swig and sitting back against the gunwale. He wore old baggy denims, brown mismatched socks and ancient dirty sneakers with dried fish scales stuck to them. His was a functional thirty-three foot Cold Water aluminum walk-around fishing boat with a jaunty white and blue cabin that Bruce had admired for some time.

Bruce eyed the twin 225 HP 4-stroke Yamaha outboard motors with their miniature sidekick, a 100 HP Honda long shaft prop, and the double down-riggers fastened to the aft transom, a setup obviously designed to get Jørgen to his honey hole quickly and facilitate slow easy trolling once he'd arrived. He had his fishing down to a science, and often shared his bounty with Bruce. The older Yamaha's covers were chipped and dented, but their fittings gleamed.

"They're my best buddy's kids. He and his wife have gone to Asia for a few weeks." He wondered how much longer it would be now.

"Asia." Jørgen nodded. "Big responsibility."

Bruce drew a great breath, sighing. "Yep. Bloody inconvenient. But Simon's my best friend. I couldn't let him down."

"Is that what's troublin' you?"

Bruce shot him a glance. "What makes you think anything's troubling me?"

Jørgen pursed his lips, peering closely at Bruce, then looked away, at the kids. "It shows. You're carrying the weight of the worrld on your shoulders. Is it the childrrren?" His accent got stronger, his w's becoming v's.

Bruce pondered the suggestion. "No. I've had discipline issues, but... I'm getting the hang of it."

"It seems you are. You know they want no more than to please you. To be part of your worrld. But you have to be in charge, so they look up to you. You're a smarrt boy. Don't let them outsmarrt you."

"You're right."

"Ya. When I was a boy in Norrway, big kids worked, and little kids followed their parents and older brodderr and sisterr around, watching them worrk, waiting their turrn."

Bruce snorted. He couldn't say he idolized his own father, but he understood the feeling. He couldn't wait to be big, like his three brothers. To have competence, skills, independence, respect. To be a man.

"When the kids are happy, they are easy. Nice to be with, really. I like kids."

Bruce nodded, detecting a melancholy note to Jorgen's voice. "Me too, actually. But they can be a challenge. They have minds of their own. Did you have kids?"

Jørgen picked up a bit of tangled fishing line and pulled at the knots with his gnarled fingers, shaking his head no. "Of course they are missing the parrents. You have to be their leader. Set a goot example, let them know you care and what you expect them to do. Don't forget they are small. They want you to be in charge, it gives them security."

Hmmn. Bruce sipped his beer, serenely watching the children on the dock, holding their rods, whispering and pointing at the little fish that were their prey. He returned his gaze to the old man.

Jørgen took a drink of his beer, astutely eyeing Bruce, patiently waiting for explanation of his troubled mood.

"I mentioned that I'm renovating my house this summer." He swivelled on the bench and pointed up at the ridge to the east. "Up there."

"Oh, ya."

Bruce ground his teeth. "The building inspector stopped work, because I didn't have my permits." His heart rate increased as he remembered the scene. "But that damned woman went and told him the house was designed by some famous architect, back in the sixties, and now it's not so simple. I can't do what I want. There are restrictions. Can't knock down walls, change things too much. I'm hamstrung. It's pissing me off." He heard his own voice rise in volume and feeling. "And furthermore, the whole thing is going to take longer. I don't even know if I can have it ready to move in by October, never mind September."

Jorgen's head shot up, a question in his pale eyes. "Ya?"

A squeal rose up from the kids, who jiggled and jumped around on the dock, Maddie jerking on her rod and madly spinning the reel.

Jørgen chuckled and slowly rose, stepped over the gunwale and strode over to them. "Gentle. Gentle," he crooned.

Bruce stood up but held back. Jørgen had the situation under control. Bruce watched as he calmly showed them how to bring in the line, gently deposit their catch in the bucket of seawater. He lifted the flashing fry up in the cup of his large palms for them to examine.

Bruce smiled. The expressions of fascination and delight on their bright, innocent faces were priceless. He pulled out his cell phone and snapped a couple of pictures to send to Simon and Kate, and set it down beside him to keep it handy.

Jørgen supervised as Maddie placed another worm from the coffee tin onto her hook, and tossed the line back in the water. She hauled on the reel, and Markus imitated her, pulling out more and more line. "Remember. Not too much line. You don't want to hook the bottom." Rejoining Bruce on his boat, he sat down slowly, giving Bruce a sharp look. "Tell me about this woman."

Bruce grimaced.

"She is who?"

Bruce let out a gust of air in disgust. "It's complicated." He summed up their situation, and how she happened to be at his house the day the inspector was there.

"Oh, ya." Jørgen pulled on lower lip, nodding. "So tell me, why don't she help you with the problem she helped to make?"

Bruce grimaced. "Oh, no. Jørgen. She's too busy, anyway. She's so... such a..." His pulse roared. He closed his eyes in exasperation. "I cannot imagine working with her."

"But you are already working with her." He gestured to the kids.

Bruce frowned. "Not by choice. Why would I want to spend even more time with the bossy, bad-tempered–"

"She is a spitfire." Jørgen smiled enigmatically. "But you like her."

"Not... really. She's not what I normally like in a woman. She might be tolerable if she was friendly, and showed me some respect. She's so condescending, I couldn't ask her advice."

"Why doesn't she respect you?"

Bruce's cheeks and neck heated. "Who said she didn't respect me?"

"You did."

"Oh. Uh." His eyes wandered over to the kids.

Markus had long ago gotten bored with holding the fishing rod, and squatted leaning over the ice cream bucket persistently poking at the one poor fry that swam its desperate laps. He'd handed his rod to Maddie, who held his and hers, determined to add to their first thrilling catch. She watched Markus over her shoulder.

Why didn't Alexa respect him? Other than the fact that he deliberately provoked her by behaving like an ass? She'd never seen him at work, for one thing. He'd met her through Simon and Kate, so he was never trying to impress... Hmm.

"You would like to win her."

His heart accelerated further. "You've got to be kidding!" He coughed. "I'm not the least bit interested in her." He lifted his feet to rest them on the opposite lazarette, crossing his ankles. All she really knew of him was that he used to be a computer geek, that he lived like a bum and totally messed up his house reno. It was the one thing she valued, besides taking care of the kids, which, admittedly he'd approached with neither enthusiasm nor skill. He scowled.

"She does not appeal to you." This was a matter-of-fact statement, and yet it somehow irked Bruce. There was something provocative in Jørgen's placid countenance. A teasing smile under the surface.

Bruce shrugged. "She's attractive, in her way. But I'm not interested in a serious relationship, and there's no way she'd go for something casual."

"So you look the other way."

"Well, I look." He grinned at Jørgen, feeling an involuntary twitch in his groin. "But I don't touch."

"You do like how she looks."

Bruce sighed, exasperated, rolling his eyes skyward. "She is sexy. And her voice boils my blood, man. But..." He waved a dismissive hand, laughing. "There's no point going there. This woman cannot be charmed."

"Hmph. Maybe she doesn't want to be."

The bench was hard. Bruce shifted his weight, twisting, then dropped his feet to the deck. He picked up his beer. It was empty. He set it down again.

"Another one, son?"

"No thanks. I've got to drive in a bit."

"I helped with the resistance during the occupation, you know. Did I tell you?"

Hell, no. He shot a pointed look at Jørgen, tilting his head.

"Back home, in Norway, during the warrr, I volunteered to carry messages into occupied territory. I was underage– sixteen, almost seventeen. But I was a small, skinny boy, and I looked even younger." He fingered his chin, a wry smile on his face. "I had no bearrd yet, just fuzzh."

Unsure why Jørgen was telling this tale, Bruce sat back, watching the kids, eager to indulge an old man's reminiscences. Anything to change the subject.

"The Krauts easily mistook me for a young farrm boy, maybe twelve or thirteen I looked. I took risks, saw horrible things, had experiences both thrilling and terrible. They gave me a medal." A blush rose to his sagging cheeks and bald pate, as though he hadn't meant to reveal that detail.

Bruce's eyebrows shot up. "No kidding?"

"No kidding. There was this girl, Hilde, in the village beyond the woods, where I often passed through. Sometimes, I stay the night at her fadder's farrm."

Oh-ho! The plot thickens. Bruce grinned to encourage Jørgen to continue.

It took a moment. Jorgen's eyes took on a faraway look, and misted over. "Ya, how in love we were."

The sounds of the children laughing and squealing faded into the background. "But... you never married her."

Jørgen moved his head a smidge. "I was young and determined to have adventure. I had to choose between marrying her and settling down right there fifty kilometres from my home, or emigrating to the new worrld. I wanted to better myself and I wanted to have adventures. I chose to leave."

"What happened to her?"

"She married my cousin Arte."

Bruce sat up, his heart pounding again. "Is she still alive?"

Jorgen's gaze flew upward. "Ya, sure. Arte's gone, but she's still there."

"You never...? I mean, maybe...?" His voice faded away in response to Jorgen's wry glance.

A moment of silence passed, as though they stood at the graveside of cousin Arte, looking but not looking across at his mourning widow, wondering, what if...what if? Wouldn't it be fun to fly the old guy over there for a visit.

"Do you regret your choice?"

"I've learned many lessons in my life, son."

Bruce waited.

"One is this. You have to take risks. To live a full and rich life, you have to risk everything. Not once, but again and again."

"And did you?"

Jørgen nodded. "Ya and ya. I came to Canada. I worked in construction. I was a commercial fisherman. I flew planes–"

"Eeeeeee! Help!"

Bruce's heart slammed into his ribs. Both he and Jørgen jumped up at the sudden and desperate scream from Maddie. He lurched forward, leaping off the boat onto the slip. Both kids were still there, thank God. Maddie wrestled with both rods, jerking them up and down wildly. As Bruce approached, she dropped one of them and hung onto the other with both fists, yanking up with all her might, reeling in the line as fast as she could.

"Fish! I gotta fish! A big one!" she screamed, jumping up and down. "Help me!"

Markus screamed alongside, caught up in her hysteria.

Adrenalin surged through Bruce's veins. Everything was in motion. He attempted to hang onto anything and everything that moved. Keep them safe.

Markus clutched the rod along with Maddie, trying to help, tugging. The rod jerked back and forth, up and down. The hook remained stubbornly embedded in the bottom of the marina seabed.

"Calm down!" Bruce shouted. "It's not a fish. You're just–"

The rod Maddie'd dropped slid off the dock into the water. Its reel hung up on the edge for a second. Then it broke free and bounced into the water. He lunged forward. He had to catch Jorgen's rod before it sank.

"Arghhh!" He dived forward, reaching out with a wild fist, missing by inches. The rod sank below the surface of the water. It's line tangled with the one Maddie and Markus still grasped. Surely it would pull them in too. He squatted and leaned out further to grab the tangled line. Maddie's wild swinging of the rod knocked Markus off balance. He teetered on the edge, flailing his arms, screeching.

Bruce spun on his heel, lunging at Markus's lifejacket, but missed that too. His own balance hopelessly lost, he tumbled over backwards into the water, feet and hands flying.

Splash!

"Urgh!" Bruce grunted.

"Eeeeaah!" Maddie screamed again.

The last thing Bruce heard as he sank were great whoops of laughter from Jørgen.

Bruce spread the roll of original building permit drawings out on his cracked patio, where the morning light was sufficient to make out the faint lines on the old blueprints. He'd gone by City Hall and requested a set, knowing that he could not avoid the problem any longer. Somehow, he had to figure out how to satisfy the City's requirements and get on with his house project.

His cell phone beeped. It was a text message from Simon. He read the message and smiled. The photos of the kids fishing were a big hit. It was a good thing he'd left his phone on Jorgen's boat when he jumped off to rescue them, or those photos would have been lost when he fell in.

Knew you'd find your groove, buddy. I especially love the pic of U all wet. LOL. Thanks for being such a great uncle. How goes it with AJ?

Bruce grunted. How indeed? He texted back. *Excellent!*

I sensed some tension the other night. No conflict?

It was hard to hide anything from the sensitive Simon. *Nah. Just tired after a long day. No worries, man.*

He tried to force his attention back to the drawings, but his eyes wanted to cross from staring at them so long. He could read floor plans well enough, but what the hell was he supposed to do with them? He stared at those tiny bedrooms and dens clustered on both sides with no storage to speak of, stared at the layout of the old, now gutted kitchen, wondering how to make a functional modern home out of it all. And though he'd picked up a copy of the inch-thick municipal bylaw governing heritage buildings, he hadn't the heart to read it, and so he still didn't know what he could and could not do. The burden of home ownership sat like an anvil on his chest.

No matter how hard he tried, he couldn't seem to disentangle the problem of his house from the problem of his relationship–if one wanted to call it that–with Alexa. She may have inadvertently been the cause of his dilemma, but she was also, potentially, the solution.

Though he tried to ignore it, he was staring a gift horse in the mouth, and if her teeth were sharp, they were also made of gold. He had an architect at his disposal. If he could convince her to help. Though she said she was too busy, he figured the real obstacle was their relationship. Which was… confusing at best.

That and perhaps his pride.

Bruce ground his teeth together, not for the first time today. In fact he had a dull pounding headache from the gnawing frustration. He scrubbed his face with his hands, yanked on his hair, and groaned. How could his plans for the summer go so terribly awry?

His mind kept coming back to his conversation with Jørgen the previous day.

What was Jørgen trying to tell him with that story about his lost love? That he's happy he left Hilde behind in pursuit of his independent adventures? Somehow, that wasn't the impression Bruce came away with. Life is taking risks, Jørgen said. What kind of risks? What had Jørgen said? Why doesn't she respect you? Well…

Maybe he could bridge the conflict with Alexa, give her reasons to like him, and engage her help with the drawings and permits. She was interested in his house. It could be a win-win. And, they could go their own ways in a couple more weeks.

A gust of wind blew up from the bay below, ruffling the trees, and threatening to lift his roll of blueprints like a sail. He heard a voice, a high-pitched carping sound like the cry of a seagull, and turned towards Gillian's house.

"Hi there!" Even though she was apparently shouting, her voice broke and wavered on the moving air.

He waved. "Hi!" he shouted back without enthusiasm.

"Are you busy?"

He made a face that she surely couldn't see at that distance. Well, duh. I guess so sweetheart. He shook his head. "Looking at my plans."

"Oh, that's nice. I wonder if you could help me. I have a little problem."

Again! He wondered what she did before he bought the house next door. "I'll be right over."

When he arrived at her door ten minutes later, she explained that she was cleaning the blinds, and although she had managed to take them down and wash them, she was utterly frustrated in her attempts to re-hang them.

"The hooks are so fussy, and when I climb the ladder, I swear my arms will fall off, and I'll fall down, or I don't know what."

"Where are the kids?"

She smiled, and he would have to say, yes, she actually batted her eyelashes at him. "Matt's at school, and DeeDee's at a friend's, up the street."

Resigned, he climbed the ladder and allowed her to pass up the blinds. Then he examined the fasteners and figured out what he had to do. *Why do we always climb the ladder first, he wondered, and then figure out how the damned thing works?*

"I sure do appreciate your help, Bruce. I don't know what I would've done on my own." She leaned against the ladder support, pressing her amazing breasts oh-so-near his shin.

"No problem," he grunted, struggling with the stubborn blinds. "My pleasure."

"Have you had lunch?"

He frowned. "It's only ten-thirty."

She made a discontented squeaking noise. "Well, then you can stay for lunch."

"No. Actually, I can't. I have work to do, and I have to pick up Markus at one."

"Well, couldn't you–"

"No. Thanks, anyway Gillian. I can't."

She sniffed.

He paused and looked down over his shoulder. Her face was pinched, and she was blinking rapidly.

Give me a break. She wasn't going to cry? "Gillian?"

She looked up at him through her lashes.

"What is it, sweetheart?"

She shrugged and sniffed again, and he sighed, wishing he could be anywhere else, while he finished the row of blinds, then stepped down to the floor. He inclined his head and peered at her with his brows raised. "Speak."

She crumpled. "I'm sorry, Bruce." She cast her damp eyes up at him, her expression imploring and pathetic. "Don't you like me?"

He wasn't an idiot. He knew he was being played.

He raised his hands, palm up, as if to say: What do you want me to do? It was all the invitation she needed to collapse against his chest, pressing her face against him, sliding her arms around his waste like insidious tentacles. Her full round breasts pressed up against him, soft and inviting. He felt an involuntary stirring in his groin, but kept his hands up and away from her curving derriere. He closed his eyes. Shit. While it was flattering to have a women throwing herself at him, this was too easy. "Gillian. You're overreacting, sweetheart. Just because I can't have lunch with you, doesn't mean–"

She pulled away, turning her back to him, brushing her thigh against his groin. "Oh. I know. It's okay. You're right. It's only that I wanted to do something to repay the favour." She peeked over her shoulder. "Dinner?"

He took a step back, his hands still raised in self-defence. "It'll have to wait. I have a lot–"

"It's okay, Bruce," she snapped, folding her arms across those luscious breasts, pushing them up and together.

He flinched. God he hated being manipulated. He flashed a cool grin.

None too soon, he finished hanging Gillian's blinds and made his escape. Back at his house, again staring sightlessly at his drawings, he wondered what had just happened. That wasn't like him. Used to be, not so long ago, he would have gone for that.

In contrast, Bruce was surprised at how much he preferred Alexa's sparkling intellect, her fiery passion for her vocation, even her harsh criticism over Gillian's manipulative wiles. Strangely, and contrary to his expectations, Alexa was by far the better caregiver to the children. And not just responsible and efficient but nurturing and gentle. It would be in his better interest to hook up with Gillian, or someone like her. She wouldn't be going anywhere. That was the safe choice. So why did Alexa intrigue him more? Getting attached to someone who had made no bones about giving her career priority was asking for trouble. That was just plain foolish. He'd end up all alone and worse off than before.

It was enough to drive a man completely around the bend. Women! A friendly loyal dog would be so much simpler.

The image of Gillian's breasts stubbornly flashed in his mind's eye, her soft femininity, combined with her charm and artifice. But despite the more obvious sexuality of Gillian, Alexa still drew him in a mysteriously sensual way.

Again he recalled the quiet moment he'd shared with Alexa when she was first at his house. She'd tried so hard to get him to understand the value of this place.

He stood up, tucking the roll of drawings under his arm, and strolled from room to room through the house. She really appreciated its unique design qualities, the relationship of these little rooms he loved to hate, and the wide blue vista beyond the walls of windows. As he gazed beyond overhanging roofs, out to the horizon, a hush penetrated to his soul.

She'd drawn his attention to the natural world outside his window, to the admittedly very unique, almost spiritual setting of his house. He knew he loved the view from the house, through the forest at the sea, the boats huddled in the marina below, the islands in the distance, the low afternoon sun sinking toward the horizon. But he'd never looked at his *house* that way, as a part of a conversation. Or as a kind of intermediary between himself and that beautiful world out there. It reminded him of why he loved sailing, why he loved living on his boat, why he loved Vancouver. Being outdoors, being out in nature, in this most beautiful of places, made him feel centred, strong, at peace.

That was why he couldn't move to San Francisco with his friends, charming as that city was. He loved his home. This place was like no other. The view from this ridge had spoken to him when he'd first seen it, as it did today, despite the grey, unsettled weather, the gusting wind, threatening a sullen summer storm.

And in that moment, he knew Alexa understood that about him, and he understood something about her. He'd looked at her looking at him and marvelled at her eyes, soft as the mist in the trees. He was drawn to them like he was drawn to the view out his windows.

She'd smiled at him, wide and joyful and uninhibited, and for the first time he'd noticed her full lips, the top one upturned and contoured, the bottom one full and pouting like a pillow, the little moist gap at the corners where they almost met. The gleam of her even white teeth pressing into the soft flesh of her bottom lip. Had she ever smiled at him before?

It had undone him. He'd almost, almost leaned in and kissed those lips, that smile. He just about couldn't stop himself. The sudden shift had thrown him off balance, and he'd been disoriented around her ever since. Jørgen was right about one thing. He would make an effort to remove whatever irritants he could from their encounters. He would give her reasons to like and respect him. And he would beg for her help with those damned building permit drawings if he had to. Simon and Kate would be pleased that their best friends could be friends, at last. But letting himself fall for Alexa? Not a chance.

∽

Alexa looked up from her computer screen when she felt someone surge up beside her. Two sharp lines sliced Stephanie's brows. She was breathing heavily through flared nostrils, and her mouth was outlined in white. Stress? Aggravation? Anger?

Exactly what she needed. A distraction from her own heaping workload. Alexa pushed her glasses onto her head. "What is it?" Hopefully she hadn't misjudged in giving Stephanie more responsibility with the Squamish school project. "What's wrong?"

Stephanie leaned forward slightly and thrust a sheaf of papers at Alexa. "This."

She glanced down, trying to make out what it was.

"This is the Arts Centre code analysis. What are you doing with it?"

"How can you ask that?" Stephanie pulled back. "You assigned it to me. Nathan said–"

"Why would I..." Alexa let her words trail off. Huh. "Let me see that." She took the pile from Stephanie and perused it more carefully. It was Nathan's marked-up copy, with a CD clipped to it, and a sticky note asking Stephanie to make the noted changes on the file copy. "Ah. I see." This was how he was doing it.

"Well?" Stephanie's desire to speak her mind seemed to war with protocol and respect for Alexa. "What... how...?"

Alexa filled her lungs and sighed deeply. "Leave it with me. Don't worry about it. And if Nathan brings you any more work, bring it to me before doing anything. Okay?"

The expression on Steph's face morphed from anxiety to perplexity. "Are you saying... Don't you want me to do it?"

Alexa smiled and lifted her brows. "Do you want to do it?"

"I...I...No! I've got more than enough on my hands with the school. The elders want–"

Alexa stood up. "Fine. Go back to the project I gave you." She squeezed Stephanie's arm. Stephanie shook her head and stalked away.

Alexa drifted silently up behind Nathan's workstation. He was leaning back from his computer screen, scowling at the drawing displayed there, chewing on the end of his pen. Was it just a pose? Did he actually do any work himself? Entitled little prick. "Hey Mini-me." She tossed the heavy document down on his layout table with an intentionally loud *thwap*.

He jumped, flipping his pen into the air and jerking upright as he swivelled toward her in his office chair. "What the–!"

She stood with her arms folded and slowly cast her gaze at the offending document. His gaze soon followed hers, and before he schooled his expression, his brows went up, his lips thinned.

"Do your own work and leave Stephanie to do hers. Please."

He glared at her. "What's the big deal? I delegated–"

"I know you're a senior architect, Nathan. That's why I know you were at the senior associate's meeting where staff allocations were decided. And that's why I know you know better than to mess with people's workloads without consulting the other job captains." She gave him a tight smile and walked away. There was little point in harassing him further. He'd been caught out. But what other tricks did he have up his sleeve? She'd been foolish trusting that he wouldn't use subversive methods to create havoc for her on this project. He'd been too quiet. Too agreeable. Perhaps she ought to find out if he'd pawned off work on any of the other juniors.

Alexa picked up her empty coffee cup and strolled the aisles of the studio, quietly greeting several of the younger architects and interns as she passed by, surreptitiously glancing at their computer screens to see what they were up to, asking if they had questions or problems.

She didn't notice anything to do with the Arts Centre project or any of Nathan's other projects. Offloading work and shifting personnel around was strictly forbidden without consultation with project architects. Nathan knew this. Therefore, he was obviously trying to annoy her, or just freeing up his own time. Probably so he could go to the gym or take longer lunches. Not that work actually ever got in the way of those things.

She filled her coffee cup in the kitchen.

It only took one jerk to mess up the culture of a workplace. If she were in charge, someone like Nathan would never have been hired, despite his credentials and connections. Character was more important. She remembered her days back in architecture school. It was a very egalitarian environment. Half of the students were women, even though the majority of the instructors were still men, a carry over from an earlier age. There was this one transfer student from Toronto, what was his name? Kirk or Kent or something? As far as he was concerned, there was no place in the profession for women, and it was his duty to single her out for harassment and humiliation. Presumably because she was smarter than him by half, and a much better student. But being a swaggering, macho guy, he got away with it, prompting sniggers and sly glances between the other guys, as though they hadn't been her friends and colleagues. The old boys club at work, then as now. Damn this profession to hell.

If only she could have picked a field more welcoming to women. But no. Some things can't be helped. This was where her passion lay. This was her chosen battleground. She sighed.

Returning to her workstation, she removed her glasses, sipped her burnt late afternoon coffee and gazed out the window. She shivered and rubbed at her bare arms. The air conditioning was working overtime again. It was a beautiful sunny summer day, and she was cooped up here with artificially arctic air and misogynistic assholes. Another deep sigh overtook her. It was happening too often. Work was getting to her today. Somehow the trouble with the Arts Centre amplified all the little things that drove her crazy about her job, and made her realize how generally frustrating and unfulfilling her work had become lately. She still had to struggle every day to prove herself.

Alexa checked her email for critical messages. Peter with a quick question on the project, Jim St. Giles from the City, and a cryptic message from Krys– *The meeting you wanted on the Arts Centre may have to happen Friday evening. My schedule is very full until then. Can you work late?* Right. She knew that meant he wanted to have dinner with her. She caught herself as she was about to exhale loudly again. Longing for the day to be over, she sent brief replies, including a tentative yes to Krystof, and scanned through the remainder of mostly mundane or junk messages from product reps.

An unfamiliar name jumped out of the mix: *Koczynski*. Koczynski? Was that...? Is that how Bruce spelled his last name? She clicked, wondering why he would be sending her an email at work.

A photo popped up on her screen. Bright sun, colour, splashing water droplets and laughing faces. Maddie and Markus in swimsuits with wet hair plastered over their smooth brows. She scrolled down. There were more photos of the kids frolicking amongst sprays of water, other children visible in the background. Her heart swelled in her chest and she laughed. Mister fun and games was at it again. They were obviously having the time of their lives. One more photo at the bottom included Markus and... Bruce. He wore only plaid surf shorts hugging lean hips, and he was... wet.

She removed her glasses and leaned forward, squinting. Her eyes skipped from his strong chest with its dusting of dark hairs and nipples taught from the cold shower, to his amazing cut abs glistening with water. Wow, he really was buff. She forced herself to look up, away from his body. To his dark hair draped in wet ringlets, sun glinting off of beads of water on his broad tanned shoulders, his face alight with a huge grin, his dark chocolate eyes sparkling with fun. Oh, man. Her bones liquefied.

Markus was pummelling Bruce with a fireman's hose, and enjoying every minute of it. The photo was oddly cropped, with the subjects in one half of the frame, the other half showing the chopped off limbs of several children. Apparently the photographer was Maddie, or someone equally unskilled.

Alexa scrolled up and scanned the other photos again, returning to the last one, her eyes involuntarily raking up and down Bruce's toned, masculine torso and limbs. Her eye, like iron pins to a magnet, traced the fine line of dark hair that disappeared below his navel into the waistband of his shorts. Her pulse quickened, and a tingle crawled up her arms and neck and over her scalp. It was impossible to take her eyes off of him. This was a very different man than the one who carried a few extra pounds at Simon and Kate's annual dinner last Christmas. She'd never imagined he could be so... so appealing. So sexy. She sat back, chewing on the arm of her glasses. Then she noticed a brief text message at the bottom and swallowed.

Missed you this afternoon at the water park. What time will you be home for dinner? BK

Oh, yeah?

"Ummmmm," came a nasal voice from over her shoulder. "He's yummy. No wonder your jaw's hanging open."

Alexa jerked, dropped her glasses and jolted back in her chair at the sound, her heart pounding. "Oh my God!" She turned. "Oh, it's you, Pete. Christ, you scared me!" Her pulse skittered down to near normal.

Stephanie sidled up beside him and peered at her screen. "Is that the same guy who I met? Your co-whatever?"

Alexa laughed and glanced at Stephanie. "Yes. It's Bruce."

"Your co-what?" Peter asked, his voice rising with curiosity.

"I can see why you weren't paying attention to your environment." Stephanie smiled suggestively. "Hey. I didn't realize. Are you and he... um, you know. An item?"

"Oooh! Tell me, tell me," purred Peter.

Alexa opened her eyes wide in shock, and replaced her glasses firmly on her nose. "What? God, no. What gave you that idea?"

Stephanie's eyes swung back to the photo on Alexa's screen, and she waggled her brows up and down. "That's a pretty tempting invitation."

Peter leaned in to read the text, or perhaps to ogle Bruce's abs.

Alexa twitched and clicked the close button on the message. "I guess he's cooking dinner. Or maybe he wants me to get there to feed the kids. That would be more like him." She tried to scowl, but it was difficult to keep the laughter from bubbling up at her friends' lascivious curiosity.

"So when are you leaving the office?"

She pressed her lips together to suppress a smile. "Um. Shortly?"

Steph nodded. "My questions can wait 'til tomorrow." She grinned and sauntered off. "Have a nice dinner."

"You go girl." Peter laughed and strolled away.

Alexa re-opened the message, trying not to stare again at the, um, yes, inviting photo, and focused on the message itself. When will I be home for dinner? She hit reply –*You're cooking? Half an hour*– and send.

Then she shut down her computer, grabbed her purse and left.

∽

Twenty-five minutes later Alexa pulled into the driveway and entered the house. It was eerily quiet, and she wondered if she'd misunderstood.

"Honey, I'm home!" she hollered as she set down her bag, glancing into the empty living room as she strolled down the hall toward the kitchen. "Hello?" The house was rather tidy. And she didn't smell or hear any signs of dinner. Hmm.

"Hey. You're here already!"

She staggered back at Bruce's sudden strode through the patio door leading to the backyard. He held a pair of long-handled barbecue tongs in one hand, and a plate in the other. He had a pronounced five o'clock shadow, and his white smile was warm and welcoming. A real live version of the hunk in the photo.

"Dinner will be ready in a few minutes. Come on outside, kick off your shoes." Bruce was wearing knee length cargo shorts and a tank top with a Vancouver White Caps logo on the front. He had changed, was dry, but huge expanses of his sun-kissed golden skin were still exposed, and she found it difficult not to stare. He's still a jerk, she reminded herself sternly. A very sexy jerk. She sighed.

She swallowed. "Uh. Sure."

He set the tongs and plate in the sink and swung around to open the fridge, emerging with a pitcher of... sangria? He caught her eye and raised his brows in question.

"Yes. Thanks." She slipped out the open glass door to find the kids on the rear patio, Maddie wearing a too-long apron, supervising some wieners or sausages on the grill, and Markus sitting at the small table munching on an assortment of finger food. "Hi kids."

They turned toward her voice, smiling. "Auntie Al!"

Alexa's face heated as a wave of emotion washed over her in

response to their enthusiastic greeting. The whole scene made her nostalgic for the companionship, warmth and sense of belonging that being part of large family had always provided, despite all the hard work and sometimes desperation. Her life had been all about her work and herself for many years now. At least until one of her siblings called with a problem to solve.

Bruce reappeared and handed her a tall, frosted glass of sangria, the ice cubes clinking, and returned to grill duty. She took a sip, hiding her sudden embarrassment behind the glass. When had she last been greeted so warmly, and had her needs cared for? It had been a long time since she'd been welcomed home to a houseful of smiling, loving children, and seldom that she'd returned to a meal that someone else had prepared. This reminded her of the years at home, with her younger sisters and brothers all around her, and she and her mom making the evening meal. She'd long ago left all that behind. It was disorienting.

She took refuge in a lawn chair, reluctantly tore her eyes away from Bruce, standing at the grill like a freaking male model for a yard and garden issue of GQ, instead letting her gaze rest on the children, who appeared to be clean and well-cared-for as well as happy in Bruce's care.

"You guys had fun today, hey? Tell me about the water park."

"It was thoooo fun, Auntie Al," offered Madison.

"Fub!" agreed Markus, stuffing another piece of cheese into his already full mouth, cracker crumbs spraying everywhere.

"We thure wish you were there with us," said Maddie. "It was so much fun."

Alexa nodded. "Me too. It would have been better than the day I had by a long mile."

At her words, Bruce glanced up, his brows drawn together in concern. "Trouble at the office?"

She sighed. "The usual. I just don't get no respect," she tried to laugh it off, but her smile felt forced.

"That's a shame. Maybe I can cheer you up later. Let's get the kids fed, and then I want to talk to you." His smile was warm and inviting, and she had to reign in her imagination. Surely he didn't mean anything… romantic by that. Did he?

Oh? "Okay." What on earth would Bruce want to talk to her about? He usually skipped out the second she got home from work to relieve him of child care. This, today, was a huge change. She narrowed her eyes, studying him. What was he up to?

Soon they were all seated around the patio dining table eating sausages and deliciously marinated steaks, baked potatoes and Caesar salad like one big happy family. The irony was not lost on Alexa, who stayed quiet, soaking up their happy exhaustion, and their lazy camaraderie. A thread of melancholy wove through the tapestry of cheerful sensations. Her normal existence didn't include this kind of warmth, and she missed it.

"Something wrong?" Bruce asked, his eyes warm on her face.

She shook her head, trying to smile. "No. Just tired."

Dinner was excellent, and she appreciated it doubly after her trying day. She gestured at the salad with her fork, and met Bruce's eye. "You made this?"

Bruce lifted his eyebrows, grinning, about to reply.

"It came from a box," Maddie said, and then she jerked. "Hey!"

Bruce had obviously kicked her under the table. He made a funny, conspiratorial face and said, "That was supposed to be a secret. Thanks a bunch, Scallywag."

"Oh, thorry." She giggled. "I forgot."

Alexa recalled the delicious meal he'd magically pulled out the other night. "You've been getting meals prepared by... someone?"

Bruce put on an innocent face, his dark eyes twinkling. "I have my ways."

She threw back her head and laughed. "Well. I like your ways very much. I appreciate it, even if it's unconventional." It was pretty smart, actually. He had the money to burn, and they certainly didn't have any time to spare.

After sliced watermelon for dessert, Alexa helped stack the dishes in the dishwasher and herded the kids upstairs to get ready for bed. They didn't need baths after their afternoon in the water, only a face scrubbing and tooth brushing. There was barely time for those ablutions before their eyes drooped, they were so exhausted from their day.

Bruce appeared in the doorway of Markus's room. "Everything alright?"

"Yeah. They're really worn out."

"Boos." Markus lifted his arms towards Bruce, and they flopped down again onto his sheets. Bruce strode into the room, bent over Markus and gave him a kiss and a nuzzle. "'Night, buddy. Sleep tight."

They walked together to Maddie's room, to find her already in bed, a story book open on her chest, her eyes shut. Alexa bent to kiss her forehead, and she stirred. Looking up, she saw Bruce bending over her as well.

"I wanted a story, Auntie Al." She could hardly keep her eyes open.

"Next time, sweetie. Not tonight."

"G'night, Uncle Bruce. Thanks f'the water park." Her voice sounded drugged.

"Goodnight, Scallywag." He kissed her cheek, and she wrapped her skinny arms around his neck briefly before they slid down again, limp. She was almost instantly asleep. Bruce smiled and Alexa quietly left the room with Bruce on her heels, his gentle hand at the base of her spine.

In the hallway, she whispered. "Want some help with the dishes?"

She saw his dark curls shake slightly. "Thanks. All done."

"What?" He sure was efficient tonight. "What's gotten into you?"

He chuckled softly as they reached the bottom of the stairs. "You could show me how to drug that cat, tho."

"Sure." She led the way to the kitchen and got the gear from the vet out of the fridge, then explained how to load the syringe.

"How much?" he asked.

"Five micrograms. Kate just had her blood sugar measured before they left." She showed him how to rub and lift the skin and inject the needle.

"You're really good at that," he said. "I wouldn't mind if you had to be my nurse. Would you like another glass of sangria on the patio? Or maybe in the living room?"

"Thanks. Even though it's a lovely evening, I need to kick back on the sofa. I'm exhausted, too."

"Go relax, I'll be right there." He strode to the fridge.

Alexa took a seat on the sofa next to a sleeping Oscar, a guest in her own house. Well, technically not her house, but it had begun to feel like her home over the past weeks. But tonight, Bruce had taken charge, and taken care of everything, including her. It felt really good to be taken care of. It was hard not to be impressed with his effort, and his success with the kids. Lucy jumped up, and Alexa settled her onto her lap, gently stroking and rubbing the back of her neck, where she knew she'd be sore.

She sat back and removed her glasses, rubbing her eyes, and sighed, a different kind of sigh than the ones that had chased her all day. One of contentment and ease, and a delicious kind of anticipation.

Bruce returned with two glasses, and a roll of drawings under one arm. She tensed and her face drew taut in a smile. Aha. So he had an ulterior motive, after all.

CHAPTER 11

"What are you smiling at?" Bruce asked as he sat down between Oscar and Alexa, setting a glass of sangria in front of her and leaned back, nestled against her. He watched as her gaze slide down his body and back up with a sigh. He smiled and flicked a brow suggestively to let her know he's caught her ogling him. She tensed, pressing her lips together, and steadied Lucy with one hand as she leaned forward to reach for her drink. He marvelled at the talent she had for soothing all the creatures around her.

"I've been puzzling all evening over what could possibly motivate this transformation." She gestured with one hand in a sweeping motion. "Engaging e-mails, dinner, drinks, dishes, happy kids and cats. You must want something."

He offered her a coy grin, and then sobered. "Can't I want to make peace? I'm tired of fighting." He gazed into her skeptical eyes, trying to convey his sincerity. She shot a sideways glance at the drawings he'd carried in.

Their eyes met, and once again he was floored by the intensity of focused energy and intelligence in her smoky green eyes. The familiar spark of attraction flared whenever they were together, and his blood stirred in his veins. He canted toward her, then stopped himself. A kiss would be premature to say the least. It was a safe bet that that overture would not be well received. Not yet, anyway. He forced himself to grin and look away, picking up his own glass, sipping.

He cleared his throat, laughed a little under his breath, and gestured to the roll of floor plans laying on the coffee table. Then he turned to her again and grinned. "Uncle?"

She shook her head with a tsk. "Is that your way of saying 'please Alexa will you help me with my renovation permit drawings and get me out of this huge muddle I got myself into so I can finish the project and move in before winter'?"

He expelled a gust of laughter, and threw his head back. There was no beating around the bush with this woman. He could always count on her to speak her mind, and waste no time about it either. It was oddly refreshing after Gillian's coquettish behaviour.

"That's exactly what I'm saying. I'm sorry I blamed you for my problems with City Hall. I was unprepared, and an arrogant idiot." He stretched his arm across the back of the sofa, and reached toward her, tucking a wild strand of hair behind her ear with one finger. His eyes kept wandering to her mouth. It was becoming an obsession. He met her gaze directly and said, his voice reflecting his mounting desire. "Yes. Please, Alexa, will you help me?"

She gazed at him for some long moments, he wasn't sure how long, because her focused attention was unnerving. Without her glasses, she was lovely and vulnerable. Again he noticed her smooth olive skin, her slightly broad nose and full, sensual lips. That little gap at the corner that glistened with moisture. His pulse quickened, and his breath rattled with a suddenly rising desire to touch her again.

"Alright, Koz," she said on an exhale, replacing her glasses like a shield. "Let's have a look."

He pushed some books aside and unraveled the coiled drawings on the coffee table, weighing down the corners. They both leaned forward to peer at them, their thighs pressing together, generating a sizzling heat that he tried his best to ignore.

Suddenly her phone beeped, and she turned to pick it up. "Sorry. Just a sec. I've got to deal with this." She dialled and lifted the phone to her ear while he sat and watched her. "Hi Owen." She turned to Bruce and mouthed the words *my brother*. "When do you have to let them know?" She listened a moment. "Did you ask Mom? Un-huh."

He watched as she absently smoothed her fine, long-fingered hand across the blueprint. Her hands were small, but elegantly formed, with short, neatly trimmed, unvarnished nails. They looked competent. The way one imagined an architect's hands should be.

"Well maybe Dylan or Megan could look at it with you... What? Why didn't he tell me? ...I know, honey, but..." She nodded. Then she laughed, closing her eyes, and Bruce decided his new life goal was to make her laugh. "Okay! I'll look. Email me the short list of courses. And the list of baby names. Honestly it doesn't matter what I... okay, okay. I know they do. It's okay. I'll find time. I love you, too. Bye." She hung up and set her phone down, then turned her attention back to Bruce.

He raised his brows in query.

She sighed. "They still defer to me in so many things. University courses."

"Baby names?" he said.

She nodded. "My second brother Dylan and his wife are expecting. Apparently I have to weigh in."

"How many are there?"

"Six." She counted them off on her fingers. "Rhys, Dylan, Megan, Bronwen, Jack, and Owen, the youngest. That was him. He's twenty-two."

He gazed at her, stroking his lips with the tips of his fingertips. His eyes danced over the contours of her face, becoming so familiar to him. Somehow he'd never seen this tender, nurturing side of her, or any side of her except the judgmental scold that looked at him with disdain, that failed to respond to his attempts to charm or humour her. Kate had been right when he said they'd got off on the wrong foot years ago. It had somehow prevented them from getting to know each other at all.

A blush rose to her cheeks and she dropped her gaze to the coffee table for a long moment. He could see her attention shift as her eyes rested on the blueprints. She stared with fascination at the drawings. "Oh. My. God. These are drawn by him." She breathed, *sotto voce*. "What am I saying? Of course they're hand drawn. Look at the date. 1961. But he did them himself. See. There are his initials. Look at the lines. They're a work of art." She looked up, her eyes flashing dark behind her glasses with a passion for something he couldn't appreciate, and yet it was contagious. "You should have these framed."

"Well, I might, when this is all over."

They shared an intimate smile, and both turned their attention back to the drawings. He sat quietly while she perused them, flipping through the pages forward and back, back and forward, tracing one long, purposeful finger across the drawings, as though she were walking through his house in her mind. And she was, he supposed, able to imagine the space in three dimensions from these two dimensional representations in a way that he could not. Although it was not unlike reading computer code, another language that became so familiar that one could picture a real kind of space, though in his own case it was a digital place that he moved through in his mind's eye. They were not so very dissimilar, he and Alexa, really. The ways their minds worked, the focused attention, discerning patterns and relationships, the creative problem solving. She nodded and mumbled to herself. He leaned back, watching her, imagining what was going on in her brain, waiting for whatever came next.

At last she pulled her eyes away from the drawings, sat back, pulled up one knee and turned her attention to him. Shoving her glasses into her hair, her gaze drilled into him, puzzling. He felt suddenly exposed. Vulnerable.

"What?"

"Okay. Tell me what you want? What are your needs?"

"Uh. Um. Well, according to Mr. Glenn, I need–"

She waved an impatient hand. "No, no. I mean *you*. What do you want this house for? What do you want it to do?"

He opened his mouth to speak, then closed it, shrugging. "I wanted to do the work myself. As a kind of... of challenge. And I guess... I want it to be liveable?"

"But what does livable mean to you? *How* do you want to live? Who are you, really?"

Bruce's heart did a drumroll in his ribcage. What was she asking? She was intense and demanding, and her driving questions felt vaguely like he was being interrogated.

"Let's cut through the crap, Koczynski. I'm not going to beat around the bush trying to drag information out of you. Despite our bickering, we know each other pretty well. Is this house just an investment for you, or is it going to be a home?"

He drew a breath. What a question! "Well. Initially I meant it as an investment, but..."

She nodded knowingly. "That's what I thought. You're tired of drifting. Tired of being a too-big kid with no roots, no stability in your life."

Christ almighty! Was this a normal interview between an architect and her client? Couldn't be, and yet, perhaps, like she said, she was simply dispensing with the diplomatic dance.

"I... I... guess so."

"So you'll be staying awhile. What are your plans for the immediate future? Will you work from home?"

His brow furrowed. She was miles ahead of him. He'd only recently entertained the notion that he might design software on his own. He had time to do that. "Maybe. Possibly."

Alexa tossed her glasses down onto the drawings and peered at him intently. "What about family? Are you planning to get married and have kids?" She laughed. "Never mind. You don't know the answer to that, do you?"

Bruce's ears and neck flushed with heat. He dropped his eyes and shrugged, glancing at the drawings without seeing them. Why didn't she ask him about his dating life? Whether he'd be throwing wild parties for dozens of beautiful women, or watching hockey and playing poker with the guys night after night? Why was she zeroing in on family, for Christ's sake? "I don't want to rule it out, but I mean, it doesn't seem likely at my age, or... or..." He gazed out the dark front window, at the middle distance. "But, at the same time, I'm not looking for some impractical bachelor's pad. I want a home that feels..." He hesitated. *What?* "Homey?"

She nodded, waiting, her knowing eyes burrowing into his.

He couldn't push away the sense of mortification. He tried to sound mature and detached. He tried and failed. "Even if... and I suppose, like I said, it's unlikely that I will... I still want my home to feel welcoming to others who... like my brothers, for example, or my buddies from San Francisco when they come to visit, or Simon and Kate."

"Warmth," she said with conviction, her voice dropping in volume and pitch, stirring a powerful warmth within him.

"Yes." He tried to shutter the part of his mind that was playing erotic pictures of him with Alexa.

"Accommodation."

"Yes, that too." He knew exactly in what sense she'd meant that word.

"You need a place to put down roots, a place you can feel you belong, a refuge, a place to work, to play, to relax, to be creative and to dream."

Her voice was sultry now, a siren's song of hoarse, shifting sand. A coil of heated excitement twisted in his gut, sending rays of energy down his limbs, making his fingers and toes tingle with anticipation and fear. How could she know him so well, when he hadn't yet figured out himself what he wanted? "How do you know…?"

She shrugged, and the corners of her mouth pulled in slightly with a wet click. A secret, intimate smile. "Isn't that what we all want?"

He glanced around the living room, gesturing with one hand. "Yeah. But, I mean, I don't want flowers and frills and kitsch, but at the same time I want…" He stopped, unsure how to put into words the feeling he was searching for.

"A worldly sophistication? A kind of understated elegance."

He tried to imagine what she meant by that. What it might look like. He shrugged, narrowing his eyes at her. "Maybe. But nothing pretentious or showy. Can I have elegance *and* warmth?"

She nodded again, smiling again. "We'll get to that. You'll see what I mean."

"O-kay…" All he could see at the moment was him, kissing her, touching her, in his mind's eye. His gaze swept over her, coming to rest again on her luscious mouth with a sigh.

She seemed flustered, and looked away, touching her forehead with her fingertips, all business. "I–I believe you picked the right house. You may think it doesn't meet your needs now, especially given the limitations of the heritage bylaws, but we can do something that will satisfy you."

"So what now? What do we have to do?"

"The heritage committee's requirements are different from the building department's. There will be one set of drawings with two very different sets of notations. One that satisfies the current building code, structural and life safety requirements and such. And another that demonstrates a sensitivity to the heritage value of the original design and the site. That doesn't mean they are incompatible. We'll find one solution that satisfies both of them, and, most importantly, you." She pressed the tip of her forefinger into his chest, then pulled it quickly away.

Bruce's eyes combed over her face, meeting her serious, intent eyes again. His chest swelled with warmth and optimism, and a tinge of excited expectancy. She was really good at this. He trusted her. His voice came out gently. "I believe you."

She smiled and replied, "Don't worry. It'll be fine."

After Alexa ran upstairs to check on the kids, and Bruce got them each a mug of steaming tea, they poured over the drawings, and Alexa made copious notes in a slim black notepad she'd pulled from her large bag. They walked, figuratively, through every room and closet of the house, imagining every possible use, identifying every imaginable obstacle to good function and aesthetically pleasing experiences. With the enthusiasm of playmates and co-conspirators, they planned hypothetical baths, meals, parties, houseguests, holidays, work projects, gardens, and lazy, relaxing days lounging on the deck with a beer and a book, admiring the view in solitude and silence.

"Look at this here," she said, pulling out a compact roll of flimsy tracing paper and laying it over the blueprints. She sketched modifications to the plan, and variations on small additions here and there, which she also expertly sketched in three dimensions, so he could visualize their effect on the form and shape of the house from the outside. "A small addition here would accommodate some extra storage, and at the same time, balance this form, and echo this roof shape here. This in no way diminishes the original harmony of the composition. In fact it enhances it."

Alexa leaned forward, her eyes dilated. She was visibly excited, vibrating with enthusiasm and passion. She pointed out the house's unique features, and explained to him why they were special and significant, and how they affected the way the space and structure were experienced by its users. He believed every word.

His hands lay on the drawing where he had pointed out certain features, and her hand brushed his lightly as it darted by, a bird in flight, pen gripped firmly and intimately, an extension of her creative mind, sending a shock up his arm. He turned to look at her, their heads bent close together as they worked shoulder to shoulder.

Bruce admired her confident hand and the strong, bold, black lines that flowed from her fountain pen as she effortlessly tossed out one idea after another. He could watch her all night. Is this what it felt like to fall in love? Did one hang on every velvet word and gesture and breath? Did you need to be so close to someone that you were almost inside their skin? He was so energized, his body felt that kind of pulsing demand. He was hard as a ship's mast, and thrumming with suppressed need, like his boat on a close haul, channeling the power of the sea.

His breath quickened, and he leaned closer to her, feeling their thighs and arms touch, aware of her heat, the scent of her skin and her hair next to him, like vanilla and exotic spice, and it made him feel weak, out of control, adrift from his body as though larger forces were sweeping through him.

He was afraid, not of his physical arousal, but by the way he was moved beyond logic by her words, her presence, her voice.

She noticed his lack of attention and glanced up, her brow hitching in question. "Are you okay?"

"Have I ever mentioned the effect your voice has on me?"

Her eyes darted, puzzled by his change of subject. "N-no."

"It makes me... " he swallowed, frowning, "...horny as hell."

She licked her lips, blinking.

He leaned forward, his eyes intent on her mouth. That wet gap.

"I see." She smiled, laughed nervously, blinked. She lifted one hand and rubbed her ear.

He pulled back, a crack of logic forming in his bubble of euphoria. What was he doing? He'd scare her away. He was scaring himself. "I guess I should... be heading home."

"Um, yeah. I have to get up early." She swallowed and stood up, turning away. "I'll need to come to the house sometime this week. To walk through, take some measurements and photos. We could... go over these ideas on site, brainstorm a bit more."

"Uh-hmm."

"Thursday? Late morning?"

"Sure." He stood.

Then he moved. He closed the distance between them and covered her mouth with his own. Tenderly. A soft, gentle, chaste kiss on those amazing lips. She hesitated, then leaned into him ever so slightly. He leaned in too, increasing the pressure of lips on lips, the tip of his tongue grazing the corner of her mouth. She shuddered and moaned softly, and his heart pounded in his throat, his breath stolen away. The heat exploded between them, and they pulled away as though burned.

"Thank you," he whispered.

Then her eyes darted away, and he pulled back, giving her some space. She glanced at him, uncertain. He smiled and shook his head. "Good night, Alexa."

∽

"What's up with you, girlfriend?" Peter asked Thursday morning, setting a fresh cup of coffee beside her.

"What do you mean?" Alexa leaned back from her drawing table, flicking her pen back and forth, tapping it on the tabletop.

Peter gestured at her hand. "That. You're a bundle of nerves. And you don't hear people talking to you. It's like you're a million miles away."

She tried to focus her gaze on his face. "I do have a lot on my mind, Pete. Krystof still hasn't dealt properly with this project. All three of us are juggling work. He met with George earlier this week didn't he? Did he say anything to you?"

Peter shook his head, no. "Is that really it?"

"It's enough isn't it? You know how important this is to me. He's not handling it. I'm worried."

"Worried about what? You know your job is secure. He can't manage this place without you."

She frowned. "Not good enough. I want more and he knows it. So far I'm already running the job, and running interference around stupid scheming Mini-Me. I'm worried about his cozy relationship with the Roses, and that Krystof will give the title to Nathan because of that, and leave me sweating behind the scenes doing all the heavy lifting and getting none of the glory. If this doesn't go my way, I don't know. I don't know what I'll do."

Peter leaned back, scowling. "Not something drastic I hope. I couldn't stand this place without you."

She squeezed his hand, leaning in and whispering, "Wherever I'm going, you're coming with me, Petey."

Peter's mouth twisted. "Even to the bottom, girlfriend?"

"I have my eye on the top," she quipped.

He quirked his brow and sauntered off, leaving her to her thoughts. She hadn't lied. She was fretting about Krys. The longer things went on as they were, the weirder they got. And the more anxious and uncomfortable Krystof made her feel. But that wasn't truthfully what she'd been chewing on when Pete had asked.

Alexa was disconcerted. Hell, she was bloody disordered. Tuesday night, somehow, Bruce had snuck up on her so gradually. She was feeling so welcome, so valued, so relaxed, and their conversation so stimulating. His change of attitude and attention had made her as nervous as hell, so after dinner she'd hidden behind a sturdy wall of professionalism. She had begun to feel confident and in her element as they discussed his house and his needs. But as the conversation progressed, sexual tension built, and it had begun to feel too intimate. He had seemed so vulnerable and open.

Her gut knew what he wanted, and she was pushy, perhaps too pushy, with her questions and comments. Presumptuous actually. She'd never talk to another client that way. But he wasn't like other clients, was he?

And then their brainstorming had been so stimulating, their minds so in tune, it was as if they were completely synchronized, like the gears in a finely tuned Swiss watch. Instead of pulling away as she had expected, hoped, even, he stared at her until she'd melted under the intensity of his heated gaze and her skin tingled where they touched.

But still…

He'd taken her off guard. His disconcerting comment about her voice, his arousal, had astounded her. Putting into words what she had felt building between them, but never acknowledged. Then, the shock of his kiss.

And it was a shock. She'd been lit on fire. A current of electricity had jetted through her body like a lightning bolt, immobilizing her. As though a puppet, she had swayed toward him, unable to control her own limbs, her desire flaring. She shook her head to clear the memory. If he hadn't left, there's no knowing what she might have done, might have allowed him to do, feeling as she did.

Then last night, he'd been cool. Or, well, back to normal, whatever that was these days. She'd got home relatively early, and the kids had been running around. He seemed on edge, and they'd had no chance to be alone, as though that was a good idea. And then he took off, saying he had to rush to the bank and run some errands before the stores closed. Now, she didn't know what to expect when she saw him later on. She glanced at the time. It was time she got going.

As she stood up and gathered her things, Krystof strolled up. He stopped in front of her, his cool silver eyes assessing. "Going somewhere, Jenner?" He tugged on his sleeves and fiddled with his cufflinks in a habitual gesture, one hand coming to rest over his jacket button. As ever, his suit was immaculate, his custom tailored shirt crisp and new, his tie perfectly coordinated. It was a shield, this uniform of his. His self-consciousness was a kind of self-defence. She narrowed her eyes at him, feeling more distance, more perspective than she'd ever felt before this icon that she'd always admired so much. Worshipped, really, if she was honest about it.

"Site meeting." She rummaged in her bag, avoiding his piercing gaze.

"Hmm. Everything okay?"

She stopped moving and lifted her eyes to meet his without smiling, without saying a word.

"I see. Well, perhaps we could talk about that later on. Over a drink? When you get back?"

She deflated. Is that what he really wanted? Or was he hoping to hook up after work. She could hardly avoid him after hounding him to answer her questions. She had considered not coming back to the office this afternoon, depending on, well, how her meeting with Bruce went. She wasn't quite sure what she meant by that. But perhaps it was time to have a chat with Krystof.

"We'll see. I might be back late. I'd have to arrange a babysitter for the kids. Why don't we meet somewhere?"

He nodded as he turned away. "I'll text you."

She scowled and headed for the door. Her phone beeped with a message before she even got on the elevator.

Lumiere. Seven o'clock.

"Do you have a chair?" Alexa asked, glancing around Bruce's empty house later that morning.

"No. No furniture here. Why?"

"I want to..." sit down. She strode out the open front door. Around the south side of the house, she saw an old wooden crate, overturned, half covered in ivy and moss. She grabbed it, it was heavier than she imagined, and dragged it backwards to the front of the house.

"Oomph!"

"What the–?"

He'd crashed into her behind as he rounded the corner. She felt his hands catch her around the waist, holding her derriere snugly against his groin for a heart-stopping moment before he stepped back. Her muscles went taut, and a shiver raced up her spine. He was so... large and strong. So exceptionally masculine. She stood abruptly and spun to face him, jerking out of his grasp.

"Where did you find that?" He looked innocent enough.

"Hold on…" she grunted, tugging the crate along. She felt her face flush, and kept her gaze averted. *Why can't I stop drooling over his body?*

"Let me. Where do you want it?" He picked up the heavy crate as if it were a cardboard box.

"Right here." She strode to the side of the front walkway, her heart fluttering, and he carried the crate over and set it down.

Alexa swept the surface clear of clinging dirt and moss clumps, turned sharply and sat down.

Bruce stood, hands on his hips and grinned at her. He shook his head.

What? Her stomach fluttered at the way he looked at her. She suppressed a corresponding smile, and glanced up ever so briefly at him. She used to have no trouble at all resisting his good looks and charm simply by reminding herself that he was a callow player. Somehow, that wasn't enough anymore to shut down her libido.

Her pulse raced remembering Tuesday evening at the house. She couldn't remember the last time she experienced that kind of instant heat. Perhaps as an adolescent, when her body had just awoken. Perhaps never.

Against her own better judgment, she wanted him near again. She slid over, patted the crate beside her, said "Sit," and turned away to pull her sketch pad and a 4B pencil out of her shoulder bag, to pull her nerve endings together.

He sat down beside her, hip to hip, thigh to long, muscular thigh, and observed. She pushed her glasses up with the heel of her hand and sketched. The familiar and beloved activity calmed her and took her mind off of the too-sexy man beside her. Her hand was confident, and her lines were quick and sure as she laid out the dominant lines of the house. Soon, the side of his house emerged on the white page. She had placed the entry canopy to the right of centre on the large drawing pad, with the bedroom wing receding beyond it. Then she squinted at the house and added some lines.

He looked up at the corner of the house, back at her drawing, at the house again, frowning. She imagined he was trying to place the imaginary piece of building that she now rendered.

He sat upright. "Aha! I get it."

She smiled, and continued to fill in windows and doors, textures, and outlined the trees beyond. Then she attempted to explain. "You see, wrapping the mass around the front entry actually enhances your experience upon approach, creating an outdoor room. And here, keeping the roof form complementary, but subordinate to the main roof, supports rather than detracts from the original design. I could imagine it, but now that I'm here, I'm sure it's good, and the heritage committee will like it."

Bruce studied the drawing, but his eyes darted back to her face. She looked at him in anticipation, waiting for his response to her ideas.

"There's a bit of dirt…" He reached his right hand up, licked his thumb, and gently wiped her cheek with it, leaving his warm hand resting lightly against her face and neck.

Her breath caught in her throat. Her eyes darted up to meet his, then down at her drawing, feeling her face heat, tingling where his hand still touched her. What would it be like, she wondered, to surrender to the powerful physical attraction that she felt for him? Even if it were a short term fling, it would be incredible to indulge in that gorgeous, sexy body. When it ended, would it be a huge mess that would negatively impact Kate and Simon? Would they be furious?

How odd, that she should become shy around him, when she was always so bold and confident, aggressive even. She looked up to see Bruce's dark brown eyes drop to her mouth, and rise back up to her eyes. Their gazes locked, and she a hurricane of heat charged the air between them. He leaned forward slightly and the earth tilt as her heart hammered. She leaned in as well, anticipating…

"Bruce! Bruce are you here?"

Alexa's pulse pounded in her chest. They both snapped back, throwing distance between them, and Alexa had to lurch to catch her glasses before they fell off the back of her head. Her! It was that woman, the neighbour. Gillian.

Bruce groaned, stood up, looked at the ground, brushed dirt from the seat of his jeans and adjusted them. He glanced toward the voice, and back at Alexa, who tore her eyes away from the bulge at his fly. She fiddled with her pencil, making small marks on the sketch.

He swore under his breath and took a few steps away.

"Yeah! Gillian? I'm right here." His voice rose, louder, but reticent. Was he embarrassed that Gillian almost caught them kissing? If he were involved with her, that would be awkward. In so many ways.

How could she let herself feel this way about a man she knew was a player? She was such an idiot.

Gillian appeared on the street at the end of the drive. "Oh, hi. There you are. Can you help me out?" She wind-milled her hands in the air, taking several strides down the driveway. "I've got an awful crisis happening. My garburator is jammed–"

Bruce winced. "Can it wait a bit Gillian? I'm… uh, in the middle of something. I'll come by to check it out in a while, okay?"

Gillian's arms dropped to her sides. "Oh. Okay, well… right. Okay." She turned and walked slowly away, out of sight, her curves swaying in a pair of cute, tight-fitting cropped pants.

Bruce and Alexa turned toward each other, and she read the embarrassment in his dark eyes. Minuscule muscles in his jaw, his cheek, his nose twitched as he clenched his teeth.

"Sorry about that. She's incredibly high-maintenance." He laughed, but it was a tense, uncomfortable sound. How was a neighbour someone you were responsible for if you weren't also…? "Where were we?"

Alexa licked her lips. Oh, shit. No. She didn't mean to remind him precisely where they were, what they were about to do. "Um." She glanced down at her drawing. "I wanted to talk about the other wing as well." Her voice sounded strangled in her ears. She stood up, lifting one hand to gesture limply at the other side of the house.

He nodded stiffly, and they walked in that direction, a good two feet of space between their shoulders, the moment of intimacy shattered. The eddy of energy that had engulfed them had dispersed. A tense, terrifying moment of connection was lost.

Don't be ridiculous. It was probably your imagination anyway. And furthermore, if he had kissed you again, what then? She dared to glance up, and found him gazing at her expectantly.

She cleared her throat. "Yeah. So. On this side, since you'll likely use one of these rooms as a home-office, and the other as a guest room, I thought we could–"

"Bruce!"

They both turned toward Gillian, who stood on her deck, waving her arms frantically. Bruce scowled.

"Sorry…" he mumbled, at no one in particular.

"Bruce, honey, if you don't come now I don't know what I'll do. There's yucky water pouring out of the sink all over the floor!"

Bruce seemed to be anchored to the ground, his whole frame shrinking as he cringed. "So call a plumber," he grumbled under his breath. "Do I look like a fucking plumber?" He sighed.

"You'd better go."

"Please come." Gillian's voice was a high whine, and she stood hunched and helpless, waiting for her hero. "Hurry!"

"Jesus Christ," Bruce mumbled. "I'll be right there," he replied with a wave, his voice louder and a broad, a tight smile pasted on his tanned face. Then he turned to Alexa. "I'm so sorry. I'd better go give her a hand or she'll never leave me alone. I'll be right back." He gripped her shoulder and released it. "Don't go anywhere; okay?" His mouth quirked to one side, a feeble, half-hearted attempt at a conciliatory smile.

She pulled her mouth tight in an attempt to reciprocate, but instead was overcome with discomfort and alienation and... loss? A feeling of shrinking and wishing to disappear. And a low, simmering anger. At him? At Gillian? *Please don't tell me I feel jealous. That's ridiculous.* Now the anger was directed at herself for being so incredibly stupid.

It was no surprise that he was involved with Gillian. Alexa might scorn his taste in women, but it was utterly predictable that he would be attracted to... to that. He was a normal, red-blooded male, after all. Most men much preferred *that* over her own androgynous severity. Isn't that why she cultivated the image? To neutralize her sexuality, to avoid distracting the males of the species so she would be taken seriously? Still, she'd allowed herself to believe in the unnamable feeling of mutual attraction she increasingly experienced whenever they were alone together.

But now she realized, that wasn't attraction. That's the way he is with women. Accustomed to having his way with them, charming them with his smiles and smart-mouthed banter. Except she'd always been immune. She had always kept her head clear, and never been vulnerable to it.

She laughed at herself. He'd used her passion for architecture to get under her skin. He'd tricked her! And she'd fallen for it. He only wanted her help with the house, and he didn't know any other way to ask for help, but to seduce and to charm and to manipulate.

Well, fine. She'd woken up. She knew him. He wasn't her type anyway. She couldn't take a man-child like Bruce seriously. How could she have allowed herself to believe that there was something more there? A real connection.

Hmph. She knew him alright.

And she'd do his drawings. But not for him. For herself. For the pleasure of salvaging and enhancing a priceless work of art by a noted architect. Because she cared about the house. Not because she cared about him.

Alexa shook her head, sighed and strode to her car. She got in and pulled out of the driveway, heading down the narrow lane and onto the main road, toward her office in town, her knuckles white on the steering wheel. Toward a world she understood, where she knew her role, and though it was cutthroat, where she, too, could be a player. She spent the afternoon chiding herself at her foolishness, her carelessness, despite his text asking, *Where did you go? We weren't finished were we?*

Alexa reproached herself for getting distracted by his charm, and succumbing, however briefly, to her attraction to his pure masculine physicality. She had to put some distance between them. A frivolous, physical fling with the likes of Bruce Koczynski would be the height of idiocy. Doomed. Inappropriate. Awkward.

And from her perspective, just plain stupid. There were more important things. Like the Arts Centre. Dealing with Krystof. Getting through the rest of this babysitting stint and getting on with her life.

CHAPTER 12

"Hey, there you are," Bruce said as she entered the house after work later that day.

"Yeah. Sorry to leave so suddenly this morning." With a businesslike smile, Alexa offered the excuse she'd spent the afternoon formulating. "I got a call on my cell, and had to dash to the office."

His brow knotted and he nodded. "Oh, I wondered…" He pulled back, no doubt sensing her cooler, withdrawn manner.

Good. That was the idea.

"I left you a message," he said, and she read hurt in his tone.

She ruffled in her briefcase, anything to avoid those puzzled, unguarded dark eyes. "Hmm? Oh, yes sorry, I had a hectic afternoon."

"I see… well. It's early. I haven't done anything about dinner yet. The kids are watching TV."

She looked up. "Oh. Right. I'm early because I need to go out tonight. There's one more critical meeting I have to squeeze in before the week's over. So we're doing it over dinner."

Bruce's face fell. His mouth opened, twitched a little. "We?"

"Krystof. My boss? You can manage, can't you?"

His brow lowered, and his eyes narrowed. "I suppose. But I was hoping we could carry on our–"

"Oh. That reminds me. I managed to squeeze in your design drawings this afternoon between meetings. Here." She reached out and handed him the tube of drawings that she'd slung over her shoulder.

He took it tentatively. "So quickly? What's going on?"

"You need time to look them over. And we can review anything you want changed before I finalize them. 'Kay?" She offered him a bright smile.

He appeared puzzled, then his face darkened, and his jaw twitched as his lips thinned. He dropped his chin, smirking. "Oh, I see. You have a date with your *boss*."

She lifted her chin. "It's not a date. We have to discuss the project. There wasn't time this week to fit it in."

"Ri-ight. Did you ask whether I'm available to babysit while you dash off to tend to your boss's needs?"

Alexa tensed. Her chest tightened at his accusation. "I beg your pardon?"

He let out a gust of laughter. "Maybe I had plans."

I'll just bet. With Gillian. She pinched her lips together, lifted her brows. "Well? Do you?"

He scowled, his dark eyes narrowing further.

She stiffened under his cold gaze, then drew herself up and smirked. "I shouldn't be too late. A few hours should be enough."

His laugh was bitter. "Plenty of time to make sure the boss hasn't forgotten how special you are, hey Al?"

"Watch yourself, Koczynski." She lowered her voice to a hiss. "Where are the kids?"

He shook his head. "I told you. Watching TV."

She peered at him. What was happening? She ground her teeth, her ribs tight, her neck stiff. She felt tears rising, burning her throat, the back of her eyes.

"Why do you do it? You pretend to take yourself and your career so seriously while you let yourself be manipulated by him." He snapped his fingers in illustration.

"How dare you? You know nothing about it. And you're one to talk. You haven't such high standards yourself. Your idea of a relationship doesn't hold a candle to mine."

Bruce recoiled with a grimace. "What are we talking about? Sex?"

"Krys and I are colleagues."

Bruce snorted.

"Unlike yourself, my employer is an intelligent, accomplished, sophisticated, well-dressed–" She waved her hand in a vague outline at

Bruce, "...attractive man and I enjoy his company." *Oh, my God. Did I just admit to having an affair with Krystof?*

He rose up and faced her with his chest pushed out, his hands on his belt and spat, "That oily little shark I met? You wouldn't recognize a real man if you *fell* over one, sweetheart."

She ignored him and carried on. "We're like-minded professionals who respect each other. We have an understanding that suits both of us perfectly. No one is getting manipulated. Unlike your little bimbo next door. Or maybe it's you that's getting used." She changed to a falsetto voice, flapping her hands in the air. "Oh, Bruce. Help! Help!"

"What are you talking about?"

She pulled a face at him. "Don't play dumb. Anyone can see what you're up to with Gillian. And God knows how many other brainless buxom blondes." A humourless laugh escaped her. "I know your type, Koczynski. You can't help yourself."

His shoulders rose up to frame his ears. "You are so mistaken. There's nothing between Gillian and me." His hands tensed in front of him, as if he wanted to grab her around the neck and squeeze.

"Yeah. Sure. Don't waste your breath."

"Alexa. Because she simpers and tries to–"

"Yes, well. Save it for someone who cares. I have to go. We have a reservation at *Lumiere*. Kiss the kids good night for me." She tossed him a counterfeit smile as she turned to the door. "And don't forget to give Lucy her insulin shot."

As she stepped outside, she heard him gasp and curse softly under his breath, a note of incredulity to his tone.

"No need to keep a light on. I'll spend the night at my apartment," she said into the crack.

Well, that was done. Her stomach felt a tad queasy, and her shoulders slumped as if a heavy load had landed there. She sighed.

Once in her car, she pushed her limp hair back from an oily brow, and realized she had intended to freshen up and change her clothes before dinner with Krystof. She stared at the door. There was no going back in there now.

But, her apartment was only a few blocks away, and there was more selection in her own closet. Dinner at *Lumiere* was worth a stylish turn, she decided, and headed for home, a place she'd be glad to get back to permanently. It was a good thing she and Krys would have this quiet time alone together. It had been too long, and she was starved for mature male companionship, and a little understanding.

∼

The house-made fig compote with aged cheeses and rich French sauces on delicately cooked meat and fish was a welcome treat after too many days of macaroni and wieners with the kids, ketchup on everything. Alexa ate up the subdued modern atmosphere as well, a respite from Kate's too-sweet mix of Martha Stewart and Laura Ashley. Tasteful but alienating to Alexa. She took another large swig of her cabernet.

She'd opted to wear a flattering black jersey skirt and a simple white blouse with French cuffs, an indulgence not practical when going home to sticky fingers and smelly diapers. She even popped in a pair of contact lenses, for a change. Krystof's appreciation flashed in his eyes.

In the end, they'd talked of work in general, people and events, rather than the Arts Centre project specifically, perhaps both of them sensing that it was not to be a simple conversation. Implicit was the shared knowledge that they would have private time together after dinner. It had been ages since they'd been together. Since the luncheon.

Back at Alexa's apartment after dinner, where earlier she'd taken a few moments to put a bottle of champagne in the fridge, and drag a rag over the most obviously dusty surfaces, Krys kicked off his shoes and fell back on her leather sofa as though coming home.

"It has been too long, Sasha, since we were here together."

Her jaw clenched at his pet name for her. She'd never liked it, yet she'd never told him so. She flicked on her stereo, set to an all night jazz station.

The last time they'd been together flashed across her mind's eye, a not altogether pleasant memory. That was the origin of her troubles, her worries. Until that day, she had not suspected that the Roses could be such fossils –that anyone could question her right to lead the project that she had spearheaded from the outset. That perhaps Krystof was not her most vocal advocate.

She narrowed her eyes and smiled at him, removing her own shoes, and sliding into the kitchen. "Champagne?"

"Yes, thank you."

She brought the bottle and two glasses to the living room and sat beside him. He took them from her and expertly opened the bottle with a pop, and poured two glasses, handing her one.

Meeting her eyes, he said, "To us," and clinked glasses.

She brought it to her nose, feeling its effervescence dance on her cheeks, sipped, and sighed. She brought her legs up and tucked her feet under her, leaning back. It was a relief to have a respite in her own world, including the collegial companionship of her friend and lover. What were they, exactly, toasting to?

Why do you do it? You pretend to take yourself and your career so seriously while you let yourself be manipulated by him.

She pushed aside the remembered words. With Krystof, there was no need to explain herself. They understood each other. No compromises. It was ideal, and yet, a knot of discomfort lay under the surface of her contentment. Waiting.

"It's good to see you, Krys. I like to look at you." It was true. He was smooth, refined and urbane. His grooming was immaculate. His dark shirt and trousers tasteful and fashionable. His body slender and lithe. She ignored the voice in her head that said, cold, calculating, conceited.

So unlike Bruce, with his faded, rumpled shirts, baggy trousers and wild hair, with the heat of his muscled body, his raw, masculine scent, his touch that lit her on fire. She shook off the images, swallowing.

Krystof set down his glass, then took hers and set it down beside his own. He slid closer on the sofa and took her face in his long, manicured hands, bringing his cool, champagne tinged mouth down over hers. His tongue, also cool and smooth, probed her mouth, pushing, presuming.

He was a skillful lover. She emptied her mind of questions and doubts, and forced herself to welcome and appreciate his touch. His attention. After weeks of starvation. It wasn't quite doing the trick.

When she'd had enough of the kissing and fondling, she led him into her bedroom. Krystof tugged down the bedcovers and strode over to undress her. Again she stood and allowed him to remove her clothing, item by item.

"You are changed, Sasha."

She winced. "How so?"

He shook his head as he unbuttoned her shirt. "You're distant. What is bothering you?"

"Don't you know?"

"I know what you want. But there is something…"

She shrugged a little, and lifted her brows. Ignoring the disturbance under the surface.

Krystof went through the motions, taking charge, slowing down and distilling their lovemaking into a precise and familiar ritual. Then, when they were both stripped to their underwear, he stopped, his arms falling to his sides. "Not this."

"What?"

"I want you to tell me what to do."

She stood in silence. He liked it that way. She was often willing to role play with him. It wasn't what she wanted tonight though. It felt forced and false compared to the raw naked desire she felt whenever Bruce came near her. She exhaled deeply. Digging down deep, she pulled up the energy to give him what he wanted and take what she needed, too. Placing one hand on his bare shoulder, she gripped his bones and pushed back. "Lie down, then."

A hint of a smile curled his thin lips. He obliged her, crawling backwards onto the bed, his silver eyes never leaving her face.

She knelt on the bed and crawled forward toward him, leaning over him and pushing him down as she advanced.

"What do you want, Sasha?"

"Satisfaction, Krystof."

"How can I please you?"

"Not with words. With action. Show me."

"I am your servant." He lifted his hands to her breasts, gently kneading, circling. He lifted his head and licked between her breasts.

She allowed him to touch her for another minute or two. When he reached back to undo her bra, she sat up, stopping him, and wordlessly stared into his eyes.

After several long minutes of silence, he sighed. "So. Ask your question."

She stiffened and scampered back to the edge of the bed. "I can't do this Krystof. I can't pretend. I need to know what's going on."

Silence.

She slid her legs over the edge, lowering her feet to the carpeted floor, peering at him in the dim light, her brow furrowing with worry. She curled her toes into the soft pile, and her hands fisted in the sheets at her sides. "Should I be afraid?"

His thin shoulders twitched. An undecided shrug.

"What's going on with the Arts Centre?"

"I want to give you the title, Jenner. You deserve it."

"But?"

"But... I don't know if it is within my power to do so."

If he couldn't do it, who could? She twisted to look directly at him, sliding one knee onto the bed, tucking her ankle under her other knee. "Explain."

He sighed again, pulled himself into a sitting position, struggling with the pillows, pushing them into place, leaning back. Finally he looked up at her.

She waited. Her heart lurched, limping, stuttering. Her jaw tightened, and a heavy weight descended on her chest, constraining every attempt to breathe.

"Krys?"

"You must believe I am on your side, Sasha. I am doing all I can." He reached for her again, and she moved away.

"Please stop calling me that. Are you telling me they will *not* accept me? Even though I'm doing the work?"

He nodded, thin-lipped. He dragged one finger down her arm. "They have certain expectations about how it should go. And all the power.

"But you're the principal consultant. They've awarded you the contract. You run your firm. *You* decide."

"They... have threatened to take the project away."

The shock of his statement hit her like a brick, jolting through her, knocking her back. "It was awarded fair and square. That must be illegal. They can't openly discriminate against a woman."

"Of course not openly. They would not say so, directly. Only that they had lost confidence in us. It would look very bad for the firm. That Rose, he speaks in tongues. He is very politic."

Rage bubbled up inside her, urging her to strike out, to punish him. "But so archaic. He must realize I'm the one who brought it this far. Doesn't he want the best building?"

Krystof's head waffled back and forth. "It's complicated. He's a pompous ass. And a control freak."

"Ch...yeah." She threw herself off the bed, strode to the bathroom door for her robe and wrapped herself in it. "He knows it's my design? He knows I've been running the job all along? Even now?"

"Yes, well. I believe so. Perhaps he doesn't care. He knows the design cannot substantially change now. It's his."

"That's wrong! It's mine."

"Of course it is."

"What are you going to do?"

"I… uh, I have a plan. I will meet with him again next week. We're having lunch to negotiate the terms of the contract."

She sat on the edge of the bed and leaned toward him. "Let me be there."

"Ahh. Jenner. No. That would not be wise."

"Krys. What are you saying to him? Are you fighting for me? Are you?"

"Of course, I am. I'm on your side, Jenner. You have to believe I'm doing the best I can here."

Something in his voice made her doubt him. Bitter resentment washed over her. Their playacting was all in fun, and she had never questioned it before, but in fact the power lay firmly in Krystof's hands. It had never been an issue, as long as she trusted him. But did she still? Now, with so much at stake, she realized she was ultimately vulnerable. She was at his mercy.

He took her arms in his hands, tilted his head to peer into her eyes. "You will not punish me, Sasha? No matter what happens?"

"Punish you…?"

"Stop loving me."

"I can't do this, Krys, with everything unresolved. Especially now. I don't feel supported."

"Are you saying you'll only have sex with me if I give you the job? That's not what this was about."

"No! It wasn't. It isn't!" How could he suggest that? He was turning the tables on her. "I'm the one getting screwed here, Krystof. I would never do that. That's not who I am. You know that!"

His lip curled. "Well you were willing enough when you thought you were going to be rewarded."

Her jaw clenched. "Like you said, that's *not* what this is about! You promised me. Purely on merit. It's you that's letting *me* down. Going back on your word." *Stupid, stupid girl. No more. Never again.* "Maybe you never meant it at all. Maybe it's you that's been using me!" Her own words echoed Bruce's earlier accusations, and her skin crawled at her foolishness. It wasn't true. It wasn't. "I thought we were friends. You respected me. I trusted you."

"And I thought you were a professional, Jenner. Don't be naive. You can't have everything you want." He got up to dress.

Later, when he was gone, she lay awake in her bed, too shocked to cry. Too upset to sleep.

She had placed too much trust in Krystof. She'd been wrong to believe that they were kindred spirits who understood each other so well. Oh, he understood *her*. Well enough to manipulate her. For years her career had been in *his* hands, not her own. How could she have allowed that? She had always prided herself on her independence and strength. On not needing anyone. How could she have surrendered her own destiny to another? To a man whom she'd allowed to seduce her, her employer, it must be said, when it was so important to her, when it was all that she lived for? Bruce was right. She had no-one to blame. She'd betrayed herself.

∼

"That's not how Daddy does it."

Bruce exhaled, set down the wooden spoon with which he was heating spaghetti sauce, refraining from shaking it at her, and glared at Maddie. "I'm not your Dad."

"You're not as nice as my Dad."

"Maybe so." He shook his head. Maybe so.

She pouted, her little brown brows pulled low over her green cat eyes. Green eyes that, strangely, reminded him of Alexa. Alexa the hypocrite. Or witch. What was it about green-eyed women? Maybe there was something behind all those myths and stories about sorceresses and witches. He lifted the lid on the pasta and gave it a stir, plucked one strand from the roiling mass. "Tell me if this is done."

"Don't you know?"

"I asked you." What had gotten into her tonight? She'd been peevish all evening, since Alexa left to go to her meeting. Meeting. Right. He'd been irritable, too. Maybe Maddie was picking up vibes.

She took the sticky tendril between her fingers, blew on it and nibbled the end. "It's chewy."

"Good chewy or bad chewy?"

Maddie was standing on a footstool, bringing her up, not to his eye level, but closer to the devastatingly beautiful, demanding, high-maintenance woman she would one day become. She rolled her eyes expressively, tossing her chestnut waves back off her flushed face. "The way Daddy likes it but too hard for Markus."

"Okay. Thanks for that bit of advice. You're a big help with your little brother, Maddie, you know that?"

"Sure. He's not really my brother, y'know. Only half."

"Same thing. What's bugging you, little witch?"

She scowled. "I'm not a witch!"

"I'm teasing. You're acting like one tonight. What's on your mind?"

Her lips protruded. "What day is it?"

Bruce frowned. "Friday."

She shook her head, exasperated. "On the calendar, stupid."

"Don't be disrespectful, kid." He set down his spoon and took one long stride over to the calendar pinned to a cork board next to the fridge. He pointed to today on the calendar. June fifteenth.

Two weeks had passed and he'd made almost no progress on his house. The summer was passing him by, and he still needed to submit drawings to the city for approval before he could resume construction. He remembered the drawings Alexa had handed to him last night. He'd been so shocked and embarrassed by the realization that she was sleeping with her boss, he'd completely forgotten about them. He'd make time to have a look at them later tonight.

"How much longer?"

He smiled, understanding. "Until school lets out?" He was intentionally obtuse. "Less than a week."

"No-ooo. 'Til Daddy comes home."

"It's hard to say. Maybe another week." Thank God. Although the idea didn't bring the elation he'd expected. "They're having a bit of a rest before flying home, until everyone feels better."

"Is that all?"

He turned back to the stove, shut off the heat and carried the pasta to the sink to drain it. "Are you trying to hurt my feelings, Scallywag?"

She was silent.

"Go get Markus for dinner. Please."

During dinner, conversation was limited, as Maddie continued to sulk, and Markus faced the daunting challenge of getting the spaghetti onto his fork and into his mouth. He was already covered in sauce, from prow to stern.

Bruce, in his turn, pondered Alexa's hazy green eyes, her emotional reserve, and yet her unbridled passion for her work. She was fiery but her energy, her emotions, were carefully caged and directed. As though she'd made a pact never to be distracted from her life's work.

Almost never.

A pang of discontent, of deprivation, of despair, shook him, as though he'd sampled the smallest taste of something unimaginably wonderful and had it snatched away. With no warning, she had shut him down, turning as cold as a figurehead, beautiful but lifeless. Rejection. Not his favourite sensation. He wondered if that were it for them. If, in fact, they'd started anything. Why the sudden shift?

He'd started to feel something different, to open up a little, but letting his guard down was hard. It was too easy to believe that no one could love him for his true self, underneath all his bravado. Was he a fool to think someone as smart, accomplished and kind as her would be interested in him? She was a challenge, but not in the ordinary way.

And now he understood why. Why the stupid, paradoxical affair with the oily boss? Didn't she realize how it looked? He could imagine what the snake was in it for, why and how he kept her strung along. She was so smart. How could she fall for such a scam?

Was she in love with him?

His gut coiled, his shoulders pinched, making his neck and back ache.

After dinner the kids splashed contentedly in the bathtub. Bruce brought the roll of drawings to the bathroom, and unraveled them on the floor to look them over. She had made a copy of the original drawings he'd acquired from the city, and done an overlay of darker lines to indicate where changes were proposed.

A blob of suds landed with a splat on his drawings. "Hey!" He quickly swept the moisture away with his hand. "Settle down." He glanced at the kids, who negotiated the rules of a suds-monster and motorboat game that suited them both. Maddie was in charge, of course, and Markus was content to squeal with each attack. Bruce's attention returned to his house.

She'd added on a small wing to the master bedroom, where a new ensuite bath and closet would be located. The two small bedrooms on that side remained unchanged, although it seemed she was enlarging one window. On the other side, she was moving a wall out to enlarge the end room, which she'd labeled Home Office. Inside were both a new work surface and storage cupboards, showing how the room would be used. The desk was placed to allow a view over the ocean, and avoid glare on his computer screens. Each place she'd suggested a change, there was an alpha-numeric code and a small note referring to another page.

He flipped the large sheets over, reading her mini-essays describing how the changes complemented and respected the original design, her words eloquent and persuasive. Small three-dimensional sketches were added in boxes, showing how each change would look from the exterior. He flipped back to the main floor plan and studied the rest of the layout. The living room was essentially unchanged, and a new kitchen was laid out on the half level above, where it used to be, but expanded and much more central and open, with a view over the living room and out to the patio. It looked grand. Enough to make him want to cook and entertain. Certainly he could picture himself shuffling in there from the bedroom and standing with a cup of hot coffee, admiring the gorgeous view.

She'd managed to incorporate everything he needed, in all the right places, and yet she'd really removed nothing and added very little. Certainly the open flow of spaces remained unchanged, and the house would look basically the same. She had reworked the patio extensively, adding some edgier geometry and levels stepping down that he quite liked. He sat on the closed toilet lid and released the drawings, watching them coil back into a loose roll, marvelling at her designs. Yet, strangely, Bruce found it difficult to feel much enthusiasm for the project. He'd been expecting, hoping even, that she'd show him the design herself, and explain it to him.

He studied the pattern of tile and grout on the floor, his hands dangling between his knees, fists clenching and opening, clenching and opening. Even if Alexa were in love with Krystof, Bruce was certain Krystof could not be in love with her. Not that she wasn't lovable. But if he were, he would not use her this way. He would respect her too much to have an affair with an employee. Bruce could imagine what they were doing right now and it filled his body with seething rage. Bruce wanted to pulverize Krystof. An irresistible violent urge to step on his neck shot through him, and he shook off the image.

The sound of rushing water made him glance up. Maddie stood up in the tub, water streaming down her skinny naked body, staring him down with those accusing green eyes.

"Are you and Auntie Alex going to make up?"

"What?"

Maddie narrowed her eyes at him. "Why are you fighting?"

"We're not fighting. Mind your own business."

"What did you thay to her to make her mad?"

"You shouldn't eavesdrop on other people's conversations, Maddie. It's rude."

"You shouldn't thay things to make people mad."

He glared at her, but she was right. He couldn't explain his own feelings, or his own behaviour. And he had no business criticizing Alexa or questioning her motives.

Once they were in their pyjamas and tucking Markus into his bed, Maddie peered at him with large sparkling innocent eyes. "Can you tell us a thtory, Bruce?"

Oh. So sweet she was now. When she wanted something. As though she were not telling him off a few minutes ago. The vixen.

"I'm not much of a storyteller, Scallywag."

"Sto-wy," added Markus, his eyes already heavy.

"You can make it up, or read one," she suggested. "Or do what Auntie Al does. She reads a fairy tale and changes thtuff and acts it out. It's funny."

He smiled. That was so like Alexa. To rewrite the story according to her own rules.

He went to the bookshelf searching for inspiration. Scanning aimlessly, his eye fell upon a dog-eared antique tome entitled: *Romances of the Middle Ages*. Trust Simon to have such a thing on his kids' shelf. Perhaps inviting misery, he pulled it out and scanned the table of contents. Some of the stories he was familiar with, others, he merely knew the names and not the stories behind them. He picked one he knew less.

"Okay," he said, sitting upright. "Tonight, we're going explore a classic love story."

"I know," said Maddie. "Like Romeo and Juliet?"

"No. Tristan and Isolde," Bruce replied, and recounted the medieval tale in which King Mark of Cornwall sends his trusted nephew Tristan to escort his bride home from Ireland, only to discover, eventually, that on the way, they have fallen in love, a relationship they do not end even after Isolde's marriage to King Mark. Mark inexplicably forgives Isolde, but bans Tristan, who then travels to Brittany.

"Where's Britt'ny?" asked Maddie.

"Um. In the north of France," answered Bruce. "But it wasn't really France yet, in those days." His eyes scanned ahead to see how the story worked itself out. When he discovered that not only had Isolde been forgiven, but that Tristan married another woman who betrayed him when he fell ill and asked for Isolde to come to his aid, he frowned and stopped reading.

"Finish it," said Maddie.

"Finis," echoed Markus, yawning.

"Whath the matter?" asked Maddie.

"This is where I make stuff up," said Bruce pensively.

The kids waited expectantly. "Well?"

Bruce squirmed. "How would you like it to end?"

Maddie narrowed her eyes and tugged her nightgown over her knees. "I want Itholde to rescue Tristan in Brittany and... and Tristan gets all better, and they live happily ever after in a pretty castle. In Disneyland."

"Markus?"

Markus stared silently for a moment, and Bruce wondered if he even understood the story thus far. Then Markus whipped his stuffed cat out from under the covers and slashed it back and forth. "Twistan sword fight."

Bruce chuckled. "I'm with you, Markus." He glanced at Maddie's scowling face. "Sorry, Scallywag. Women are too fickle." He laughed. "So... Tristan sends his wife to see if the sails on the returning ship are black or white. And she lies, and says they are black, meaning that Isolde has rejected his invitation and isn't coming."

"That's the same."

Markus slashed his stuffed cat again. "Sword fight."

"Hold on, buddy. So Tristan is so disappointed in both Isolde, and in his wife Iseult, for betraying him, that he swears off women and love forever. He rises from his sickbed, becomes a Knight Templar, and rides off to the Holy Land to fight in the Crusades against the Eastern Hordes."

"Who?"

"Saracens who held Jerusalem in those days. They fought for hundreds of years. So Tristan spent the remainder of his days riding his mighty steed and fighting sword fights against enemies of Christianity. The end."

"Sword fight," insisted Markus sleepily.

"There were enough sword fights to please any man, Markus. A lifetime's worth."

Maddie frowned. "I don't like your ending. Your thtories are even worse than your cooking."

"Well, thanks so much, Madison. Time for bed." He bent to kiss Markus on the forehead and tuck him in. "G'night, little buddy. Come on, you."

Bruce stood in the doorway, waiting while Madison kissed her baby brother goodnight, and followed him out to the hall. When they got to her room, and she climbed in her bed and frowned as she said, "Auntie Al's thtories are funnier, but they aren't very romantic either. There's something wrong with both of you."

"Oh, yeah?" That was interesting. "No knights in shining armour rescuing maidens in distress?" Was he surprised?

"Are you kidding? Auntie Al's princesses kick butt. But they don't like princes."

He laughed out loud, and continued chuckling to himself until he fell asleep on the sofa an hour later. He jolted awake near midnight to the phone beeping. It was Alexa, texting.

Since I have to go to work early in the morning, would you mind dropping the kids off at school. Etcetera.

Right. Sure. Like he hadn't already figured that out.

Remember to pick up the birthday gift for the party. Instructions on Kate's list. –M.

Bruce set down his phone. That was all she had to say in her curt text message? As though he were the nanny, and she too busy and important to bother with civility.

CHAPTER 13

Next morning, Bruce consulted the list to decipher Alexa's message. Kate had apparently emailed about a forgotten birthday party on Saturday. Alexa had added, in her neat block printing, that there was a particular set of Playmobile that the birthday girl wanted, and Wal-Mart ought to now have it in stock.

Bruce pulled into the parking lot at Wal-Mart and got Markus out of his car seat. They had dropped Maddie off at her friend Ella's house for a play-date at nine-thirty, as previously arranged. At least, if Alexa was going to stay out all night, and work all day, she'd only stranded him with one kid, for now. It was a relief to get a little space from both sets of judgmental green female eyes.

Inside Wal-Mart, Bruce set Markus down, and held his hand. It didn't work so well, as Bruce was too tall, Markus too short, and Bruce ended up bent over and hobbling along like the Hunchback of Notre Dame. Soon enough, Markus tugged free.

"Stay close to me, Marky. It's a really big store."

Before they could shop, they had to locate the washrooms and change Markus's pull-up. Since when did three-year-olds wear diapers? What he ought to do is stay home and put Markus in the back yard with no pants on. That'd teach him. He tried to remember when he was that small, but couldn't.

And he couldn't call his mother and ask her. It's a good thing he didn't have kids of his own, because he didn't have anyone he could go to for advice. Except Simon who was in Asia and didn't need to be disturbed. And Alexa. But he wasn't going there.

He took a moment to ponder in awe all his best friend had dealt with when Maddie was born, all that he had accomplished as a single dad. He'd been married, but Rachel had been an absentee mother. She was never there, and probably would have terminated the pregnancy if Simon hadn't begged. But then Simon had to learn it all and do everything himself. And he'd been amazing. He was a wonder-dad, totally committed to his little girl. It took balls. And sacrifice.

"Come here, buddy." Bruce led Markus into the handicapped stall and set down the diaper bag. He quickly stripped off his pants, cleaned him up and popped on a fresh pull-up diaper. He was getting pretty good at this. It wasn't such a big deal, really. They washed up and headed out into the shopping aisles in search of toys. Markus waddled off ahead, and Bruce followed. Maybe he had some kind of built-in toy radar.

What would it be like to have a person in his life to whom he was that committed? Someone for whom he would do anything, for whom he would sacrifice everything. It left a hollow ache in his chest, not knowing the answer. Not having such a person. But then, not everyone was cut out to have a family. He was not Simon. When it came to relationships, Simon expected rewards, whereas Bruce saw only the risks.

After Alexa had awakened him with her terse text at midnight, he'd been tempted to phone Simon in Bangkok or Phuket or wherever he was, just to hear his familiar, reassuring voice. He imagined all those lonely nights that Simon spent with Madison sleeping, Rachel out of town on business, or out with her 'friends.' He scoffed. Simon would understand. Bruce and Alexa may not be involved, not really, but in the wee hours, especially last night, his situation seemed oddly parallel to Simon's in those days. Instead he'd pulled himself together and sent a cheery text to Simon: *Sleeping at the house tonight to give Alexa a night off. All is well.*

Not so well.

Strangely, Simon's reply text had been almost instantaneous. It had been around dinner time there, he figured.

Terrific. Hey, let's do another video chat tonight, okay? We want to catch up with you both. After the kids are in bed? Around eight.

Bruce wondered idly why they'd want to talk *after* the kids were asleep instead of see them. Probably just about their return travel schedule. Well, that was one good thing. At least this babysitting stint would be over soon. He expected Simon and Kate due back on Thursday. Just a few more days and he wouldn't have to deal with Alexa anymore. Unless he wanted to.

His resolve of the previous week was crumbling. Why would he want to win over Alexa? He didn't want to feel anything for her, but couldn't deny that he did. Or was starting to. Maybe it was just the proximity. What would he do if he found himself in a serious relationship with a serious woman? Why would he want to get entangled with her? There would be compromises. There would be expectations. Inevitably, there would be disappointments.

He must be out of his freaking mind. That wasn't Bruce Koczynski. Bruce Koczynski was a free agent, a rolling stone, a lone ranger, like Aragorn in Lord of the Rings. His mind filled with the romantic image of Aragorn astride his dark horse, his robes fluttering in the wind, his mighty sword in hand.

He shook his head. Bad example. That dude had heaps of baggage, and ended up with the ultimate responsibility for others. Damn!

The prospect of returning to his old ways –his self-contained, autonomous, solitary state– left a longing melancholy behind, as though he knew he wouldn't relish it nearly so much as he once had. What was happening to him? He felt compelled to rescue Alexa from that smarmy villain Krystof, rescue her from her fickle self-destructive self, teach her something about real love, and real men. Ha. Something he didn't even know himself.

There was potentially something special between them. They were more compatible than either realized. And had a level of understanding that was... unique. They could have something profound, with a mutual respect and admiration and attraction that outshone anything they had previously experienced. He felt confident that he could say that about her despite what she said about her boss. Bruce certainly felt that way. Ever since that first moment at his house, when she'd shown him how to see the relationship between the house and it's setting, he'd sensed a connection. Then later, when she'd interviewed him –if that's what you call it– about his desires and needs, as if she'd seen into his soul, and understood his very essence, even more than he did himself. Her response was to turn a house that barely met his practical needs into one he could hardly wait to transform into a home. More than practical, it shouted and sang out to him to live in it. To live fully. And to love.

And Alexa, he was convinced, had felt something similar at those moments of connection. And yet, despite his sense of harmony and rapport, she had turned cold and hard and pushed him away.

But why?

Had he mistaken her passion for architecture for a romantic interest in him as a man? Was it only his house she cared about? Perhaps she fell in love with every building she designed. Perhaps she was so married to her work, and so fulfilled by it, she had no need of human connection.

But though that was probably partly true, his gut told him otherwise.

She was so insightful and sensitive to others.

So then why pull away?

Because she was in love with that creep Krystof? Bruce didn't want to believe it. There was something else. She had put up a wall, a prickly protective barrier that had always managed to keep him at bay in the past. Not that he'd tried very hard to get past it. His flirtations had always been fun, frivolous, and half-hearted. Mostly he'd been poking fun at her seriousness, her earnestness, her self-conscious posturing. Now that he knew her better, it seemed plain to him that her hard veneer was a sham. A shield to keep people at bay. Or maybe just men. But now, now that he was looking, it was as transparent as glass. And maybe, just maybe, it was as fragile as glass, too. Fragile enough for him to break through.

Preserve his soul, he should get out while he still could.

∼

It turned out Markus's sense of direction was no better than Bruce's. They ambled the aisles for quite a while, until Bruce got his bearings, and was able to finally locate the toy section.

Once he'd found the Playmobile display, he consulted the list and searched and searched for the specified Dressage unit, or failing that, the Horse and Carriage, while Markus squatted on the floor. He could locate neither. He'd have to ask someone. He looked and looked and waited, but no staff person appeared.

"Hey Markus. Stay here for one sec. I'm going over there to get some help. I'll be right back."

Markus, squatting on the floor, was engrossed in a boxed toy with enough exposed parts to keep him busy for several minutes.

"Markus?"

He finally looked up. "O'tay."

"Okay what?"

"Stay."

"Right." Off Bruce went, but when he approached a clerk in a blue vest, he was busy, and he had to venture a little further to find another. He was gone for, he was sure, no more than four minutes.

"We have some additional stock over here," the saleswoman said.

But when he followed her back to the toy aisle, Markus was no longer there.

His heart slammed in his chest, accelerating to an insistent tattoo that hammered in his ears, drowning out ambient noises. With his breath caught in his throat, he whipped his head back and forth, desperate for a glimpse of Markus's familiar flaxen head. Nothing. He dashed around the corner, up and down several more toy aisles.

"Damn!"

"What's wrong?"

No Markus. "My little boy." How could the kid vanish in four minutes? "Markus," he shouted, "Markus!"

Leaving the baffled clerk behind, he dashed out into the main aisle nearly crashing into a mother pushing a stroller, a couple of older kids in her orbit.

"Have you seen a little blond boy?"

She glanced up.

"I'm sorry. Excuse me. Did you see a little blond boy around here? Three years old?"

She appeared disoriented, and looked up and down the aisle.

Bruce shook his head. She was so preoccupied with her own kids, she wouldn't even notice someone else's. "Never mind."

He loped down the main aisle, across the way, wading into a mixed clothing section, children's merging into women's morphing into men's, row upon row, circular rack upon circular rack of blouses, t-shirts and summer shorts. All of them taller than Markus. He'd never find him this way. Damn, damn, damn! He needed more eyes.

Returning to the aisle and down to the row of cashiers, he barged in front of an elderly East Indian woman in a sari, arguing with her daughter or daughter-in-law, about how many packages of paper towelling they needed.

"Excuse me," he said to the clerk. "I've lost a little boy. Is there—"

"You'll have to ask at the customer service desk, sir." The thin-faced man pointed across the acres of store.

"Where?"

He ignored Bruce, scanning items like an automaton, his chicken neck oscillating like a clock pendulum, counting out the hours until quitting time.

"Hey! Where is it?"

The skinny man shook his head, as though he'd already forgotten what Bruce had asked. "Oh. By the other entrance."

Bruce took off, racing diagonally across the store, his pulse pounding in his throat, looking wildly this way and that as he navigated through the aisles, hoping to see Markus. And that image came back. The icy look the day-care teacher gave him when he'd dared to ask, *Why would anyone want someone else's three year old kid?* A snake of terror coiled in his gut, squeezed, shivered. A kind of fear he had never contemplated before. Pushed down. Surely Markus was only misplaced, disoriented. It was easy in a place as huge as this.

At the customer service desk, he had to wait in line for the clerk to deal with several returns and questions before getting his turn. When he'd explained his problem, the stout older woman's lips thinned, and her eyes narrowed at him. He stared at her, waiting. Her wiry hair was pulled back into a ponytail. Mostly steel grey. Her brows were thick and black like a man's, her square face full, deeply creased and jowled. All business.

"I can't tell you how many people lose their kids in the store every day. People never learn. Little kids move around. They wander off. You have to keep your eye on them all the time." Her voice was gravelly, from long-years of smoking. She picked up a telephone from her desk and punched some buttons. "Parents these days," she breathed, leaving her sentence incomplete.

She pulled a pink sheet of paper from a file drawer and set it in front of him, along with a Bic pen with a well-gnawed end. "Fill this in please." Then she turned her back and spoke in a hushed tone to someone on the line, first clearing her throat in a violent rumble.

Bruce loosened his jaw, stretching to release the tension, and squeezed his eyes tightly shut for a moment, swearing under his breath. Markus was somewhere lost in the store, terrified, all alone, or being tossed into some pervert's van in the parking lot, and he was filling in a fucking form. He blew out a shaky breath. "Can we speed this up please? I'm really worried about him."

"Oh. Of course you are, dear." She paused, her smile condescending. "Now."

A freight train of rage hit Bruce, filling his blood with adrenaline, his eyes with blood. His hand slammed down on the counter with a loud whump. Vaguely, he sensed people casting furtive glances their way. "Hey! This is no joke. Who the hell do you think you are? Judging me. You know nothing!"

The woman set down the phone, stood taller, pulling her shoulders back, and lifted her chin. "Do you want my help or not?"

Bruce wanted to spit. He leaned forward, using his size to intimidate. "Do you want me to call the police and tell them you're obstructing the search for a missing toddler?"

She stepped back, withdrew her pompous glare. It was replaced by a sneer of contempt. "It's people like you who spoil things for everyone."

"You should talk!" effing Nazi! He wanted to shake her until her bones rattled.

"For your information, all the department heads have staff searching the store for your little boy. If they don't locate him in ten minutes, I'll broadcast a message while staff search the perimeter of the building." She sniffed. "We do have systems in place for this eventuality, you know. Sir."

He felt a stirring of remorse, but she wasn't being very sympathetic, either. The standoff lasted the remaining four minutes or so, Bruce and the woman glaring at each other in silence. Her phone trilled, and she snatched it up. "Mavis."

Bruce leaned in.

"Uh-huh. Okay." She hung up the phone, her eyes traveling up to his face. "Nothing yet."

Bruce's throat tightened and his eyes burned in frustration and rage. There must be something he could do besides wait here for these incompetent people to muddle through his problem. He needed to take control. He needed… he needed to talk to someone. He needed help. He pulled out his cell phone, touching it to illuminate the time. *Oh my*

God! It was already past twelve. He was supposed to pick up Maddie at twelve-thirty so the mum, whatshername... Joanne, could go out to an appointment. Damn it!

There was no other option. Much as he loathed to contact Alexa after last night, someone had to get Maddie. He touched her number and waited. In truth, there was no one he'd rather talk to.

∼

Alexa kept her distance from Krystof that morning, despite her desire to throw herself back into work with a vengeance. He'd left her condo last night after their aborted date. She arrived at work without knowing if he were here or not. They were accustomed to this, coming together and drifting apart like strangers. It was part of the cover, to keep their affair secret, but it was also an expression of their relationship. Two individuals with common interests, mutual affection, but no spoken commitment. She had never questioned it, in fact, she had defended it as ideal. At least ideal in terms of her goals.

She ignored the slightly bitter taste it left, the sense of hollowness and falseness. Today, it hardly seemed worth the trouble.

The whole team was meeting at the office this morning, to go over design development issues, and review the budget. She didn't relish meeting with Nathan, as he invariably found ways to be unpleasant, to challenge her authority, or insult her, but this was her team, like it or not.

"Hi, hon."

She greeted Peter with a kiss and a brief hug.

"Oh, aren't you sweet. Look at the lovebirds," Nathan said, sauntering out of Krystof's office and passing them.

"Grow up, Nathan," she responded, glaring at him.

"Ooh. Someone's bitchy today."

Peter stuck his head in the door of Krystof's office. "We're starting without you, Krystof." He always found one more thing to deal with at his desk. Something to detain him. She wondered if he didn't like to make an entrance, to even the most casual of meetings.

They sat around the table in the small boardroom, a pot of coffee between them.

"Did you bring the budget analysis?" Alexa asked.

Nathan poured himself a cup and sat down. "Yes and no."

She peered at him. "Meaning what?"

His expression was bland, insipid, arrogant.

She raised her brows. "Well?"

"Well, if you must know, it isn't quite done."

She made a face, shook her head at him. "Nathan?"

"What?"

"You know that's why we're meeting today. We need to know where the numbers are before we lock onto this version of the design. What if we're way over budget?"

"He waved a dismissive hand. "Oh, don't worry. We'll be fine. It's early yet."

"Says you. You know there's no such thing as carte blanche. They always come back squealing."

He shrugged.

She narrowed her gaze at him. "You delegated it, didn't you? Who's been working on it?"

His jaw twitched. "Kim Nguyen and Roger whatshisname. The new guy."

"He's a technician, Nathan. He shouldn't be–"

"He's got tons of experience. Very good with pricing. Used to work for Cobb Brothers."

Contractors. "Anyway, Nathan. You were supposed to be responsible for that yourself. You have to quit seconding staff that've been allocated to other projects. You'll mess up everyone's schedule and budget. Furthermore, you're supposed to be focussing your efforts on the Arts Centre. Have you been spending all your time at the gym? I'll have to speak to Krys about it."

Nathan shrugged.

"Speak to Krys about what?" said Krystof, entering the office at last, coffee mug in hand.

"It's staffing, Krys," she replied, turning to him. "Nathan seems to think he can enlist help anywhere he pleases. He's taken Kim off of Cottonwood Mall revisions to work on the budget for the Arts Centre. He shouldn't–"

"I cleared it with Krystof, actually," said Nathan.

She spun back to Krystof, a question in her eyes.

He cleared his throat. "Yes. He did. Nathan has other work to do."

"Without mentioning it to me?"

They both shrugged, sat down, shuffled papers. "You were busy," Krystof said, as though that were the end of the topic.

Alexa ground her teeth together, her breath quickening with ire. How dare they? Bloody arrogant men! Well, obviously Nathan figured he could get away with it as long as he had Krystof onside. She'd speak privately to Krys later. She pressed her mouth tight and narrowed her eyes at them both.

"Alright. Let's begin with what we have. How do the numbers look on the site work and envelope, so far?" She placed emphasis on the last two words, levelling her gaze at Nathan. Let him crawl out of his own hole.

He passed some papers around for everyone. "Actually I have an agenda typed up that we might want to follow. Before we discuss the constraints of the budget, if there are any, there are some programmatic and thematic changes the client wants that we should consider. It might require some more fundamental changes to the design concept."

"What?" Alexa's stomach tightened and twisted. She was about to challenge him for hijacking the meeting. Who was the project leader, anyway? It was her meeting. But this complaint was superseded by his last comment. "What were you doing speaking with the client?"

Nathan and Krystof exchanged a furtive glance. "I bumped into the Roses at the country club and he wanted to talk about it." Nathan shrugged, but she could sense a gleam of satisfaction in his lazy gaze. "What could I do?"

"Defer to me, obviously."

"Well. Rose *seemed* to want to talk to me specifically. He and Weinstein had some ideas, and he asked me to sketch them up and see if they were feasible."

Alexa shook her head, dumbfounded. "And it never occurred to you to bring this to my attention until now?"

Nathan shrugged again, and Alexa nearly threw herself across the table to wring his neck. "It was late. You haven't been around much lately, so I dealt with it. It was the right thing to do."

"You could have called me, Nathan. The right thing to do is to inform the project architect, and you know it."

Nathan heaved a great melodramatic sigh. "That's still to be determined, as you know."

"It's a technicality, *as you know*."

"Maybe. Maybe not."

If he shrugged again, she'd spit. "Show me what they asked for, and what you've done with it so far." She stuck out her hand, expectant, and Nathan reluctantly passed her his project file, scowling. "This meeting is a waste of time. Krystof? I'd like a word with you in private please." She stood, spun and left the room.

A few minutes later, Alexa's blood pressure had come down a notch, but she was still fuming mad. She'd reviewed Nathan's notes, and his new sketches. Krystof had dismissed the others and joined her in his office, where she sat, one leg crossed over the other, swinging rhythmically.

"Please tell me what the hell is going on here, Krys. It feels like a bloody mutiny, and if it weren't beneath you, I'd say you were in on it."

"Jenner, please. Calm down." He raised both hands, palms toward her. "We have to keep the clients happy."

She continued to stare at him.

"Okay, okay. I admit I've given Nathan some leash."

She waved the file at him. "You can say that again. It's going to his head. This is a virtual re-design and I'm only finding out about it now!"

Krystof blinked. "The clients are being bloody difficult, Jenner. Rose has asked repeatedly for Nathan, and seems to have assumed the little twerp's in charge. I had to keep things moving. I wanted to see what fresh ideas Nathan could come up with. One way or another, we have to please both the donors and the planners at City Hall."

"Everyone was *quite* satisfied with the original design, as I recall. It did win the competition, after all."

"They loved it. But things change. Rose talked to some cronies and they put ideas into his head. You know how it goes."

She pursed her lips. "And we, the experts, should bend over and let them have their way with us, changing our design at their whim."

Krystof said nothing. The corners of his mouth curled up slightly, then dropped. He took two long strides and stood above her, bent over, and took her hands in his. "Come away with me next weekend. We both need a break, Sasha. We haven't had any time alone together lately. You're the only one who can help me unwind." He smiled and his silver eyes heated, filled with invitation. He touched her under her chin. "We'll go to Galiano Island and stay in that nice B & B. Maybe we can look at the design changes. We'll come up with something even better. You know how well we work together."

Alexa's tension eased, and she dropped her eyes to their joined hands. That's the way it used to be. They would go away, talk, sketch, eat, make love, and time would stand still. She sighed. "I can't, Krys. I have too many responsibilities at home right now, with the kids. They need me."

"These kids!" Krystof stood upright, dropping her hands. "I need you. You haven't made any time for me lately. No wonder we are at odds, darling." His face darkened, and he turned away. "I am wondering, Sasha, if you are committed enough to your work to handle the Arts Centre. You've been very distracted."

Alexa shot out of her chair, her heart pounding. "Krystof! How can you say such a thing? You know there is no one more committed to this profession, to this life, and especially to this project than me." That was a dirty shot.

He harrumphed.

He's more concerned about his own needs than the project. He was so different from Bruce, who set aside his own problems to help his friends. He was a team player. He was supportive. Except... of her relationship with Krystof. He might have a point, she conceded.

"Try to understand, Krys. I had no choice but to help my friends with their emergency. And besides, I love these kids like my own."

His expression was incredulous. "You don't want kids. Don't even like them."

"No. I just love my work so much that I'm willing to give up having a family of my own. I *am* devoted to my career Krys. Never doubt–"

She was interrupted by the ringing of her cell phone. She stopped, looked at the screen. Her heart lurched. It was Bruce. She should be annoyed at his interruption, but she felt only a sense of relief. She was reeling from Krystof's cruel words, and her eyes burned with tears. She could only glare at him while she picked up the call.

"Alexa Jenner."

"Al. It's Bruce." He sounded agitated. Yet her lungs filled with warmth at his familiar voice, and she hesitated, gathering her ruffled emotions.

"Oh. Hi."

"Yeah. Listen, I've got a problem here. I'm at Wal-Mart and Markus has wandered off. We're searching for him, but I can't leave the store."

Alexa's pulse slammed into her throat, her breath catching. "What?" Oh my God, Markus was gone? "How long has he been missing?"

Bruce sighed heavily. "I dunno. Probably half an hour now?"

"Shit Bruce! Shit. Shit. Shit. How could…?" She almost ripped into him for his idiocy, but stopped herself. It could happen to anyone. She knew it.

"I'm not leaving this store without him, Alexa, if I have to stay all night. I swear I didn't turn my back on him, he just– vanished." His voice broke.

He sounded beside himself with anguish, on the verge of tears. She sighed, dropping her voice to a whisper, conscious of Krystof standing nearby, listening to the entire exchange with a disapproving frown. "Okay, I understand. It'll be okay. Don't panic. Take a deep breath. What can I do to help?"

Bruce expelled a long breath. He asked her to retrieve Maddie from her play date at her friend's house. Time was of the essence.

"Ella's the one that lives on Maple? Near Sixteenth?"

"Yeah. That one, the blue house."

"I'm on it. Keep me informed." She didn't hang up right away. She wanted to reach through the line and give him a big hug. To let him know it would be okay. But, she didn't know. Would it?

She hung up. "I'm sorry, we'll have to talk about this later. I have to go. It's an emergency." She avoided meeting Krystof's eye as she left the room.

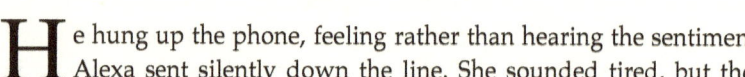

He hung up the phone, feeling rather than hearing the sentiments Alexa sent silently down the line. She sounded tired, but they were in this together.

"Are you finished?"

He sent the clerk a quizzical glance, his lip curling.

She picked up her telephone again and held it upside down to her mouth, like a microphone, then dialled another number.

Her voice echoed in the air around him, shrill and loud.

"*Attention shoppers. A small boy has been lost in the store.*" She glanced at the pink form. "*His name is Markus. He's three years old. He's blond and is wearing khaki shorts and a red t-shirt, with white running shoes. If you see him please bring him to the Customer Service Desk.*" She paused, pursing her lips. Her voice went up a half octave, taking on a simpering mewl. "*Markus, if you can hear this message, please come out and show yourself to*

the nearest person in a blue vest. They will bring you to your... Uncle Bruce."
She hung up.

Bruce scowled at her. "Now what?"

"Now we wait again. They usually come out eventually."

"What do you mean come out?"

She wobbled her head. "Kids hide. They get scared and hide. Or they're playing a game. We teach them how to play hide and seek, and then we wonder why they do it."

"You've got to be kidding. This is normal? And yet you–"

Her smile was far from friendly. "Remember who was responsible for him in the first place, sir."

Bruce's teeth ground together with a shrieking sound that, hopefully only he could hear in the cavern of his skull.

"Maybe we should be calling the police anyway."

"Well. There you go." She said, her face suddenly lighting up, its harsh geometry and deeply shadowed lines softening. "That must be your little fella now."

Bruce spun, following her gaze. Far away, down the main aisle, he could see a blue-vested employee carrying a tiny blond-haired bundle.

Tears rushed to his eyes, his throat constricting painfully. He lunged forward, then dashed across the remaining yards separating him from Markus.

"Markus!"

"Boos!" Markus blubbered through his flushed, tear-streaked face.

"Marky," Bruce sighed, taking him from the employee. "Thank God, you're okay, buddy. Where were you? Where did you go?" He heard his own voice crack.

Bruce held him tightly, burying his face in Markus's soft neck, wiping away the tears that he realized had escaped unbidden. He lifted his face and kissed the boy's soft cheeks again and again, tucking his towhead under his chin, rubbing and patting and squeezing him in relief. Never had he been so happy to see anyone. Never had he adored another creature quite so much. His chest swelled and he nearly lost it again, fresh tears welling in his eyes.

"Thank you," he said to the woman who'd brought Markus back. "Thank you so much," he repeated, returning to the Customer Service clerk. She was gracious enough to simply nod, and turn to her next customer, preserving his dignity.

CHAPTER 14

Ella's mother Joanne wasn't in such a hurry after all, and had time for a coffee and a chat with Alexa when she went to pick up Maddie. Alexa filled her in on the crisis, but played it down, all the while gnawing with tension over Bruce's predicament. She tried not to worry. She'd been in this situation before and it usually resolved itself. She didn't need the whole neighbourhood talking about how incompetent she and Bruce were. How they'd lost Markus. Wouldn't Kate and Simon love to get wind of that.

An hour later Alexa pulled into the driveway at home. The SUV was already there. She chewed her lip. Bruce hadn't called her again, but he was here. Alexa's gut twisted. What did that mean? Had he found Markus?

Maddie jumped out of the car and ran toward the front door. Alexa drew in a breath and quickly followed her, afraid of what she might find. Opening the door, the house seemed quiet and empty, and her heart sank. Maybe Bruce wasn't here after all.

She moved quickly through the house, searching, trying not to alarm Maddie with her concern. The drawings she had left with him were lying on the kitchen table, half furled. They were covered with small yellow sticky notes, scrawled in a dark, slanting hand and... she leaned forward and squinted at them, question marks. Lots of them.

Then she heard them. Giggles and squeals emanating from the back yard. Bruce's deep belly laugh. Releasing her held breath in a long sigh, she inched toward the partially opened French doors to peek out, unseen.

Bruce squatted on the lawn, shirtless, and aimed the garden hose sprayer up into the sky, forming a waterfall. The muscles of his bare, bronzed back gleamed and rippled in the sunlight. Markus, wearing a red t-shirt but no pants, ran and jumped through the cascading water, squealing. A rainbow hung above them in the airborne droplets, not quite touching down on the sparkling green grass. They both laughed, their joy contagious. Alexa found her face stretching into a huge grin of relief, of pure happiness.

Hallelujah, was she happy to see those two guys.

As she was about to step forward and open the door, Markus charged Bruce, knocking him over onto his back, his arms grasping Bruce's neck. The hose bucked and coiled onto the lawn, spurting water into a flowerbed. They rolled, and Bruce's arms came around Markus and held him tightly, so tightly. Bruce kissed his face again and again and again, smoothing back his wet hair. Tears sprang to Alexa's eyes, seeing it. She could imagine how he felt at this moment. She'd been there.

Giving them another moment alone, she went in search of Madison. "Hey Mads! You wanna run through the sprinkler? Maddie?" She ran up the stairs to help her with her suit.

Moments later, Maddie was bursting outside, joining in the fun. Alexa hung back, her arms across her chest, swelling with pleasure. When Bruce saw Maddie, he turned to look at Alexa over his shoulder. Their eyes met for one intense, heartfelt moment. His smile was huge and warm and sincere, and she couldn't help smiling back, her heart swelling with joy.

A little later, the sprinkler fun finished, and the kids wrapped in towels, he approached her. She handed him a beer she'd gotten ready from the fridge.

"Thanks."

"Rough day?" she asked.

"Oh, Al." He shook his head, his Adam's apple sliding up and down, his eyes speaking volumes about the emotional rollercoaster he'd been riding. "I lied. I did leave him. But only for a couple of minutes, but Al..." His voice cracked. She saw his eyes glisten with moisture, and she moved toward him, ready to embrace him. She got no further than laying her hands on his broad bare shoulders, looking up at him, and realized what she was doing. He was warm and cool, slick with water, and smooth and hard. An electric shock of sexual awareness shot through her. She swallowed, dropped her hands and stepped back.

He cleared his throat and took a long pull of his beer. Then he grabbed a crumpled t-shirt from the table and pulled it on over his wet skin.

They sat down at the patio table.

She tried to smile, a trace of awkwardness intruded, and her smile fell. "Tell me what happened. Where was he?"

He explained that, as the customer service clerk had foreseen, Markus had been spooked and had hidden in the centre of a rack of clothing. The longer he stayed there, the more afraid he was to come out. He heard his name being called repeatedly, and feared the consequences. He knew he'd be in trouble. It took a knowledgeable employee to sweep the racks one by one to find him.

"I'm so glad. So relieved. It must have been terrible for you."

He nodded, his eyes closing briefly. Then his head tilted, and he peered closely at her.

"What's up? You stressed? Or is something else bothering you? You seem low."

The events of her own day came flooding back at her, everything still wholly unresolved. She dropped her gaze, sighing. She would have liked nothing better than to pour out all her worries to him. To fall into his arms and feel the warmth and comfort of his strong embrace. To close her eyes and stay there for a long, long time, until everything was right again with her world.

"Al? You okay?"

"I'm fine. Challenges at work."

After a moment of silence, Bruce reached across the table and briefly brushed his fingers across her hand. His dark eyes peered into hers, earnest and kind. "I'm sorry for what I said last night. I have no right to judge you."

Alexa tried to remember what he'd said. He'd been critical of her affair with Krystof. *Why do you do it? How can you take yourself or your career seriously while you let yourself be used by him?*

She expelled a deep breath. "Maybe you were right."

Bruce peered at her, frowning, puzzled. "Sorry. About what?"

She shook her head, dropping the subject. "Did you manage to get the gift in all that chaos?"

He laughed. "Yeah. I almost forgot, but in the end I did. It's wrapped."

"The party's at one tomorrow, right?"

"Yeah. I should get going, I guess." His gaze fell, and he tongued the inside of his cheek, pensive.

"You don't have to leave yet. Stay for dinner with us."

He shrugged, then lifted his face, his eyes popping.

"I forgot in all the madness. Simon texted last night. He and Kate are calling tonight. They want to talk to us *after* the kids are in bed."

She frowned. "That's... weird, isn't it?"

He nodded. "Maybe just travel details for Thursday?"

It was a strange request though. "Why don't you chill and I'll make dinner for us."

Their eyes met and they exchanged a small smile, but it was a warm one, filled with understanding.

After dinner, Alexa joined Bruce and the kids downstairs to watch a movie before bed, since the water play had made evening baths unnecessary. The four of them snuggled up on the sofa together, Markus on Bruce's lap, tucked into his arm, Maddie between him and Alexa, content to be safe at home. In the dim flickering light, she snuck surreptitious glances at Bruce's profile. In repose, it seemed softer than it had been in the past. Or perhaps she'd never seen him with his guard down. Now and then he lowered his face to kiss Markus's hair and give the little boy a squeeze.

Bruce was really quite a good looking man. Completely different from the smooth metro-sexual that Krystof was. Bruce's perpetual five o'clock shadow and manly bulk lent him a slightly dangerous air, which she rather liked. Or was growing used to. She doubted his curling dark hair had ever met a lick of hair gel. He was enormous compared to Kristof's trim tidy physique. Completely different from her own. In fact they were a study in opposites. Next to him, she felt tiny, and almost feminine.

His brow was high and smooth, and his lips exceptionally well formed. She shouldn't be looking at his lips at all, she realized, and tore her eyes away. But not before a subtle smile stretched his face, and not in response to Nemo, she was quite sure. He lifted a hand and rubbed the back of his neck before lowering it and hugging Markus again. Fortunately the darkness hid the flush of heat that bloomed on her cheeks, and she shifted in her seat, tucking her feet under her.

Enough of that. Her mind wandered back to her afternoon at work, and the conversation she didn't quite get to have with Krystof. Everything had happened so quickly, she hadn't time to ponder why he suddenly suggested a weekend design retreat just when she was about to nail him on the slipping parameters of the Arts Centre project. She was about to lash into him for even worse insults when Bruce's call came in, distracting her.

Had Kristof's timing been coincidental? Or had it been strategic, attempting his own distraction from Nathan's encroachment on her turf. Nathan's endorsed encroachment! How dare he redesign her award-winning project without even telling her, never mind involving her. Her agitation, her teeth grinding as she puzzled it out, until she felt Bruce's strong fingers grip the back of her neck and squeeze, firmly but gently.

She glanced up to catch the glint of his eyes, concern evident in his slight frown. He shifted his hand and slowly began to massage her shoulder, and her neck again, until she was forced to let go of her tension and relax. She dropped her head forward to allow him better access, and let herself enjoy his persuasive touch as his fingers dug into the base of her skull, chasing away the stress headache that had been sneaking up on her. He eased up from squeezing to rubbing gently, and then stayed like that until the end of the movie, which came all too soon for Alexa's taste. His hands were magical.

The kids were bustled off to bed, Alexa tucking in Maddie while Bruce had another snuggle with Markus. She came downstairs before him, and poured them a couple of glasses of wine. It was nearly time for their scheduled call from Kate and Simon. Alexa hoped there was nothing wrong. She really needed to turn her attention back to her own life, her project and her job, before things went even further awry.

Soon Bruce was back downstairs and booting up the computer in Simon's den.

Alexa brought in the wine and handed him one, and was treated to a grateful smile. They sipped and sat in silence for several minutes waiting for the call. When it came, they both jumped.

Simon's face appeared on the screen. Blue smudges under his eyes suggested fatigue.

"Simon! Hey man. How you guys doing?" Bruce said.

"Hey Bruce. Hi Alexa. I'm really glad you're both there. I was worried it was too late for you."

Alexa noted that he hadn't answered Bruce's question. Something was off. Something in his voice was triggering a sense of foreboding.

"What's wrong Simon? Where's Kate?" she asked, her hand darting out to grip Bruce's arm.

Bruce shot her a sideways glance. "You okay?"

She shook her head minutely and indicated with her eyes to focus on Simon.

"Kate's right here with me. Don't freak out, Alexa."

"Let me talk to her."

Bruce frowned at her and murmured, "What's up with you?"

She took a deep breath and released it. "Call it women's intuition."

The image on the screen wobbled, blurred and resettled. Kate's pale face came into view. Her hair was mussed. She was obviously reclining in a bed. She was surrounded by white pillows, but it didn't look like any hotel Alexa had ever stayed in. The head of the bed showed wires and tubes against a pale wall.

"Where the *hell* are you?" Alexa heard her voice rise in panic as her pulse accelerated, thumping in her chest and head. "Kate? Where are you?"

"It's okay, Alex. I'm okay. But yes, I'm in hospital. We're in Phuket, so it's okay. A really good hospital. I'm alright."

"What? Hospital? Simon, man. What's happened?"

Alexa's eyes burned with unshed tears, her mouth quivering as the possibilities flooded through her head. "The baby?" she squeaked.

The screen wobbled again and Simon reappeared. "...is okay."

"Diagnosis?" Alexa managed to get out.

"Incompetent cervix," Simon replied, and Alexa felt Bruce's hand cover her own.

"What does that mean?" he whispered.

"Put Kate on? Katie? Symptoms?"

"At first it was just a backache," Kate said. "And mild abdominal cramps. I was very tired. I knew I'd been on my feet too much, but I didn't worry too much."

"Then?"

Kate sighed heavily. "More pelvic pressure. And a very little bit of bleeding. Nothing much, but Simon insisted I come in for some tests."

"Good man, Simon," Bruce mumbled.

Alexa felt her breath shake as the tears she'd tried to suppress forced their way out and down her cheeks. Bruce squeezed her hand, and she felt his other hand come to rest on her lower back and rub in gentle circles.

"So the baby'll be alright, then?" Bruce said.

"I can't believe this is happening," Alexa said.

Simon came back on. "Yeah. The trouble is Kate needs bed rest. They want to keep her here for a few days, under observation. Then, they think the Trans-Pacific flight will be too long, too stressful right away. The cervix will stabilize if she rests. So they're recommending another week or so of bed rest."

"And you can stay there? At your hotel?"

"We have two adjacent rooms. To be honest, my Dad could use a bit longer himself, and Kate can kick back until she's stronger. They'll check the baby again before she comes home."

"What do you mean, before *she* comes home, Simon?" Alexa asked.

A stern expression fell over Simon's face. "Well, we talked it over. I figured I'd head home sooner. We've been away from the kids too long already. Maybe in a week, once Kate's settled at the hotel."

"You can't leave her!" Bruce said, leaning forward.

"Your folks will stay with her?"

"No, they'd come back with me," Simon replied, "So I can help them."

"Then what?"

"Who will be with her then? Who will fly home with her?" Bruce said.

Simon's reply took a moment too long. "Depends. Maybe a... maybe we could hire a nurse or something? The insurance might cover it."

After another awkward silence, Kate took the phone and said, "I'll be fine, guys. Really. It's okay. Simon needs to get home to the kids. You guys need–"

"No, man," Bruce said. He turned to Alexa, his expression fiercely determined. "He's got to stay with her. Right, Al?"

She looked at him. Their gazes locked, and a wealth of information passed wordlessly between them. All the consequences of his words sinking in, filtering through their minds. She nodded slowly in agreement. She couldn't even process what that meant, would mean. But he was right. There was no way Simon should leave Kate behind in freaking Asia to fly home alone after this.

"Right. You're not leaving her, Simon," Alexa replied.

"Aw. I don't know guys." Simon ran a hand through his hair, his gaze cast down. His loyalties were obviously torn. "It's too much. Too much to ask of you. I can't even say for sure how long–"

"Doesn't matter, Simon. And it's not too much. You know we'd do anything for you. We've found our groove here. The kids are fine. They're used to us now. We'll be okay." Bruce squeezed her hand again, his touch reassuring her more than he knew. They were committed to this. And they were in it together. For better or worse.

Bruce ended up staying the night, sleeping on the sofa in the den. After the call ended, they sat up for a long time. At first in silence, processing, and then, Bruce holding her hand to comfort her, talking. Talking about Kate's condition, the risks to the baby, the logistics of the trip. How could one family have such a streak of rotten luck? Then they analyzed their own situation every which way they could.

When the kids got up in the morning, Bruce hushed them and fed them breakfast so Alexa could catch up on her sleep. At some point, they'd have to tell them about Kate's illness, and the extension to the trip. Another two weeks!

When Alexa finally got up, he had coffee waiting and they sat the kids down to explain, as simply as possible, that their parents wouldn't be home on Thursday as planned. The night before, they'd agreed to minimize the amount of delay, and break it to them a little at a time, as if the plans were shifting "a few more days" at a time. Which, in essence they were. But they didn't need the children getting hysterical because the trip was now twice as long.

Maddie cried, though Bruce could tell she tried not to. She seemed to sense that it wouldn't do any of them any good to upset Markus, who really hadn't a clue how much time had passed, or what day it was. They both gave her big hugs.

"You're a good girl, Scallywag. Dad would be proud of you."

Alexa made a big deal out of gift wrapping the toys he'd bought at

Wal-Mart. With the birthday party to go to in the afternoon, there was no point him driving home and back again, so he just hung out at the house. The mood was subdued. To pass the time, he browsed in the cupboards and scanned the contents of the fridge, pulling out a cold beer and cracking the top open. The late night and stress were taking their toll.

He sat down at the table. "Do we need anything from the grocery store?" he asked, hoping to find something to do and score a few brownie points with Alexa at the same time. They were skipping lunch since there would be ton of food at the party, so there wasn't much to do.

"Nothing major," Alexa replied absently, fussing with ribbons and bows. "But don't worry about it today. We've got enough going on." She sighed heavily.

"Are you worried about Kate?"

She nodded, meeting his gaze, and frowning. "I keep wanting to call her, or text, to see how she's feeling, but... really the less we bother them, the better."

"Yeah. That's what I think every time I go to text Simon. Just send them happy news, that's what I tell myself."

"We should take some pictures at the party."

"Good idea. I guess I should put Markus down for a snooze before we go, eh?" He dug the heels of his hands into his burning eye sockets. God he was tired.

"Good idea. Why don't you lie down with him." She smiled and cast him a warm glance from beneath her dropped lashes. "You've earned it."

Bruce tossed back the last of his beer and stood. "Okay, I will."

"I'll wake you up when it's time to get ready to go."

He let his fingers caress her arm as he walked away. He put Markus to bed, then cruised into Maddie's room and flopped down on her bed. An instant later, he slowly surfaced from a deep sleep, strands of images pulling away as he made sense of his surroundings.

"Hey. Wake up."

Bruce felt a hand jostle him, and he mumbled, "Not yet."

"You have to get up. We have to go."

Go? He tried to roll over and go back to sleep. It was the best sleep he'd had in ages, and he fumbled to catch the frayed remnants of a dream. Go where?

"Koczynski!" The hand shook him vigorously.

His eyes shot open. Alexa's green gaze met his, inches from his face. "Hi-ya, beautiful." His voice cracked. Then it came to him. The party. He sat up, scrubbing his face with his hands. "Wow. I slept like the dead." Bruce looked around Maddie's pink and green bedroom, getting his bearings. "Where's Markus?"

"The kids are all ready to go. Get up. It's almost four."

He groaned and stood up. "Man, this is the last thing on earth I feel like doing. Give me a sec. I'll be right down."

When he'd taken a leak and splashed cold water on his face and hair, he jogged down the stairs to find the three of them dressed and ready to go. Alexa had scrubbed and dressed the kids neatly, and she herself looked hot in a sleeveless white shirt, pleated taupe walking shorts that showed off lean tan legs he hadn't seen in years, and sexy flat gladiator sandals. His gaze scanned up and down, admiring her new look. "I have a clean shirt in the truck."

He dashed out, retrieved the shirt and changed in the powder room. "All set."

Alexa eyed him, smiling at his only slightly wrinkled but clean shirt. "You look... nice." She leaned in and narrowed her eyes at his shirt. "What... what are those?"

Bruce followed her gaze to his chest. "Red flyers."

She nodded slowly. "Oh."

He scraped his palm across his two-day beard. "Maybe I should have shaved. These people..."

"Never mind. We're not trying to impress anyone."

"Right. That's why you're dressed like a suburban mom."

She made an indignant face at him. "I beg your–"

He laughed. "I meant that in a good way, Al." He grinned and bent to give her a peck on the cheek. "It's not your usual don't-mess-with-me style." He snapped a quick picture with his phone, chuckling.

"Hmph. I'm trying to look approachable."

He grinned and lowered his lids, twitching one brow at her. "It's working."

She quickly averted her gaze, and he detected a hint of pink on her tan cheeks.

After their flirtatious exchange in the hall, a shy awkward silence descended. Everything they did now seemed to be loaded with the mutual knowledge that they had weeks of this yet to go. Bruce had nothing to say. His mind was too busy swirling with images of shared meals and late night talks. It was a short drive, a dozen blocks to Brittany's house, another little girl that Madison knew from school.

"You remembered the gifts?" he asked.

"Yes. You needn't have bought both, though. They cost too much."

He shrugged.

"And Mads signed the card. Didn't you Maddie?"

"Yup," she confirmed from the back seat.

As they maneuvered into a parking spot a half block from the house, and prepared to get out of the car, Bruce said, "You two be on your best behaviour, okay? Make your Mom and Dad proud."

"Yup."

"And have lots of fun, okay?" added Alexa.

He glanced at her. "Kids don't normally need to be reminded to have fun, eh?"

"You'd be surprised. Kids can get very serious, and get weighed down with worry and stress, just like adults."

He shot her a skeptical –*you've got to be kidding*– look.

Before they reached the gate, the noise level rose exponentially. A clamour of voices filled the air, punctuated by laughter, squeals and shouts. Inside the back yard, pandemonium reigned. Kids ranging from Maddie's age or a bit older down to toddlers younger than Markus ran back and forth madly. Adults clustered near the house, around the patio and barbecue. A few intrepid mothers swarmed amongst the kids, trying to impose some order, but there seemed to be none. As far as Bruce could see, it was a free-for-all.

"What a madhouse!" he said to Alexa over the din.

Maddie and Markus dashed off to join the melée as soon as they were through the gate. They seemed to know everyone and be comfortable in this crowd.

"There must be forty kids here," she ventured, surveying the yard, already strewn with half-eaten hot dogs, paper cups and stray items of clothing. Not to mention streamers and balloons, many of which had been pulled down. "They must be nuts inviting this many."

"Do you recognize anyone?" he asked, scanning the unfamiliar sea of faces.

Alexa peered into the crowd. "Oh. There's Joanne. That'd be a good place to start, since we just had coffee."

They moved in that general direction, smiling at various people along the way, though they were strangers. Bruce, gifts in hand, trailed behind Alexa, who weaved her way between clusters of parents buzzing with conversation. Before they reached Joanne, however, a hand gripped his arm, and he stopped and turned around, expecting to see someone he knew from the school.

Instead, an attractive blond he didn't know zeroed in on him, standing close enough to be heard, her hand lingering on his bare bicep.

"Ooh. Muscular," she said, glancing at her hand and up at his face.

"Erm. Hi, there." He offered her an and-who-might-you-be grin.

"I'm Lizbeth. I've seen you at the school. You're Simon's friend, right?" She cast her appreciative blue gaze up and down his body, making ants crawl up his neck. Cripes! He didn't know what he was expecting from this party, but he sure wasn't expecting women to be checking him out. He glanced at her left hand, to see if she was a married or single mom. At least that would give him some idea what he was dealing with here. No ring. Hmm.

He turned his body toward her, moving a little closer, gazing down her t-shirt appreciatively. "Yeah. That's right. I'm Bruce. Nice to meet you, Lizbeth." He smiled and offered his hand, and she took it, hanging on. She smelled good.

"I hear you had a mishap at Wal-Mart yesterday morning."

He flinched, pulling back. What? "Where did you hear that?" His smile froze on his face like a mask.

"Oh, word travels," she said coyly.

Bruce chilled instantly. "It sure does. Excuse me." He peeled himself away from her possessive proximity and tried to find Alexa and Joanne. They'd shifted position, and he finally saw them, by a picnic table laden with chips, canapés and presents. Aha. He moved in their direction, cringing at the close press of bodies. He wasn't in the mood to mingle with strangers, especially if everyone knew what he'd done yesterday. He deposited the gifts and turned. Alexa's familiar presence called to him like a beacon in the dark, the only place of comfort and warmth in a cold sea.

As he approached them from behind, however, he caught part of their conversation with a third woman.

"–reluctant to leave the kids alone with him, Alexa. I mean, you're responsible too, even if it's him that screws up. How would you feel?"

Bruce hung back, curious to know what Alexa would say. Her

rebuttal was terse.

"That could happen to anyone, Joanne. You can't tell me, with three kids, that you've never misplaced one for a few minutes. I lost my brothers and sisters a dozen times. It doesn't imply neglect."

Bruce's chest swelled with a pleasant warmth.

Joanne sputtered, "Well, I…"

Alexa continued. "I felt so sorry for Bruce. He was more distraught than Markus. You should have seen him afterwards. He was so relieved and glad to see Markus. It's obvious to me he loves him like his own child."

Bruce's stomach clenched at her words. That was true.

"In my opinion, it's good for the kids," said the third woman, a full-figured brunette with large teeth and dangly earrings. Her eye darted to Bruce hovering outside their circle, and away again. "It builds character. They learn to be independent."

"You can't really mean that about a three year old, Barb," said Alexa.

"Or even older kids," said Joanne. "They all need structure and discipline. They don't thrive with too much freedom."

"Oh, here's the man himself," said Barb, as if she'd just noticed him, and hadn't been checking him out. "You're Bruce, aren't you?"

Alexa spun around, her eyes wide.

"Yeah. Hi."

"Barb," said Barb, shaking his hand.

"Tell us your opinion, Bruce. I gather you think kids ought to be given a long leash." Joanne took a step back to make room for him.

He moved into the gap, and a tall bald guy in a Hawaiian shirt handed him a cold can of beer.

"Thanks." He turned, but the guy had vanished into the throng. He opened the beer with a pop and a satisfying hiss, taking a moment to process the loaded question and figure out what he would say. What he believed. "I guess I agree with both of you, a little. I take the middle ground." He tipped up his can and took a sip of beer.

"But look at them," Barb gestured at the wild swarm of children scampering around in the back yard, engaged in no organized activities that Bruce could discern.

He shook his head. "I grew up with no structure, and total freedom, as did my older brothers, and I can't say that was a good thing." He glanced at Barb, and then at Joanne, one hand out in supplication.

"Sure they need room to explore, but they also need security. They need to know you're there when they need you. Otherwise…" he shook his head. He dropped his eyes to the lawn. Otherwise they suffer unspeakable heartache and they're bloody insecure.

"But too much structure and control is no good either," said Alexa to Joanne with a glance at Bruce, her sea green eyes warm with empathy. "My life growing up was so regimented, and my parents' expectations of me were unreasonable. That doesn't give kids the opportunity to figure out who they are, and the freedom to be what they want to be."

Curious, Bruce searched her face. Interesting. Their experiences were so different. Is that why she fought so hard to do what she wanted? Why she took herself and her work so seriously? Was it won at a great price? "You did alright."

Joanne frowned. "I don't know, Alexa. I don't believe kids are capable of making sound decisions without guidance."

"Don't be too sure. You can't box them in, and you sure can't force them to be what they don't want to be."

Bruce turned to Alexa, tilting his head. He recalled old man Jorgen's cryptic advice. "Kids are happier with adult role models. Someone to show them… hmm, I don't know, how to be competent, confident and kind, for example, and then be there while they have the space to make their own decisions, and also to be there when they make their inevitable mistakes?"

Alexa gazed at him for a long moment. "You make a persuasive argument, Koz." Her warm smile radiated up at him like the sun. "I actually agree with you."

He laughed at the irony and turned his head to include Joanne and Barb in their discussion, only to find that they had both vanished into the crowd. He turned back to Alexa, laughing, and their eyes met in understanding. If they weren't in the middle of a huge crowd, he would have leaned in for a kiss just then.

Gazing around, he located Joanne scolding and chasing after Ella and a couple of other girls who were squealing and running around in circles, nearly knocking people over in their hysteria.

"Jesus this place is a zoo." He looked at Alexa again. "Someone should organize some games or something."

"Yes, they should." She paused with a challenging –why-don't-you-do-it?– smile.

He opened his mouth to protest, to splutter the response that sat at the tip of his tongue, that it wasn't his job, that he had no experience, that someone else could do it. But the words fell flat before they were spoken. Why didn't he?

"Okay. I will," as if she had spoken her challenge aloud. He waded into the throng, found Maddie and a group of her closest friends, including the birthday girl, Brittany, and squatted down to propose a game of Freeze Tag. With their help, he managed to get a dozen or so kids involved, and as the game progressed, as he suspected, more and more kids came over to find out what they were doing that was so much fun. Freeze tag having some limitations, it was soon over, but he now had the attention of most of the kids.

Next he suggested a game of Manhunt. Some of the kids were familiar with it, and the usual hopelessly disorganized discussion ensued as everyone tried to explain the rules to everyone else, with very limited success. A couple of dads got involved, and at least one mother got dragged into it. Even the most experienced players disagreed on the fundamentals. Nevertheless, a game ensued, took up the entire back, side and front yards, and lasted quite some time, with much fun had by all. The younger kids, like Markus and his contemporaries, hadn't a clue, but ran around in circles pretending to be involved in the purposeful pandemonium.

Eventually, the kids became winded and losing interest, and it seemed it was time for Brittany's birthday cake and gifts. He rounded up the kids and herded them toward the back patio, where Barb and a couple of other adults were setting out paper plates and plastic forks. She caught his eye as he settled the kids down, and made an approving face. He nodded in acknowledgement. Barb's husband, the thin-haired guy who had given Bruce a beer, and whose name he still didn't know, emerged with a huge birthday cake topped by prancing plastic ponies and a wax '7', leading them all in song.

Once Bruce had scored a couple of pieces of cake, he slipped to the fringe of the crowd, and sure enough, soon spotted Alexa loitering there, under the shade of a chestnut tree by the fence.

He handed her a piece of cake, and she smiled at him with thinly veiled admiration and –was it his imagination?– possessiveness.

"Thanks." They stood side by side, silently eating cake for a few minutes, before she finally spoke. "Well. As you can see. I'm speechless."

"What?"

"You're amazing! Your unsupervised childhood left you with some awesome skills. I didn't really expect you to organize games. But I have to say I've never seen anything more impressive. I underestimated you. Look."

She flicked through her phone, showing him the pictures she'd taken of his games with the kids. They were pretty funny.

"You really are Mr. Fun and Games. All that wasted creativity and talent."

He frowned and then smiled, puzzled. "What makes you think it's been wasted?"

Alexa's lips thinned and she chewed cake for a few more minutes before answering. "I always felt that you, well... lacked initiative, for one thing. And furthermore that you lacked organizational and social skills. Now I see how wrong I was."

He laughed out loud. "Honestly, Al. There's a lot you don't know about me."

"Like?"

He shrugged. "Well, for instance. How do you suppose I ran my own software design company for eight years, and sold it for fifteen million dollars?"

She raised her eyebrows, obviously shocked by the number. "I guess... you got lucky with the dot com craze?"

He laughed. "I did. But you can't get lucky if you're not in the right place at the right time, with the right product."

She nodded, acknowledging his point.

"Oh, by the way. I looked over those drawings you did for me."

"And?"

"Well. I like what you did. I had some questions."

Alexa raised her eyebrows, waiting.

Bruce pursed his lips and shook his head. "Ah. Little things. I don't remember without looking at them. But I wanted to tell you that I like what you did. I don't need more significant changes, and you seem to have made everything work without knocking many walls down."

She laughed. "Well, that is the general idea with a heritage project, you know."

"Maybe so. I guess I'm impressed at how well you incorporated the things we talked about. It takes a lot of insight and sensitivity, things that I guess I didn't realize were part of the job."

"You mean traits you thought I lacked."

He laughed, his dark eyes scanning her face, and he reached up and tucked a wild wisp of hair behind her ear, gently grazing her with his fingertip. She shuddered and he smiled, pleased that she was no longer immune to his advances.

A flush of pink stole up Alexa's cheeks, and her eyes darted away, monitoring the activities of the crowd. She scooped a forkful of cake into her mouth, even though she looked as though she wasn't really enjoying it. "It wasn't hard. We've been given such a great house. And you gave me pretty clear directions. Some clients think they know what they want, give all kinds of contradictory instructions, don't understand my feedback, can't read plans, or are daft..." her voice tapered off, and their eyes met with a twinkle of amusement.

"Well, how long before I can work on it?"

She tilted her head. "That depends on what all those little sticky notes are about." Her grin was warm and generous, and Bruce was caught once again by her beautiful smile, her full lips and gleaming white teeth.

"We should try to find a time to go back to your house and go over the finer points. I can make the revisions to the drawings quickly and submit them for you. It should take no more than a couple of weeks for the application to be processed."

"Excellent news." He cleared his throat. "And perfect timing."

They were standing close together, and had finished their cake. He took her empty plate and fork from her hands, and reached to wipe a tiny smear of icing from her lip with his fingertip. Instead of bending to kiss her, which he was sorely tempted to do, he simply licked his own lips, and smiled and winked.

She dropped her eyes to the lawn.

"Hey, you lovebirds. Come and watch Brittany open her gifts," said Joanne, passing by.

Both of their heads shot up, startled.

Bruce's pulse quickened. Lovebirds! Is that how they appeared? Wait until Simon and Kate got wind of it. He'd never hear the end of it. The way rumours travelled through this crowd, it was inevitable.

Too bad it wasn't true.

"Let's go. I'm about ready to grab the kids and say *sayonara*. What do you say?"

They walked side by side toward the patio. "Absolutely," she agreed.

It was a shame that his getting closer to Alexa wasn't as sure a thing. His heart pressed, and his chest tightened. Bruce wished he knew how serious Alexa was about her boss. She seemed low yesterday, before the video call threw a wrench into their lives. She'd been really fretting about something during the movie. If she were in love with him, or even if she weren't, her taste in lovers obviously didn't run to scruffy unemployed computer geeks living on sailboats, his millions notwithstanding. It was a shame. He was beginning to believe they could have something rather good together, even if it wasn't forever.

~

Bruce, carrying Markus who was already sleepy from all the exercise and excitement, followed Alexa into the house, pondering the party. They'd connected again. And he felt himself wanting more time with her. It was a new experience for him, to feel such powerful attraction and not to act on it. This was different. More complicated.

"They don't need dinner. Just a bath and early to bed," said Alexa.

"You want a hand?"

"Sure. Why don't you run the water, and I'll strip them."

They all trooped upstairs and soon the kids were up to their chins in bubbles. A lot of bubbles.

Alexa walked in. "How much bubble bath did you use?" She laughed, meeting his gaze, amusement sparkling there in her green eyes.

He screwed up his face, feigning chagrin. "Too much?" Then he winked at Maddie.

"I love it!" said Maddie, piling a crown of suds on top of her head.

Markus could hardly be seen. He was buried in a cloud of suds over his head, giggling hysterically.

Alexa shook her head. "You kids. You mind supervising while I throw their clothes in the wash?"

"No problem." He grinned and planted himself on the toilet seat. Things had sure improved since the last time he sat here. He and Alexa were getting along better than ever. Which was fortunate, since this had turned into an open-ended deal. She seemed quite open to his advances, tentative though they were. He was still a little afraid of her. But then, there were too many unanswered questions about that Krystof dude.

Alexa gave the kids a bedtime snack of milk and bread and butter, and tucked them in. "They're exhausted. Kiss them goodnight and come downstairs. I'll fix us something to eat that isn't a hot dog."

Bruce saw that Madison was quietly leafing through a book, and went to Markus first. "Well, my little friend. We had quite a busy couple of days, didn't we?"

Markus lifted up his chubby arms. "Boos."

Bruce perched on the edge of his bed and bent to kiss his downy forehead, closing his eyes, refusing to contemplate what might have been yesterday. He thanked his lucky stars. He thanked God. He thanked Simon's Hindu deities with the thousand eyes who adorned the wall-hangings in their den.

"Lie down wif me, Boos."

Bruce shifted his weight, carefully wedged himself in beside Markus on the narrow bed, and draped an arm across his tiny, warm body, snuggling him close. The two of them had forged a special bond. Alexa's words at the party echoed in his head. *It's obvious to me he loves him like his own child.*

"Good night, Markus."

"G'night, Boos." Markus sighed and closed his eyes.

The glow of weak light from the hallway illuminated the blue-tinged translucent skin of Markus's eyelids, the soft, angel hairs of his brow. Bruce caressed his smooth, round forehead rhythmically, wondering who he was soothing.

"I wuv you, Boos," mumbled Markus.

Bruce's throat tightened and his eyes burned with a sudden intensity of feeling. "I love you, too, Markus." It wasn't hard to say it. Not when you meant it with all your heart. Closing his eyes, he imagined another kind of life, one that was more like this, every day. He had an inkling of a profound depth that more than compensated for the breadth of his current freedom. A nano-second later, his eyes shot open and he gasped, awakening from brief and deep sleep, and recalled where he was. Markus slept soundly. He slowly extracted himself from Markus's bed and tiptoed to Maddie's room. She slept, propped up on her pillow, the book tipped over in her slack hands, Lucy curled, as always, by her side.

He put the book away, stroked the cat, shifted Maddie down and bent to kiss her goodnight. She murmured and stirred slightly, rolling over, but didn't wake. Lucy resettled and tucked her head down.

Downstairs, Alexa moved gracefully in the dim light of the kitchen. She'd set two places at the island. "Hi. Everyone down?"

"Yeah." He stifled a yawn. "Including me."

Her eyes lit up and crinkled as she sized him up. "I've made a salad, and reheated some pasta from last night."

He perched on a stool. "Sounds perfect." A bottle of red wine stood waiting, with an empty glass for him. He was more of a beer drinker, but he'd been enjoying the wine Alexa shared with him lately. He poured it and took a sip. The warm, rich cabernet tasted like nectar on his sleepy tongue. He rolled it around, savouring the tart woody flavour. "Mmm. Did I ever need this." He took another large gulp.

Alexa brought her glass to the table and sat, setting salads in front of them both. "Dig in. You look like you're not going to last long."

"Thanks."

They ate in silence for several minutes, Bruce enjoying the crisp textures and tangy vinaigrette on the mixed salad she'd prepared. She stood up to get some bread buns from the oven, and laid a plate of pasta in front of him. He sighed, feeling supremely well-cared-for and comfortable. He lifted his glass.

"To a satisfying end to a long and trying couple of days." Their gazes met for a long moment. And to… connection.

"I'll drink to that," said Alexa. They clinked glasses, sipped wine and resumed eating.

"Hear from Kate today?" he asked.

She shook her head no. "They've got enough on their minds, I guess."

After a few more minutes of companionable silence, Bruce said, "I've been rehashing something you said this afternoon."

"Mmm?"

"At the party. You said your parents had unreasonable expectations of you growing up. The word you used was regimented. Will you tell me about it?"

She stopped chewing and gazed down at her plate for several long minutes before looking up, meeting his eye and speaking. "My parents are very loving. And very hard-working. But also very traditional.

Around *our* house, roles were always very clearly defined. There were pink jobs and blue jobs, you know?"

He nodded. It was the way he grew up until Mom left. After that, there were no rules. And not much housework got done either.

Alexa sipped her wine and continued. "From about the age of nine, I was systematically taught to cook, bake, clean house, do laundry, sew and take care of my younger siblings. Like I had any choice with Mom working two jobs after Dad's accident. Even with his pension there was never enough money, or time."

"That's rough for a kid, wow."

"My brothers, thank goodness there were three older ones, did all the manly jobs. My sisters and I, all the housework. And since I was the eldest, I ran the whole show while Mom worked, including practically be a mother to little Owen. We were a very efficient tag team, Mom and I. All of us really. We were like an army."

"And your Mom wanted you to give her a dozen grandchildren?"

Her eyebrows shot up. "Not at all! Quite the opposite."

"What do you mean?"

"She was overwhelmed, and though it was far too late, wished she hadn't had seven kids. I mean, no one expects their husband to be suddenly taken out of the equation when there's a houseful of children." She shook her head.

He sensed from her expression how sorry she felt for her poor parents and their lost dreams. No wonder she was so nurturing and empathetic, and at the same time, ambitious for herself. She'd grown up caring for her parents as well as her siblings.

But who had ever taken care of her?

"She wanted a different life for me." Alexa snickered. "She hasn't a clue what I do, but she's proud of me, and happy that I've pursued my career."

"You obviously like kids, though."

She smiled. "Sure I like them. But they are, as you now know, a lot of work."

"There's still time to change your mind," he said, and laughed when she swatted him with her serviette. He smiled sympathetically.

Her story got more and more complicated the better he got to know her. He'd certainly underestimated the degree of her determination and commitment to her career. It was starting to make sense now. "I'm sorry you had such a rough childhood. That must have really sucked with the schoolwork. And I guess you didn't have much of a social life as a teenager." In a way, they'd both grown up alone, and, in many ways, abandoned.

"Yeah. None. And schoolwork… well there's always a bit of time after the kids are asleep. I got by."

"Not much time for yourself. Or appreciation for your intelligence and talents. You really are talented."

She smiled. Her mouth pulled tighter, and she gazed into his eyes. "But look at me now."

"Look at you now. Did you ever want it to be different? That with the right partner, you could have it all? Your career *and* a family?"

She made a face. "Yeah. No. Not really. Didn't seem possible. Men do it all the time. Easy for them. But someone has to make the sacrifice." Her sultry voice was low and marked with melancholy, and his heart ached for her.

He shrugged, picked up his glass of wine and tossed the rest down. "It doesn't have to be a sacrifice, if that's what they want to do." Alexa refilled his glass, and he drank again.

"Who's they, in your scenario?"

He lifted a shoulder. It wasn't such a crazy idea, that a man might want to have a quiet life, and devote his time and attention to raising his kids, supporting his wife, was it? Maybe do a little creative work from home? It sounded kind of nice, to him. "Are you sure you're not still trying to compensate for lost time, instead of going after what you really want?"

Her jaw dropped in feigned shock. "Why you nervy bugger. How would you like me to psychoanalyze you?"

He laughed. "Okay, I deserve that. Shoot."

"Alright. How is it that you grew up with total freedom?"

He grunted. "The correct term would be neglect."

"You had both parents?"

"Yes and no. I was close to my mom when I was small, but she… left." Bruce's chest tightened, and he sucked on his lower lip. He blinked and shifted his eyes away from hers, to the window, the stove, his wine glass. "I was eight. Not quite eight." He took a long swig of wine, and swirled it around in his mouth, remembering.

Alexa watched him in silence, waiting, a tiny frown line between her dark brows discernible above her glasses.

"That's it. End of story. She was gone. I never really understood why or where. I didn't see her until... until it didn't matter anymore."

Alexa inhaled and reached across to take his hand.

He laughed, but it felt forced, and he knew that didn't work on her anyway. "And my Dad, who is an asshole, by the way, he had an interesting hands-off approach to parenting. My three older brothers were more tormentors than protectors. I basically raised myself from that point. I learned to survive." He shrugged and met her eyes, grinning. "I turned out pretty good, don't you think?"

"It's a miracle you didn't join a gang or become a drug addict."

"I came close, believe me. But strangely computing science had greater appeal. It was still a rebellious thing to do in those days." Bruce's tongue thickened. It was harder to form words, and yet easier to grasp onto the feelings he was trying to express.

Alexa stood and cleared away the dishes, and Bruce poured more wine into their glasses. He sat drinking and admiring her lithe brown limbs and narrow hips, her tight little ass, while she rinsed and loaded the dishwasher. It was easy to imagine her clothing stripped away, his hands roaming all over that smooth skin. She was so small and light, he could easily lift her. What couldn't they do? A liquid heat seeped through his veins.

"Where's your mom now?" she asked, returning to wipe the countertop.

"Uh." His attention snapped back. "Denman Island, apparently. My brothers have visited, and she comes to town once in a while, which I manage to evade." He swallowed thickly. "They say she wants to see me."

Alexa paused in front of him, a tea towel in one hand, peering intensely into his eyes. Hers were serious and shaded dark, like tree shadows on a pond, deep and unfathomable. She placed a palm gently on his cheek. "That's good, isn't it? You want to see her, don't you?"

Bruce tried to shake his head no, but something short-circuited. Instead he twitched, blinked, nodded slightly. Salt flooded the back of his throat. "I don't know."

"You should. Poor baby."

Blood drained from Bruce's head, and rushed to his groin, as a kind of madness overtook him. He inhaled sharply and pulled her to him by the ribs, kissing her at first tentatively, inhaling her scent of soap and wine and musk, and then covering her mouth with his own, his desire to possess her suddenly so overwhelming he wasn't in control. He plundered her mouth with his probing tongue, questing for– something, some kind of satisfaction, fulfillment of his desperate need.

Her sudden intake of breath against his mouth signalled her shock, and then a sigh, her surrender. She melted against him, and he felt her respond to his demands, her hands sliding into his hair. He felt the heat explode in her, as it did in him. Their mouths fused hungrily, small urgent grunts and moans escaping their throats as their hands roamed, grasped for purchase.

Then suddenly, without warning, she pulled away. Her eyes were large and bewildered, and she dropped her gaze and stepped back. "I'm... sorry."

Huh?

"I... shouldn't have..."

"You... didn't."

She shook her head, her body language stiff and withdrawn. "I felt, momentarily..."

Sorry for him. Something shrank inside him. Some door slammed shut. He felt the deadbolt slide into place. "No, I'm sorry. It was my fault. I didn't mean to make you uncomfortable. I drank a bit too much wine." He smiled lightly, rose and moved toward the door. "S'late. I should get going, eh?"

"I suppose so." She averted her eyes, and stood awkwardly in the middle of the kitchen, arms at her sides.

Bruce took another step toward the door and the room spun. He stumbled and grabbed the doorjamb to catch himself. "Whoa."

"You can't drive home, you fool. You're drunk."

"I'll be fine." He turned to her and wobbled again. He smiled crookedly. "You could take advantage of me, and I wouldn't even mind."

She reached for his arm to steady him. "Don't be ridiculous. You'll have to sleep on the couch again."

He stopped in his tracks, swaying. His head spun dangerously, and he blinked to clear his fuzzy vision. She had a point. He turned, leaning back against the kitchen wall and grinned at her. "Promise not to hurt me, baby." Geez his words sounded slurred and stupid even in his own ears. He must have really sucked back a lot of wine.

Alexa rolled her eyes to the ceiling and went to fetch a couple of blankets and a pillow, and soon Bruce was lying back on the sofa, his breathing slowing, falling into a deep, sheltered sleep.

CHAPTER 15

"You can't keep taking this crap, Alexa." Peter stood with his back to her in the staff lunchroom the following week, stirring his coffee. "What are you doing? You have to stand up for yourself."

"What are you talking about, Pete?"

He turned to face her, his expression sober. "Don't pretend you don't know. This whole Arts Centre project has gone sour on us. This isn't the way it was supposed to be."

"I know, Peter, but it's not settled yet. Krystof's working–"

"You stupid beyotch! Quit making excuses for him. The writing's on the wall. I know why he's penalizing you…" Peter shot a furtive glance toward the hall, and lowered his voice. "It's none of my business what goes on between you two after hours. But I care about you and your career. And this is affecting me, too."

Alexa's blood turned to ice. Her denials died in her throat. But Peter was her friend. The only work colleague she could truly call a friend. "How long have you known?"

Peter gazed at her and expelled a frustrated breath. "Since that trip to Portland." His lips curled up sadly. "You can't hide that kind of chemistry from me, girlfriend."

"Oh, Pete." Alexa sighed. Three and a half years, and he'd never let on, never compromised her secret. "What do you mean, he's penalizing me? Are you serious?"

Peter threw up his hands, and hissed under his breath, "This is precisely why people don't get involved with their bosses, honey. Your house of cards has come crashing down."

Alexa froze. "But... Pete. Are you saying my success is undeserved? You know me better than that. I've worked—"

"I'm not saying you didn't deserve every project, every award, and every promotion you've gotten, honey. Despite discrimination and nepotism, you've always come out ahead. But the line is blurred. Who can say what Krystof thinks?"

She pressed her fingers to her mouth, her eyes stinging. She'd asked herself that question a million times. She could not now say she believed he had the integrity she had always credited him with.

"What should I do?"

"I don't see that you have any choice. It's ultimatum time, Al."

"But what if...?" She couldn't finish the question. They both knew what she feared. But so what? Peter was right. It was her turn to show what she was made of. She'd made her bed, literally, and now she had to lie in it. Now wasn't that ironic?

"Then wherever you go, that's where I'll be, girlfriend. You're a strong, smart, supremely gifted architect, Alex. You're the only reason I put up with Penis-head and Mini-Me. It's your talent and passion that make this job worth doing for me. I'll follow you anywhere." He opened his arms, and tilted his head to one side.

Alexa's eyes burned as she slid into his comforting embrace and held on tight as he rubbed her back.

"Don't cry, honey. It's not over yet. The bastard may come through for you."

Her voice cracked and wavered. "Oh, Pete. I've been such a fool."

"Hey, girlfriend. Love makes fools of us all."

She pulled away and peered at him, confused. "I'm not in love with him, Pete. I'm not sure I ever have been."

Peter wrinkled his nose. "Then what the hell are you doing?"

What indeed?

∼

Late Friday afternoon, Alexa and Krystof were the only one's left in the office. She shut down her computer and put away her files. However this conversation went, she wanted it to be the last thing she would do this week. She couldn't concentrate on work anymore. And she had a feeling she'd need time to herself afterwards.

Krystof sat at his desk, writing. He didn't move when she entered.

"Krys? Got a minute?"

He raised his head, smiled, and set down his pen. "Of course. Of course. Come in."

She stepped in, stopped in front of him, crossed her arms, turned and paced. "I need things settled, Krys. I'm not happy."

He sighed. "I know, Jenner. I have nothing to tell you yet."

The muscles of Alexa's face tensed, and she ground her teeth, trying to stay calm. She faced him, hands on her hips. "Stop lying to me, Krys. I don't know what you said to Weinstein and Rose, but I don't believe you're still trying to sell them on me. I suspect you've made a deal with them and you're stringing me along to keep me working on the project like a patsy."

"Jenner." His face was pained. He stood and came around the corner of his desk. "You are distraught. You must not imagine such things. I would not do this to you. You are my star."

Alexa expelled a rush of air. She recognized the pattern of their conversations. He diffused her concerns and complaints with his soothing compliments and half-truths every time. Playing to her ego. But in the end, he never addressed her concerns at all. "Have I done something to make you angry, Krystof? Have I screwed up somehow? Is that why you've lost confidence in me?"

"Jenner, no! What are you saying?" He strode forward and gripped her shoulders in his strong wiry hands. He tugged gently, trying to pull her into his embrace, but she resisted, turning away, her gaze darting out the windows.

"I'm not stupid, Krys. I know you're using Nathan to placate the clients, and to shield me from them." Her words rang true, and made her breath come quicker. A bloom of sweat rose on her palms and forehead, tingling. She turned toward him, earnest. "It's ridiculous! I won't slave away in the back room. I want to meet with them myself. You have to set up a meeting. Let me talk to them. I know I can persuade them to work directly with me. Surely to God they know I'm running the job behind the scenes anyway. Isn't it logical that a direct line of communication is best?"

Krystof pulled back. He withdrew, his silvery eyes cooler than before, and she felt a corresponding shiver. "You have to let me manage the client relationship, Jenner. The more I push, the worse it gets. You have no idea."

"If you didn't hold me back, I would know. Why are they making unnecessary changes? I've gone over Nathan's notes. It doesn't even make sense. I can talk them out of it. Explain what we need to do. Why is Rose talking to Nathan about changes anyway? Who told him to do that?"

"No one told him. He's being a stubborn old bastard. Thinks he can do as he pleases with consultants. It's always the way."

"No it's not. I've had plenty of great clients who respect me. This is bullshit. It's this old, old boys…" She stiffened her arms, pressing tight fists down at the floor, her blood racing. "It's *my* project, Krys. I'm the only one that truly understands it. The vision I'm trying to achieve. I need to be informed and in control or I can't do my job. And I need credit for my work."

Krystof dropped his chin, smiling and peering at her under his overly groomed brows. His voice was low and seductive. "This pains me. Let's not argue, Jenner. I don't want to fight with you. I only want to love you, darling."

She immediately felt herself soften under his gaze. His smooth charm and sex appeal always affected her. And yet she sensed a hint of condescension in his manner. He was playing her, like he always did. She kept herself detached, objective, and questioned her motives. Why did she always give in to him? Why didn't she challenge him more?

He moved toward her, his smile flashing wider.

She'd been blind and weak when it came to Krystof, seeing what she wanted to see. It was such a thrill to work with him when she first joined the firm. The great Krystof Konstantin. And he saw her talent and nurtured it. He'd stroked her ego. She imagined herself becoming like him one day, a celebrated architect who garnered the respect and adulation of everyone in the business. Someone whose clients looked up to him like a demigod. Someone who was recognized in the press and with industry awards. Someone with power and influence. That's what she wanted.

And he knew it.

His long, elegant hands came up to cup her face, pushing back her hair. His sultry silver gaze pierced hers. Her blood quickened at his touch. She resisted.

He was a good mentor. He was a good colleague. But why she'd made him her lover, she couldn't remember. She must have had stars in her eyes. Or she was more naïve than she'd imagined. Every caution and admonition of Kate's over the years echoed in her mind, along with her indignant replies.

"Krystof."

"Jenner." He pulled her face toward his, his mouth opening, ready to possess her and sway her to his will.

"Krystof." A little more resolute. She placed her hands on his shoulders and pushed him firmly away.

His neat brows came together in question, one vertical line dividing his forehead. "Jenner?"

"I need some distance."

He laughed and held her at arms length. "How much distance?"

She frowned. He never really paid much attention to how she was feeling. But in her blind devotion she hadn't noticed or cared. He was Krystof. Like everyone else, she'd been thrilled to be in his company. Except she was special. She was the chosen one. Huh.

She pulled back, walking to the other side of the room and turned to peer at him, crossing her arms, studying him, as though seeing him for the first time. "Things have to change between us, Krys. I want our relationship to be professional only."

"What?"

"I don't know why I didn't see it before, but our involvement is not good for my career. And you know there is nothing more important to me. I have to put that first."

"Your career is in no danger, darling." He laughed, a shallow, tinny sound.

Alexa pursed her lips. "I'm not so sure." She sighed. "Our affair has run it's natural course, Krys. It's over. It's a distraction for both of us. It's getting in the way of our working together."

He scowled. "No, no. It is not. This is what always allowed us to work so closely. To understand each other."

"I *thought* we had an understanding, but I see now that I projected my own ideas and ideals onto you and our relationship." In fact, he probably knew that, and had used it to manipulate her. She shook her head slowly from side to side. "Your judgment as principal is coloured by our involvement. You're not making objective decisions anymore. About me, anyway. It's too complicated, and it puts you in a position of conflict."

Krystof stiffened, stood with his legs apart. "My judgment is not affected. I am perfectly objective about my business, Alexa." He reached up and straightened and smoothed his tie, tweaking his cuffs, like a boxer warming up for a match. She could feel his anger building. A rare thing. He was typically so calm, so reserved. Totally in control.

Alexa suddenly felt quite melancholy. Sad for him. Sad for herself, sad that they had wasted so many years lying to themselves. "If it's worth the trouble, Krys, then it should affect you. If it doesn't, then it's a waste of time. It's cheap and superficial. And that puts me in a position of conflict because I question my own motives." She sniffed and squeezed her eyes shut, holding back the tears that burned her eyelids, threatening to undo her. Her throat convulsed. "I hate that. I don't want to second-guess you or myself anymore. I'm tired of lies."

Krystof took two long strides toward her and grabbed her again. "Jenner. Don't do this. I still want you. How can I work with you and not have you? I love you." His mouth covered hers in an urgent and hungry kiss, hard and demanding, bruising her lips.

She pushed hard on his chest, moaning but unable to utter her protest against his passion. How could she trust him? She didn't trust him.

Finally she broke free of his embrace, her eyes locked on his, resolute and miserable. "No. We have to stop seeing each other this way. Out of the office. Completely. It's the only way." She stormed out the door, grabbing her bag as she passed her desk, and hurried down to her car without looking back.

How she drove home, she wasn't sure. By rote. She had no memory of the streets or intersections, but suddenly there she was, sitting in her car in the driveway. Only then did she allow herself to feel the torrent of raging emotions that had swirled in her head and in her chest since Krystof's office. Burning hot tears welled up and spilled over, and she put her head down on her hands, across the steering wheel of her car, and let them flow. Sobs escaped her, and her nose ran.

A tap on the driver's side window made her jump, and she glanced out, then quickly whipped her head away, hiding her tears. Bruce stood there beside her car in a running tank and shorts, his longish curling hair hanging in damp shiny ringlets. He knocked on the glass again, harder.

She sniffed and swiped the heels of her hands against her wet cheeks, dabbed under her leaking eyes. Then she dared to look at him, and lowered the window a couple of inches.

"Al? You alright?"

Her mouth buckled as she tried to hold back more tears. "Do I look alright?"

Bruce opened the door wide and reached in, grabbing her arm and hauling her out. He folded her into his strong embrace and held her tight. "Sshhh, baby. It'll be all right. Shhh."

She wrapped her arms around his waist and held on, letting the tears flow, letting the sobs and convulsions run their course. Finally she calmed, and could breath again without gasping for air or shuddering. She lifted her head. His shirt was smeared with her mascara, and she rubbed at it with no affect.

"Tell me what happened."

She shook her head, unable to speak. Finally she managed, "I broke it off with Krys."

Bruce's breath caught, then he expelled a huge slow sigh. "I'm glad, Al. You don't need him. He wasn't good for you. He wasn't what you need."

"I don't know what I'm doing anymore. I don't know what I want or need." Her voice broke, and he gathered her into his embrace again, holding her, saying nothing.

Then she felt a stiffness rising in his groin, pushing against her. Her own breath stopped for a heartbeat. She swallowed. Then some of the tension eased, and a warm current of heat flowed through her own veins in response to his obvious arousal. She lifted her face to peer at him, and he looked down at her, his kind face gentle and full of concern, his dark brown eyes shadowed with desire. Then she couldn't help herself. She reached her hands up to his neck and pulled his face down towards hers, opening her mouth and pressing it against his. His hands lifted off of her back in shock, and then settled back down, pulling her closer against his erection with a growl.

A rush of primal heat flooded through her core from her scalp to her toes, consuming her, overtaking her judgment. She wanted him. Desperately and immediately. She kissed him again, and this time he kissed her back, their mouths fusing, their teeth clashing and their tongues duelling with the sudden urgency of their mutual desire.

Bruce's embrace tightened, lifting her off the ground, and she pressed her aching need against his hardness, clawing at him. One leg wrapped around his in her desperate drive to merge with him, to become one flesh. One of his hands dropped to cup her rear, lifting her against him. She heard herself moan, gulped air and went in for another deep kiss.

But he pulled away suddenly, his dark eyes piercing hers, searching. "Jesus." His nostrils flared, and his breath came in ragged gasps. "No, Al. Not like this." He peeled her off of him, holding her wrists out. He pushed her away. "Al, stop. We're on the street for God's sake. The kids are in the house. Stop!"

His sharp voice penetrated the fog of her animal need. She stepped back, shrinking into herself. She was breathing heavily through her open mouth, her lips swollen and throbbing from their kisses. Her heart raced wildly, but she knew he was right, of course. She'd gone mad.

His voice was deep and hoarse. "God knows, I want you, Alexa. But, I can't– we can't. You need time. I don't want you like this. I don't want you to do something you'll regret."

CHAPTER 16

Bruce carried the grocery bags from his truck and snuck around the side of the house to the back yard the following afternoon. He used his key to enter by the patio door, and set the bags on the kitchen counter.

He'd sat in his truck, a block away waiting for over an hour. Bruce didn't know for sure, but hoped that Alexa would take the kids out at some point in the afternoon, to go shopping or for a little exercise. That would make the surprise all the better.

Bruce had lain awake half the previous night reliving that fevered kiss in the driveway. Not a hundred percent sure she would be home after work, since it was Friday, he'd been surprised to hear her car drive up fairly early. When she didn't come in, he'd gone outside to see if Alexa was alright, discovered that she was anything but, and ended up with the shock of his life. She was like a wildcat, uninhibited and ardent. He'd nearly exploded in an ecstasy of delight. Until he'd pulled back to look in her eyes.

They'd been hooded, veiled, shuttered and fogged with grief and desperation, an impenetrable deep green-black like polished malachite pebbles. And he knew, even though this was what he wanted from her, it wasn't right. She wasn't choosing him with a clear mind and a calm heart.

He wanted her to want him, but not that way. If he'd taken advantage of her vulnerable emotional state, not only would she likely regret it and withdraw before they'd gotten very far, but he would never know if it had been a true choice. He didn't want that.

Instead, he'd tossed in his berth, remembering the sensation of her hungry mouth plundering his, her clutching grasp, her leg wrapped around him, pressing her heat into his erection, and he'd suffered. He'd suffered until, hand on his throbbing cock, he'd given himself release. But before he'd finally fallen asleep, he'd come up with a plan. He'd change her emotional state. He'd give her reasons to celebrate her freedom. He'd give her reasons to want him and come to him with a clear head. He'd give her another opportunity. One neither of them would regret.

Having put his plan into action, therefore, it was with a sigh of relief that he'd finally seen them emerge from the garage with bicycles. They turned, fortunately, in the opposite direction and woven off down the sidewalk, their pink and orange helmets bobbing. He suspected they were going to the neighbourhood park. That meant he hadn't a great deal of time to prepare.

Rolling up his sleeves, he washed his hands and got to work.

Over an hour later, he heard noises outside the front door. Thuds and muffled voices. His skin prickled with anticipation, and a lump of tension sat in his gut like a lead fishing weight.

Now that the moment had come, he hung back in the kitchen, waiting for them to park the bicycles and get in the door, unsure of his reception. A burst of louder voices and the sounds of the kids' feet scampering upstairs met his ears.

The next moment, Alexa stood in the doorway with her mouth frozen in an O, her hands at her sides. "Bruce?"

His heart pounded. "Hi?"

Her dark brows pinched over her green eyes, darting around curiously. "What... what are you doing here?"

"Um. It's a surprise. I went shopping."

Her head tilted to one side, and her full mouth pulled into an amused but cautious smile. "Why?"

He dipped his head, stood a little taller, and gave her a lopsided grin. "I'm going to make dinner."

She blinked rapidly, naturally skeptical. "You mean, you brought gourmet food from your secret source?"

He swallowed. Well. Here he was. Nothing to lose, now. "Nooo. I'm going to cook from scratch." Well, mostly. "Myself. But first," he raised a finger. "I have an afternoon treat. You've been to the park?"

She nodded.

"Excellent! Get the kids. Wash your hands." He rubbed his hands together.

She squinched up her face as she ducked back into the hall. "Ooo-kay."

He took out the new parfait dishes he'd bought and set them on the counter, pulled the multiple small tubs of ice cream from the freezer, and peeled bananas. Moments later, the three of them tumbled into the kitchen together.

"Boos!" Markus ran to him and hugged his legs.

"Hey, little buddy. Hi, Scallywag. Okay, everyone, first thing, the sundae bar. Gather round. I went to my favourite little Italian gelato bar. I've got chocolate, strawberry, vanilla, spu-moni," he looked at Markus, "lemon and mango sorbets and... I can't remember." He opened the lids to the tubs one by one. "Ah. *Dulche de leche*."

"What's that?" Maddie asked.

"Caramel. Kind of," Alexa said.

"So," Bruce wielded his ice cream scoop. "I'm making custom banana splits. You get three kinds of ice cream and two toppings of your choice. Madison, you go first."

Excited, Maddie scrabbled up onto a stool and looked at the array of choices, her face alight. "Okay. I want Strawberry, Mango and... um, and I guess... oh, it's hard. I can't decide."

Alexa smiled, lifting Markus up beside her. "Come on, Mads."

"Oh, okay. Vanilla."

"Right." Bruce arranged the banana slices in a dish, carefully scooped out her three choices and arranged them on top, and then offered her the toppings. After a sprinkle of sliced strawberries and a drizzle of chocolate sauce, she was deposited at the kitchen table with a spoon and a huge grin.

"My tuwn," Markus said. "I want pas-moni–"

"It's spu-moni, Marky," Maddie said through a mouth already full of ice cream.

He ignored her. "Chocklit, aaaaaan'..." He stretched up onto his knees, peering at the tubs. "An' doo, um..." He pointed. "Dat one."

"Okay, Markus." Bruce assembled another banana split, discretely making Markus's smaller, with half a banana and small scoops of ice cream. "There you go."

Alexa lifted him down and set his sundae in front of him.

"And you, Alexa. What'll you have?"

Alexa's eyes twinkled with delight at the entertainment he'd concocted. "Let's see now." She slid up onto a stool and he watched her closely as she considered her options.

He puffed up at little because he'd succeeded in putting a smile on her face already. Just wait until she saw what else he had in store. Her eyes shone with delight.

"I'll have something similar to Markus. Chocolate, of course."

"Of course."

"And *Dulche de leche.*"

"Mm-hmm." He scooped and smiled, waiting.

"And vanilla."

"Coming right up." He finished up her sundae. "Toppings?"

"Nuts."

"Seems as though you're sweeter than you let on."

"Hah. Maybe I am."

As she dipped into her treat, he made his own.

"What're you having?"

Bruce ate the remaining half of Markus's banana with his fingers, and scooped a huge mound of lemon sorbet into his bowl, winking at Alexa.

"That's it?"

"That's it." He scooped some of the cool, tart ice into his mouth and savoured its intense lemon flavour.

"You're pulling my leg."

"What do you mean?" He took another spoonful, closing his eyes.

"That's not really–"

"What?" He opened his eyes and glanced at her, but she had stopped talking, and was filling her mouth with banana split, her full lips glistening with melted ice cream, her mouth working as she moved around the contents of her mouth. Uh-oh. It was early for this, but his libido suddenly perked up and insisted on a kiss. He leaned in and pecked her on her luscious, wet lips, trailing his tongue for a split second.

"Hey!" she protested, but her expression was pure flirtation. For once, instead of blushing and hiding, she was meeting him straight on, and the chemistry between them sizzled. When she let down her guard, she was one hot little mama.

"Hey, yourself. I needed a little taste of caramel." He licked his lips and continued eating his lemony treat, his chest puffing out, his heart lifting like a hot air balloon, feeling large and light.

"What were you saying?"

Alexa gazed at him. "Seems you're more evolved than I gave you credit for." She gestured with her spoon at his bowl of sorbet, quickly disappearing.

"Nah. I'm a sucker for anything tart." He paused, winking. "Like you, for example." He let his gaze slide down her body and up again.

She threw a peanut at his head, laughing.

"Anyway," he said, "how do you know I haven't always been this awesome?"

She smiled into his eyes with obvious admiration and a delicious heat that warmed him to his toes, despite the icy temperature of their tongues.

The afternoon continued to be a success. After ice cream they all went out into the backyard for water play and a wild, unruly game of hide and seek. Once everyone's energy flagged, Bruce ushered them all inside, and sent them upstairs for baths while he prepared dinner. He'd taken extra care to research recipes, buying special ingredients so that nothing could go wrong. When he heard their footsteps descending the stairs, he met them in the hall and suggested board games while they waited for dinner to be ready. They settled on a game of mousetrap to please Markus.

Alexa went along with the whole thing, only a hint of a curious smile playing at the corners of her mouth all evening. Her sparkling eyes kept darting his way, and when he raised his to meet hers directly, she smiled, shook her head and looked away. It's a good thing he was alone in the kitchen so his simmering state of arousal wasn't so obvious to her eyes. Oh, he couldn't wait for the kids to go to bed tonight.

He was making some progress. There was little sign of yesterday's trauma, though obviously it would be on her mind. But only time would tell.

Like the sundaes, he'd planned a dinner that could accommodate the eccentric tastes of all four diners, ranging from kid-friendly pedestrian to gourmet. The only thing Bruce hadn't left to chance and choice were the tubs of pre-made pizza dough, which he'd kneaded and shaped, and were now rising nicely in individual rounds. He was quite proud of himself, and his plan was going perfectly. Now it was time to gather in the kitchen to choose their toppings.

"Okay, everyone. Custom homemade pizza for dinner. What's your favourite topping, Markus? Let me guess…"

"Cheese," he answered.

"Oh. How'd I know? I bought some cheese. Mozzarella cheese."

"Yum."

"And you Scallywag?"

She narrowed her eyes at him. "Betcha don't have pineapple."

He raised his chin. "Betcha I do. What do you like with that? Ham, maybe?"

Her face lit up. "How'd you know?"

Bruce tapped his temple with one finger. "Oh. I'm a much smarter fellow than I look."

"Indeed you are," Alexa said. "But I bet you don't have my favourite toppings."

"Well, try me." He winked at her with a grin.

"Hmm. How about artichokes?"

"Got 'em."

Her eyebrows shot up. "Really? Okay. How about sun-dried tomatoes?"

"Got 'em."

She laughed. "Is there anything you didn't buy?"

He made a wry face. "What, and lose this game?"

She chuckled. "Okay, did you buy anchovies?"

He sighed and pulled a long face. "I didn't expect any of you folks to want anchovies."

"What's choovie?" Markus asked.

Madison curled her nose. "Thtinky little fishes, Marky. You don't like 'em. Trust me."

"However," Bruce continued, "…I bought a tin just in case."

"Oh, I know," Alexa said. "I bet you did not buy goat cheese."

"I did."

"Spinach?"

"Got it."

"Holy mackerel," Alexa said.

Bruce grimaced and snapped his fingers. "Dang it. No mackerel.

Now that would be an unusual choice." He pursed his lips. "Maybe with a touch of ginger and soy? Next time."

Alexa laughed again. "I'll let you off the hook, so to speak. Tell us what else you bought."

Bruce cleared his throat and peered at the ceiling. "Let's see... pepperoni, salami, chicken, barbecue sauce, béchamel–"

"You've got to be kidding."

"Nope. Don't interrupt or I'll forget something. Um... pesto and tomato sauces of course, and peppers and onions, roasted garlic and shrimp, mushrooms, olives both green and black..." his voice tapered off.

"Okay. Enough. I believe you. What are we going to do with all this food?"

He shot her a sardonic look. "Eat gourmet pizzas tomorrow and the next day?"

"And the next."

Forming and assembling the individual pizzas was fun, and everyone took part with much laughter and mess. He and Alexa even made several smaller pizzas for themselves so they could sample the array of ingredients he'd purchased. They ate one while the next ones were baking. The kids loved it.

"Well. I can't eat another bite," she finally groaned, holding her stomach.

"Me, too," mimicked Maddie.

Markus's eyes were glazing over, and he teetered a bit on his chair.

"Big day, Markus?" Bruce asked.

"Bed now," he replied, and they all laughed.

"Wise little man." Bruce turned to Alexa. At last they would have some time alone. The sooner the better. "My honours?"

She shook her head no. "You've done enough today. I'll take them up."

"Let's both go." He picked up Markus and tossed him over his shoulder like a sack of spuds.

They trooped upstairs, all four of them, and split up, boys and girls, to don pyjamas. A rendezvous in the bathroom for tooth brushing and then they gathered in Markus's room to tuck him in first. All was going according to plan, and Bruce's blood was heating as he planned his next moves.

"Can we have a thtory?" Maddie said, her voice a plaintive whine, as though she knew she was pushing her luck.

Bruce closed his eyes and groaned just as Alexa said, "Sure, Maddie," so he smiled and nodded. Damn it! How long would this take?

"Alright. Who will choose?"

~

"You choose," Bruce said, meeting her gaze and nudging her with his arm. Cozying up while they told the story could be conducive to his plan.

Alexa lifted her eyes, but before she could speak, an idea shot into Bruce's head. "Wait. I've got it. I'll start and you see if you can figure it out. Sec." He dashed over to Maddie's room and returned a moment later with a book in his hand, quickly flipping through it to find his page.

With their eyes focused on him, he sat at the foot of the bed, making space for Alexa to sit beside him, but not so much space that she wasn't snugged up close, and began. He told a tale of a rich man who had many large splendid houses, impressive carriages, fine horses and much silver and gold. "Unfortunately, the man had a blue beard, which made him so ugly and fierce-looking that all the women in town ran away from him. Nearby lived a noble lady with two beautiful daughters, and the man asked permission to marry one of them. Neither of them wanted him, especially since he had been married several times before."

Maddie looked bemused, as though she wasn't sure what to make of the story so far. A quiet smile lurked behind Alexa's eyes. "Mmm." Bruce began to slowly caress her back while he read. Maybe this would work out alright after all.

"Ith he a pi-wit, Boos?" Markus enquired.

Ak! "No-no, little buddy. Not a pirate. He was a scary guy, though. But people were also fascinated by all his riches. One day, he invited the noble lady and her family for a visit to his grand country house. He entertained them with sumptuous meals, country rides and hunting parties, games and musical performances, and they were awed by the beauty of his house and rich possessions. They stayed for a whole week, and had so much fun, that by then Bluebeard's beard didn't seem quite so blue, nor did he seem so fearsome as before. Impressed by the luxurious lifestyle it would bring her, at last, the younger daughter agreed to marry him."

"Foolish girl," Alexa mumbled, and Bruce glanced at her but didn't hold her gaze. He did, however, slide his hand down to the sexy dip above her cute little butt. She wiggled a little, settling in.

Maddie narrowed her eyes.

"Doeth Boobeed have a thowd?" Markus asked, leaning closer to Bruce with wide eyes.

"A what?" Alexa asked.

"A sword." Bruce smiled. "He sure does, buddy. That's coming. Hold on."

Markus slunk down a little deeper into his blankets.

"After a grand wedding in town, Bluebeard took his new bride back to his magnificent country house. A month passed, and then Bluebeard announced he must go away for several weeks."

"Like Daddy and Kate," Maddie said.

"Yuh. Ahem. He told her to have her sister, brothers and friends to keep her company, and invited them to luxuriate in all his wealth, and to enjoy themselves to the fullest while he was away."

"In other words to have a big party," Alexa said, flashing him a grin.

He nodded. "He gave her a large ring of keys for every door and cupboard in his grand house, inviting them to eat, drink, dress in fine clothes and play games and music to their hearts' content. But he warned her that she must never use the smallest key on the ring, which opened his private room at the end of a long hall. *'If I find you have disobeyed me, there is no knowing how angry I will be, or what I might do,'* he threatened before he rode off in one of his fine carriages."

"What's in the room?" Maddie whispered.

"Secret, Scallywag," Bruce said with a sinister smile.

"Oy," Alexa said, rolling her eyes.

Bruce continued. "So the young bride's sister and friends came, and they partied hard for a couple of weeks. They ate and drank, danced and played games until they were bored. They explored the grand house, and she led them from room to room, opening the doors to sumptuous ballrooms and luxurious bedrooms full of beautiful carved furnishings, silver mirrors and gold picture frames. She opened up the many store rooms that contained Bluebeard's ample riches, and they were awed by his gold and silver coins, his chests of precious jewels, tapestries and silks, antiques and fine art."

Bruce paused for air, then cleared his throat. Whether they understood every detail or not, the kids were rapt, waiting no doubt for the promised sword fight. "The young bride became tired of her friends' greed and silliness. Besides she couldn't stop thinking of the secret room that Bluebeard had forbidden her to open. The more she thought about it, the more curious she was, until finally she couldn't resist."

"Oh, no!" Maddie moaned, covering her face with her hands, and Markus slid down and pulled the sheet up to his chin.

"Hey! How d'ya know it's going to be bad?" Bruce asked with a shrug.

"Smart kids," Alexa said, and Maddie leaned closer to her, pulling Alexa's arms around her.

"Hmph," Bruce said. "So, she turned the little key in the old-fashioned lock and opened the door. Creeeeek!" Bruce mimicked the sound of the hinges. He lowered his voice to heighten the suspense. "Inside, she found the floor was covered with thick, clotted..." Bruce darted a glance from Maddie to Markus, "...blood!"

Markus disappeared completely under the covers with a squeak. Maddie's green eyes grew wide. "Here it comes," Alexa said with dread.

"All around the room were the bodies of Bluebeard's other wives, each with her throat cut." Bruce slashed his hand across his throat and rolled his eyes back in his head.

"Oh, Bruce. This isn't—"

"Shhhh. The young woman was so frightened she dropped the key on the bloody floor. She quickly picked it up, locked the door and ran back to her friends, her heart racing at what she had found."

"Ewwww," Maddie said.

"Ew, indeed," echoed Alexa. "Bad man."

"The key was covered in blood, and the young woman wiped it and washed it and polished it, but the blood stains would not come off. It was a magic key."

"Double-ew," Maddie said.

"That night, Bluebeard returned from his trip, explaining that his business dealings had been unexpectedly resolved. His bride was terrified, but put on a smiling face and pretended that everything was fine.

He asked for his key ring back the next day, and noticing the little key was missing, he asked her about it."

"Oohhhh," Maddie moaned, leaning into Alexa. A muffled off-tune humming came from beneath the covers, which was probably just as well, or they'd be up all night with nightmares.

"The young woman made excuses and delayed, but finally she had to bring the magic key to Bluebeard. He asked how it came to be stained with blood, and the young woman said she didn't know. 'I know you have gone into my private room,' Bluebeard said. 'Now you will join the others, and die at my sword.' The young woman pleaded for time to say her prayers, and Bluebeard agreed. Instead, she ran to her sister, and asked her to look out from the tower to see if their brothers were approaching, because they were supposed to be coming to join them, and they were both brave soldiers."

A muffled mumbling came from under the covers.

Bruce pulled them back to reveal Markus with his eyes bugged out. "Do the bwothers have thwords?"

"Yes, of course, Markus. Don't worry."

"Pish," Alexa said.

"What?"

She waved him on. "Nothing."

"Bluebeard called for her over and over, and she pleaded with him to give her more time. Then she called to her sister, 'Are they here? Are they coming?' Each time her sister said, no. It seemed they would not arrive in time, and the young bride knew it was time for her to die, so she slowly descended the stairs to where Bluebeard waited, sword in hand. Finally, the sister called out, 'I see a cloud of dust on the horizon!'"

Maddie and Markus both leaned forward eagerly awaiting the arrival of the avenging brothers.

"There was a loud thud and a crash as the brothers broke down the door to the house. They rushed in with their swords drawn–"

"Yay!" shouted Markus.

"That'll show'm," Maddie said.

"There was a big fight," Bruce acted out the dramatic sword fight, "–and finally–"

"Okay. That's enough."

Bruce sat up and stared at Alexa. "We're getting to the–"

"I've heard a very different version of that story," Alexa said. "But, the brother's never came."

"No?" Bruce wrapped his fingers around her ribs and squeezed affectionately, pulling her closer to his side.

Alexa shook her head. "In fact, the young woman had no brothers or sister. She was all alone, except for her mother. And when she was married, she was very lonely at the house, and had nothing to do but play the piano."

"Oh. That's very different," Maddie said. "I don't like—"

Alexa held up a single finger to silence her. "Bluebeard admired his new wife's musical ability, and so he gave her the gift of a piano tuner. He was a young blind man from the village near their isolated country manor." Her eyes slanted over to Bruce's face, and her beautiful lips twitched with a suppressed smile.

"Where'd you get this?" Bruce's face twisted skeptically. "Is this one of your—"

"Shh." She pressed one slender finger to her pursed lips and it felt almost like a kiss. Mesmerized, he watched her mouth as she continued. "The young bride and the piano tuner became friends, because they were both gentle, creative souls, and they had no one else to talk to. When the young woman discovered the horrors of the secret room, she told the piano tuner all about it, and he consoled her."

Bruce smiled then, and met her sparkling green eyes tentatively. Was she trying to tell him something? He continued gently stroking her back with his fingertips. She shifted a little closer to him, and leaned back.

"Then when Bluebeard returned, the piano tuner vowed to stay and protect her from his violent fury. But he was blind and weak and powerless to do anything when Bluebeard drew his long sword and dragged his bride to the courtyard to cut off her head."

Oh. Bruce's heart sank. His brow drew down a little as he replayed her story in his mind. Where was she going with this?

"Oh, I don't like this!" Maddie whined.

"She knew it was the end of the line for her, and she had a moment to reflect on her life and the decisions she'd made, and she had some regrets. She realized her marriage to Bluebeard was a mistake, and that she should have trusted her love and her talent for music to get by, instead of being captivated by his great power and wealth."

"That'th what you always thay, Auntie Al. No princes."

"S'right, Maddie. But it was too late for her now." Alexa shook her head sadly. "She bent her head meekly, and Bluebeard raised his sword high…"

Markus climbed under Bruce's arm, and buried his face in Bruce's shirt, whimpering. Bruce narrowed his eyes, listening intently for what came next.

"Suddenly, they heard rapid hoof beats echo on the cobbles, and a crash at the courtyard gate. A single rider galloped into the courtyard and reared up in front of them. Bluebeard hesitated, his sword overhead, and then with a loud CRACK! he crumpled to the ground. The young woman looked up to see her mother astride the horse, a smoking gun in her hand."

"Oh!" said Maddie.

"Her mom?" Bruce said, squinting at her in disbelief.

Alexa laughed aloud, as three pairs of incredulous eyes locked on her face.

"But Auntie Al!" complained Maddie. "The princess has to rescue herthelf."

Alexa sniffed and nodded. "Yes, Mads. But in this case, her mother had betrayed her. She had forgotten to teach her that important lesson, and so her work was unfinished."

"What happened to the piano tuner?" Bruce asked.

"Did they fight wit thowds?" Markus asked.

"In a manner of speaking." Alexa smiled coyly at Bruce, and his pulse picked up at her veiled reference. *Hoo-boy.* "The young widow inherited all her husband's wealth, and so she married the blind piano tuner, and they lived quietly, and happily, ever after." Then she added, "With her mother, of course."

It was Bruce's turn to laugh out loud. He playfully gave her bottom a pinch and was rewarded with a squeal as she jerked back into his lap. Now they were getting somewhere.

CHAPTER 17

The children, thankfully, were too exhausted to be kept awake long by images of blood and beheaded women, and Alexa's alternate ending diffused some of the tension. Bruce followed Alexa downstairs on tiptoes, his breath coming fast and shallow. This was the part of the evening he'd been looking forward to all day. Their time to be one-on-one. Their time to be alone.

He refilled their wine glasses and rolled up his sleeves.

"Have a seat. I'll have these last few dishes done in a jiffy."

She pursed her lips, suppressing a smile. "I'll help. Then they'll be done quicker."

He liked the sound of that. "Alright, then."

"Hey, does coffee keep you up? I'm in the mood for coffee and biscotti."

"Okay."

They got the machine warmed up and ground the coffee beans, and Alexa made the coffee while Bruce rummaged in the pantry for biscotti. He knew as well as Alexa they'd be there somewhere, since Simon and Kate, despite being daft tea-totalers, offered them to guests without fail.

As they settled side by side on the sofa, Bruce said, "Hey, do you feel like going over the house drawings?" A little bonding over his house could warm up the atmosphere. At least it had last time.

"I saw them on the table earlier. Sure. Let's do it."

Bruce retrieved them from the kitchen counter and sat down beside

Alexa again, unrolling them on the coffee table, and holding down the corners with his coffee and plate of biscotti. Alexa sat her coffee down as well, and bent over to read his sticky notes.

"Where do you want to start?" Alexa asked.

"Uh, well. I was wondering where the laundry went, and the hot water tank and stuff. It used to be in a utility cupboard right here, where the new kitchen is."

She smiled and pointed at a large cupboard off the new master ensuite bathroom.

He squinted down. "Oh. I didn't know what that was for."

"That's where most of the laundry is generated anyway. And it's not far from the kitchen in this case, either."

He nodded. "Logical."

"The domestic hot water is right there too, and the electrical panel is over on the other side, in the study. That's where the existing main comes in, but since all the wiring will be redone, I've placed a new, larger panel on this wall here, behind the door."

Okay, this wasn't as romantic a conversation as he'd hoped. "Oh, speaking of hot water. I was hoping to add a hot tub, on the patio somewhere."

"I didn't draw it, but I think this would be a good place for it. The view is excellent, but it's out of the way of outdoor dining. And access is easier from the bedroom."

"I see. So the deck could wrap around that side of the house."

"Yeah. Maybe. You probably want to involve a qualified landscape designer. I can recommend a couple if you like. But this is all that's necessary to get the permits in place and get you going."

Bruce lifted his eyes from the drawings to her face, and their eyes met. "Thank you so much, Al. I don't know how I would have gotten through this without your help." He grinned. "I probably would have been in jail by now."

She waved his comment away. "You would have hired someone. I happened to be in the right place at the right time."

"Well. I'm glad it was you. I owe you. This is so important to me."

"I know." Alexa seemed pensive, her gaze unfocussed on the drawings before them.

After a lull in the conversation, Bruce found the nerve to ask, "So what happens Monday, when you go to the office?"

Alexa's lips pressed into a firm thin line, and she dropped her eyes.

"I really don't know. I pray he's adult enough, and professional enough, that this change in our personal relationship won't affect his behaviour towards me."

She threaded her splayed fingers into her hair, rested her forehead on the heel of her hand, and sighed deeply. "I can't say I'm not worried about it. I don't trust him as much as I used to."

"Men aren't very good at break-ups," Bruce said. "It's always about ego."

Her head shot up, and her face filled with incredulous laughter. Her green eyes sparkled with amusement. "I can't believe you said that, girlfriend." She elbowed him. "You're so savvy."

He laughed. "Well. It's the simple truth. Even when a guy's not very invested in a relationship, his ego does not like to get dumped."

"You'd be an expert on that subject, I guess?"

He pursed his lips. "No, not really."

"You usually do the breaking up?"

"I... I don't usually get involved at all." He shot her a wry smile, but couldn't hold her eyes.

A moment of quiet hung between them, the air thinning and the temperature rising, before he looked up and met her eyes, and held them.

"Have you ever been in a serious relationship?" Alexa asked.

Serious. Not even close. "Nnno. I can't say that I have. Not that I'd... you know. I can't speak for..."

"Heart breaker, huh?"

"Hardly. I don't believe in that shit."

"What, love?"

He shrugged. "Yeah. I guess that's what I mean. Not for me, anyway."

She frowned. "I used to agree. And maybe I still do, for me. There's not much room in my life for a committed relationship. But seeing Kate and Simon together, it makes me believe it exists. For some people, anyway."

Simon and Kate were different that was true. "How about you? Leave a trail of broken hearts?"

"No. I didn't date in high school, because I didn't have spare time. In college, I threw myself into studying. Most guys my age were turned off by that."

"So, what, you were virginal and celibate?"

Colour rose to her cheeks. "Not quite. I had a couple of brief affairs with advisors and one with a prof."

"Why older men?"

She seemed frowned before responding slowly. "I suppose it wasn't that I had a thing for men who were more accomplished and powerful than me, but rather that... I envied them. I wanted what they had, so that drew me into their orbit. And one thing led to another."

"Hmm."

"Looking back, now I see that I was, subconsciously trying to usurp that power somehow. Not logical, I know."

He laughed. "I guess that's why you were never interested in me, although, you know..." He pressed his palm to his chest and raised his brows to ham it up a little, "...I am quite successful."

She studied him intently for a moment, as usual seeing right past his every attempt at a charming veneer. "So I hear. I never saw you that way. To me you've always been a perpetual boy."

Whoa. That knocked him for a loop. He swallowed and deflected with, "And Krystof? Another powerful man. Not that I believe you were serious about him. I can't imagine..." he broke off, peered into her eyes, his breath stuck in his throat. "Were you?"

She guffawed. "Oh, very serious. Not a frivolous moment between us." She sobered, her eyes drifting away from his. "I might have imagined we had a future, at one time."

Bruce waited. He wanted to ask her, why then? But he didn't want to threaten or upset her. He'd worked hard to lighten her mood all day. To make her feel appreciated. To help her forget her worries. This wasn't what he wanted now. He bit his lip.

But she continued speaking, as if he had asked the question that was burning his tongue.

"I've been trying to figure out why I got involved with him." Her eyes darted to his, then away. "It's... it's hard to remember now. It was four, almost five years ago." Alexa pulled her heels up and tucked them under her butt, dipped her biscotti, stirring it around in her espresso before biting off the tender end.

"We'd worked together for almost a year, after he hired me. There was chemistry right away. It was so exciting. He really is something you know. Not just his reputation, and the talent that made it, but also his... his charisma, I guess you'd say. It was almost like I'd been promoted to Olympus, to work side by side with the gods every day. It was euphoric. The level of ideas, the stimulating brainstorming and design *esquisse's*–"

"What's that?"

"Oh. Like a group design session–brainstorming. Everyone throws ideas out, but also sketches on large sheets. It's very exciting. The ideas would flow. The adrenaline was pumping. Krystof and I were always so in tune, on the same wavelength. Our ideas building on each other's. I was finally playing in the big leagues. It was terribly affirming, for me. As a designer."

"So. You grew. As an architect. And... your confidence."

She nodded energetically.

"We never really talked about it. We fell into bed one night on a wave of...of endorphins."

"I remember what that's like. When my buddies and I really hit on something great, a new software concept, and worked through the initial design stages, so we knew we had something exceptional, we'd work through the night, many nights, fuelled by passion and caffeine." He chuckled. "They were all butt ugly and scruffy, though, and by then they stunk, so, you know, I was never tempted." He smirked.

She gave him a you're-too-sweet smile, acknowledging his attempt at humour without giving in to it.

"I did love those guys, though. I miss them."

Alexa sighed. "I wonder if..." she shook her head, pressing her lips together, and he sensed her embarrassment.

"What? You can say it," he softly urged.

"Well. I wonder if it was all a big case of hero worship. You know, me wanting to grow up to be just like Krystof?"

"That's understandable."

"But what was in it for him?"

His breath caught. He peered at her, but she seemed both sincere and as innocent as she sounded. "Are you serious? You have to ask?"

Her face buckled. "But that sounds so sleazy. So cheap. I really didn't–"

"Hmm. Well, I can tell you, most guys won't look a gift horse in the mouth. But that's not what I meant."

She appeared puzzled, scrunching her face at him.

"You really don't know what you have to offer, do you? You're so smart, smarter than the average bear. And you're talented and creative." He gestured to the drawings she'd done of his house. "Look what you've done for me in a week. You're so energetic and capable both with your work and with the kids. And…" Bruce locked eyes with her. "You're so gorgeous. So hot." He leaned forward, slipping his arm around her shoulders. "Alexa…" he swallowed, his eyes caught by the glint of moisture at the corner of her full lips, now slightly ajar, as though awaiting his kiss.

Her eyelids fluttered over eyes that darkened a shade, and he made his move.

His mouth covered hers, and he heard a groan of pleasure escape his own throat. Yes. Yes, at last. The memory of yesterday's fevered embrace fuelled his desire further, and he reached for her, caressing her hair, letting his hand glide down, around one delicate ear, along the curve of her perfect neck, tracing the line of her collar bone, and let his hand slide flat over the soft mound of her breast, pausing there. He could feel her heat, feel her nipple harden in the palm of his hand. She was so small, so exquisite.

It was as if a floodgate opened. She responded in kind, her hands flying up to his chest, smoothing and kneading his muscles, sliding around him, reaching down to grip his butt tightly. Another groan escaped. They slid sideways onto the couch, instantly an uninhibited tangle of limbs, groping, panting, pressing, peeling away clothing in a desperate search for more skin. Where their groins touched, the heat was intense. She slid her hand down, over the bulge in his shorts. He gasped. Then she tucked her hand between his shorts and his abdomen, down inside, gliding along the burning, stiff shaft of his cock. It was like silk, like fire, making his head spin.

Oh, God, Alexa. Alexa. The heat. The desire pulsing within him was unprecedented. She was as frenzied with passion as he was.

But then, as suddenly, she pulled out her hand and pushed him away, her eyes dilated and wild. A fine shimmering strand of saliva hung between their swollen mouths, linking them, suspended.

"Oh, my God." She pulled further away, panting. "This is too…this…We can't do this!"

"But…" Why the hell not? He was too strung out with desire to form the words. He reached for her. He wanted more.

She allowed him to pull her in for one more kiss, both of them sucking and probing tongues as though their lives depended upon it, as though it was a final good-bye, pausing to breath deeply, their teeth pressed against each others.

But she pushed him away again, shaking her head.

"It's too complicated."

No. He shook his head, groaning. No. But she was right.

"We can't get involved while we're taking care of the kids. What if it goes sour? We have to work together. Kate and Simon are counting on us."

That was true, but... "What's that got to do with–"

She stood up. "No, Bruce. It's a bad idea. We can't."

He didn't understand her logic. In his mind, what was left functioning, there was nothing to keep them apart. She was so alive with sexual energy, he felt supercharged with his awareness of her physical presence. Her smooth, tawny skin, her perfect small hands, her delicate pointed chin, the angle of her jawbone, the tiny near-invisible hairs that dusted her cheek. Especially the line of her full lips, the implicit invitation of her wet mouth. It was all too much. He wanted all of it. By the shell-shocked expression on her face, the shadows in her green eyes, she obviously wanted him as badly as he wanted her. And he wanted her bad. Now.

"Al. I want you." His voice cracked, a near-moan.

She turned away. "We can't, Bruce. We're getting along fine now. Let's not ruin it."

Ruin it? How could the hottest, most excellent sex he'd ever imagined, as he imagined it would be, ruin anything? It would be heaven.

Alexa stomped out of the living room, returning a moment later with an armful of blankets and a pillow. She tossed them on the chair. "You can crash here."

Don't do this to me. He gripped his throbbing hard penis through his shorts with his hand, rubbing and squeezing it, his eyes closing involuntarily with a moan as he tried to control his rampant desire. When he opened them, she was staring at his crotch, a distracted, worried expression on her face, her nostrils flared. He could see she was still hot and bothered, but she tore her eyes away. "Don't..." She pointed a finger at his nose. "Don't even *think* about coming upstairs."

He glared at her accusingly. What kind of woman would deny herself what promised to be the most amazing sex of a lifetime? Surely she felt the same.

She turned away.

The light flicked off.

He sighed, lay back in the dark, his hand still gripping his erection through the fabric of his shorts. He was trembling. Un-fucking-believable.

For the second night in a row, Bruce found himself letting off sexual tension caused by Alexa. This time in Simon's guest powder room off the hall. Damn her!

It was an angry and frustrated pair of burnt brown eyes that stared back at him from the mirror in the semi-darkness. He was a fool to let any woman do this to him. He'd never put himself in this vulnerable position before. A tense shiver ran through his spine, like a subterranean quake. It felt dangerous. Bruce knew better.

Appeased but not satisfied, he returned to the sofa and lay back, staring into the darkness, his eyes following the ghostly white skeleton of the stair railing leading upstairs to where she slept. Alone. Her hot little body throbbing for him.

Her calm, cool control was undeniably threatening, especially in light of how badly he wanted her. Yesterday, he did the honourable thing by pulling back. And after the day they'd shared, he knew she reciprocated his feelings. At least physically. She wanted him too.

But now that she was in control of her faculties, she wouldn't let herself go. Did she mean to play with him. Even though Alexa was now unencumbered romantically, she still rejected him. So much for making clear-headed choices. Her decision was plain.

Despite their obvious mutual physical attraction, it seemed he wasn't someone she could take seriously. She'd never approved of him or his way of life. She'd always denigrated his character. Whatever they might have together, it wasn't a future. Fine. Fine with him. He punched his pillow and flipped over.

But a little mutual dalliance, especially after their conversation earlier, wouldn't be bad, would it? They were on the same page. The chemistry was undeniable, and after yesterday's tangle in the driveway... Clearly he'd been wrong about her. She would never agree to a fling with him, and obviously wasn't interested in anything more serious. She was too uptight, too focused on her career and her image to ever risk getting involved with someone like Bruce, even though it felt so right. Was he wrong to want her? His dream was just that, a stupid fantasy, and he would let it go while he still could, before he was too invested in the idea. He'd obviously mistaken her professional attention for romantic interest. It was his stupid ego. What a fool he was. If she couldn't... Damn it! If she couldn't give him the love and respect he deserved, then she could go to hell. He didn't need her. And he didn't want her, either.

∽

Monday morning came, ready or not.

When Alexa awoke, Bruce had gone. She'd stood in the doorway to the living room and stared at the neatly folded blankets with the pillow stacked on top. Did she feel remorse? Guilt? This was the kind of thing she'd normally share with Kate. Not this time. For so many reasons.

Her feelings were unsettled at best. On the one hand, she was still tingling with the thrill of Bruce's touch, still throbbing with unsatisfied need. Never had she experienced such mad desire. The sum of the attraction that had simmered since she'd first seen him at Kate's dinner table, that had flashed and flared and finally erupted the evening she'd split up with Krystof, had been unleashed last night. So much so that she fought an overwhelming terror.

What was that, exactly? Alexa had had her share of flings, even a few unbridled one night stands. Even Krystof, for whom she felt –used to feel– a kind of unwholesome adoration for years, never inspired in her the kind of mindless lust she felt last night. There had been no methodical, systematic seduction. No intellectual appreciation.

Only animal instinct.

She'd barely been able to hold on to her rational mind and drag herself away from his kisses. He had evidently felt the same way. She had never felt so desired in her life. His eyes, when he glared at her, were accusatory. Incredulous. Betrayed. How could she *not* want to continue? To culminate such feelings? How indeed?

But she couldn't allow herself to dwell on those questions now.

Her stomach roiled as she approached the office. How would Krystof be today? Would he push aside his feelings and carry on as though nothing had changed? Or would it affect him as it was affecting her? Alexa couldn't remember feeling less in control of herself.

What she felt was truly fear, but also a simmering anger and resentment. She could only blame herself for getting involved with her boss and complicating her life, and risking her beloved career. Embarrassed, she pushed away recollections of all the scoldings and disapproving faces Kate had given her over the years. She'd seen the truth, and let

Alexa find her own way through. But Krystof was not an innocent. Suddenly she was able to see him in a new light.

The moment was anticlimactic. She entered the office, exchanged greetings with a few colleagues, tucked her bag in a drawer and sat down at her workstation. There seemed to be a normal amount of activity around the design studio, no more nor less than usual.

She glanced at Krystof's door. Closed. Maybe muffled voices. Maybe he was on the phone.

Then she grabbed her cup and strolled to the kitchen to get a coffee, eyeing Nathan's workstation as she passed by. His computer screen-saver danced by in a flash of psychedelic colours. A tumble of papers and drawings were strewn across his desk. It appeared to be a normal workday. But as usual, he wasn't around.

She walked to Peter's workstation. He sat there, hunched over his keyboard and mouse, busily drawing, intently mumbling to his screen. He'd drawn a picture of Mini-Me with Nathan's moustache and beard, and put it in a red circle with a slash through it, propping it up on his desk. She snickered. He didn't notice her standing there, so she opted not to disturb him and returned to her own desk.

Her attention was scattered. Her breathing was shallow, a tightness gathering under her diaphragm, and she stretched and tried to relax. She wouldn't be able to work if she was so wound up worrying about Krystof. But she had to go on as though nothing had changed. What choice did she have?

And yet everything had changed. She knew it in her gut. Her restless mind kept jumping back to Bruce's words. *Men aren't very good at break-ups. It's all about ego.*

That didn't bode well. It seemed clear to her that her entire relationship with Krystof was about ego. His enormous ego, that she'd gladly fed with her hero-worship. All along she'd felt he was supporting and nurturing her confidence and her career, when in fact, she saw clearly now, she was massaging his ego, while he manipulated hers. He'd taken the brightest and best talent in the office and bent her to his will. Made her into his personal noviciate, bowing down at the altar of Krystof the Great.

A burst of bitter laughter escaped her, and she cast a furtive glance around to see if anyone had noticed, but no one looked up from their own concerns. How ironic. Krystof's favourite sexual game to play was to be her servant. To worship her. Often insisting that she act the role of the dominatrix. And she fell for that, soaking up the attention, the favours, of her own personal god, letting it feed her ego.

Suddenly Krystof's door was ajar, and a gust of male laughter streamed out, disturbing the quiet concentration of the studio. She looked up.

Nathan emerged, his face alight with amusement, turned, noticed her glaring at him. His smile fell and was replaced by a supercilious expression. He lifted his chin and strode by without a word.

What the hell?

Her eyes slid back to Krystof's open door.

Something was going on, and she didn't like it. Her stomach tightened into a rock-hard knot. The skin on her neck prickled with fear.

Amy Lo, a twenty-something intern architect that had been hired a few months ago, approached Krystof's door tentatively, papers clutched tightly to her chest, a hesitant, questioning expression on her young, unlined face. She lifted her slender hand, clenched in a loose fist, and knocked on the open door.

"Yes?" Krystof's familiar hoarse voice emerged from within.

"Um, Mr. Konstantin? Can you spare a minute?"

Krystof's laughter. "Please. Call me Krystof. Everyone does. We are all peers here. Come in, Lo. Close the door, sit down."

Alexa sat, staring at the closed door, chewing her lips, for about fifteen minutes. Remembering. Remembering what it was like to be a relative newbie in the office, in awe of Krystof the star, and eager to please. Remembering his words and manners, how encouraging and inclusive he was. How optimistic her own bright future seemed in the halo of his reflected glory.

The door opened and Amy emerged, her face aglow.

Had she ever been quite that naive? Alexa nodded knowingly and stood up, stepped to the door. She'd have a word with Amy later.

"Krystof?"

He looked up, his expression grim. She saw his shoulders slump. "Jenner. Come in."

Alexa's skin shrank, as though it was too tight for her body. Her sphincter clenched and her bowels turned over, sending a shiver through her. She told her heart to stop racing, tried to control her breathing. She willed her voice, when it emerged, to be calm, normal.

She forced a determined smile as a protective barrier. "Nathan seems pretty chipper."

Krystof's brows darkened over his silver eyes, hooding them. "Yes. He has cause to celebrate."

Alexa was afraid to ask. Her lip quivered and she clenched her teeth to control it. "Because?"

Krystof expelled a long, slow breath. "I had to give him the project, Jenner. There was no other way. I'm sorry."

Bile rose in her gorge, and hot tears seared the back of her eyelids. But she held it all in. Her head felt hot, and her vision darkened with the effort. "Are you? Really?"

"Of course I am, Sasha."

"Don't call me that. Don't ever call me that again."

A moment of tense silence passed, during which Krystof appeared to draw himself up, stiffen his spine, compose himself.

"This is best for everyone. Rose and Weinstein will be happy, and we will ensure they still get the best possible project. That's what we all want, isn't it? Nathan will be Project Architect on paper, and handle the public, social exchanges. Just fluff. But in the office, you will still be in charge. Even Nathan, pompous puppy that he is, concedes that it must be you to carry the project through to realization. It's your concept. You are the brains and vision behind this."

Really? He believed she'd go for that? She spoke carefully. "That is true. But. No one will ever know. I'd do all the work and get none of the credit, my career would stagnate, and nothing will ever change in this damned business." She turned to him, her hands on her hips, and her voice rose. "Krystof! I don't deserve this! If you believe I'm good enough then you have to stand up for me. You have to push me forward as Project Architect. I'll make sure our names are in the magazines, and on the awards. But I have to be there. I won't hide in the shadows. I've worked too hard for this. I can't."

"If you will not accept work on the Arts Centre team according to this plan, then you'll have to take on another project. Perhaps the Millstream condominium towers for Quadrant, or you could take over Nathan's industrial park."

"No! You might as well let me go."

Apprehension flashed in his silver eyes. "I don't want to let you go. You're too valuable. But you are not being team player, Jenner. That has always been problem with you. Take it or leave it. This is way it must be. I cannot make it work any other way." He was stressed, his Polish syntax was showing.

"You mean you won't."

He shrugged, his eyelids drooping to half-mast with a lift of his chin. "Take it as you will."

"Do you think I'm a fool? This has nothing to do with Rose. Or at least he's only a convenient excuse for your vengeance."

Krystof's face folded into a sneer. "Vengeance is strong word, Jenner."

"Yes, vengeance. And you dare to suggest that *I* might be punishing you." Alexa shook her head. "I don't suppose you're even aware of it. You're so accustomed to manipulating people."

Krystof stood up, leaning forward onto his palms on the desk. "Enough. I won't listen to this."

A red rage rose up through Alexa in a flood. "You will listen." She stepped forward, thrusting her face near to his. "I've stupidly toed the line and played your game for five years now, giving you the best of me. You can damned well listen to me for a few minutes." A fine spray of spit chased her words into the tense air between them, settling on his chin. He didn't flinch. Their gazes locked, and she peered deep into his cold grey eyes. The she laughed, her voice dropping into a seductive purr. "You may not like it, Krystof. But I know you."

Krystof's chin jutted forward in a comical way. Alexa stepped back, crossed her arms and appraised him. "Yes. You're a complicated little man, but I understand you very well. It's a shame really. You have talent, intelligence and charisma, but you lack one very important thing. And you know it." She shook her head, the whole picture finally falling into place. "Without integrity, Krystof, you're nothing. It's the true measure of a man's worth. But you'll never redeem yourself by using others. You only dig a deeper hole."

Krystof drew himself up taller. "You cannot take back these words, Jenner."

"I don't intend to. I mean them with all my heart." She turned toward the door, but as soon as her hand touched the lever, he spoke again, a wary note to his voice.

"What are you doing? Where are you going?"

She turned back. All of her hot rage was spent. Ice ran through her veins and a deep calm stole over her. "You know, my friends have long wondered what I saw in you. Why I was involved with you." She drew her lungs full. "And I was always perfectly clear about why– I adored you." His eyes flashed, and she held up a hand to stop him from responding. "I wanted to be just like you." She swallowed. "And I guess I owe you thanks. You were a wonderful mentor. I've learned a great deal from you. I'm a stronger designer now because of it. But…" She shook her head sadly. "I no longer want to be just like you." She turned and set her hand on the door lever, and cast a cool glance over her shoulder.

"I don't need you anymore. I quit. You and Nathan can have the Arts Centre and do with it what you will. Ruin it. See if I care."

And with that she left the office, and she didn't look back.

Bruce had been out of sorts all day, and consequently kept the kids to a routine. He'd taken Markus around the park in the jog stroller, too grumpy to banter and tease the three year old, pushing himself to run farther and faster than usual, trying to drive memories of Alexa from his mind as well as his body. The housekeeper he'd hired was working her wonders on the house today. After he and Markus picked up Maddie from school, he took them to the neighbourhood park for a bit of play, but left them to their own devices. When he brought them home, he was feeling guilty for resisting their urgings to participate in games and keeping to his own brooding thoughts.

It didn't matter, he'd finally concluded. If Alexa could contain her physical desire and maintain a platonic, professional pose, then so could he. For the sake of the kids. For the sake of their duty to Simon and Kate. For whatever damn reason she chose. If she could do it, so could he.

The trouble was, she was right. His madness the night before had been just that, a momentary loss of self-control and common sense. Hadn't he just determined that falling for Alexa would be the stupidest thing he could do? So what was wrong with him?

And the fact that he didn't dare call Simon to ask his opinion just reinforced the fact that she was right. They were treading into territory that had no precedents, no rules. There was too much at risk.

By the time he heard Alexa's car pull into the driveway mid-afternoon, he'd prepared himself as well as he could. He believed he could withstand the sight of her, lean and tawny, the smell of her, sweet and spicy, the maddeningly sexy sound of her sultry voice, and, if not be unaffected, then at least goddam-well not show it.

CHAPTER 18

One sight of her face challenged his resolve.

She neither stormed in, nor greeted him with cheer, nor did she sit in her car weeping onto her steering wheel. Bruce stood in the foyer looking at her as she walked in, slow and calm, set down her keys and her bag, and floated past him to the stairs, eyes dead in a mask-like face. She trod listlessly upstairs without a word.

He was still standing in the foyer puzzling when she descended, having discarded her work wardrobe in exchange for a pair of soft black pyjama pants and a black camisole, elegant even in apparent distress. Then she threw herself down on the sofa in the living room and plopped her bare feet on the coffee table, her unfocussed eyes trained on the front window. And there she continued to sit in stony silence.

Bruce stood in the doorway for several minutes. He tried clearing his throat once or twice, but she didn't look up. She didn't acknowledge him in any way. Finally he turned and went out to join the kids in the back yard. Whatever happened at work today, it looked like she'd need a little help getting through the evening. He could do that. He could man up to the job. Be a friend. It didn't mean anything.

About an hour later, Bruce came in to start dinner. He'd prepped some ingredients for fish tacos earlier, and it looked like he'd be finishing the job alone. He peeked into the living room, not surprised to see Alexa lying on her back, staring at the ceiling, her arms clutching a pillow across her stomach. Again he cleared his throat, but she didn't move an eyelash.

"Erm. Can I get you anything? A glass of wine? Something... stronger?" A nervous laugh escaped him, like a hiccup.

Still no reply. Her chest rose and fell steadily, and she closed her eyes like a door in his face. Okay then. He shrugged and returned to the kitchen. Fine. It was nothing to him if she had a bad day at the office. He didn't need to know about it.

It was so unlike her, though, to succumb to any weakness. It was freaking him out. This withdrawal was worse, almost worse, than her breakdown in the driveway last week. Nothing's worse than a woman in hysterical tears. *I guess I'd better make dinner, then, if she's just going to lie there.*

He heated the frying pan and dredged the fish, slipping it into the pan. Then he opened the patio door. "Kids! Come in and wash up for dinner." Whining was their retort. "Now. Please."

Maddie looked up, scanning his face. "Come on, Marky." She took his hand and led him inside.

Bruce assembled the tacos and plated them as the kids came back to the kitchen and sat down. He poured them each a cup of milk. "Eat."

Returning to the living room, he glared at Alexa's inert form, crossing his arms. "Are you eating with us or what?" His voice came out irritable and impatient. Not what he'd intended.

She pushed an exaggerated sigh out of her nostrils and turned her face away.

"Al. Answer me." Trying for sympathetic.

She sat bolt upright and turned her head in his direction. Her eyes were dark and bleak, but they did not meet his. "Why are you hassling me?" Her voice was hoarse and shrill, as though she'd smoked a case of cigarettes in one day. Maybe she'd already shed her tears today.

Bruce flinched. Then he blinked and gritted his teeth. *I'm not hassling you, you crazy bitch. I'm trying to help you.* He sighed. "Do. You. Want. A. Taco."

"No, asshole! No!" That time she screamed. "I. Do. Not. Want. A. Fucking. Taco."

"Watch your dirty mouth around the kids." He retreated to the kitchen and sat down to eat his own dinner. It took four large angry bites. To hell with her, anyway. He didn't need to put up with this. They weren't in a relationship. She wanted distance? Good. Fine. That's the way he liked it, too. Much safer this way. "I'd stay out of Auntie Al's way tonight, kids, if you know what's good for you."

They stared at him with wide, uncomprehending eyes, like two little frightened rabbits under the porch light.

He made up the leftovers into tacos and covered them with plastic wrap, tucking them into the fridge. Likely she would want to eat later, if she didn't commit suicide before then. Or murder. His eyes darted to the wall clock. It was long past time for him to go. He wondered if it was safe for him to leave the kids with her. "Bath time."

He glanced into the living room as they trooped up the stairs. No change, except... was that a trail of tears he could make out on the side of her face? *Fuck! Stay away. Stay out of her life. That's what you both want, isn't it?*

"Is Auntie Alex gonna be okay?" Maddie's voice was plaintive as she hunkered down beneath a wall of suds in the tub. She sounded scared.

"Sure she will, Scallywag."

"Did you make her mad again?"

The muscles of his face tightened. "No, I did not. She had a bad day at work. She needs a little time. She'll be back to normal by morning, I'll bet." He wanted to believe it, but he wasn't convinced. Something terrible had happened, and the urge to go down to her and find out, to hold her and comfort her was tearing him apart.

But he knew that she didn't want his help. And he'd be damned if he'd stick his nose in and get it bitten off again.

Once the children had drifted off, he lingered upstairs, picking up discarded clothing destined for the laundry hamper, rinsing the bathtub and mopping up water and messes, folding towels. He knew he was stalling. Part of him was hoping that she would go to bed. He was afraid of what he might find when he went downstairs, and his whole body was tense with the prospect of dealing with it. Or not.

Again his heart squeezed with concern for Alexa. He tried to push the feeling away. He wasn't used to getting tangled up in other people's problems. He wasn't used to caring about anyone. It only brought heartache.

A wave of protectiveness squeezed his chest, but he fought against it.

Reluctantly, he shuffled downstairs, paused in the doorway. She was curled in a fetal position on the sofa, staring glassy-eyed into space, hands clenched into fists across her pillow. Strands of her usually tidy hair lay across her face. Her glasses were missing.

Poor kid. She'd obviously had the day from hell. Whatever happened with that turd Krystof was clearly worse than expected. A surge of anger had images of his fist in Kristof's face flashing in his mind's eye.

He chewed his lip for a moment. Then he went to the kitchen, put the kettle on and, with a racing pulse, wiped down the table and the counters. *What am I doing here? This is not my thing. I don't know how to handle this.*

The teacup rattled on the saucer as he carried it to the living room. He paused in the hall to take a deep breath and steady himself. Pulling back his shoulders, he pasted an encouraging smile on his face and strode forward. She hardly seemed to notice him enter. He sat quietly on the edge of the sofa near her feet, and set the teacup down in front of her. Then he waited.

A flash of white beneath the curtain of her dark hair alerted him to her awareness, her darting eyes. He braced, half expected the cup of hot tea flung in his face.

Bruce reached forward and pushed aside a lock of hair the better to see her eyes. "Al? Will you talk?"

Her eyes slid to his face, wide and scared.

He cupped one hand around her knee. "Alexa?"

She sighed and pulled herself slowly upright, clutching the cushion to her middle, her shoulders hunched, her hair hanging forward across her face.

"Drink some tea, huh? It'll make you feel better."

"Why are you being so nice?" Her voice was emotionally flat and hoarse from crying. More hoarse than usual.

He shrugged, his eyes darting to her face.

"I don't need your help."

His jaw jutted and he leaned back, crossing his arms over his chest. "Right. I know that. I'm here anyway. So…"

Alexa reached for the tea, pushed her hair out of her face and took a tentative sip. Blew on it then took another. Then she took two large gulps and set the saucer down on her knee, her hair falling forward again. Her hands trembled. The cup wobbled and clinked against the saucer, and her shoulders quaked. She tried to set the cup down.

He quickly took the cup from her, setting it on the coffee table. Then he placed one palm on her thigh. He whispered, "Al?"

And as though he'd pushed a lever, the sluice gates opened. She turned to him, leaning into his chest, keening sobs tearing from her throat.

Bruce tensed. He placed his arms around her shaking shoulders. Patted. Rubbed. *Oh, Christ! Now what have I started?* "Tell me what happened today."

Her crying intensified and continued unabated for several minutes, while he held her. She was an ugly, noisy crier. Not much practice, he figured. Gradually her sobs faded and her body softened and stilled.

The tension lifted. He became more at ease rubbing her back, relaxing into their shared body space, despite, or maybe because of, the pillow sandwiched between them. Maybe all she needed was a good cry. Uncomfortable as it made him, he supposed it was the least he could do. They were friends, he reasoned, and she had no one else to comfort her.

"Did you get fired today, kiddo?"

Suddenly she pushed away and shot to her feet, clutching the pillow. "No. I quit." She paced the room in long angry strides. "How could he fire me, the coward? It would be sexual harassment. Or post-sexual harassment, or something." She swung her arms around, pillow in her fist, and he glanced around for breakables. A bitter laugh broke from her throat. "Cause of dismissal –withholding sexual favours. How would that look? No. Nooo. He simply castrated me!" Spittle flew from her twisted mouth.

"Erm." He wanted to point out that castration was not technically possible. But, it seemed highly irrelevant under the circumstances. He decided the better course was to let her vent. He swallowed, hoping her fury wasn't turned on him.

"Bastard!"

Bruce flinched. Krystof, he assumed, but he wasn't taking any chances. He kept his eyes open and trained on her, braced for unexpected movements.

Alexa approached him and leaned toward him, shoving her face near his.

He pulled back and swallowed. Man, she was furious.

She shoved the cushion into his lap and shook a clenched fist. "That sonuvabitch had the nerve to give the project to Nathan! Nathan! That spineless, scheming little snake. Of all people. He can't do the job! He even acknowledged it. What is Krystof thinking? The whole thing will disintegrate. But they don't care about the project," she hissed, sneering. "It's all politics. It's a conspiracy. I'm sick of it."

Bruce held his breath, clasping the pillow to his stomach now.

Alexa stood up and paced again, flinging her hands. "I'm finished. I might as well resign my license and get a secretarial job until I find a husband at the mill. That's all I'm good for. What will my mother say?"

"That's ridiculous." Whatever it meant, it sounded ridiculous.

She spun toward him. "What do you know about it? You're a man!"

"Alexa. It's only one job. You're at the top of your field. There will be others."

"You're wrong! I've been working toward this my whole life. I had a plan. Fighting an uphill battle. Taking on the old boys' club. This is the project that was going to propel me into the big time. It's been one long steady climb. One rung, one bloody hoop at a time. Hard, back-breaking, soul-crushing work all the way. Years of sacrifice. And for what!"

Bruce's blood pumped. Heat radiated from his pores, and acid roiled in his stomach. It took everything he had not to respond to her aggressive hostility with either fight or flight. He fought the urge to react, to defend, to strike back. Her hostility wasn't directed at him. He knew she was processing intense emotions. He could feel her grief and fear, oppressive and needy like a soul-sucking space alien, demanding something from him in response. Something unfamiliar and terrifying. Something he had no access to. He kept his voice calm. "You love your work. That's why you do it. You're forgetting how far you've come, babe."

Her laugh was chilling. "I've come to the top!" she screamed. "For me. I've hit the bloody glass ceiling! That's how far I've come."

Bruce's hands trembled, his ribs squeezing tight. He tried to find encouraging words, but his voice sounded choked and rigid. All this emotion was wreaking havoc on his nerves. "You can't assume it's the same everywhere."

"It is the same. Everywhere is the same. Everywhere is controlled by men. And they don't want me there."

"You're upset. It'll look different after you get over the shock." He stood, taking a tentative step toward her, lifting a hand, dropping it. "Maybe you're over-reacting? You've been through a lot of stress lately."

"I am not in shock!" she spat, shaking her head in disbelief. "I did this! I foolishly assumed the rules were the same for me. But they're not."

He was in over his head. He was not good at this. "Well... maybe take some time. Something else will come up."

"Something else will come up? That's your advice for my uncertain future?"

He shrugged. "Maybe."

"And what will that be, Koczynski? Another mentor I can sleep with? You don't understand. I played with fire and got burned. I've wasted five years of my life. Five years I'll never get back. And what do I do now? Who will want me? How do I explain this on my resume, hey?"

"No one will ever know. And it wasn't wasted. You don't have to start over."

"People will figure it out. Why else would I leave such a great position with a top firm, just when I won a prestigious competition? Any idiot can add that up."

"I don't agree. You're still good at what you do. Stay at home with the kids for a while and just chill. It'll work itself out."

"Stay home with the kids? That's your idea of comfort? I need time at home with the fucking kids! They're not my kids! Goddamit!"

"Shhhh." He cringed, imagining the kids listening in to her rant.

"There's a reason I don't have kids. A husband. A home." She stepped closer, dropping her voice. "If I'd been at work, paying attention to what was going on, this would never have happened. You're not innocent."

Shit. Here it comes. What'd he do?

"You're part of the problem, Koczynski, with your helpless, pitiful, perpetual adolescence. You're just another selfish, arrogant man, crashing around taking what you want from life and expecting me to pick up the slack." She swung her arms around. "Stepping on everything and everybody in your way. I'm sick of you all."

Bruce went rigid, holding the pillow up like a shield, turning his body away. He was definitely leaning toward flight now. "That's not fair. I'm not the one who–"

"I don't care! I don't care! I don't..." her voice cracked, and she shook with a sob, "...care!" She broke down, fresh hot tears flowing down her cheeks. "I hate you."

He froze, staring at her, gripping the cushion in front of his crotch with white knuckles, trying to breath without shaking, without screaming, without crying out– STOP! She wasn't making sense. He had to get out of here. Away from this crazy harpy.

Her body slumped, her shoulders curved, defeated. He could see she was shivering, but he couldn't bring himself to move toward her now, still stinging from her harsh words. She hugged herself with her thin brown arms and looked up at him, her eyes dead flat. This was not the strong and capable Alexa he had come to know and admire. This was some angry creature that he couldn't understand or deal with. He couldn't give her what she needed.

She glared at him with contempt, turned to the side and tilted her face down, her eyes on the floor. "Why are you still here, anyway? Go away, Bruce. Go and leave me alone."

He cringed inwardly and his extremities grew cold. He felt his heart shrinking, freezing, cracking. "Right. Not staying." He strode to the door and opened it. Why was he here? She didn't want him, and he didn't need this. There was nothing here for him. And he wasn't going to stick around for more abuse. His efforts to comfort her were a disaster. Obviously he wasn't cut out for this relationship stuff. Anyway, they were never a thing. She'd made that abundantly clear.

"I stayed for the kids, since you seemed incapable of taking care of them this evening. But now that you're back on your feet, and since you'll be available…" he made a snap decision. "I'll be away tomorrow. The weather looks good, so I'm going to take the boat out sailing. It's been too long since I had a day to myself. I guess you'll manage without me, since I'm so useless anyway."

Their eyes met across the room, cold and shielded.

She stood and took one long stride toward the door, grabbing the throw cushion on her way, and hurling it at him with the force of a hurricane. "Yes. Go on. Run. Run away, Peter!"

Bruce ducked. He paused in the doorway and turned his perplexed face toward her, *–What the hell is that supposed to mean?*

Alexa shook her head. "That's Peter Pan, in case you aren't clever enough to figure it out on your own. Look it up, genius."

∼

Bruce felt sick. He found himself driving around the neighbourhood, circling the block again and again and again. Something was pulling him back, preventing him from making the long trek across the bridge to the marina.

A fist of guilt grabbed his gut and twisted cruelly.

But that wasn't all. His breathing was shallow, and his heart was as heavy as an anchor, weighing him down, mooring him to the spot.

He knew she was distressed and didn't mean what she'd said. He knew she'd been through the worst day of her life. He *knew* she needed him. And damn it, despite the lies he tried to tell himself, he knew he'd failed her. He didn't know how to make it better. He needed to do something to help her but he didn't know what. He was afraid to go back.

But he couldn't leave.

It was just that he couldn't stand to be pushed away like that. It hurt too much. It was bad enough going through life always feeling inadequate and unlovable. He of all people didn't need rejection thrown in his face. He'd spent most of his life finding ways to avoid being put in this position– giving other people reason and opportunity to reject him. It had worked. Until now.

But it hadn't worked, had it? All he'd accomplished by keeping people at bay was to inscribe a safe zone around himself, around his heart. Trouble is, he was all alone in here. He wasn't a fool.

He circled around once more and pulled up in front of the house, cutting the engine. Then he sat, gripping the steering wheel tightly. Thinking about his life. Thinking about all that he'd done, and all that he'd avoided doing.

It had been one long joy ride. Always looking forward, never looking back. No ties. No regrets. But the truth is he was always looking over his shoulder, running to avoid the fate he most dreaded.

Being left behind.

Alexa was right. He was Peter Pan. Afraid to grow up, afraid to accept grown-up responsibilities, or feel grown-up feelings. He'd felt enough pain to last a lifetime when Mom left. And he prided himself on his survival skills. His independence. His detachment. But he could see that it went both ways. If you wanted someone to be there for you, you had to be there for them. Even when it got ugly.

What he hadn't realized, until Markus and Maddie and then Alexa had wormed their way into his unguarded heart, was what it had cost him. Now, he knew. Running away again, avoiding and disappointing the people he loved, hurt more than anything they could do to him. Whatever the risks, he was tired of running.

Enough!

Using his key, he entered the house quietly. It was possible Alexa had finally succumbed to fatigue and gone to bed in the time he'd been circling the block. He paused in the foyer and listened to the sound of his own heart beating like the ticking of an epochal clock counting the minutes to the end of time.

"Koz? Is that you?"

Alexa's velvet voice was tremulous.

"Yeah."

"What are you doing?"

In answer, he moved silently toward her voice. She still sat on the sofa, now ramrod straight, eyes wide. In a pool of low light from a single floor lamp he could see the flutter of her pulse racing on the delicate skin of her throat, and sense her trepidation, like a butterfly poised to flee.

"It's only me," he whispered. He stood and took her in. She appeared oddly vulnerable, no longer hunched and tense, but still soft, so slight, so feminine. She had never before seemed to him so defenceless, his urge to protect her never so great.

"Did you forget something?"

He stared at her for a long moment, admiring the way the light limned the edge of her hair, her beautiful, if puffy, face, and his heart skipped a beat. "Yeah." He moved toward her. He discerned her furrowed brow, her eyes darkly shadowed, blinking. He lowered himself down beside her and turned his body to face her.

"You," he said, and paused. "Tomorrow."

"It's okay." Her head shook. "I'm sorry."

But it wasn't okay. "No."

She waited in silence.

Bruce pulled in a deep breath, strengthening his resolve. He took both her hands in his, and gently rubbed his thumb across her knuckles. "I want to take you and the kids out for a day of sailing. It's supposed to be a beautiful sunny day, a calm sea with a perfect ten to fifteen knot wind."

"It's a school day."

He expelled air through his nose. "She's seven. What's she going to miss? I'll call the teachers."

Her eyes dropped uncertainly. "S'pose." The lamplight glowed on her smooth skin. Her narrow brown shoulders rose and fell. "But, why?"

Bruce released her hands to reach toward her and push her straggling limp hair back from her tear-stained, haggard face. "Because this is what we need." He leaned closer, sliding his palm down her cheek, along her finely angled jawbone, and curved his fingers behind her lean, delicate neck. He inhaled the warm spicy scent of her body, her fragrant hair. As much as he longed to kiss her, he held back. If all she wanted was a friend, then he would be that friend. "Time to play. Time to heal."

Alexa moved toward him, so slightly he might not have noticed if he had not felt the muscles of her neck flex slightly and the pressure ease away from his hand. He increased the pressure, pulling her closer, and edged his face toward hers at the same time. Her eyes glinted forest-black with flashes of gold in the dim light, darting over his face, from his eyes to his mouth and back again. He placed his thumb on her throat, on that spot that fluttered like a nervous wing, keeping time with his own wild heartbeat.

He heard her draw in her breath and hold it.

Time stood still as he closed the gap between their expectant lips, brushing his lightly against her full sensuous mouth, revelling in her softness, in the slight saltiness of her taste. They stayed like that, touching, breathing against each other, absorbing each other like a drug for another timeless moment before he reluctantly pulled away a few inches.

"Come to the marina as early as you can manage."

She didn't reply, kept her eyes on him, hopeful.

"I'll get everything ready in the morning. Bring a change of clothing. Something warm for the kids. Mmm. Marky's sippy-cup?" He pulled back so she could see his slight smile –*You see, I know. I've changed*– he wanted to say. "Okay?"

She nodded and whispered. "Okay."

He kissed her again, swiftly, like a promise. "Until tomorrow."

CHAPTER 19

Alexa and the kids strolled down toward the gate once they'd arrived at the marina. It was locked, so she paused, expecting to have to call Bruce on his cell phone. He didn't appear to be around, but Maddie was convinced she knew where the boat was moored.

Just then a group of teenagers stomped up the ramp, triggering the motion sensor and opening the gate.

"Come on!" shouted Maddie and took off down the ramp, causing the teens to quickly side-step her.

"Hey, watch it!"

"Maddie!" Alexa called after her. She hesitated. She'd rather wait here for Bruce, but now… "Come on Markus." She took his hand and they followed tentatively. "Excuse me. Sorry." The group of teens parted to allow them to pass, and she caught a soft wolf whistle.

They caught up with Madison as she stopped in front of an older man in a striped blue windbreaker. She overheard him say, "Well. *Gød mørgen*, Miss Madison." He looked up. "*Hallo*, Markus."

"Hi, Mr. Jørgen," Maddie replied, and Alexa smiled warily at the man, stepping forward.

"Hello. Are you a friend of Bruce's?"

He stepped toward her, gnarled hand outstretched. "Yah. I am Jørgen. Jørgen Pedersen. You are Bruce's lady friend, Alexa." The way he said her name, it sounded like a song, with a long round vowel and a skip at the end. "It's a pleasure to meet you at last."

Why would he know anything about her? She took his hand, mumbling. "Well, friend, yes."

"And a lady also." A warm smile lit up his creased face, and his pale eyes sparkled with amusement and a knowledge that made a blush rise to her cheeks. "The boy was here a moment ago. I'm sure he'll be right back. Would you like to visit my boat while you wait?"

"Oh, uh. Well, we ought to wait here." She turned to the boat Markus was now tugging her towards in his attempt to climb aboard. "Is this his boat?" She was amazed. She knew he was living on it, yet it was somehow larger than she expected, and more... elegant. It had a long beautiful white hull, and lay like an arrow in the water, sleek and swift-looking. Graceful black letters were painted on the bow that read, *Belle-Etoile*. Beautiful Star? She wondered if he'd named it himself. More surprises.

"Hey there. You showed up."

Alexa's heart skipped a beat. She turned at the sound of his voice, cheerful and lilting. He was so determined to cheer her up, she hadn't the heart to be grumpy, nor could she stop her face from mirroring his grin. Besides, the sight of his smiling face, his broad chest in a clean blue t-shirt, his wrinkled plaid shorts, his long, tanned, muscular legs stretching all the way down to his bare sexy feet in flip-flops, was almost enough to lift the weight that pressed down on her heart today. In fact, her bones melted at the mere sight of him.

"You had doubts?"

His smile twisted playfully– *I wasn't sure*, he seemed to say.

"How could I resist?" she reassured him. "Is this really your boat?"

"This is her." His smile was proud and affectionate.

"She's beautiful."

"I'll show you inside, but I'm not quite loaded up. It's messy."

"I invited your guests to visit me while you get yourself ready," piped up Jørgen.

Alexa glanced up to see Bruce meet Jorgen's eye. The corners of his mouth tugged in slightly, and some silent message was exchanged. A flush of colour worked its way up Bruce's neck and cheeks before he looked at her. "Would you mind? I only need a few more minutes and we'll be ready to go."

"Sure." She ushered the children with her and they followed the old man to his shimmering aluminum fishing boat a few slips away, feeling an odd excitement rising at the day that lay ahead.

After a brief tour of his space and equipment, Jørgen sat her down and offered her a tin cup of strong black coffee.

"Thank you. How well do you know Bruce?"

"Oh. We are neighbours, ya?" He gestured at their proximity. "We go fishing sometimes."

She felt bashful, not knowing what he knew about her. "Bruce told you about me?"

Jorgen's almost-smile was enigmatic, and his pale blue eyes sparkled in the morning sunshine. "Aah. He is not so talkative. It's what he has not said that tells me the most. You are important to him. He is ready–" His eyes darted across to Bruce where he loaded stuff onto his sailboat, the muscles of his arms and back bunching in a way that made Alexa warm. "I have said too much."

Alexa took a sip of coffee and cleared her throat. "You're from Sweden?"

"Norway."

"Oh, sorry."

He waved a hand in dismissal.

"How did you come to Canada?"

Jørgen needed little invitation to tell his story about the war. She listened politely, attending to the kids, who played with some fishing lures under Jorgen's watchful eye, comfortable in his familiar boat.

She was warmed by the fact of Bruce befriending this lonely old man. It wasn't the kind of thing she pictured him doing. It seemed he was always surprising her lately. He wasn't the unfeeling rogue she'd always taken him for. Quite the contrary.

"Okay!" came Bruce's shout a few minutes later. "I'm ready over here."

She stood up, rather too quickly. "Thank you for the coffee and the chat." She handed him the empty coffee cup. "It was nice to meet you, Jørgen."

He chuckled. "You will have a wonderful day. Enjoy." He helped her step over the gunwale to the dock, and handed the kids over to her care. "Bye for now, kiddies." He waved them off. Bruce lifted the kids on board *Belle-Etoile* and handed Alexa over the gunwale, letting his hand slide gently down her back, resting it there and giving her a little push while she stepped on board. But it wasn't exactly flirtatious, she reflected. Rather more protective. Proprietary. Certainly nothing she would complain about. It made her feel rather cherished, actually.

Once they were out of the slip and underway, Bruce asked if she had any experience sailing before.

"Um. A very little. Years ago... maybe ten. I'm not sure I remember very much. Is it... do you need help?" Now she was worried that they should have had this conversation before she agreed to come.

"Nah. I sail her single-handed all the time. Just wondering." Bruce stood at the wheel, and they motored slowly out of the marina. "If the wind is light, we might want to lift the spinny, that's all. I could use a hand with that."

She was relieved to discover that Bruce had already purchased child-sized life jackets for the kids. Apparently they'd used them last time they were hanging about on the dock. Both of them appeared very comfortable on board, and seemed lulled into a calm and still state that was uncharacteristic.

"Fish?" Markus asked, hope in his eyes.

Bruce took in their eager faces. "Not today, sport. Sailing."

"Aaaww," was Maddie's response.

"Hey, can you hook up the little one?" Bruce said.

Alexa looked at him, questioning.

"See that halyard there, the green and white one with the carabiner on the end?" He gestured at a pile of coloured ropes and she inferred that's what he meant. She recalled now how much jargon was involved in sailing.

Alexa squinted and fumbled at some lines, which all seemed to be a variation on green and white, blue and white, green, red and white, finally presenting one. "This one?"

"Yeah," he offered her an encouraging smile. "You mind hooking that on the back of Markus's life vest? That loop there. Right."

She did as he asked.

"Good, you take direction well." He winked at her eager smile, and his eyes slid appreciatively down her bare legs and up again, his smile widening. Okay, now he was flirting. "Now tie it off at about four feet. That should be enough rein."

"Tie...?"

"Lock it into that cleat there. Right."

Markus tugged at his leash, grumbling.

"Never mind, little buddy. There's nowhere to go anyway." Bruce laughed, and Alexa quietly admired his carefree, white smile.

"Hey, Scallywag. Can you go round and pull the fenders up onto the deck, please?"

She squinted at him, uncomprehending.

Bruce pointed over the gunwale. "Those big white ball things hanging on ropes along both sides. Pull them up and lay them there, inside the lifelines."

Maddie, incredibly agile and sure of foot on the gently rocking deck, moved to the first one, pulled it up, and searched his face for approval. He nodded, and she went about her job without further instruction.

Alexa was impressed at the ease with which Bruce maneuvered the large vessel out of the marina while seemingly occupying his mind with other matters, and chatting effortlessly with them. She envied the efficiency of his movements. He shifted his body with ease and confidence on the swaying deck of the boat, without waste or hesitation and she watched his muscles bunch and flex. It was sexy in a way she hadn't considered before. Masterly. Manly. The way, she reflected, one would want a man's body to move. It inspired trust. A prickle of appreciation for his strong, masculine body shimmered through her. His physical strength and informal, sporty clothes were utterly appropriate in his world.

Maybe all this time she'd been looking at him through the wrong lens.

She inhaled deeply and looked around her at the sparkling blue water and the boats bobbing in the marina. As they glided past the red buoy and between a rocky outcropping and a small island, the sea opened up all around them, and Bruce increased their speed slightly.

A buzzing in her pocket disturbed her peace. She withdrew her phone and glanced at the screen. There was a text from Bronwen that she'd missed. It was the office calling now, but who? Bruce glanced at her, a line of worry between his dark brows. She shrugged and answered the call.

"Hello?"

"What the fuck, girlfriend?" She released her breath. It was Peter.

"Petey." Her eyes met Bruce's, then he looked away again.

"You left without telling me anything!" He sounded distraught. "Aren't we in this together?"

"In what, Pete? What am I in, but a pot of boiling oil? This isn't what I planned."

"I hate to say it–"

"Then don't. I know you warned me. I know it." She huffed. "It just fell apart so fast. I... I don't know what happened exactly. I suddenly saw everything so clearly and I just snapped."

"Oh, honey. What now?"

"I don't know. I'm still numb. Just hang in there okay? I don't even have a plan B."

"You know I have to work *under* asshat Nathan now. He's strutting around here like a peacock. It's nauseating."

"I figured." She shook her head. "I need time. Just keep your head above water and I'll be in touch. Okay?"

"Okay. Okay." He paused. "Are you alright, really?"

She tilted her head to the side, cast her eyes around at the ocean waves and distant blue horizon, flicked her gaze toward the sexy, capable, strangely comforting Bruce at the wheel of the boat. The corners of his mouth twitched in at tentative, questioning smile. "Yeah. For the moment. I'll call you later. Tomorrow maybe?"

They signed off and she put her phone back in her pocket pensively. She had a great deal of hard thinking to do, but today, she was emotionally frazzled, and not yet ready to deal with any of it. Bruce was right, she had healing to do first.

"Is that Passage Island?" She pointed ahead.

"Yup."

"Where are we going?"

Bruce shrugged. "Wherever the wind takes us."

Alexa sat back and forced herself to relax.

"Remember all the rules we talked about, kids?" Bruce asked.

Maddie nodded solemnly while Markus looked blank. She supposed that was why he got the leash.

"I can't sail if you guys are in my way," he said. And I may ask Alexa to help me do things. So the best is for you to sit right where you're told, and to move out of the way if we say so. Otherwise, no moving around while we're under way. Got it?"

They nodded, too thrilled with the novelty of boating to question anything he said. All at once he was like a sea god in their eyes, opening a door into a new and fascinating adventure. He seemed that way in Alexa's eyes too.

A little ways out, he suddenly turned the boat, and dropped the engine to an idle. "Come here," he said, gesturing to Alexa with a flick of his fingers.

She moved toward him, and he pulled her gently behind the wheel beside him, his hands warm and firm against her sides. He pointed up. "See that little arrow at the top of the mast?"

She looked up, noting the arrow, and nodded.

"Keep it pointed straight ahead." Then he was gone, and she was holding onto the large stainless steel wheel by herself, missing his hard, warm body.

"Wha–?"

He darted over the deck with sure feet, which she noticed were now clad in smooth-soled leather deck shoes. She hadn't noticed the change until now. Suddenly he was removing and storing the fenders, hauling on ropes, and vigorously cranking winches with a handle. Her eyes followed his efficient rapid, shifting movements, trying to understand what he was doing.

The mainsail he was hauling up flapped violently.

"Keep her pointed into the wind!" he shouted over the sudden noise, jumping up onto the foredeck, dashing here and there adjusting hardware and lines.

Alexa jerked her head up, checking the arrow on the mast, and quickly corrected their course, feeling a blush heat her cheeks.

With a gentle hand on their heads, he murmured to the kids to keep their heads down, explaining that the boom could knock them clean off the boat, and left them staring up at it in fearful fascination.

Then he was at her side again. He reached down, pulled on a lever and the engine went quiet. All was suddenly silent, and the sea loomed larger. Placing a hand over hers, he turned the wheel a bit, smiling with satisfaction as the sail filled with wind, pulling them over the surface of the sea without a sound. When he had it aligned, he patted her hand on the wheel and off he went again.

The sea tugging on the hull and the rudder echoed through the vibrations on the wheel into her hands, like a living creature. He hadn't said anything, but she had the sense to hold their position to keep their angle to the wind constant. Their speed picked up, the only sound the waves lapping softly against the hull, and a soft whirring.

After yarding on the main sheet and adjusting the sideways pulley-thingies, he released another line and yanked on yet another, and the foresail unfurled and billowed with rushing air, and a thump like a base drum.

As their speed increased, the boat heeled slightly, the cool wind rushing at them, and the kids squealed with terror and delight. He reached back, adjusted the direction of their tack slightly, flashed her an atta-girl-smile, and cranked on another winch handle until he was satisfied with their trim. He was in his element. Oddly, she was filled with a kind of awe at his prowess on the sea, and her chest filled, inexplicably proud of herself at his simple approval.

At last, everything was set the way he wanted, and he joined her and took the wheel from her hands.

"It's beautiful," she said. "I'd forgotten how exhilarating it is. It's been so long."

"Did you take lessons? Or did someone take you out?"

"An old friend had a boat. I was going to join a club, but I never got around to it. Picked up a few things by osmosis." She pointed at the pulleys. "What's that called again?"

His gaze followed her pointing finger. "Traveller."

She nodded. That sounded familiar. "Can I help?"

He smiled warmly. "We're good on this tack for a while. I'll let you know when we need to change things up." After indicating a seat behind them, he sat down beside her, gazed up at the sails, peered out to sea. After a few minutes of silence, during which Bruce kept his gaze pinned to the horizon, he spoke. "How are you feeling today?"

Her gaze slid over to him, and found his warm assessing eyes resting on her face, his expression somber. She sucked on her lip a moment and said, "Perhaps surprisingly, not so bad."

"You wanna talk about it?"

Alexa pondered his question. "Not sure what I'd talk about. I don't want to rehash the final conversation with Krystof, if that's what you mean."

"Hell, no. No, I mean. Will you be okay? While you figure out your next step."

She shrugged, feeling her face heat, tears threatening.

Bruce's lifted his arm and set it on her shoulders, giving her a squeeze. "You'll be alright, you know. A change never killed anyone. It's only that it caught you off guard."

She nodded. "I have some serious planning to do for my future."

Bruce leaned toward her and bussed her on the cheek. After a moment he asked, "Is money an issue for you? ... 'cause I could–"

Alexa was startled. "No!" She was almost offended at the personal question, but then realized he was expressing genuine concern.

"If you need help—"

"Oh." She blinked, surprised. It had never occurred to her that he might... what, worry about her? Offer to help? "I... uh...No. Absolutely not. I own my condo and have a bit put away. In fact I've been saving for years, so that..." she stopped. Now why would she share that with Koczynski?

He lifted his eyes and studied her. "So that?"

What the hell. "For the day I open my own office. Start-up capital."

He nodded, his brows lifting in comprehension.

"Thank you, though," she forced herself to say, knowing that he meant well. Alexa observed the kids, who seemed strangely content to sit still and look out at the sea and the scenery passing them by. "It's odd the kids are so happy. I would have expected them to be bored and fidgety."

"Sailing does that to people. It's very soothing. I relax out here like no place else. Something about the sea speaks to me."

"That's why you bought your house where it is?"

He shrugged. "Partly. The view. Proximity to the marina. And, I wanted a place I could work too. You were right. I don't see myself working away from home anymore. I can keep myself busy there." A sparkle of mischief lit his eye. "It was also amazingly cheap. It's in pretty bad shape."

"You're so lucky to have it. I don't know if you realize."

"That may depend upon one's point of view," he deadpanned.

"No. No, it's not some architect's fancy. Do some research. You'll see how valuable it is. You might even garner some fame for discovering an unknown treasure."

"It's you who discovered it. And you who will be responsible for bringing it back to life." He seemed to ponder a moment. "Hey, maybe you could get some useful exposure out of this. To help launch your own firm."

Alexa considered his words for a long time before answering. It was her deepest desire, to one day own and run her own firm. To call her own shots. It's that it had always seemed like it would take her a very long time to get there. Now, it would take even longer. "It takes a lot of capital and good will to get a firm off the ground and to succeed. I'd like nothing better. Someday." She sighed deeply. It was more than that. She'd lost her direction. "I'm afraid my career took a serious setback, though."

Bruce's brows furrowed, and his mouth puckered, but he deigned to offer her any conciliatory words. They spoke no more until they were well out past Passage Island.

"We're going to get ready to tack up ahead. Can you handle the foresail, or do you want to steer the boat?"

Alexa froze. "Um. Do I have to choose?"

Bruce laughed. He explained what he wanted her to do, step by step. "Okay?"

She nodded.

"Keep your heads down kids. Coming about!" He turned the wheel, and the sails fluttered and then caved in. Alexa scrambled to release the foresail sheet from the cleat, and yanked hard, hand over hand on the other side. It was harder than he made it look, and she bruised her shin on the bench, and nearly tripped over the coiled lines on the deck. She wasn't fast enough, the sail continued to luff, and they instantly lost their speed.

Bruce jumped up and came to her aid, pulling the sail tight, cranking the winch handle a few times, tightening and cleating it. But once the sails were trimmed, they remained virtually dead in the water, the sails fluttering feebly, all their momentum lost.

"I'm so sorry." Alexa said, as deflated as the sails. She couldn't even follow simple directions. She dropped her gaze and plopped down on the seat, discouraged. "I've ruined our fun."

"Hey, it's okay. It's not you." He cupped her cheek in his hand, lifting her gaze to meet his. "The wind died. Unlucky coincidence. Bad timing. Whatever. It happens."

"It's alright, Auntie Alex. You'll do better next time," Maddie said.

"Maybe you'd like to try steering, Scallywag," Bruce said.

Maddie's eyes widened. "Uh. Okay."

"It's a hard job." Bruce's mouth twitched. "You sure?"

"Yeth. I can do it." Her green eyes shone with determination.

"Hang on a bit." Bruce pulled on a few lines, loosening the sails, and hauling the traveller over. "Let's see if we can find some wind." He fiddled a bit, scowling at the sails, and finally turned over the motor. "I'm going to take us a bit further out there, see if we can pick something up from the south. There's nothing here." While the engine purred, everyone sat down, and Maddie chattered endlessly about her desire to learn to sail the boat herself, and how proud her dad would be when she told him. Markus piped up from time to time with comments of his own.

Bruce asked Alexa to hold the wheel while he dropped down the hatch, and a few minutes later he resurfaced with juice for the kids and a bag of chips. "Beer?" he asked.

Alexa glanced at her watch. It was only eleven-thirty. "A little early isn't it?"

He shrugged. "I'm having one. I also have Evian and... uh, cider."

"Evian, please." Alexa shook her head. She'd never met anyone so relaxed and seemingly unworried. But even though she'd always called him lazy and irresponsible, it wasn't that at all. He certainly was both knowledgeable and skilled, and lacked neither energy nor initiative. He simply didn't get stressed out about anything. He truly lived in the moment, taking whatever life threw his way. Perhaps there was a lesson for her in there somewhere.

They made their way to the southeast, closer to Point Grey, lounging in the sunshine and savouring their drinks. The kids were more than content to sit and munch on potato chips, and Markus had even forgotten that he was lashed to the boat. Alexa lay back against the cabin wall and closed her eyes. Bruce was right. This day of sailing was both soothing and healing. It was exactly what she needed to clear her head, and as the sun warmed her skin, she closed her eyes, picturing how his muscular arms and legs stretched and bunched as he moved over the boat like a panther, and fantasized about how she might thank him for it.

The boat turned suddenly, and Alexa's face was thrown into shadow as their direction reversed. Her eyes shot open. "What's hap–?"

"Sit tight and relax. I'll handle it. I feel a little breeze." She watched him for a few minutes as he adjusted the sails again, and shut the engine off. Then she closed her eyes and let him steer. She could feel the hull tilt as the sails filled again with wind, and let her body rock gently back and forth on the hard fibreglass bench, lulling her almost to the point of slumber. A blanket of warmth stole across her bare legs as their position shifted slightly, and she was again fully in the sun.

"How's that?" came Bruce's soft voice, like a tender caress.

"Mmm. Lovely," Alexa replied. "How come some of the ropes are lines, and others sheets, and still others halyards? It's daft."

He laughed softly. "Tradition, me darlin'."

"I'm hungwy," Markus complained.

"You ate a big bag of chips, little buddy."

"I'm hungry, too," Maddie said.

"Me too," Alexa added with a sleepy smile.

"Blimey," Bruce muttered. "Oh, alright. Hold on a minute."

Alexa sat up and watched as he angled the boat downwind, loosened the main sheet and shoved the boom across to port side, opposite the foresail.

"This is called running, right?" Alexa said.

"Very good," Bruce smiled. "The wind is light but steady, and we can cruise this way while I make your lunch." He lashed the boom with a short line to stop it from swinging back, and they bobbed along at about three knots, gently enough to neither heel the boat over, nor cool the warming rays of sun.

"Where's your hat, Markus?" Alexa asked. "I should put more sunscreen on you two." She jumped up to retrieve the items she needed from below, and was met with Bruce, his broad shoulders blocking the hatch, handing up her backpack.

"Don't peek," he said.

She listened to him clattering around in the cabin while she slathered more sunscreen on the children's brown limbs, wondering what he was up to. Her question was soon answered, when he climbed up with a tray, and sat it down on the deck beside the kids.

"Oh, my God! Look at you."

Bruce had prepared veggie sticks and dip, tiny tuna and cucumber sandwiches, and a bowl of grapes, which were all laid out beautifully in coordinated nautical themed dishes, with boxes of juice, a glass of cold white wine, and folded paper napkins adorned with little anchors. The grin on his face was contagious as he handed her an acrylic wine glass frosted with condensation.

"Thank you."

"You're welcome. Dig in, everyone."

They all ate their fill, as the boat bobbed gently back toward the North Shore. Bruce sat back with a contented smile as he sipped his beer. They were better than half way, but not making terrific headway. Alexa noted that Markus's eyes were getting heavy. He'd need to have a nap before long.

"Eat more carrots and grapes, and then I can give you dessert," Bruce said.

The kids obliged with wide, expectant eyes, and soon he was

handing around chocolate chip cookies, and he was down below again crashing around cleaning up and putting things away.

"Are you sleepy, Marky?" Alexa asked.

"Nooo," he replied, yawning. She bunched up her fleece and tucked it in the corner. "You can set your head down there, if you want to close your eyes for a minute," she said.

"Are you ready to drive the boat, Scallywag?" Bruce's head popped up from the cabin hatch.

Madison's face lit up. "Drive? Really? Can I?"

"Sure you can. Come here." Bruce set Maddie on top of the seat behind the wheel, and pointed out where they were going. "Keep the bow pointed at that big white house there. Keep her steady."

Madison gripped the wheel with both hands and kept her gaze locked on her target.

Bruce slid onto the bench next to Alexa, then twisted around suddenly and lay down, resting his head on her lap, and with an impish grin, closed his eyes. "Ahhh. This is the life."

She laughed at him as he took her hand and set it on his brow. "You don't mind, do you?"

She laughed again, and he smiled contentedly, wiggling his hips. "You smell good."

"It's going to take us all day to get back," she said softly.

"Don't worry, babe. We'll get there."

Alexa eyed Markus, who had indeed set his head down, and seemed to be dozing off. Maddie was content, and well... so was she.

"Thank you," she whispered.

"You're welcome."

On an impulse, she bent down and planted a soft kiss on his smiling mouth.

"Be still my beating heart."

"Oh, shut up."

"That's shut up, *Captain*."

Alexa chuckled and rested her hand on his chest, revelling in the feel of his firm pecs and abs through his slightly sweat-dampened t-shirt, and imagining what it would be like to get really naked and really sweaty with him. Her heart thrummed at the very idea of it, and heat rose in her core like a thermal air pocket. She was having trouble remembering why she'd pulled away from their passionate embrace the other night. Seemed rather foolish now, in retrospect. At least, that's what her libido was telling her.

"I can feel your heart beating," Bruce murmured.

"Can you?"

"Mmhmm." His voice was low and husky.

An involuntary twitch drew Alexa's attention to an obvious bulge in Bruce's shorts, away from which she tried and failed to tear her eyes away. Resisting a powerful urge to slide her hand down to feel his firm, engorged flesh, instead she flexed her hand, digging her fingers into his chest, kneading like a cat, and slowly stroked the curls on his brow with her other hand, again and again. The weight of his head on her lap created the heat of an oven between her legs. His hands, lying on his stomach, clenched into fists. Her breathing and pulse quickened and she felt rather than heard a low rumble in his chest, like a moan. *Oh. My. God. We might as well be having sex. This is so hot.*

They remained like that for several long minutes, but although Alexa might have been getting closer to an orgasm, they weren't getting much closer to their destination.

∼

Jeezus, I'm going to cum in my shorts. Bruce's eyes shot open, and he locked molten gazes with Alexa. He sighed and sat up. "I'm suddenly impatient to get home," he said, and leaned over to kiss her with enough slow sensual tongue to send shivers through her hot mellow limbs, reassuring him that he wasn't imagining their mutual lust.

He'd been on his best behaviour all morning, keeping his libido under control, despite how awed he was when he saw her trim smooth-limbed, cafe-au-lait toned body in short-shorts and a tight tank top stretched over her taut small breasts. Whatever made him think she wasn't his type? He'd never seen such a simple, perfect body. He was delirious with desire.

Still not sure whether it was a good idea to follow his urges, when he knew she wasn't interested in any kind of long term relationship, and a fling gone bad could really mess up their fragile new friendship, not to mention Simon and Kate. And anyway, was that what he wanted? It's just that he couldn't seem to help wanting more of her.

Bruce blinked and looked around at the kids, squinted at their destination and said, "Come on, let's put that spinny up."

He lifted the pole and had her hold the end while he hooked it in, then dropped through the hatch to return with an armful of bright blue silk. With his guidance, they connected the sail and he dashed back to furl the headsail, haul up the spinnaker's halyard in a flurry of swishing silk, and cleat it off. A lively gust of wind suddenly filled the sail and tugged it out over the bow in a stunning, three-dimensional arc, like a brightly coloured balloon. Bruce's breath was stolen away, as much by the expression on Alexa's face as by the spinnaker's awesome beauty as it billowed in a rainbow of sun-kissed aqua and azure stripes like a strip of the summer sky gone wild.

They heard an "Oooh!" from Maddie, and turned to share a this-is-awesome smile with her.

"Good work, Captain!" shouted Bruce over the shushing of the hull past the waves. He could feel the boat surge forward under the power of the new sail, doubling their speed.

He and Alexa sat hip to hip on the bow of the boat for a few minutes, gently guiding the spinnaker with its sheet, keeping it brimming with wind. Bruce could feel the wind alive and vibrating with energy in his hand.

"This is so amazing. Just what I needed," Alexa said.

He gazed into her sea-green eyes and replied, "You are so awesome, just what I need."

"I don't know how to thank you." Her beautiful smile was huge and sincere, her limbs lean and brown, and in a flash, an idea came unbidden to his mind– *I am falling in love with you.*

"I can think of a way," he said, his reply deep-voiced with need, and he slid his hand down her back, resting it in the hollow above her gorgeous ass, tucking one fingertip under the waistband of her shorts and stroking her incredibly smooth bare skin.

She turned to face him, and his mouth came down on hers with a heat that threatened to capsize him. His tongue plundered her ready mouth with abandon and he was back again to the evening on the sofa, overcome by a wild, primal need that could not be held back. She gripped the front of his shirt with a desperate fist, kissing him back as though her very existence depended on it. Never, never had Bruce needed, or been needed by a woman like this, and all he could think of was joining, mating and possessing her, making her his.

A high-pitched scream from Madison broke through their rapture. "Maarkuuuus!"

Bruce's heart leapt to his throat and lodged there, pounding like a tribal drum. Overcome with lust, he'd neglected the kids completely for the last few minutes. In a flash, Bruce shoved the spinnaker sheet into Alexa's hands and was gone from her side. "What the hell?" Instantly he was in the cockpit with Maddie, his head whipping from side to side. It hadn't been more than four minutes since he'd seen a glimpse of Markus's blond head behind the cabin. "What happened? Where is he?"

"I don't know," Madison cried, hot tears springing to her solemn green eyes. "I was looking at the pretty sail. I don't kno-ow!" She was hysterical.

Bruce grabbed the halyard that had lashed Markus safely to the boat. His life jacket dangled from the carabiner, open and empty. Bruce's gut sunk to the bottom of the sea like a stone. No. This could not be happening. His breath was stolen from his lungs. NO!

"Madison? Did you let him out? Did you undo his crotch strap?"

"No!" she screamed. "Nooo!" Tears flooded from her eyes as she realized what had happened.

Alexa stood up. "What is it? Where's Markus?" She obviously couldn't see over the roof of the cabin to where Markus had been, but Bruce had no time to explain. He grabbed both the life ring and the man-over-board pole and tossed them overboard.

Grabbing the wheel from Madison he shoved her out of his way, shouting, "Coming about!" his voice tinged with a desperation unlike any he had experienced before.

"What happened? Is he hurt?" Alexa's voice shouted out.

He spared her a glance. She was stranded at the bow, holding the sheet, while the spinnaker buckled and flapped, twisted and collapsed onto her as the boat abruptly reversed direction. "What is it? I just saw…" She slapped at the folds of silk. "How did he…? Damn it! What do I do with this thing?"

Bruce didn't reply. He hardened his heart, knowing that he had to keep his head. He had to find Markus. He turned his gaze to the port as they circled around, their speed dropping, his eyes scanning anxiously over the suddenly dark and ominous waves. He shouted "Markus! Markus!" while Madison continued to scream hysterically.

"What do I do with this fucking sail?" Alexa screeched.

Bruce spun to her for a moment, bellowing, "Pull it in before it tangles, damn it! Get back here and help me!" He heard the anguish in his own broken, beseeching voice, like a tear opening in the sail of his soul. In that split second, Bruce saw that she understood fully what had happened. Why he'd turned the boat back. He saw in her eyes a dread and terror and grief that was as great as his own, along with tears of frustration, but there was nothing he could do for her. There wasn't a second to spare. If Markus had somehow gone overboard without his lifejacket, he would bob on the surface for only a few precious minutes before his lungs filled with deadly brine and he was sucked under.

Markus. Oh my God! Oh my dear God!

He shook Maddie's shoulders. "Stop screaming and help me look for him!" Bruce released the mainsail halyard, allowing the sail to collapse in a messy heap onto the deck. Then he released the spinnaker halyard, enveloping Alexa in the buckling blue sail. He started the engine and pushed it slowly forward, retracing their path by following what remained of their wake, shouting, "Markus! Markus, where are you, damn it!"

Alexa's attention was still preoccupied by the spinnaker twisted around her limbs. Finally she yanked handfuls and then armfuls of blue silk in on top of herself. Bruce was aware then of a tangled bundle of blue silk stumbling toward him over the roof of the cabin. She dumped the lot near the cabin hatch and glared at him with murderous intent.

"What are you staring at? Get back to the bow and look for him for God's sake! There's no time!"

Alexa cast her gaze around, took in the empty life jacket, as though she needed confirmation that all this was really happening while she was fighting with the spinnaker, then stormed back to the bow. She grabbed onto the forestay and hung over the bowsprit, scanning the water with a furrowed brow.

"Go up there, Maddie. Go help her."

Madison did as she was told, her shoulders quaking, her tears reduced to helpless gasping and snivelling. His heart in a crushing vice-like grip, Bruce continued to steer the boat back and forth slowly, looking over both the port and starboard gunwales, praying to see some flash of colour, the gleam of a small blonde head bobbing in the dark waves...

"What'th that?" came Madison's high-pitched voice.

Alexa leaned further out, squinting into the flashes of sun reflecting off the water, her face a question. "I..." She turned to look at him, uncertain.

"What do you see?"

"I don't know. A shadow. I can't tell..."

"Point at it, and keep pointing at it," he hollered.

They both did so, and he steered the boat carefully toward whatever they had seen. It had to be five minutes since he'd gone over, at least. Bruce's throat squeezed tight, choking him. What was worse, finding Markus's drowned body, or not finding him at all? Hot furious tears burned behind his eyes, but he stayed firm. He couldn't surrender.

"There he ith!" shouted Maddie.

"I don't know..." Alexa peered hard at the water, shaking her head.

Bruce wasn't going to wait around while they made up their mind. He tightened the lock on the wheel, popped the engine into neutral, kicked off his shoes and took a running, flying leap toward the bow and over the lifeline, diving into the cold water like a bolt of lightning.

His heart constricted with shock as he plunged into the icy sea.

He slashed his arms and legs through the water, trying to surface as quickly as possible, and swam hard, whipping his head around in search of anything, anything at all. As the water drained from his ears, he heard the tail end of screaming from the bow above him. "Where?" he shouted, and peered up for guidance.

Squinting up at the sun, following their pointing fingers, he swam and swam in circles, until at last he saw a shadow, and lunged toward it, diving and grasping with his hands. Breathless, his heart pounding in his chest, he nearly broke his fingers as they collided with the solid weight of a deadhead. Fuck!

Bruce hung on the slimy log for a moment, gasping for air, his heart sinking to the bottom of the sea. "Keep looking!" But he knew it was no good. It was too late. He'd lost Markus. Beautiful, innocent Markus. His best friend's baby boy. Whom he loved more than anything, who depended on him to protect him and care for him. How could he ever face Simon again? He didn't deserve Markus's love or Simon's trust. Bruce was paying the ultimate price for his years of selfish detachment. At last, when someone depended on him, he'd let them down. He was contemptible. In that moment he hated himself and everything he had become.

Black rage consumed him. He tilted his face to the sky and opened his mouth, a roar of fury torn from his throat that originated deeper than the bottom of his lungs, deeper the bottom of his heart, in the very depths of his dark soul.

He swam furiously toward the stern of the boat, latched his hand over the edge to haul himself up over the gunwales, but there was no ladder, and with wet clothing, he tried and tried and, despite the force of his anger, could not pull himself up, and fell back in defeat. He slammed his fist into the hull of *Belle Etoile* again and again and again, insensible to the pain.

Hanging from the gunwale, an unspeakable sorrow tore at his core, wrenched free of the confines of his hardened heart. Sobs of anguish wracked his chest, hot futile tears finally flowing down his cold cheeks, lost in the frigid sea.

CHAPTER 20

Alexa looked on in horror, her hands covering her open mouth as her eyes flooded with tears. What had just happened? One moment everything was beautiful, and they were lost in a bubble of desire. She'd been hypnotized by the expression in his eyes. Her heart raced at what she saw there. This was more than just a fun afternoon in the sun. They'd formed a connection. She felt seen. She felt loved, really loved, for the first time in her life. By the most unlikely of men. And it didn't scare her. She wanted more and had decided she would go there. It turned out she'd been looking in all the wrong places.

Now all she could see was Bruce's wet hands gripping the gunwale, blood seeping from wounds on his white knuckles and diffusing into the seawater that had splashed on the deck. Maddie continued to sob hysterically behind her. She felt numb and utterly alone. Her limbs trembled and her gut swirled with adrenalin. Her mind blanked. She didn't know what to do.

Markus couldn't be gone.

She didn't know what happened to a three-year old when he'd fallen into a cold ocean, but she knew it was bad. If she had any doubts, Bruce's panic and anguish should have told her how terrible this was. How could they have so utterly lost control of the situation and allowed this to happen. But still, they couldn't just lose him in the ocean and give up? Could they?

The fear flooding her own veins suddenly propelled her forward. They couldn't give up. "We need to do something!"

She leaned over the side and glared at him. "Bruce?" He'd completely lost it, his dark wet head pressed against the hull, his shoulders shaking as the waves splashed over him and they bobbed helplessly. He felt responsible. He was a good-hearted man, of course he did. But no more than she was. They were in this together. Compassion for him swamped her, but was quickly followed by a surge of rage. How could this be happening? How could he fall apart now? She needed him. Markus needed him.

Worst of all, he needed her.

"Koczynski!" She reached down, hand outstretched.

∽

"Bruce?" he heard Alexa's rasping voice. "Koczynski!" A note of desperation.

He ignored her.

"Look at me!"

He looked up. Her face appeared above the gunwale, her brows darkened in concern. "Here, take my hand." She reached down to him.

He turned his face away. "Leave me."

"Don't be stupid. Get in here. We can't give up! We have to call someone. The coast guard or something. Get in here and help me."

He gazed up at her, beautiful, intense Alexa, whom he actually thought he could love, who could love him in return, with whom he might make a life together. But he didn't deserve her.

He shook his head. His voice croaked, "It's too late."

"Fuck you, asshole! Take my hand and get in here. We can't give up!"

"Fuck you! Leave me alone!"

A sudden splash shattered the water beside him, obscuring his vision. He ducked, assuming she'd thrown a fender at him in her anger. Blinking the water from his eyes, he saw that in fact she had jumped in. She spluttered and bobbed beside him, clinging to the hull. He stared at her in shock. "Crazy bitch! Maddie's on board alone!"

Then his sea-cold face exploded in pain as her hand came across his cheek. "Exactly! Get your lazy ass on that boat Koczynski!" Flailing to tread water, she pulled back to slap him again, and he grabbed her wrist to stop her mid-swing.

"Stop it!"

"Then pull yourself together, asshole. You can't quit. It doesn't work that way." She paused, catching her breath. "Even if it is too late, we have to... we have to find him."

Resigned to the truth of her words, he grabbed her by the waist and shoved her roughly up toward the gunwale, allowing her to pull herself up. She turned and offered her hand, and he took it and hauled himself onto the boat. They both stood there dripping cold seawater over the cockpit, their eyes locked in a bleak glare. Bruce swallowed through his tight throat. He'd have to call in the SOS on the radio. He turned toward the cabin, reaching for the heap of spinnaker sailcloth that blocked the hatch.

It moved.

He froze.

The sail rustled again, and then Bruce heard it.

A whimper.

His heart slammed into his throat, and he clutched handfuls of silk and yanked it away as fast as he could.

"What is it? What's the matter?" Alexa's voice behind him shrieked with tension.

"Markus?" Bruce continued hauling the sail away, exposing the opening to the cabin below. *Please, God, don't let this be a hallucination.* "Markus! Is that you?"

"Markus?" Alexa and Maddie's voices echoed behind him.

Then he was there. His little flaxen head mussed as he waved his arms, trying to get free of the entangled sail that had buried him alive. "Boos!" he cried, his sweet, round cheeks red from tears. "He'p me. I twapped."

Alive! Bruce's swelling heart tried to burst from his ribcage. His throat slammed shut with the violence of his disbelief. Hot tears of relief burned his eyes. A gasp of joy exploded from his burning throat. The last of the sail fell away, and Bruce lunged at the little boy, enveloping him in a stifling embrace. *Oh my God! Oh my dear God! Thank you. Thank you.*

Bruce held him close, feeling the pliable softness of his small limbs. Absorbing his sweet and sour smell. Cooing and murmuring reassuring words into his tender ear. "Markus. Markus."

After a timeless moment, when they had all, at last, realized that disaster had been averted, and they had each held and kissed and patted Markus in their joy and relief, Bruce set him down in the cockpit and they looked at him.

He was perfectly okay, except for his tears of frustration at having been trapped under a mountain of sailcloth. And he was stark naked from the waist down, his chubby bowed baby legs poking out below his t-shirt.

Alexa furrowed her brow, puzzled. "Marky. Where are your pants, honey?"

Markus's face lit up with pride. "I go potty!"

CHAPTER 21

The long trip home was a disquieting denouement after the trauma of the afternoon, leaving Bruce more time than he cared for to contemplate what had happened, and to consider how he felt about it. The kids were exhausted and hungry, despite devouring what remained of the lunch and snacks that Bruce had brought aboard. Bruce himself, and Alexa too, were fatigued from the wind and wet clothing they wore, but more so from the emotional stresses of the experience, one that he would gladly never repeat as long as he lived.

They motored back, the drone of the engine over the waves lulling them all into a trance. No one spoke. Alexa stayed below with the kids, holding a sleeping Markus on her lap, a drowsy Madison wrapped in a blanket curled beside her.

Bruce alone, chilled to the bone, endured the cooling temperatures on deck, steering the boat into the marina. This was the downside of being skipper, he rued, his stiff hands gripping the wheel, every part of his body aching like the old man of Hemingway's story.

This solitary act of endurance, a kind of penance, allowed him to withdraw deep within himself. As his body stiffened, so it seemed, did his heart and his mind, like a traumatized spine that calcified and became rigid to inure itself against further insult and injury.

Once back at the house, Bruce and Alexa carried the sleeping children to their beds. Their exhaustion had outweighed their hunger in the end, and there seemed no point in waking them for dinner.

Bruce yearned for the escape of sleep himself, his limbs so heavy he could hardly drag himself up the stairs. Alexa emerged from Maddie's room and found him hovering in the doorway to Markus's, watching him sleep. His legs seemed rooted to the floor, and his eyes were glued to Markus's golden head, as though he might disappear if Bruce dared look away.

Alexa approached, blocking his exit, and Bruce found himself studying the carpet at his feet. The hallway suddenly seemed too narrow, the air too thin as he struggled to fill his lungs. He glanced at her, and her piercing green eyes intruded on his solitude and threatened to upset the tenuous equilibrium he'd restored on the way home. He nibbled his cheek, wishing he could get past her without having to exchange any false or empty words, or even acknowledge what they'd been through. He moved restlessly, not knowing where to put himself, and finally tucked his hands in his pockets. He winced and pulled the injured one out again.

She stepped closer, raising her palm toward him.

A shiver chased across Bruce's shoulders like a convoy of spiders. He exhaled and raised a hand to smooth the hair at the back of his neck, feeling the fine grit of dried sea salt and sweat on his skin.

Alexa's hand advanced, coming to rest on his chest. His heart thudded violently, and he was certain she could feel its steady drumming under her hand, resting so lightly there, igniting him.

His eyes dropped to her hand, noting her slender, shapely fingers, and trimmed even pink nails. He wanted to suck on them. He wanted to sit quietly and hold her hand. He wanted to fall asleep with his cheek in her palm. He felt a soul-deep connection to her. He loved her, he realized, but he couldn't let it go further. He had to stop it, this tsunami of emotion that threatened to overwhelm him, before it did. "I need to go."

She withdrew her hand, tentatively, as if reluctant. It hovered still in the air between them. Then she let it slide down his arm and lifted his battered hand to her lips gently kissing his raw knuckles before letting it go, and he yearned for her touch again.

He glanced up to find her brows knit, her green eyes darkening in question. "Don't go." Her sultry voice wrapped itself around him like a silky shawl, warming his skin, percolating inward, downward to his loins. "I... I want to be with you." She glided forward like a wraith, sliding both of her hands up his chest, threading her beautiful fingers through his tangled, windswept hair, caressing the back of his neck, warming him. She seemed so small, so vulnerable. "Bruce, I need you. Don't leave me now."

The breath rushed out of him like a blacksmith's bellows, fanning the flames of heat that rose in his unwilling organ, heating the blood that raced through his veins like molten metal, awakening his fingers and toes. His muscles tensed. His fingers twitched, longing to touch her, but he jerked away, impatient to put space between them.

He shuddered, suppressing the urge to grab hold of her, knowing he couldn't go to her. Couldn't risk opening himself up again. Could not endure it. Doubtless she sought comfort in his arms after their shared distress. But he went rigid, his muscles knotted with fear, his breath ragged and thick.

"No." His voice broke, the word strangling him. He turned his face aside. "I'm leaving."

"Bruce!" She whispered, but her voice carried an imploring tone, as though she shouted. "Why?"

He met her eyes, begging her to understand. "I can't. I can't do it."

"What's the matter?"

"I don't deserve..." Bruce searched for words to explain the wrenching pain tearing him apart, the chilling dread. "I've never been able to get... so close. You... terrify me, Alexa. I can't handle the... I can't be responsible for..."

She moved toward him again, and he flinched, flashing a grim caricature of a smile, his lips pulled back, baring his teeth, as if to say: Don't hurt me, please.

"Bruce, is this about Markus? Today? Or is this older and deeper? What's going on with you?"

He was unable to reply. He stood as if turned to stone, as though he had mistakenly beheld the terrible gaze of Medusa.

Alexa's eyes narrowed to green slits, peering into him, studying him like a behavioural ethologist beholding a new species of creature, a puzzle to be categorized and named.

"Is this... about your mom?"

A surge of appalling emotion arose from his core, and Bruce's throat closed up to stop it from erupting. The effort pulled at his mouth, tightening and distorting his face, the heat and power behind it building like a breach in the earth's crust. His eyes seeped febrile molten tears, and his chin and chest quaked under its fierce pressure.

Then, without knowing exactly how, she was in his arms, their mouths fused in a furious jarring kiss, as though they meant to devour each other. Her hands clambered over his chest, around his ribs, slid under his shirt, raked his ass with her nails. An explosion broke him open. He grabbed her arms to pull her closer. His hands slid up to hold her face between his palms, his hungry tongue plundering the softness of her sensual, silky mouth, his heart sprinting, thundering against his ribcage. He lifted her and thrust her against the wall in the corridor, grinding his burning need between her legs, which wrapped themselves around his torso like serpents intent on crushing the life out of him. Though her weight was slight, he almost lost his balance, staggering and disoriented. Suddenly they were in the master bedroom, tearing off their own and each other's clothing with desperate clawing hands, their mouths still joined in frenzied unrelenting desire. He flung her down onto the coverlet so hard she bounced and he kicked off his shorts and threw himself down on top of her, loath to let any space come between them, unwilling to waste one second before he could possess her wholly.

He hardly took note of her slender brown limbs, her perfect slight wiry torso, her pert breasts with their erect brown nipples calling to him, except as an image flashed on the screen of his mind's eye. He saw himself suckling them, driving her wild with the expert skill of his lips and tongue and teeth and hands, but that would have to wait for another, less urgent time. He knew in his heart there would be another time with this woman. Having at last surrendered, he would come back to her. He would stay with her, if she would have him. He would make her his.

His eyes tightly shut, as if he were familiar with this landscape and needed no direction, he entered her in one clean unbroken thrust, burying himself to the hilt to a chorus of their joined voices crying out. She was hot, liquid and tight around his pulsing cock. He could not stop himself then, but withdrew and thrust again and then again with a primitive roar, aware only of her nails clawing at his back, her slender body arching toward his, pressing up into him with as much force as he ground down, their desire to merge mutual and complete. A violent quiver shook them both as she crested, her beautiful lips open in a silent scream, only a second before he went rigid, a flash of light blinding him with its intensity, and the world went black.

A lexa lay perfectly still, stunned, under the dead weight of an unconscious Bruce's heavy leg and arm, still draped across her. She didn't mind. She could hardly feel her own body, she was so numb and euphoric from what they had just experienced. The comfortable weight of him anchored her to the earth. Her teeth still vibrated with the electrical current that ran through her like a power cable that had been supercharged and ripped from its connections, that lay thrashing with jolts of aftershock on the pavement after a storm.

Yes, okay. She knew she was responsible for what had happened.

But what had just happened?

She couldn't help herself. Some heady mix of his masculine physical power on the boat, his mellow sex appeal before the crisis, and his unexpected vulnerability afterwards made her drunk with wanting him.

Perhaps not the wisest thing she'd ever done. It certainly went against her better judgment. What would Kate and Simon say when, if, they found out? But lying here, dazed from the most mind-blowing, life-altering sex she'd ever, *ever* experienced, it was as yet hard to feel any remorse. He was a beast.

She had no answers. Bruce showed no sign of becoming conscious anytime soon. Alexa closed her eyes, trying to empty her mind of a too-confusing mélange of images, thoughts and sensations, and, utterly relaxed, fell soundly asleep.

D awn came too soon.

Bruce stirred, waking Alexa, and shifted his large, warm body, snuggling closer to her, wrapping himself around her like a big bear. She lay still, breathing in his scent of salt and musk and sex, underlain by faint traces of some spicy soap or aftershave she hadn't noticed last night.

Suddenly he jerked and shot up glancing frantically around the room, twisting to stare down at her, his expression of bewilderment giving way to understanding, remembrance and apprehension. Would he feel some regret upon awakening? Earlier yesterday, he'd apparently come to the conclusion that he wanted to pursue a relationship with her, but something had shifted when they'd lost Markus. He'd withdrawn, and obviously changed his mind, until something had given way, and they'd lost all sense of restraint.

Now, she could see plenty of thoughts racing behind his dark eyes. Processing this new, unexpected situation. His throat moved.

Without giving herself a chance to question her motives, she reached out and fingered his bare chest, raking through his soft chest hairs. Her hands slid down and encountered his already half-hard flesh, stroking and gripping him gently, giving him a little squeeze.

He sucked in a deep breath, holding it, and his eyes darkened.

"Good morning," she said.

His nostrils flared, and his chest heaved with his breathing. Between gritted teeth, he said, "Don't speak to me with that voice of yours or I'll cum in your hand."

"We really should talk," she said, making her voice intentionally sultry, knowing it would trigger him. She laughed and shoved him down onto his back, rising to sit astride his muscular thighs, continuing to caress his now proud erection, keeping her eyes locked on his. A sparkle of shared amusement flashed between them, a recollection of the thrilling ride they'd shared last night thrumming through them both.

The corner of his lips curled upward slightly, and his gaze took on a dangerous, predatory gleam.

His strong hands slid up her thighs and along her ribcage, settling on her breasts, resting there. His right hand had swollen in the night, and she raised her left hand to caress his gently. "Does it hurt?"

He shook his head, holding her gaze. "Talking can wait. I've been dreaming about this." He stroked and fingered her, gently pinching and twisting her erect nipples between his fingertips. A jolt of current shot through her, exploding in her core with physical memories of last night's hunger, sensation and ecstasy. She moaned, and Bruce rose up to latch his hot mouth over her aching nipple.

In a flash she was flipped on her back like a flapjack, and he was devouring her, his hot, incredibly skillful mouth licking, sucking and nibbling on first one breast, then the other. Wave upon wave of heat shook her to the bone. His broad, strong palm stroked down her taut belly and covered her mound, their heat merging and multiplying. Then he cupped her and his fingers slipped between her slick folds, gliding upward, pressing inside her, teasing her, heightening her need, but not quite satisfying.

A growl of frustration escaped her, and she squirmed out from under him, flipped over again, gripped his shoulders and leapt astride him like a rodeo queen on a powerful steed, smiling, she knew, like a crazy woman. Not able to wait another moment, she drove herself down on the pike of his erection.

A howl issued from his open throat. He gripped her narrow hips and held her still, his face screwed up as though she'd impaled him through the heart, his breath stopped in his throat. "God, woman, you're torturing me," he gasped, as though confirming her impression.

"Then why are you grinning like a baboon?"

He laughed, gasping. "Can't. Help. It."

A tremor of desire shook them both, and Alexa fell forward over his bare abdomen, raking her fingers through the fine field of hair on his hard chest, across his muscled shoulders and up into the tangle of his long curls, gripping handfuls and clenching her fists.

She rode him, rough and wild, while he bucked and thrashed under her. Their skin was slick with their mingled sweat, and their breathing hot and heavy as their pleasure intensified. In the back of her delirious mind, she worried that their careless grunts and moans would wake and alarm the children, but she was beyond caring, certainly without the power to do anything about it. She floated higher and higher on a wave of passion, the world fracturing and crumbling around her, her vision and hearing disintegrating into a mosaic of sparkling white light and red heat.

Then— *wham*. He flung her over again, and he was between her thighs, driving himself deeper into her core, into her heart with a rhythm and beat designed to tear her in two. Her body filled with the sound of an animal roar that she knew emanated from him but seemed to fill her from the inside out. He slammed his groin against her heat and convulsed, arching over her, his strong arms flexed and rigid, his face contorted in blissful anguish.

And then he collapsed atop her, his dead weight quite alarming, as though she were crushed by a house that had fallen in, or a giant tree toppled, that would never rise again, and she would perish there, breathless and feeble.

She gasped for air.

With super-human effort, he pushed one palm into the bed beside her and rolled himself off her, well, half-off, but it was enough that she knew she could fill her lungs and would live to see another day.

It seemed he was asleep again, but after a few moments of silent stillness, he lifted his head and turned it to peer deeply into her eyes.

His voice, when it emerged, was a broken whisper. "What have you done to me?"

"What have I done to *you*? You're an animal, Koczynski."

"Whatever I am, you make me that way. You destroy me." His mouth came down on hers, hungry and possessive, his tongue plunging deep into her mouth, sucking on hers, exploring and savouring every part of her. "God in heaven, I love your mouth. I dreamt of your lips. They slay me. And that voice of yours is like a drug."

She laughed. "What about my voice? Do you want me to say... something in particular?"

He growled, low in his chest. "You could read a laundry list and my blood would boil, woman. If you dared to talk dirty, I'll spontaneously combust."

"I didn't know."

Bruce pushed himself up, putting more space between their cooling bodies. He ran his fingertips down her body, lovingly, like a carpenter feeling a smooth plank he had laboriously sanded. "I thought I knew what a woman was."

She scrunched her face at him, puzzled.

His head swung back and forth, shaking slightly, but also letting his dark eyes rake over her naked form, taking in every curve and line and shadow. "You are perfection. You have none of the fluff and frills of a full-figured woman. In fact, I used to think you had the figure of a boy, but..." While he spoke, he ran his hands over her limbs and torso, tracing the lines of her. "...you're so much more. You're the quintessential woman, nothing wasted, every lean bit of you strong and lithe and feminine. Like... Eve, in the Garden of Eden. The first woman, with no need of padding or insulation. Your bones are feminine. Your proportions so exquisite..."

Alexa was deeply moved by his romantic words. She felt exceedingly loved. Unfortunately she'd heard similar sentiments before, and she blurted, "That's what Krys used to–" and stopped, aghast, clamping her hand over her mouth in instant remorse.

She wasn't surprised when he stopped talking, and seemed to draw inward. "I'm sorry. That was awful. I didn't mean to…" she began.

Bruce met her eyes, searching, seeking connection. She saw a little sadness there, but more sympathy and understanding. "Go on. Tell me."

She jiggled her head in protest.

"Please, Alex."

She ground her teeth together, remembering. "He… he admired my form. He said I was perfectly proportioned, and used to… used to almost draw the lines of my body, as though he wished I were something he had designed himself."

"Maybe in his egotistical mind, you were something he created."

Alexa pondered that idea. Bruce surprised her sometimes, with his insightful observations. She nodded.

"When we… when we had sex, it was very detached. Almost an abstraction. Very premeditated. Except he often wanted me to…"

"What? Go on."

"He liked me to be dominant."

Bruce's smile then was mischievous. "So do I, babe. You're…" he drew in a breath, as though feeling her all over again, and shuddered "… an animal yourself. A force of nature."

"But with him, it was artificial. I realize how fake it was. It seemed we were having fun, but really, it was all a… performance?. I went along with it, but I wasn't into it." She paused, feeling a shiver race across her skin. "Nothing like…"

"There's nothing fake about us, babe. All I want to do is fuck your brains out. It's purely primal." His nostrils flared, and Alexa's pulse raced, remembering. Her blood and her body would never forget the sensation of being with him. He bent to kiss her again, this time softly, negating his coarse words, letting his lips alight on hers like a feather, brushing, teasing, tingling, raising gooseflesh all over her body. She moaned in agreement.

"Mmhmm." He sat up. "I'll go make us some coffee."

Awareness came crashing down around Alexa. She sat bolt upright. "Oh, my God! What time is it?"

Bruce peered at the bedside clock. "Ten to seven."

She met his gaze. "You stay right where you are. The kids will be up any second."

His face went slack with dawning realization.

"I'll bring you a coffee, but you can't leave this room," she hissed, suddenly supremely conscious of the racket they had made in the throws of their morning passion. She leapt from the bed and wrapped herself in her robe, tying it tightly with the sash. "I'll get them ready and take them to school."

His smile was languorous. "No work to go to. Why don't we forget about school today? Call the—"

"No. We need to talk. About last night. And your Mom." She pointed a finger at his chest. "You stay right here. Be here when I get back."

He shrugged, his expression baffled.

"Don't you run away."

His brows blackened over the bridge of his nose.

She tilted her head to the side and narrowed her eyes at him. "Don't play dumb. You know exactly what I'm talking about. I'm not your mother." And she left, closing the bedroom door securely behind her, hoping it was enough to hold him there until she got back.

CHAPTER 22

He didn't, and yet, he *did* know what she meant. Never in his life had he fallen so soundly asleep in a woman's arms, except, of course, his mother's. Certainly he had never woken in the morning with one. Even if he'd been drinking, and passed out briefly after sex, it wasn't long before the urge to hightail it roused him and spurred him to disappear.

He sat on the edge of the bed, still nude, wrapped in a sheet, sipping his cup of coffee with an ice pack on his hand. It actually hurt like fuck now and the ice was probably too late. She'd followed through with the coffee and ice when she came back in to shower and quickly dress, and then disappeared again to drive the kids to their respective schools.

Though delayed, the desire to flee emerged like an addict's need to fill his veins with comfortable oblivion. Along with questions, millions of questions. How, when he was determined to escape last night, had this happened? He could understand, he supposed, how their mutual exhaustion and the bond created by their nearly averted disaster would draw them together for momentary comfort. Escape. Or, rather, madness. There was nothing low-key about the way they came together. And *came* together! Fuck, she had rocked him to his very foundations. He knew a thing or two about lovemaking. And then this morning, before he was fully conscious, she'd done it again. She was a wildcat. He had no conscious will, no control, as though she'd drugged him and dragged him back in time to a primitive age of instinct and impulse. It shouldn't be that way. She shouldn't have this power over him. It terrified him. And yet, irrationally, he felt elated, a stupid, stubborn grin pulling at his cheeks, his chest rising like a balloon.

We need to talk, she'd said. That ought to be enough to send him running. He swallowed, feeling his body tense. His teeth clenched, and his face twitched nervously. He could feel adrenaline mounting in his veins.

How did she know he would want to run away?

How did she know his desire to flee had something to do with his mother, for Christ's sake? How did she know him so well at all?

Bruce felt naked and flayed, like he'd been tied to a rack and lay exposed and vulnerable to examination and torture. It made him squirm with discomfort. Worse, it made him cringe with fear of what might show, what hideous, humiliating parasites might escape and expose him if she cut him open. His deepest secrets. His darkest truths.

Yesterday's experience had broken him open. When he'd thought Markus was lost forever, he'd relived every feeling of abandonment and worthlessness he'd ever known as a boy. He couldn't face his life, his friends, or himself under such circumstances. He'd wanted the escape of death.

Talk about running away. What a coward.

He realized now that for his younger wounded self, survival had meant building strong defences. Protecting his heart from vulnerability, from loss, from the love that would put him at risk. But now... well he'd be a fool to lie to himself. This time with Simon's kids, and his blossoming friendship... relationship with Alexa, he realized how lonely he'd always been. How lonely he'd made himself by choosing to keep people at a jovial distance. It had seemed safer. It had seemed like the only way to survive.

Now, he realized he craved closeness. He wanted the family he'd never had. He wanted the love of a good woman... of Alexa. But he didn't know how to do it. He didn't know if he *could* do it. What would happen if he allowed himself to love her? She wanted completely different things, didn't she? What if she left him, too? It scared him to death.

The muffled sound of his phone ringing jarred him from his contemplation. He glanced around the room. It was strewn with clothing, his and hers, torn from their frenzied bodies last night. The phone rang again. He rose, set down his coffee cup on the bedside table, and rummaged in search of his shorts. The phone continued ringing. Whoever was calling was persistent. He wondered if it was about his house, but the tradesmen he'd strung along while he waited for his permits had gradually drifted away, finding other work. Aha! The shorts had been kicked under the bed. He knelt to retrieve them and dug into the pocket for his phone, hitting the button just as the ringing finally ceased.

His breath caught, and then escaped in a rush when he realized the caller had hung up.

The screen said Derek Koczynski.

The phone bleeped again in his hand, a text.

Hey. Can't reach you. Have you talked to Mom yet?

The phone beeped again, and he jumped. Derek, again. He hesitated. He didn't have to reply. He wouldn't know.

Bruce recalled Alexa's words as she left. *I'm not your mother.* He bit down on his lip, stewing. She'd make him do it anyway, if he didn't muster up the courage himself. Did he have to wait to be pushed?

He stared at his phone, scrolled back to the message where Derek had given him Mom's phone number. Stared some more.

Then, finally, he dialled.

"Hello?"

His heart fluttered wildly against his ribs.

Silence. A tentative, soft voice that struck a chord within him, making him flushed and hot all over. "Brucey? Is that you?"

He swallowed and cleared his throat. "Yeah. S'me."

"Oh, honey. I'm so, so glad you called at last."

"I know." His throat was tight, his voice sounded strangled and unnatural. He could hardly draw a breath. When was the last time they'd actually had a conversation, one-on-one? He couldn't remember.

After a pause, she said, "Can you talk to me, Brucey?"

An irrational burst of anger flooded through him. He could hear it in his voice, though he tried to suppress it. "Why wouldn't I?"

"Well, it's only that I... you're always avoiding me."

"That's not true."

Tense silence. Of course it was true. Bruce swallowed.

"Well. I guess Derek gave you my messages... they were here with the kids last week, you know."

"No. I didn't."

"Well." She paused. "He told me he'd passed along my invitation to visit."

"Uh-huh."

"And he also said…"

Bruce wondered what Derek would say about him to their mother. His hand and ear were burning. He switched the phone to his other side, and wiped his hand on the sheet wrapped around his thighs.

"He also said maybe you'd come with a little urging."

Bruce sniffed. He examined the clashing feelings inside him. He wanted to run. He wanted the oblivion of sleep. He wanted to cry. He wanted to hit something. He also, maybe for the first time in his life, wanted it to be over. He wanted to stop feeling like a victim, pushed and pulled by his memories of pain, and his fear of the future. That was new.

"Will you?"

"Huh?" He'd realized several moments had slid by while he'd turned inward. "Oh, uh… I dunno. I'm kind of tied up right now." He swallowed again. "Commitments. I've got Simon's kids for another couple of weeks. And my house…"

"Mmm. Derek told me you'd run into some trouble with the renovation."

His back stiffened. "Not really. Minor delays." Somehow the urgency he'd felt over his house project had ebbed. Maybe it had been a red herring for him. He'd wanted to shore up his self-esteem, or maybe his image. When really what he needed to do was man up and face his past.

"So… isn't school finished soon? This is the last week, here on the island, anyway."

"Yep. S'pose."

"So bring the kids here, honey. I love… anyway, there's space for you all." She paused. "Even your lady friend, the architect, if you like."

"My–?" How the hell would she have heard…? Then Bruce remembered his last conversation with Derek. He hadn't even been remotely involved with Alexa then. But… maybe he'd given something of his disturbed state of mind away. Derek, in any case, had read what he wanted into it. And now it was true.

"I don't know. It might not be convenient. Maybe."

"Will you call and let me know? Please? Don't leave me wondering, honey. It's not fair."

Fair? Fair! Walking away from your family wasn't fair. Abandoning your little boy, whose universe revolved around you, whose whole self was wrapped up in you– *that* wasn't fair. Bruce ground his teeth and fought the urge to throw the phone across the room. He tried to calm himself, slow his breathing, steady his heart. Enough! Stop this. Grow up. His throat tightened, and his eyes burned. He clenched his jaw, blinking, trying to get a grip on himself. What a fucking mess he was!

"Bruce? Are you still there?"

"Yeah." His voice was thick with unshed tears and suppressed anger.

"You'll call?"

"Yeah. Yeah." He hung up, unable to bear the sound of her pleading voice another moment. How long he sat, gripping the phone in a stranglehold, shuddering to bring his emotions under control, he didn't know.

The bedroom door opened quietly, and he sensed Alexa slip into the room. "Oh, you're awake. I thought you might have…" She stepped toward him, peered closely at him. Then she knelt on the carpet in front of him and reached up to cup his face. Her thumbs swept his cheeks, and he felt the cool sting of moisture as she wiped away the drying tears he'd been unaware he'd shed. "Baby, what is it? What happened?"

He raised his eyes to hers. Hers were hazy green, warm and calming like a tropical sea, inviting him in, wrapping around him, faithful and sure like a safe harbour. They were filled with concern and caring, and his heart squeezed with love for her. *Fuck me. It's too late. If she left me now, I'd drown in solitude and self-pity.*

He leaned in and kissed her soundly, revelling in the return of pressure on his mouth. He trusted her.

When they broke apart, he blurted, "I love you."

Her eyes went wide, and he saw her throat convulse.

Bruce brought his hands up to hold her face. "It scares me, too, but I do. I can't help it. I need you, Alexa."

She drew a breath. Opened her mouth to speak. Hesitated. "Somehow this is not the conversation I expected to have when I got back."

His mouth twitched in a half-hearted smile. "I know. Me too."

"Is that what upset you?"

"No. Well, partly." He dropped his eyes, pressed his mouth

together, still feeling unreasonable fear. He clutched at the sheet around his waist, snugging it around him, tucking it in. "I called my mother."

"Just now? You actually called her?" Alexa stood up and sat beside him on the bed, wrapping an arm around his shoulders. She was so small, she had to reach up and could hardly embrace him, but her hand on his bare skin was a comfort just the same.

He shook his head. "Yeah." He turned to look at her. "Alexa." He pulled her into his lap and kissed her impulsively again, drawing comfort and strength from her touch. "I realize how crippled I've been. I found a way to cope when she left, and it worked– you know? But I never gave myself a chance to move beyond that."

She was silent, nodding. Listening.

"My brother Derek's been putting ideas in her head, or vice versa." He shrugged. "She wants me to come and see her. She sounds quite desperate." He paused, took a deep breath. "There's something wrong with her. Her health, you know. She's worried that we'll never... you know."

"Talk? Reconcile?"

He nodded. "I don't know if I can."

"You can. Of course you can."

He wanted to. He wanted to confront his past. He wanted to heal and move forward. He wanted to be whole for Alexa... "Come with me!"

"Me? Would that be appropriate? She doesn't know me."

He laughed, a humourless bark. "She doesn't know *me*, Al. She invited you and the kids to come with me. She says she has room." As he said it, he knew it was the right thing to do. Everyone would enjoy themselves, and he would have more courage with her by his side. "Please come with me. I don't know if I can do it without you."

She nodded, and he pretended he didn't see the haze of doubt in her green eyes.

∽

Alexa contemplated Bruce's profile through the windshield of the SUV as he leaned on the railing of the small ferry, gazing intently out to sea, his dark curls tossing in the wind. She wished she could join him at the rail; have one of those side-by-side no-eye-contact kind of heart-to-hearts that seemed to work with men. Or just hold his hand.

Ease his worry or fear about spending time with his mother after avoiding her for so many years.

But she was trapped in this oven of a car, her bare thighs dripping wet with perspiration where Markus lolled unconscious on her lap, their skin sticking together like melted plastic. Even with the windows open, and a little breeze blowing through, the hot sun baked the car, and them with it. She squinted through the windshield again. She doubted very much Bruce saw the shards of sparkling sunshine reflecting off of the pitching waves, or the darkly shadowed blue-gold outline of Denman Island as it drew nearer in the late afternoon light, lifting her with anticipation of their country retreat.

He was a million miles away.

She had been busy entertaining and feeding the children since they left the city this morning, while he became increasingly distracted and withdrawn all day.

Maddie's tangled brown curls popped up beside him, still staring down at whatever had held her interest on the deck. She kicked at it, then looked up at him, her hair whipping, her face screwed up against the glare of the sun. Her little hand slipped into his, and he looked down and gave her an absent smile. Alexa's heart swelled. At least Maddie seemed to have made her peace with him, no longer blaming him for Simon's prolonged absence.

It wouldn't be long now. They had a week for this holiday together, and then Simon and Kate would be home.

They'd emailed Simon and Kate, letting them know their plans. Alexa hadn't mention her job situation, just called it an end of school holiday. They had seemed almost relieved, clearly anxious about the burden their extended stay had put on Bruce and her. They'd had a long email from Simon yesterday. Kate's condition was stable, and they would be able to risk the long flight home at last. That was one less thing to worry about. Then it would be over, and they would all go back to their normal lives.

Except they wouldn't.

On the ferry to Nanaimo, Bruce had sat with them for short intervals, but seemed incapable of being still, jumping up on one pretext after another: "I'm going to get a coffee, you want anything?" or "I'm going to step outside for some air," or standing staring out the window with a dark introspective frown sketched on his brow.

"Are you okay?" she'd asked him more than once, but he brushed her off. "What? Yeah. Yeah, fine."

Alexa tried not to let his preoccupation alienate her, even though she missed his attentive gaze and hungry touch. Her skin still tingled when she looked at him, heat flooding through her core, remembering their first night together. They had spent last night apart, packing for the trip, and it still astonished her that she ached for his touch. His agitation had increased throughout the day, as their visit to his mother loomed. She knew what he was going through. She longed to go to him, but he was so jumpy now Alexa dared not approach him, or even speak to him unnecessarily.

She acknowledged that he sat poised on the threshold of his greatest fear, and her affection for him deepened at his willingness and determination to do this. Not for the first time, she pondered the fact that he'd actually spoken the words, '*I love you*' to her. Did he really mean it? Did he know what he was saying, and what it meant to her? Her own heart faltered each time she remembered, and she tamped down feelings of exhilaration and terror. What gut-wrenching emotions had he experienced in the last couple of days to bring him to this point? He was far less deeply entrenched in his protective distancing behaviour than she'd realized. She understood him better now.

The transformation rocked her world. And the responsibility daunted her. She didn't want to be responsible for someone else's heart.

Her phone buzzed. She'd received a stream of concerned emails and texts over the past few days, from Peter, from Stephanie, and from various brothers and sisters, all stunned at her change of status. So far, mostly, she'd replied with minimal answers, not yet ready to explain. As if she understood it completely herself, or were in a position to reassure others.

She looked at the phone. An actual call was coming in from the office. Pete again?

"Hello?"

"Jenner."

Krystof! Alexa's gut clenched with nerves. She couldn't speak.

"Alexa? Hello?"

"Yuh." Why was he calling? Her pulse raced; her mouth went dry.

"Listen, Jenner. We need to talk. We can't leave things unresolved."

She stiffened. "They're not unresolved, Krystof. I quit. That's pretty resolved."

A minute of silence passed while, she supposed, he found the words he wanted, or found the nerve to say them.

"I want you to come back. We need you here." That must have almost choked him.

She swallowed, reprimanding herself for the weakness that brought the burn of tears to the back of her throat. No. "No."

"Wait. Don't say anything yet. Let me explain." He cleared his throat. "It's the Arts Centre. *It* needs you."

She harrumphed. "You have Nathan." She didn't quite succeed in keeping the spite from her tone.

"No. The board," he released a frustrated breath. "The board have complained. They insist on having *you* back. Mrs. Rose had something to do with it."

Her heart soared at this information. But... "I'm sorry." She couldn't.

"Jenner," Krystof sounded pained. "We'll lose the project. They've threatened to take it away if you don't run it. They've realized the truth, that it's been yours from the beginning. Now they want the full value of your leadership or they'll take it to another firm."

Huh. Wasn't that ironic. Finally the recognition, the validation, the power and the freedom she'd always desired. But not the freedom. Because she'd have to go back to Vision Architecture, and Krystof, and... whatever that meant. Gripping the edge of her leather seat, she said, "I'd need autonomy. I'd have to be a partner." She wasn't even sure that's what she really wanted. But she had to ask.

Krystof sucked air, clearly taken aback. "I, uh, I can make you an associate immediately. We'd... we'd have to negotiate the rest. Is complicated. Biljiana is a shareholder."

He was willing. She was amazed, and slightly nauseated at the possibility. "I don't know. I have to think it over."

"There's not much time. The project schedule is already compromised."

"I need a week. I'm out of town anyway."

"Alright. A week." They ended the call.

Oh, my God! What the hell am I doing? She'd been dragged so unrelentingly into Bruce's messed up life, she'd hardly had time to deal with her own. She couldn't lose herself in the process of helping him. She had decisions to make. She stood at a crossroads, without a map.

Alexa watched as Bruce and Maddie returned to the car and climbed in when they approached the dock.

The fact that she'd quit her job and derailed her career felt like a paralyzing weight pressed down on Alexa, making it difficult to breath. Though she wanted to support Bruce during this challenging time, and even more just be with him in the heady atmosphere of their new relationship, she needed to spend some serious time alone figuring out her future. She knew that, in some way, her relationship with Bruce was at least partially responsible for changing her perspective. When he was persuading her to accompany him on this trip, Bruce had counselled her, wisely, to take time to reconsider her goals and dreams and how to achieve them before making any hasty decisions. And that was *before* Kristof's call, and the lure of her Arts Centre dream.

A vague sense of panic trickled through her. Should she go back? Where could her next job possibly be? She wasn't quite ready to go solo, even with Pete's support. What step would she take? Any position she could find would be a come-down from the one she'd left. How could it be anything but? And yet…

What exactly *had* she left behind, and how would her peers perceive her in the business now? Was Peter the only one who had discerned her intimate relationship with Krystof? Maybe it was common knowledge, and she was a laughingstock. People would ask why she left when she had won such a prestigious project. Whether anyone knew it or not, the truth made her intestines twist into painful knots of shame.

And furthermore, her whole world view had shifted. She no longer wanted what she had always wanted, and the feelings of uncertainty were disorienting. Sure, she still wanted to achieve greatness as an architect, and believed she had the talent. But there was a new, bright layer of expectation on top of that. She had ideals. She wanted to create a nurturing environment for young talent; she wanted to create a workplace culture that was respectful and enlightened, and she wanted to work for clients who were smart and ethical and to support causes and projects that she believed in.

She stole a sideways glance at Bruce's stoic profile as he steered the SUV up the ramp and off the ferry. His upper lip shone with perspiration. It was hot, but he'd gotten increasingly tense as they'd approached his mother's house. Markus stirred in her lap, whimpering a little, and she squirmed slightly under his warm weight.

Was getting involved in a relationship, one unlike any she'd ever had before, with a wounded, defended man-child no less, a distraction she could afford right now? She was being sucked into a role she had never envisioned for herself– nurturer and helpmate. Quite the opposite. Alexa wanted to trust Bruce, and she craved the comfort and connection from him that their new intimacy offered. But it was an uncomfortable place to be. And yet how could she abandon him?

She peered at him again, noting the tension in his set jaw, the sheen of sweat on his brow, as he cast his gaze around, getting his bearings. His dark curls were scraped back into a haphazard tail, and his jaw sported a few days dark growth.

Mountain Man. She shook her head. How far she'd come. They passed a fork in the road, past a tiny clapboard church, an old fashioned General Store with a false front and a broad leaning porch, a cluster of shops and a citron green-painted heritage house with a sign–*Arts Centre*. It was cute. Folksy and inviting. A haunting reminder of her own grand, urban Arts Centre, possibly lost forever.

Was it cowardly? Did it weaken her resolve regarding her own career, her life? Could she afford to hide from her own problems by getting involved with Bruce and his? Could she really be serious about Bruce so quickly? If Bruce was not mature enough to deal with her during her own time of upheaval, then, for better or worse, she would be truly alone.

Her musings would have to wait. After disembarking the ferry, and passing through the little village centre, they drove to the north end of the island. Bruce's brother's directions were vague, so it was more a matter of finding the right road, Northwest Road to Chickadee Lake, and then driving along reading names on mailboxes until they found the property.

"There!" cried Maddie, pointing and leaning forward, throwing her lean arms around Alexa's neck. "Is that the blue pot?"

A large cobalt blue urn, maybe four and a half feet high, marked the end of a driveway, as well as a small sign.

"*Na*-maste Pottery," Bruce read, as he slowed the SUV and pulled into a narrow, rutted dirt driveway. "That's it."

"Nam-as-*tay*," Maddie corrected, her voice haughty. "My mommy says that when she's done her yoga."

Alexa smiled inwardly that Kate's absence had secured her status as Maddie's "mommy" at last.

"What's it mean?"

"It's like 'have a good day.' She puts her hands together and bows." Maddie demonstrated. "Are those supposed to be flowers?" Maddie asked, eyeing the withered stalks and drooping purple petunias hanging limply over the edge of the urn with a jaded eye.

"Dunno, Scallywag." Bruce own qualms were obvious in his expression.

"They have a water shortage in summer. The water table is so low their wells run dry," Alexa said, gasping for breath. She pried Maddie's tight grip from her throat. "You're choking me, honey."

"What's a water table?" The questions and answers continued idly as they bumped down the ridged dirt drive. Bruce drove slower and slower as they got further in. She got the sense he would turn around and drive away had there been room.

The packed dirt track was bisected by a strip of tall grass like a greenish mohawk that went on and on as they jerked and jolted along through a wood of tall fir and spruce trees. Markus squirmed and roused, so she shifted him with a wet smacking sound. Her hot legs breathed a sigh of liberation. Alexa noticed a flash of white trillium flowers here and there, where shafts of sunlight penetrated the umbrella of evergreen branches overhead.

"It's beautiful here. Such a relief from the heat." She inhaled the cool sharp scents of evergreen needles and decaying mulch through the open windows. The understory was a deep shadowy green world, with a low carpet of salal and huckleberry amongst ferns and rhododendrons. "Magical."

"It's like a fairy tale," Maddie said, her voice awed. She withdrew and pressed her face out the rear window, sticking out her tongue like a dog.

Bruce grunted, his tone skeptical.

Alexa shot him a sideways glance. "You okay?"

"Sure, babe. Why?" He flashed her a broad thin veneer of a smile, behind which she could plainly see he was tense, anxious, panicky. His hands on the steering wheel were clenched tightly, the knuckles white, even through the redness and swelling on his right hand.

"Liar." She gave his arm a pat, chuckling.

He guffawed lightly at her accusation.

"You'll be alright. Your mom will be happy to see you. She asked you to come."

In contrast to Bruce's anxiety, Alexa found the atmosphere tranquil, mystical and soothing. It seemed that time stood still as they rolled slowly up the long drive. The only sound entering the open windows was the crunch of their own tires over the dirt track.

"Is this really your mom's house, Bruce?" Maddie asked.

"Mommy?" Markus piped up, the bumpy lane rousing him from his long nap, a note of rising excitement in his sleepy voice. He pushed himself upright, blinking.

"Not our mommy, Marky," clarified Madison. "Bruce's mommy."

"Boos mommy?" Markus echoed, clearly perplexed.

Alexa had to laugh. "Yes, Markus. Bruce's mommy. Everyone has a mommy."

Bruce made a sound in his throat– half cynical, half hopeful.

At last, some modest buildings came into view through the trees. A couple of cottages with a smattering of small outbuildings.

"Maybe there's no one home," Bruce said with a note of dread. "I should have called. She asked me to call first."

The place did seem deserted. There were no vehicles. Air pregnant with slumbering life, invisible to them, buzzed with the sounds of insects, the clicking of grasshoppers idly rubbing their legs together in the tall dry grasses that flanked the driveway as they cleared the wood. The occasional cry of an unseen bird in the forest. The dull distant drumming of a woodpecker. It was a sere landscape, scorching under the hot summer sun.

"Don't give up so easily."

"I'm..." Bruce caught her eye and stopped. She saw the muscle in his jaw working as he clenched his teeth, his brow and nose glistened with perspiration. Determined. Brave. Terrified. She smiled her encouragement and he lifted his chin a millimetre, almost nodding.

"You're not alone. You've got a whole army of people who love you."

She saws his eyes dart her way in surprise, then quickly narrow as a shadow of questioning doubt came down over his brow– *really? You love me?* She hadn't said so. Not yet.

They parked the car to one side of the building enclave where a sward of short grass stretched around behind the buildings and terminated at the edge of the wood. Climbing out and setting Markus down,

Alexa's gaze raked over a flatter area to the other side where several large lush garden beds had been laid out between railroad ties and driftwood logs, where row upon row of various mysterious greens grew, some tethered to poles, trellises and mesh frames. Alexa recognized beans and tomatoes but there were plants there that she had never seen before. The pathways were strewn with trampled yellow hay, and scattered amongst the plants were several large ceramic pots similar to the one that marked the driveway entrance, glazed brightly in blue and gold and crackled celadon green, young green squashes and cucumbers dangling over their edges.

Maddie strode up beside her, her voice low and enthralled. "Look, Auntie Al. It's a witch's cottage." She pointed at a low white stucco cottage with a romantic upward-curving roof, half-covered in thatch, or perhaps dead grasses that had self-seeded on the decaying cedar shakes, giving the impression that they had come upon a magical medieval fairy-tale landscape– within which any wonderful or horrible adventure awaited the unsuspecting intruder.

"Oooh. You'd better watch out. She's probably been waiting for some juicy young kids like you to stew up in her big cauldron."

Markus let out a shriek and flung himself into Bruce as he rounded the SUV.

"Stop that now. You'll freak him out." He looked like he more than half believed it himself. He lifted Markus, and his face showed a hint of confusion and distaste as he scanned the property.

Alexa laughed and bent to whisper in Maddie's ear. "That's probably what's in these big pots. Bones!"

Maddie squealed and giggled with complicit fright.

"Enough!" He snapped. "Look, there're the goats back there." He pointed at a rustic enclosure at the far end of the garden where creatures moved in the shadows.

Alexa pressed her lips together to suppress a smile. He sounded like a dad, but he'd kill her if she said it aloud. "Not what you were expecting?"

Bruce grunted and carried Markus toward a taller building, rectangular in plan, with a sloped roof, walls of sun and rain-weathered cedar planks, and a rustic solarium leaning off one wall, its frame constructed of sinuously curving bleached grey driftwood branches, its irregular glazing shadowed with snaking green vines and darkly layered leaves pressing against glass, fogged with condensation, almost obscuring the interior.

She joined him. "You think this is the main house?"

He shrugged, pointing to a hand-painted sign on a pole that read 'STUDIO' with an arrow pointing to the white witch's cottage. Driftwood benches perched on a low platform that protruded from one end of the other building, serving as a kind of porch before a single carved wooden door. Bruce set Markus down on the deck. The door was flanked by a huge mosaic mandala, inlaid with shattered tiles, smashed china plates and shards of mirror, reflecting slices of the green and gold landscape.

She never would have guessed that Bruce's mother was an old hippy. She gathered he hadn't either. It was like he was completely disoriented, as though he'd passed through an invisible doorway into a fairy tale world and all the rules of engagement had gotten left behind in the real world.

They stood around Bruce in a cluster, more like a gaggle of starstruck tourists than a family of visitors. Alexa glanced across at Bruce, and found him as awed as the rest of them. He noticed her movement and looked up, meeting her eye. His brows lifted, and she could imagine how it felt for him to arrive at this strange place, the home of his mother, and yet completely foreign and unfamiliar to him, as was the woman who lived here.

She sent him an encouraging smile, and with a small nod, he moved forward uncertainly. They followed him up the porch steps, with its bizarrely magnificent mandala, and the huge door that, as they approached, she could see was adorned with the sinuously carved form of a nude woman covered in part by long flowing hair. He glanced at her over his shoulder, his brows twisted in amusement.

She had heard of the unique home-grown architecture that flourished on these islands, and seen some images. But nothing could have prepared her for the overwhelming sense of wonder and quietude these natural, handmade buildings offered, as though they had grown up themselves out of the ground, or were decaying into it, bewitched by fairies rather than built from found objects and the junk piles of generations of hippies and back-to-the-landers.

Together, they slowly crossed the porch, half expecting the resident fairy or ogre to emerge. A blind-eyed terracotta Buddha squatted beside the door like a burly bouncer waiting to check their ID at a club.

For a long moment, they stood there before Bruce strode forward and knocked on the heavy carved door, dodging the woman's naked breast, targeting instead the smooth curve of her shoulder. They waited.

Again, Bruce knocked loudly but no answer came, the heavy thuds echoing in the still air. After a few moments, Maddie said, "There's a rope. Like a doorbell, maybe?"

"Go ahead. Pull it," Bruce said.

Tentatively, Maddie stepped toward the wall and yanked on the braided rope, its tail end decorated with a string of large, ceramic beads the size of her fist. They heard no sound, and exchanged glances and shrugs. Bruce stepped forward to bang on the door yet again, when suddenly it swung open, leaving him standing with his fist upraised in the empty air.

"Can't you read?" came a exasperated loud voice from the apparition before them. A large robed figure filled the open doorframe, backlit by glowing sunlight, reflecting off gleaming Mexican tiles, refracting through the wild wiry pokes of her halo of hair. Under a dusty grey vest, her flowing batik *muumuu* swirled with brightly coloured tie-dyed patterns like a fiery vortex that would suck in innocent children. The resident witch.

"What kind of inconsiderate idiots would bang and ring repeatedly? You should know to come to the studio door when I'm on the wheel!" The woman held up dripping greyslime-coated claws to either side of her face. Her smock-like vest and wild frizzed grey-black hair, that ranged out around her scowling face like a blazing aureole around an angry sun, were splattered with a million freckles of the same mushroom-toned mud.

Confronted by this terrifying spectre with eyes that flashed sparks of green fire like polished orbs of malachite, Markus promptly screamed and burst into tears, burying his face in Bruce's trouser leg.

Maddie, likewise alarmed, took one large step back and bumped into Alexa, who lost her balance, tottered, and nearly toppled off the porch.

Holyfuckingearthmother!

CHAPTER 23

Not one of them found words, least of all Bruce, who stood with his mouth ajar, his Adam's apple sliding slowly up and down.

Alexa clutched Maddie by the shoulders and held her tightly, trying to impart confidence. She stepped forward. "Mrs. Koczynski? We didn't mean to disturb your work. We didn't know."

The woman stepped toward them, out of the doorway. The warm afternoon sunlight fell on her from the front, softening her face, melting away her aura of fury. Her hands relaxed and lowered, dripping wet clay onto the wood deck with a *splat, splat, splat*. She leaned forward slightly, squinting her now warm jade green eyes, which were not so much glowing as sparkling with energy, with vitality, and now, with curiosity.

"I'm Tina Koczynski..." her voice, now softer, tapered off. "Who might you lot be?"

Alexa thrust out a hand. "My name is Alexa Jenner. How do you do?"

The woman did a double-take, seeming to wobble backwards on her Birkenstock-clad feet. She automatically responded by jutting forward her right hand, realizing as Alexa did the absurdity of the offered gesture under the circumstances. They both dropped their hands, smiling. Bruce's mother, for that was obviously who she was, peered hard over Alexa's shoulder at his face. "Brucey?"

"Yeah," Bruce croaked. "Sorry…"

"You didn't call back. I thought…" She waved a fossilizing hand, crumbs of drying clay flying off in a cloud of dust. She stepped out onto the porch toward them, taking them all in, their little patchwork family. "I hardly recognize you with that hair and…" She waved a hand around.

"Hello," she said, bending toward Maddie with a radiant smile that caused Alexa's heart to skip a beat, it was so like Bruce's. "What's your name?"

Maddie narrowed her eyes suspiciously, not willing to accept this transformation as anything but a magic trick. "Madison Sharpe."

"Nice to meet you Madison. Can you introduce me to your brother?"

Maddie's lips thinned, but she turned to Markus and laid a hand on his shoulder, pulling him away from Bruce's leg. Bruce's hand, which had lain on Markus's flaxen head to comfort him, ruffled his hair and fell away. Markus reached up to grasp a finger of his hand.

"Hey little buddy. It's alright."

Markus sniffed and looked up at him, his adoration clear in his glistening blue eyes.

"He seems very fond of you, Bruce," said his mother.

"Marky, this is Uncle Bruce's mum. Say hello," Maddie urged.

Markus turned his head toward her warily.

Tina Koczynski crouched down to his height and raised her brows, her green eyes twinkling in invitation. "Would you like to make a clay piglet in my studio, Markus?" She rubbed her fingers together, demonstrating the silky stickiness of the clay that coated her hands.

Intrigued, Markus nodded slowly.

"I'll take you there in a little while. Why don't you come in and have a snack?" She stood up. "Get your things." She paused, looking them over. "You can all sleep in the loft."

Bruce opened the back of the SUV and carried their bags to the porch. He went back for the two cats in their carrying cases and set them down. Lucy slept, but Oscar let go a skeptical throaty mewl.

Tina cast her gaze over the pile, doing a double-take when she realized that two of the suitcases were in fact animals in carrying cases, and let go a bark of laughter. "My goodness. Are you planning to stay long?"

Bruce pulled back, stiffening, and Alexa noticed his jaw twitch with tension. Clearly he was going to be as touchy as a candle flame in a gale.

Alexa gave his arm a reassuring squeeze. "I'm sorry about the cats," she addressed Tina. "It was a rather impromptu decision to come, and we're responsible for them while our friends are away. Do you have animals or... or allergies?"

Tina's half-smile was enigmatic but she shook her head in answer, narrowing her eyes at Alexa, her demeanour becoming more solemn. Her voice when she spoke was warm. "I'm glad you're here. All of you. Please come in." She turned and led the way into a large open room with a sloped, vaulted ceiling. "I've got to wash up. This clay is drying on my hands." She disappeared.

"I've never seen her... like this." He waved a feeble hand around. "I feel like I'm in a stranger's house," Bruce said, squeezing through the door with his arms full of bags.

"You are."

"I forgot she had green eyes," he said wistfully.

Alexa tilted her head to consider his baffled expression. "Are you okay?" Their eyes met and locked. "When was the last time you looked in her eyes?"

Bruce swallowed, raised his brows, screwed up his face.

"Poor baby." She stepped toward him and briefly embraced him, suitcases and all, dropping a kiss on his cheek. She shrugged and went inside, the kids trailing, their mouths open in awe as they gaped at the strangely appointed house.

"Wow," Bruce whispered as he took in the room. "Weird. She's still got the same..."

Alexa gazed upward. A large round bubble window in the gable end let in a giant shaft of bright sunlight, fading all the colours to shades of white and blurring the many textures in the simple open rectangular room. A mezzanine overlooked the tall space, over their heads, its railing draped in many tapestries and dangling green plants, their chlorophyll-green colour diffusing into the air in the dazzling light.

She stepped forward to focus her eyes better, turning her back to the blinding light. Weathered cowhide sofas were arranged in a U-shape, and draped with a multitude of exotic woven blankets, furs and patterned fabrics in oranges, reds and purples. Cushions of every shape and colour were strewn everywhere on the Mexican tile floor and sofas. She strolled toward the far side of the room that opened into the greenhouse they had seen from outside. She could see an inviting vintage table and mismatched wooden chairs tucked in amongst a jungle of plants, many of them hanging from macramé creations not seen since the sixties. Alexa was speechless.

"It's like being in a time warp," Bruce said from behind her.

Alexa laughed. "Maybe it is."

~

On Bruce's third trip from the car to the house, the sounds of Carole King drifted out, filling his head with snapshots from his childhood, flashing in his mind's eye, tugging at his newly exposed heart. Did she put it on intentionally? She must know he'd remember that it was her favourite, and that they'd sung along and danced together when they were alone in the house. But maybe not. He didn't know what she remembered. He didn't know her at all. That's why he was here, wasn't it, to bridge that chasm?

The tight knot of pain he felt, just under his collar bone, hadn't let up for days. Now it was quite sharp. He set the bags down in the entry hall and rubbed his diaphragm, trying to ease the tension.

The kids and Alexa sat at the kitchen table around a plate of cookies. Somehow the moment of terror when his mother had answered the door had been diffused with music and warmth. His throat thickened suddenly, and he turned to go outside again for another load of luggage. A pitiful mewl came from one of the cat carriers sitting in the front entryway. He crouched to poke a couple of fingers through the mesh gate.

"Hang in there, Oscar. I'll let you guys out in a sec," he murmured, not wanting to draw attention to himself. He was grateful to be busy, and let Alexa break the ice. It was cowardly, but he also had a sense she was doing it quite deliberately, to give him a chance to get his bearings. A wave of gratitude swept over him, intensifying his feeling of vulnerability. He'd never had anyone, except maybe Simon, who understood him so well. He stepped outside to get another load of bags as the familiar lyrics of *So Far Away* drifted from inside. He paused on the deck, his hands at his back, raising his burning eyes to the crests of the trees surrounding the clearing in which the house sat, and drew a lungful of clean dry air.

With stinging eyes, and a mouth flooded with the taste of salt, he exhaled and stepped off the deck to stride around the side of the house. The little white cottage door sat ajar, and he stepped inside the empty building to peer around the dim interior. His nose filled with the wet mineral scent of clay. The perimeter walls were lined with rough wooden shelves, stacked with ghostly pale pottery. Large urns and barrels crowded the corners and encroached on the central work area, where battered old wheels squatted in coronas of splattered clay. Damp dirty canvas draped over various incomplete projects. He recognized the elements from the small pottery studio his mom had set up in their garage, though this one was larger, more crowded, and better equipped. Frowning and scratching his hair, he squeezed his eyes shut, trying to force images of shattered pottery from his mind. Piles of it. His head throbbed with the echo of his father's angry voice and violent gestures. It was all a blur, and he shrank from the memory, just as he had scurried from the scene of chaos and recrimination, and tucked it away in a dark corner.

With another deep breath, he turned and walked outside, ambling through the yard, his gaze flitting from hanging planter to glazed pot to rusted pitchfork, trying to make sense of this alien place, where every object tugged at him like a friend, though he'd never seen any of them before. It all hung together like a tapestry woven together from strands of old familiar emotions, long forgotten, the pattern made by the interwoven weft and warp achingly recognizable. And it all seemed to be bunched up in his chest like a knot of rough jute cord, scratchy and stiff.

He shook off the feelings and hurried to the car for the last of their bags, bracing himself to re-enter the house. Nothing had changed, no one got up or looked over. He filled his arms with bags and lugged them up the stair to the mezzanine above, an open space under the vault of the roof, where various mattresses lay on the plank floor. Neatly folded piles of patterned sheets and patchwork quilts, a rainbow of towels sat on top, awaiting the next houseful of grandkids, he supposed. Again, he was stopped in his tracks by the force of emotion that drove the air from his lungs as though a band had tightened around his chest. Another quick trip down and up the stairs and he was able to release the frustrated cats, setting up a clean litter box for them in a corner, and putting out food. They'd need water, too. And Lucy needed her insulin shot, which was in the small cooler they'd brought.

A flurry of muffled laughter drifted up from downstairs, causing a twist of longing in his gut. What were they laughing about? He wanted to be included, but he fought a powerful urge to evade the entire thing. Raking his hands through his hair, he grabbed and pulled. He couldn't hide forever. He grabbed the cats' water dishes and skipped down the flight, pausing at the bottom to take in the scene again, bolstering his courage.

"Come and have a cup of tea, Bruce," his mom said.

He sauntered over. "I need to give the cats some water, and Lucy needs her shot, I guess."

"I can do it," Alexa said, moving to rise.

He set a hand lightly on her shoulder. "Stay put. I'll do it."

He felt his mother's eyes following him as he went to the kitchen sink. More strange things surrounded him, and he tried to blur his focus and not really see any of them. He filled the dishes and carefully carried them back across the living room and upstairs to the cats. Forcing breath out to release tension, he didn't let himself dawdle, and went back down.

His mother stood with a pitcher of water, and set it down on the corner of the tiled countertop. "You can take this up later. So you don't have to carry the bowls up and down."

He nodded and turned to Alexa. Their eyes met, and hers radiated compassion and encouragement. Lifting his chin, he sat down next to her at the table and squeezed her hand.

"You like hibiscus?" she asked with no hint of the amusement that he knew lurked under her cool exterior.

"Sure. Love it."

She poured a cup full of steaming pink liquid and slid it over to him, while his mother returned to her seat. She kept her eyes on the children, who were done their milk and cookies, and looked like they were getting jiggity.

"That's quite a nice studio you've got out there," he said, taking a sip of the tart fruity brew, wincing.

"That's my church," his mom said without explanation.

"Can we see it, Tina?" Alexa said.

"Of course. We'll take the kids out to do their project in a little while."

"They need to let off some steam," Bruce said. "We were in the car a long time."

"You can take them outside when you've had a rest. Have a cookie."

Bruce blinked at the half plateful of homemade cookies, darted a glance at his mom, and back at the cookies. Could he stand it? He swallowed and took a cookie, tentatively bringing it to his nose. His eyes closed when the sweet, buttery, nutty aroma hit his lizard brain and flared, nodding in anticipation of the melting flavour on his tongue. Pulling himself together, he bit, tasted, chewed, swimming in a secret pool of memories as the sensations filled him. Without knowing how, he was reaching for another one.

"Lawrence should be home soon," his mom said, and his head shot up, questioning.

"My husband," she said.

His brow drew together, remembering something Derek said. "He's a... some kind of monk?"

"Rinpoche. Rin-po-*shay*. A Buddhist teacher."

Bruce blinked and darted glances at his mother. He somehow couldn't let his eyes rest on her, though he was burning with curiosity that drew him to her. More than curiosity, he was powerfully attracted to her, but something, some invisible wall of resistance held him back. He had to fight it if he were to accomplish what he came for. He'd been running for too long. Alexa's hand slid over his thigh, gripping warmly, and again he felt gratitude that she seemed to know what he was feeling.

"Tell us about him," Alexa said. "How did you meet?"

∽

Alexa took things one minute at a time. Tension radiated off of Bruce, and she felt empathy for him, but she could also see that he was making it harder on himself by being so stiff and resistant. He couldn't help himself, she supposed. She was sure Bruce very soon would feel better about being here, if he could get past his nerves. She really wanted him to get what he needed from this visit. Meanwhile, she would help as much as she could by filling the time with get-to-know-you chatter. Even though her thoughts kept snagging on her own dilemma. She couldn't put off dealing with it too long.

The weird thing was, she really liked Tina. It was instant, barring that unsettling moment when she opened the door, and the light had framed her from behind. The older woman was so warm and generous, with a huge spirit that immediately soothed and comforted Alexa. Tina was like some kind of goddess, filled with compassion and wisdom, and anchoring everyone in her presence to Mother Earth like the sheltering branches of a big protective tree. She would be so good for Bruce, if he could let her in.

But she understood he had a deep tender wound, and needed to pace himself.

"I met him here, on the island. I came here as a retreat, and to explore, because I'd heard it was a haven for artists."

"You've been into pottery for a long time?" Alexa asked.

Tina nodded, lifting her cup to sip. "I always did it. Bruce will remember. But... it was hard with four kids. There wasn't enough time, or space, for my things." She glanced Bruce's way as she spoke, though he kept his eyes lowered. She emphasized the word *things* as though it were loaded.

Bruce's eyes lifted warily and met his mother's for just a moment before he looked away again. Something was being remembered and not spoken about. A touchy subject.

"So all these huge urns are your work, I guess?" Alexa veered the conversation to safer ground.

"Yes. It's my signature creation now. But I do smaller pots too, plates, bowls, beads, the usual stuff. It's a different kind of clay."

"I love them. Have any landscape designers commissioned your work?"

Tina shook her head. "Tell me about your work, Alexa."

Speaking of touchy subjects. She cleared her throat. "I've designed all kinds of buildings, but I like civic work, and schools, especially."

Bruce drew an audible breath, as though he were going to speak, but changed his mind.

Alexa swallowed. "I was responsible for winning a competition recently for my firm, for a prominent Arts Centre on the waterfront in Vancouver - the Rose Centre for the Arts. I'm quite proud of it." She heard the melancholy in her voice. It was hard to say out loud. Her beautiful project was tainted now.

Tina nodded, interested, waiting for more.

"But... I had a falling out with my boss, so I left the firm. That's why I have time off right now." She glanced at Bruce. "He called me today, when we were on the ferry, actually, to ask me to come back."

"What? Why didn't you tell me?" Bruce suddenly lost his shyness, and she met his earnest, concerned gaze warily.

"Yeah. It just happened." She shrugged. "I want my project back, badly, but... not sure if I'm prepared to go back there."

Tina frowned but kept her peace. She stood up to clear away the tea things, just as the sound of the door opening interrupted any further need to elaborate. "Lawrence!"

"Hello, my love," came a lovely soft tenor from the entryway, and they all turned to greet him.

The man that walked toward them in no way met any expectations that Alexa might have had. He was fairly tall, though rather thin, but presented an imposing image nonetheless. His full head of thick tangled hair extended past his shoulders, the coppery gold faded with strands of grey. His frizzy full beard extending to his chest, was capped with a magnificent faded gold moustache that flared and merged with the beard.

As he approached, the golden beard and moustache parted to reveal a flash of white teeth in a welcoming, magnetic smile that instantly won her over. "And who's this motley crew?" he asked.

Tina made the introductions, and Bruce stood to shake his hand. Lawrence wasn't that tall after all, as Bruce towered over him. But he still managed to fill the room with his charismatic presence. Alexa noticed then what he was wearing, which was as unconventional as his coiffure. A double breasted white linen blazer over what appeared to be women's pyjama bottoms, since they were covered in small coral pink rosettes, terminating in grey wool work socks and, what else, Birkenstocks. A white scarf was nattily knotted around his neck as though he'd been to the races. He reached to shake her hand too, and her palm was enclosed by his warm, powerful grip. It was as if she'd been infused with a little bit of the energy that he seemed to carry with him like a summer wind. She felt it pulse through her, after which she felt a bit more awake and alive than she had before. Her gaze locked on his vivid blue eyes, which crinkled and twinkled with wisdom and humour.

Lawrence pulled up a chair and sat down opposite them. Tina

brought a large mug of steaming green tea and set it down in front of him.

"Madison, Markus," she called softly. "Come and see what I have in here."

As though they were pulled by a cord, both children immediately rose from the table and followed her out, now a more-than-willing Hansel and Gretel.

Bruce twitched and followed them. "I'd better go with them."

Alexa glanced up, puzzled, but he didn't turn back to look at her, only scurried from the room after the kids. She looked back at Lawrence, found him still gazing at her with his piercing blue eyes, an enigmatic smile curling his golden moustache up at the corners. She lifted her brows and shrugged. "It's just us, I guess."

"So that's Bruce. Are the children yours?" Lawrence asked.

"Oh! No. They belong to my best friends, Kate and Simon," she quickly explained. "Well. Bruce's best friends too. That's how we ended up in this situation. Together, I mean." She cleared her throat.

Lawrence nodded. "I see."

What did he see?

"Bruce's brother Derek told us you're an architect."

"Yes, that's right."

"Why?"

"Pardon me?"

He flashed his teeth at her again. "That's a big commitment. A lot of schooling and hard work. Why did you choose it?"

Taken aback by his abruptness, she paused to think of the right way to explain with equal honesty and frankness. "It chose me. It's inside me."

He nodded slowly, as though that were a perfectly normal and obvious thing to say. "Have you ever designed spiritual places?"

"You mean, like a church or a mosque?"

"Or a monastery."

A monastery? Where would a modern architect get the opportunity to do that? "No. Uh... sometimes a space will take on a kind of spiritual quality. A public space, or an outdoor space, can feel like a church. It asks for a contemplative quality, if you know what I mean."

He nodded again. "I do."

Wow. No frills. This guy said exactly what he meant and not a syllable more. "Tell me about your monastery. That's what you have here, is that right?"

"Yes. It's old and simple. Rustic, like the island. I'll show you, if you like."

It was her turn to nod. "I would like. Thanks."

"Perhaps tomorrow." He got up and began pulling things out of the refrigerator. "We're vegetarian here. Is that alright for you?"

"Of course."

"What will the little ones eat?"

"Good question. Peas. Carrots. Eggs. Rice?"

"Okay. I'll see what I can do."

"Need any help?"

"Sure."

She got up and began to wash the veggies he'd pulled out while he chopped and mixed some seasonings together. They were instantly companionable, and Alexa couldn't help but imagine how simple and pleasant life could be without anxieties and pretensions. Tension fell away and she sighed.

Tina came back in, drying her hands on a towel. "Look at you two. Like an old married couple."

Lawrence laughed, and Alexa followed suit. "How are they?"

"Fine. Kids love to squish wet clay through their fingers." She smiled. "It's doing Bruce some good too."

Their eyes met in understanding.

"It's hard for him to... let go of his..."

"I know, sweetheart. It's hard for me, too." Tina went about setting the table for the six of them. The plates, of course, were her handmade creations in swirling blue and green glaze.

"Those are beautiful," Alexa said. "Do you sell your stuff from here or in shops?"

"A bit of both. And craft fairs. I thought you were tourists coming to browse, earlier."

"I gathered that." Alexa sensed an apologetic air, as though Tina were aware she'd scared the pants off of them earlier. "I actually assumed Bruce had called to tell you we were coming. Or at least told Derek. I'm sorry."

Tina shook her head. "Nope. Kinda caught me by surprise." Her words seemed to stick in her throat, and when Alexa met her eye, they were swimming with tears. Alexa's promptly filled in sympathy, and she dipped her head, focused on her task. Of course she'd be shaky. Apparently she'd been wanting to see Bruce, to reconnect, for quite some time. Lawrence reached over and squeezed Tina's arm, and they kissed sweetly. It was a tender moment that made Alexa wistful, and a little jealous of their uncomplicated devotion. In a perfect world, she could have that too. A partner that understood her so perfectly, she'd never have to compromise who she was to share that kind of intimacy. But she'd never found it. And she wasn't convinced anyone existed who would accommodate her commitment to her work.

Movement outside the window caught their eye, and diffused the thick emotion that permeated the kitchen. Bruce chased Markus past the window into the backyard, shaking a rag and hollering. Pottery time was clearly over. Maddie tailed them, skipping and giggling. Soon whatever hand-washing protocol Bruce was trying to enforce was abandoned in a spontaneous game of tag, with much laughter.

"It's lovely to see him with the children," Tina said.

"Kind of a shock, for me," Alexa said. "Until a few weeks ago, it's a side of him I'd never seen."

"Really?"

"Yup. I found him kind of immature, actually."

Tina's eyes narrowed. "And now?"

Alexa pondered her answer. "My whole world has shifted in the last couple of weeks. I don't know what I think about anything anymore." She pressed her wet fingers to her mouth. "But I do know that Bruce has been a rock for me, stepping up and being there when I... when I kind of lost it. He stayed calm and quietly put everything into perspective. Held me together. I've grown to respect him, and we're closer now."

"Hmm. I see."

"Now we just have to figure out a way for the two of you to grow close again," Lawrence said, meeting Tina's eyes.

"Maybe I can help," Alexa blurted. She looked up, from Lawrence to Tina and back.

"Maybe you can," said Lawrence.

~

Bruce managed to spend a long time with the kids outside, exploring the property, even disappearing into the forest for some time. Now they loitered under the gnarled canopy of a cluster of old apple and plum trees that snuggled against the backdrop of evergreens, their boughs bowed low with ripening fruit, the ground redolent with their rotting flesh. He avoided looking back at the house, even though, when their activities carried them past the many windows of the solarium, he could see them with his peripheral vision, in the kitchen, talking and talking with Lawrence while they prepared dinner together. Wraiths moving within the cage of green light and twisting vines, unknowable.

Of course he was avoiding them. He told himself he wasn't needed to help with the chore, since keeping the children occupied and out of the way was an important job, too. Never mind that their energy was flagging, and he knew it was past time to take them in to wash up before eating. He was tired too, though he knew, in addition to the long morning of traveling, he was mostly flagging from the constant anxiety of arriving here. From all the pent-up emotion.

What were they talking about all this time? He felt them looking his way from time to time and knew they'd be talking about him, at least some of the time. He felt uneasy, and that everyone else had a leg up on the situation over him. But that was his own fault, he supposed, being the avoider that he was.

He bent to pick up a fallen apple, shining on its surface, its bottom side carved by insects, and pitched it into the shadows of the trees.

"Time to go inside, Scallywag. C'mon Marky, let's go." He lifted the toddler onto his hip and took Maddie's hand.

"How come you don't wanna talk to your mom?" Maddie asked, jarring him out of his introspection.

"Hey! Whadya mean? Of course I want to talk to her. We'll catch up later, after you kids are gone to bed." He ruffled her hair, marvelling at the perceptiveness of children. "Besides, I want to hang out with you guys. This is our vacation. Our time together is almost up, you know."

"Mommy come?" Markus asked, his grubby soft baby hand on Bruce's chin.

"Yeah. One more week and everything'll be back to normal. I'll go back to building my house, and Alexa will go home."

What would happen then? They hadn't really figured out what they were, yet, or what would happen between them next. Would anything happen? Was he kidding himself that this was something different? Something special? Did he really want it to be? What did Alexa want? What he was feeling now went against everything he'd expected. From a relationship, certainly, but from life in general. He felt different. Unsettled. Strangely hopeful.

Markus wrapped his little arms around Bruce's neck and dipped his head, butting his forehead against Bruce's ear. "I miss you Boos."

Bruce squeezed, his heart flipping over. "I'll miss being with you all the time, too, buddy. We've had a good time together, hey?" He gave him a squeeze. "But I'll come and see you like I always did. Don't worry."

He'd miss Alexa too.

And the old fear reared its ugly head, threatening. If this didn't work out, either of these relationships that he was so tentatively exploring, where would that leave him? Alone. More alone than ever.

Somehow his house project had slipped from the top spot. The permit drawings were being reviewed at City Hall, thanks to Alexa. He'd deal with that when he got home. Whenever. Right now, all he wanted was to sort out whatever needed sorting with his mother. And work out something longer term with Alexa, though he knew he couldn't hold on to her too tightly. And for some reason, those two problems were tangled together in his mind. Or maybe in his heart. But either way...

"Will you come thee the new baby when ith born?" Maddie asked.

"You bet. Wouldn't miss that for the world." Another kid for Simon. Another addition to the Sharpe clan. Bruce shook his head, wistful. It was a lot of work, for sure, but it didn't seem like such a nightmare anymore, having a family. He was almost envious.

They shuffled into the back door, and he herded them both to the nearest bathroom to clean up, taking a moment to prepare himself for more Mom time. He'd been rude, before. He wasn't stupid. But he couldn't deal with this strange man, her husband for who knew how many years, who undoubtedly knew all his secrets. How was he supposed to be with the guy?

"There you are," Tina said when they entered the main room.

"Just in time. I was going to go looking for you," Alexa said from across the room, glancing up from flipping through a magazine at the kitchen bar. He glanced up, met her amused gaze, noted the slight turn of her lips, and felt himself blush. His heart swelled in his chest at the sight of her. God, she looked good. He strode closer to her, wanting to scoop her into his arms and kiss the breath right out of her, but settling for a small peck on the lips while he wrapped one hand around her lower back, pulling her against him. He pressed his nose to her hair, inhaled her familiar exotic scent. Yeah, it was no secret he'd been cowardly. But no more. He'd come here for more than a break for Alexa and the kids.

CHAPTER 24

Dinner had been surprisingly relaxed after all the earlier tension. He'd forced himself to make a genuine effort to participate in conversation, though admittedly, he'd paid more attention to getting to know Lawrence than to his mother. Every time he moved to speak to her, ask a question, or even meet her eye, his ribs rattled with tension and his pulse shot skyward. But it was a start. At least he wasn't bottled up and sullen as a teenager.

As both his mother and the children were flagging before the last bite had been taken, Bruce had offered to clean up the dishes to allow everyone else to get ready for bed. It had been a long and emotional day. Perhaps more for him than for anyone else, but he didn't say so. He was glad to have a few minutes to himself while he washed the dishes and tried to figure out where to put things, alone in the big room, the lights low, the soft murmur of voices drifting from other parts of the house.

His mother's house. How strange that felt. After all these years.

And he had Alexa to thank for that. He tiptoed upstairs in anticipation of quiet time alone with her. As he'd hoped, the kids were out cold, flaked out on the narrow mattresses tucked against the sloped ceiling of the loft. Alexa was bent over, murmuring and scooping cat food onto a plate, Oscar swirling between her ankles.

He slid up behind her silently and placed his hands on either side of her slender hips, pulling her to him. "Is Lucy's shot done?" He didn't see her.

"Yes. She's curled up with Maddie." As she stood up, smiling at him over her shoulder, he wrapped his arms around her in a tight embrace and pressed his face to her neck and hair, inhaling her familiar scent, spicy and musky after a long day in the sun. His body responded immediately to the feel of her, and his desire swelled. "Mm. I want you." It was true, he wanted her, but in more ways than just sexually. He had yet to learn how to say half of what he was feeling. He was bursting with the need to show her.

She slipped out of his embrace and turned to whisper. "I'm going to slip down to the bathroom to wash up."

Reluctantly, he let her go. He'd better do the same, even though he wanted her just as she was. He'd love to lick the salt and musk from her smooth brown skin. She probably wouldn't appreciate the reverse. He probably stunk. He grabbed his toilet kit and a towel and followed her downstairs to take his turn at ablutions.

When they at last slipped between the cool, crisp sheets, he pulled off his shorts and reached for her, stripping her panties and camisole from her and setting them aside, leaving the sheet pulled back so he could gaze at her, thankful the kids slept so soundly. Liquid moonlight gleamed through skylights on the sloped ceiling, and cast a soft blue glow over the bed, and her slender limbs, highlighting the contour of her ear, cheek, jaw, shoulder. Her eyes flashed in the darkness, and he moved closer to press a slow, deep kiss on her mouth, reaching to stroke her tongue with his own. Every time he did, he revelled at his good fortune and change of circumstance. This was Alexa the untouchable, with the mouth that he dreamed of, and the voice that turned his blood molten. And now that he knew her, so much more.

He pulled her close, running his hot hand over her cool back and taut buttocks. "You. Are. Amazing. Come here."

"I'm as close as I can be." Her sultry voice hinted at laughter.

"Oh, no you're not. Not yet," he murmured as he dragged his lips, and stubble and rasping tongue over her smooth skin, enjoying each dip and curve, while conscious of hitting those spots he knew she especially liked. It hadn't taken him long to learn her body, she was so responsive to his touch. His fingers slid into the tight crevice between her cheeks, and dipped down, grazing her delicate heat, teasing, and she squirmed and bucked against his hand.

He took his time licking, nibbling and sucking on her erect nipples, taking his time with them. The heat built between them, until she was trembling and arching toward him, and his own need rose up joyfully to meet hers. Tonight would not allow them the noisy, frenzied frolic of their first time together, but somehow, that's not what he wanted anyway. Tonight he wanted to show her, with his body, a tenderness and depth of caring that he had never wanted, or needed, to express in the arms of a woman. He wanted to love her body with his body, and convey, without the words that were so foreign to him, something of the intensity of feeling that welled up inside him.

He lifted himself over her and slipped in between her thighs, sighing as she opened to him, guided him, and he slid slowly home with a moan. Her slick heat welcomed him, and he shuddered with the sensations that coursed through him. "Ah, Alex. My Alex. I love the way you feel."

Breath rushed out of her, but she remained silent, lifting her head to kiss him, opening her luscious mouth to accommodate his searching tongue. She seemed to sense what he needed, and came to meet him halfway, her shadowed gaze intense and locked with his as their bodies undulated in synchronicity and their breaths mingled. Then all he could do was move with her, tongue to tongue, sliding in and out of her silken sheath, heart to heart, deeper and deeper, while his muscles shook and she trembled and arched silently beneath him. He kept his eyes on hers, despite the dim light, wishing she could know how she made him feel, trying to show her his love with tenderness, and passion, hoping and praying she felt the same, feeling that she must. Sweat dripped from his face and neck, slicked and pooled between them and they climbed together toward a silent, shuddering climax, all the more intense because they could make no sound.

He rolled to the side and pulled her back to his front, wrapping her tightly in his embrace, planting soft kisses on her shoulder, arm and back. "Thank you. Thank you for everything."

"You're welcome," she whispered. "For what?"

"I don't know. I only know that you've changed me. I've never felt this way before." He was thirty-nine years old and he'd never had a serious relationship with a woman. He'd never let himself feel this way, or get vulnerable enough with another human being to come close. And he knew why, of course, but the risk was worth it. He hoped. God, he hoped. He knew he was putting himself, his heart, at risk. And it terrified him. But what else could he do? He no longer had any choice. He was hers to love, abuse or discard as she chose. He only hoped she would choose him, because now he needed her to stay. He pressed an open palm against her flat stomach, holding her close, aching inside with his need for her.

She sighed heavily but said nothing, and his heart squeezed in fear.

"Alexa?"

She made a sound in her throat, but remained facing the wall. It seemed to him she went very still.

"What happens now?" he asked.

"What do you mean?"

"Simon and Kate come back in a week. We all go... back to the lives we lived before?... But..."

"But nothing is the same."

A bit of the tension drained away as she acknowledged what he was hinting at. "Right. Nothing is the same. What will you do?"

Her head shook against the pillow, her hair caressing his cheek. "That's what I'm trying to figure out. Nothing has turned out the way I expected it this summer. My grand plan has been blown to bits." She went silent for a few beats, and he waited. "I have huge decisions to make, and no idea what I'm going to do. It terrifies me. My entire future hangs in the balance."

She was talking about her job, her career. Of course she was. Sighing, he deflated. She wasn't on the same page as he was. For her, the question of the future had nothing to do with him or his dreams. With them being together.

The wall of tightness started in his throat, and rolled down his chest to his belly. "Is there anything I can do to help?"

Another head shake. "What can you do?" Her hands came up and rubbed her face in frustration.

Right. What could he do? He was irrelevant in her life. She didn't crave the intimacy or security that he did. She had ambitions. She wanted freedom to pursue her dreams, and to exercise her passion. And it wasn't him. He was being foolish. What did he expect? He was walking, eyes wide open, toward his own heartache, but he couldn't stop himself.

A few minutes passed in silence. Something of the closeness he'd felt dissipated, and a wave of sadness swept through him. A hint of heartbreak lodged under his diaphragm.

Her soft voice broke into his darkly spiralling thoughts. "What about you? What now?"

"It will be strange not to live with the kids and have them around all day, every day. I'll actually miss them."

"Me too."

"I never thought I'd say this, but... my feelings about having a family have changed." He laughed softly to lighten his tone. "I never wanted a family of my own, but now... I don't know. It's not so bad."

"I knew you had it in you, Koczynski."

"You did not," he scoffed. "You thought I was a waste of space."

"We-ell. Not exactly."

"Liar." He squeezed her around the ribs playfully.

She chuckled and rolled towards him. "I've often wondered, lately, why I always thought you were... childish. Like, not a fully grown man."

He groaned and buried his face in his pillow. "Thanks," he mumbled.

"I'm sorry. But seriously, whenever I saw you, you were lounging around, mooching off of Simon, generally behaving like an overgrown teenager."

Laughing, he said, "Well. I guess it's kind of true. Simon's house was always my real home. A safe place where I could relax, let down my guard, play." He lifted one shoulder. "And that's the only place we ever met up, right?"

"It is. But I realize I'd judged you on appearances alone." She set her palm against the side of his face, gently. "Well, I've changed my mind about you. You're incredibly capable. You'd make a great father."

He was silent, just looking at her looking at him, his questions backing up in his throat. Why was she saying these things about him? What did she want? Was she trying to tell him that maybe... he swallowed.

She rolled away again and tucked her butt up close, spooning. "Anyway... I sensed you wanted things you weren't able to talk about, when we planned your house, I mean. I could feel it."

"Yeah. I guess deep down I've always been jealous of what Simon has, and wanted the same." He paused, held his breath. "With the right person, of course."

She stiffened slightly, and he heard her swallow.

"How about you? Will you ever make room for them?"

"I can't see how." Her tone was not what he'd have hoped for. It was filled with bitterness and scorn.

"You're such a natural with kids."

"I've had enough experience to last a life time," she replied, and went silent again, for so long, he assumed she'd drifted off to sleep. "I love kids, but I don't love what they do to your options. To your life."

He chewed on that awhile. They could have been his own words but a month ago. But now they spoke more to him about the speaker than the truth of having a family. The conversation wasn't going the way he'd intended. His timing was bad. Mentally he shrugged. "It doesn't have to be that way."

"It pretty much does. Somebody has to spend their time and energy parenting. And I don't believe in hiring people to do it all for you. Don't bother, I say. Decide what's important to you, and do it right."

Better to drop the subject before he created more tension. "You're right." He kissed her bare shoulder. "Go to sleep. Forget about it." He shifted his weight back and sunk his head into the pillow, sighing deeply and trying to breath evenly, giving the impression of sleep, though he lay awake for a long time, fighting an unwelcome heat that pressed the back of his eyes, and a tightness in his throat. Alexa, too, lay awake, the little catches in her breathing, and small muscle twitches giving her away. He wondered if she had given his words further reflection, or was too busy laying out her illustrious career as Krystof's partner at Vision Architecture.

He was a fool. He should have known better. He did know better. But he'd let his guard down, he'd let her slip inside and wrap her tendrils of feminine caring around his scarred, soft heart. And he'd foolishly let her do it. And now he was going to get exactly what he deserved. Which was nothing. Nothing at all. She'd rip those tendrils away like a cruel bandage from a wound, and leave him bleeding, to start all over again.

∽

Alone in the loft, the sound of voices down below telling her that everyone was gathering in the kitchen for breakfast, Alexa rose from bed slowly in the morning, pondering Bruce's heartbreakingly tender lovemaking the night before. Again he said that he loved her. He'd waited until he thought she slept, then whispered the words against her neck until she finally heard his breathing even out with sleep.

She shed silent tears then, her heart aching with a sense of loss. Does he know what he's doing? What does he know about love? What makes him think he can just try it once and he'll get his happily ever after? How long will he stick with it before he realizes it's not that easy? How long before he realizes it's not her, but a stage of his own growth? How long before he realizes she hasn't got what he needs, and leaves her to look for someone else? He still hadn't dealt with what he came here to do. When he did eventually reconcile with Tina, it would change everything in his world. He would realize he didn't need her anymore.

I'll be okay. I need to figure out my own path before I fall into a trap and lose my focus. She didn't have to complicate things by declaring her love and raising his expectations. She could love him and let him go. It's what she did. She'd turn her focus back onto her true self, her career, which is all she'd ever cared about anyway. What would she do with a man in her life full time? It would be a spanner in the works. Too hard. The way he was going on last night, he'd probably want kids of his own. He obviously loved the kids. Then what would she do? She'd have to disappoint him. How could she keep her career and be a partner and a mother? It couldn't be done. She'd end up paying the ultimate price, one she was not prepared to pay. That was a decision she'd made long ago.

CHAPTER 25

After breakfast, as the sun rose higher and hotter in the summer sky, Alexa sat with her morning coffee as Bruce took the kids out for a drive in search of a lake. Apparently Chickadee Lake wasn't too far away, and had a good swimming spot.

While Lawrence sat in lotus pose in the far corner of the living room, absorbed in his meditation, Tina refilled Alexa's coffee cup and sank into a chair opposite her with a settled air that told Alexa she wanted more talk.

"Are you still interested in visiting the Hermitage for a bit?"

Alexa nodded. "Yes, of course."

"Have you talked to Bruce about going?" Tina set down a plate of apple slices.

"No. I don't know what I'd say... I mean. He doesn't..." Alexa picked up a piece of apple and gnawed her lip, glared at her coffee, wondering how she would tell him. What would she say to him to make him understand that she needed some time alone?

"What kind of understanding do you have?" Tina asked.

Alexa looked up at her. "None. We're very, very new. Perhaps fleeting."

"You don't seem like... a fleeting thing."

Alexa let out a heavy sigh. "We've known each other through Simon and Kate for years, even before that, but somehow, this summer, everything changed. The timing's not great. I have a lot going on with my career. Decisions to make. There's no worse time to get involved with anyone. Not that I've ever really..." She shook her head. No, she'd never made room in her life for a real relationship.

"You feel like you have to choose?"

"I've always chosen my work. Always." She felt something akin to panic flutter in her chest.

Tina nodded, and her silence seemed to invite further confidence.

"It's true, I'm confused. About so many things. I'm doubting myself. I feel unsure." Alexa hesitated to confide in Bruce's mother. "I feel a... a closeness to Bruce that I've never felt with a man, even though he isn't even my type. I mean, he isn't anything like the men I've always admired, anyway. I feel like I don't know myself anymore."

"Why is that a problem for you? Feeling something for Bruce, I mean."

Lawrence rose from his corner and drifted over, hovering nearby, tending plants.

Alexa explained to Tina how her own mother urged her to pursue her own passions. How she'd spent her youth caring for her sick father and her brothers and sisters. "I love kids. But I've always felt a powerful calling to my design work. Even when I was young, the family sucked that energy and drive out of me until I was desperate to escape. And no one understood or cared how much pain it caused me to be pulled in a thousand directions, to feel conflicted between passion and duty."

"Was your father always sick?"

Alexa filled her lungs with air and let it go slowly, picturing her father a permanent fixture in his chair in front of the television. "No. Things were fine until I was about nine. I mean Mom had her ideas about gender roles, and there were too, too many kids. But things were okay. It was an accident at the mill. My Dad's back was broken. He spent the rest of his life in a wheelchair."

"Oh, I'm so sorry." Tina grimaced in sympathy.

"He was never really himself after that. He could have done more, maybe. Could have rehabilitated. But his spirit was broken. His pride was broken. He had ideas about manhood that he couldn't reconcile with his wreck of a body. So he made everyone else suffer along with him." She frowned, remembering. "Mostly my mother. She never stopped trying to do the right thing, take care of the family, compensate for him. And she gave up everything."

"Did your mother have a dream?"

This woman was frighteningly insightful. Maybe that's what came of living with a Buddhist teacher all these years. Alexa nodded. "Mom was an artist, of sorts. She used to paint. She loved it, and it made her so happy."

"I certainly understand that." Tina's voice was a mere whisper.

"But she gave it up completely. She worked two jobs, while I filled in the gaps at home. And so I had two broken parents. I had to break out of that… that…"

Tina sighed. "Your mother made a sacrifice, of course, Alexa. She had children she loved and cared for. She had a husband that she presumably loved. She made a choice."

"What choice? Martyrdom?" Alexa cried, her face hot, waving her apple slice through the air. "There was no way I was ever going to let that happen to me. I had to follow my own dream!" Against her bidding, tears pushed up and escaped, flooding her eyes and blurring her vision. A sob broke loose from her tight chest.

Tina rose and shifted to a chair next to Alexa so she could wrap an arm around her. Her hand came to rest on Alexa's overheated head and pressed it into her shoulder. "Good. This is good."

After a few moments, Alexa's pulse calmed and she sat upright, wiping her face with the heel of her hand. "I'm sorry. I don't know where that came from. It's not like me. I do as I please, anyway."

"Hmh," Tina squeezed her closer. "I've seen you on your phone with your brothers and sisters every day. And I've only known you for two days. But you haven't abandoned anyone." She sat back and gently pushed Alexa away to gaze into her eyes. "You grew up believing that you had no choice. And in defying those expectations you came to believe you could have only one or the other. That binding yourself to a family meant you'd have to give up your art. One or the other."

Alexa said, "And isn't that true? Really, to be exceptional at anything, to devote yourself to it, that you have to commit to it wholly?"

Tina took a long time replying, sipping her coffee. "Every woman is different, Alexa. Not every woman is cut out to be a wife or a mother, or to follow a vocation either. For some, nurturing is their business in this life. Only you can decide. But don't feel that you have to choose. You can have your work, and a companion for your life as well. Or you can have a family and your career. That's a choice too."

She leaned back, resting her cheek on her palm. "When I was a young woman, things were changing, but not quickly enough for me. I fell into a traditional role, and came to regret it. I felt I hadn't explored who I was, my own potential as a person. Suddenly, I had four young sons and a husband with expectations. I felt misunderstood. I craved freedom. But..." Tina's gaze drifted off, and Alexa could see her painful memories reflected on her face. "But I wanted my children, too, Alexa. Don't ever think because I left them, that I didn't want them. Especially Bruce. He was so young, and we were very close. But I wasn't strong then. It took every bit of courage I had to leave that stifling place. I couldn't do both, but it was because of my marriage, not my children. Now my sons are grown men, and they don't need their mother anymore, even though I still need them."

"Bruce needs you," Alexa said, sniffing and wiping her eyes.

Tina nodded. "Maybe. Maybe not."

Lawrence had drifted closer as they spoke, and now he placed a hand on Tina's shoulder.

She sighed heavily. "Now I have my art, and I have a life companion in Lawrence who knows me and accepts me for all that I am, and all that I am not. That's important." She glanced up and met his gaze. "It's on his urging that I've been trying to reconcile with Bruce. He knows my loss." Tina fell silent as her glimmering green eyes welled with tears. She sat, crying gently, letting the tears slide slowly down her cheeks unchecked. Lawrence sat down next to her, rubbing her hand. "And while I can try to build bridges and move forward, I can never go back and undo the past, despite my regrets. Neither can you. You need to take some time to go deep inside, and ask yourself the questions, and listen very carefully for the truth. For your truth, Alexa."

Alexa took a bite of apple. "Oh! These are really sweet."

Lawrence cleared his throat. "Why don't you take a few days right now and come to the Hermitage. You can stay as long as you need to. A day or two, or three. There are people there who can guide you to find the answers you seek. I can work with you myself. I have time."

Alexa smirked. "Are you trying to get me out of the way?"

Lawrence's magnificent moustache tipped up, and she saw a flash of white teeth. "You're not the only one who needs a little space, my dear."

∼

Bruce returned from swimming with the kids to find Alexa, Lawrence and his mother heads together, again, at the long dining table. He hesitated at the door. Was it just his imagination, or did they collectively give off an aura of guilt, or conspiracy? Whatever they were doing was making him very uncomfortable. As if he weren't already in way over his head. *Coward. Remember why you're here, dude.*

"Hey!" Bruce said, dumping wet towels and bags into a pile by the door, striding in, resolved.

Tina leapt to her feet, offering to feed and bath the kids, who were shivering in the entryway, dirt sticking to their wet skin. She ushered them down the hall to the bathroom and he sighed in relief, his heart lifting as he turned toward Alexa's welcoming smile.

He approached her and bent to plant a quick kiss on her lips. What he longed to do was grab her and lift her into a tight embrace, tell her again that he loved her. But he fought the urge. He felt altogether too needy. He wanted time alone with her. "I just heard from some people down at the lake that the tide's super low right now. There's an island you can wade out to, apparently, a kind of refuge?" He glanced at Lawrence.

Alexa lifted her brows. "Refuge?"

"Tree Island," Lawrence clarified. "It's a provincial marine park and bird sanctuary. There's a small camping area on the sandy spit, accessible by foot only at low tide. You can see a community of bald eagles, many sea birds, and rare plant species."

"That sounds lovely. We'd have to go right now, though? Won't the kids be tired?"

"Just us?" Bruce smiled, hoping she got the hint.

Alexa turned to Lawrence. "Do you want to go?"

His eyes gleamed meaningfully as he shook his head and smiled. "No, no. You two go. I'll help Tina entertain the little ones until bedtime. I promised them we'd feed the goats tonight. If you hurry, you might even get a bit of the sunset before you have to wade back."

Bruce felt relief that Lawrence had the sensitivity to realize he'd intended the outing as a romantic escape for just Alexa and himself. He caught the man's eye and nodded his thanks.

"Ok, then. I'd better change my clothes quickly. I'll be right down." She dashed up the stairs to the loft.

Lawrence sauntered into the kitchen. "Would you like to take a small picnic?" he asked. "Something to drink, perhaps?"

Bruce slanted his gaze toward him. "That's an idea."

"We have a bottle of chilled rosé in here," he said, opening the fridge door and peering in. "Would that do?"

"That would do perfectly." Bruce accepted a small pack from Lawrence with the bottle and a few other items in it, and went to grab a couple of fresh beach towels and an old blanket from his mother's cupboard.

~

Alexa's thoughts swirled as they pulled the SUV up beside a few other vehicles parked in a dirt patch next to some woods. They exited the SUV and started down the narrow dirt trail.

"All the parks on this island look the same to me," Bruce said. "If you don't know where you're going, you'd never know they were there." He pointed. Almost obscured by the undergrowth, a small, faded signpost marked the trail to Sandy Island, the official name for Tree Island.

He waved her ahead as the path narrowed. She felt his eyes burning into her back.

She knew he was unhappy with her. He'd been swept up in a new feeling and he wanted, not without justification, to dive into that euphoric place where new lovers dwelled. Who wouldn't?

Alexa, that's who.

His passion and focus on her made her nervous. Clearly he wanted exactly what she feared. Maybe he wasn't aware to what extent he'd expressed his feelings last night, with his tender lovemaking and whispered words of devotion. Though, if she were honest, she'd felt it too. Whenever she remembered, an exquisite lightheadedness overtook her.

Suddenly he rushed forward, laughing, and gripped her around her middle, lifting her off the path, and nuzzling his face against her neck, his lips cool against her sweaty skin. "At last, I have you to myself," he growled.

She squealed in surprise and then laughed. "Put me down, you lunk!"

He obliged, letting her slide down against his hard body, keeping her pressed closely to him, letting her feel how much he wanted her. His voice was teasing, sexy when he said, "Lunk?"

She rotated in the circle of his arms and he bent to kiss her, moaning as though her mouth were a delicious indulgence, some decadent dish of ice cream. Or lemon sorbet, she amended, remembering his closed eyes and ecstatic expression when he ate his favourite treat.

Her breath quickened, and she felt her heart race in the space where her breasts pressed against his chest.

"I like your... lunk-ness." She smiled.

He chuckled. "Some honeymoon we're having, eh? Surrounded by kids and geriatrics." He kissed her again and set her down.

"Honeymoon?"

He shrugged. "Courtship? Or whatever you wanna call it. We just hooked up and we haven't had a single day to ourselves. It's torture."

"True." She turned and continued walking, but stayed closer to him, so they bumped arms and hips as they shared the narrow path.

He slid his fingers between hers and squeezed. They walked on in silence, a vague sense of guilt gnawing at her. Before too long, the trees thinned and they emerged onto a sandy stretch of beach, framed on both sides by the ocean, waves lapping softly.

"Oh, look!" she said, releasing his hand and striding forward. "It's so pretty!"

The island, such as it was, was really just a long, low stretch of sandbar, the beach sloping up on both sides, littered with drying detritus of the sea - sea grasses and bull kelp. It bulged in the middle, growing both wider, and taller, into a hump. In the centre, where a small forest of evergreen trees grew crookedly from the crest of the ridge, he could see and hear the movement of birds.

He pointed. "There really are a lot of birds here."

Weathered driftwood logs and twisted roots and branches sparsely furnished the high tide line, the sand fine and silvery-white, and studded with bleached white shell fragments. A small group of day campers in bright clothing hunched at the far end of the beach, a tendril of smoke wafting up into the fading blue sky.

They walked forward until they found a clear and sheltered spot in the crook of two large, crossed logs. "This looks alright." He glanced at Alexa, his brows raised in question and she nodded her approval. He bent to spread the old blanket on the sand, set down the pack and turned to her.

She sank down onto the blanket, hugging her knees. He joined her, leaning back against a log, and they just looked out at the peaceful scene. The minutes stretched.

She sighed. "God, it's nice to get away from everyone. It's so quiet. This is what I needed."

"You could have come swimming with us."

"That would have been chaotic."

"It was nice actually." He paused, his eyes roaming over her bare arms and legs. "It would have been nicer with you there in your little shorts." His brows flicked up suggestively. "Anyway, better than having to entertain my mother and Lawrence all day."

She shook her head. "It was okay. I'm enjoying getting to know them. We had a good talk."

"Oh? What about?"

"Don't sound so freaked. We didn't talk about you. They've been really helpful to me, sorting through my shit."

"Yeah?"

"Yeah." She went silent again, leaning back on her elbows, gazing distractedly out to sea where a trio of kayakers were passing the spit, a hundred yards or so offshore.

A vein popped in Bruce's temple, and his jaw moved with tension. Every time he tried to get closer, she couldn't stop herself from pulling away. Self-preservation, she told herself. Necessary, she told herself.

"Hey, look what I have." He opened the pack and withdrew the bottle of chilled rosé, beaded with condensation.

"Aha." She took it from him while he rummaged further, pulling out two acrylic glasses, a few plastic storage tubs, and some paper napkins.

He spread everything out, opening the tubs to expose crackers, sliced cheeses and some raw veggies. They poured the wine and toasted the sky and the beach. The sun had already dropped in the faded blue summer sky, a wash of soft pinks bleeding up onto the thin clouds at the horizon to the west. It wasn't a spectacular sunset, pale and translucent, but it was soothing and added a hint of romance to their quiet evening.

He leaned in and pressed his mouth on hers, wet and tangy from the wine. "Mmmm."

She lifted her face and kissed him back. "This is wonderful. Thank you."

"My pleasure," he murmured between kisses. He wrapped his hand around her narrow ribs, pressing her back onto the blanket, supporting her with the crook of his other elbow. As usual, she thrilled at the largeness of him. His power. She'd been with Krystof so long, with his narrow limbs and tidy grooming, his precise, calculated seduction. She never knew what a turn-on it would be to touched and held by a big, rough, beast of a man. It stirred deep inside her a matching wild, untamed desire.

They lay back, kissing languidly, until she felt a surging heat rising in herself, as well as the evidence of his own desire. It may be true that they'd had little time alone during the days, since the night of the sailing mishap, but they had slept together almost every night since, making love every which way, exploring each other's bodies, discovering a common language. Incredibly, it just got better and better, feeding her sense of panic that it was out of control, and she'd be swallowed whole. He clearly wanted it to go on. Part of her did too, but the very idea terrified her.

They lay, arms entwined, gazing up at the evening sky. Her limbs and her core buzzed with a gentle, pervasive desire.

"So have you–" he began at the same moment she said, "I have to–" They both stopped and laughed, sitting up. Their gazes met, until she slid hers away, her chest squeezing.

He rubbed the heel of his hand against his upper chest absently, a gesture she'd come to associate with moments when he was feeling anxious. "Go ahead. Tell me."

She picked up and nibbled a bit of cheese, and sipped her wine.

"I've decided I have to go away."

"What? Home?"

"No, I mean right now. Tomorrow, actually."

"No!" His face flushed red, and she watched his Adam's apple move as he swallowed and gathered himself. "I mean... we've only got three days left here. What's the rush?"

She turned to face him, meeting his gaze directly. "Bruce. I've got to give Krystof an answer by the end of the week. I have to choose, and I don't know what I'm going to do. Do I go back as a junior partner, or less, so I can have my project? Or do I give up the project and look for another job? And where? The optics are so bad. What will I say when people ask me why I left Vision and the Arts Centre? I have to figure it out. This is the rest of my career. The rest of my life. I can't..."

"But why go away?" His voice sounded small. Defeated.

She sighed. "I just need to think. I need to be alone and work it all out. I know the timing's bad. I don't want to ruin our holiday, and I hate to leave you alone with the kids. But you'll have your mom to help. And Lawrence I guess, although he'll be helping me, too."

"Helping you? How?"

"I'm going to the Hermitage."

"What? Here?" He pointed emphatically at the sand beneath them.

She nodded. "I can do a three day retreat. Lawrence will guide me. Talk to me."

"Can't I help you? Talk to me." He leaned forward, grabbing a seashell fragment and whipping it toward the water with a vicious flick of his wrist. "I can be supportive. I've been through this before. I had to make tough career choices, too. Not that long ago."

"I know, but no, I have to go. This is exactly what I need, and it just happens to be available here, right now. I need to be alone. I need some space to think. Weren't you listening to what I said last night?"

"I was. But I can help you. I won't hold you back."

"You already are."

His nostrils flared in anger. "How? How am I?"

She shook her head, fighting tears that pooled in her throat, and pressed her hand against her mouth. She knew if she let herself feel love she'd be torn and her career and her freedom would suffer. Her work was too important to sacrifice. She couldn't have both. "You distract me from what I have to do."

He froze. "I don't have to. I won't. I promise." He shifted to his knees, taking her upper arms in his hands, peering intently into her eyes. "Alexa, listen to me. I get it. I understand what's important to you. And I won't get in the way. I want you to succeed. I want to help you and support you. In whatever way I can."

Her gaze dropped to the blanket, her lips pressed together to stop the trembling that threatened. She exhaled through her nose, long and slow.

"Bruce. Listen to me." She raised her eyes and met his gaze, dark, almost black with the intensity of his feelings. "You have to believe me when I say I have to do this away from you." She paused for a moment. "And sweetie, listen. We came here to your Mom's for a reason. And you're not dealing with it. I'm as much of a distraction to you as you are to me. You can't hide from it anymore."

His hands dropped from her arms and hung at his sides. She was right.

After a moment, he rose and packed up their picnic things without another word. They were silent all the way back to the house.

～

The next morning, Bruce stood with his hands shoved into the pockets of his shorts, silent, stoic, as Alexa packed her few things in her bag, preparing to leave for her *retreat* at the Hermitage. He couldn't speak. What was there to say? She'd decided. It didn't matter what he wanted. How much he hurt. How angry her decision made him. How panicked he was at her leaving.

Why? Why? Why? Why?

They hadn't made love last night. The first time they'd slept together without touching, the air between them charged and fraught with recriminations. It felt ominous, and now he fought the press of hot, angry, helpless tears behind his eyes.

When she was ready she set her bag at the top of the loft stairs and turned to him. "Come here," she whispered, taking his hand and leading him to the edge of their mattress on the floor, tugging him gently until he sat beside her. She wrapped her arms around her shins and gazed across the room toward the dormer windows in its sloped wall.

His gut swirled with acid, his chest fluttering and pinching with tension and a kind of premonitory grief and loneliness as he waited for her to speak. He absently pressed the heel of his hand against his diaphragm to ease the pain. He was powerless to change his circumstances. All he could do was allow her to say her piece, do her thing. He spoke anyway.

"It's fine. You do what you have to do."

"You don't understand why I'm leaving, do you?"

He glared at the floor. "I'll be fine. The kids'll be fine. We're good."

"How do I make you understand? This isn't about us. About you."

He raised his eyes to hers and dropped them again, clamping down on his jaw. No matter what she said, he couldn't help feeling betrayed. Abandoned. Furious. Old wounds flared in his heart, burning hot and raw. He should have known better.

"I want you to know, the time we've spent together has been

wonderful. But… the circumstances, around my job and everything… it was a mistake to get so involved so quickly. It's distorted things."

"Distorted?" he blurted. *What is she saying?* "I know what I'm feeling."

She stroked his arm, his rigid shoulder. "I know. I feel it too. But it scares me."

"It scares me, too. This hasn't happened to me before, you know. I don't do this!"

"I know. It's not who we are. It really, *really* isn't who I am. But my life was falling apart, and I felt weak. Scared. And you were there. So kind and supportive and… manly. That's why I don't trust my dependance on you. That scares me more than anything. I really, really don't want to be saved, you know? I need to rely on myself."

He shook his head. "I wouldn't stop you," he murmured.

"Please try to understand. I just need time to figure out who I am and what I want. My whole life I've been afraid of being trapped." She clenched her fists on either side of her head and shook them. He swallowed at the intensity of her expression. "Getting caught up in a romantic relationship is not going to help me do that. That's the myth that all women fall victim to. Our whole society is set up that way. We aren't given the power or the desire to stand alone. And it enfeebles us so we come to think our identity is limited by our attachment to a man."

He rubbed his eyes, listening to her words, that didn't seem to have anything to do with the pain in his heart.

She stood up and lifted her bag.

"I can't belong to you. Or anyone. I'm sorry this comes at a bad time for you. But you'll be okay. You need to be strong, too." She exhaled and descended the stairs, disappearing from view.

CHAPTER 26

"There's optional meditation in the mornings before breakfast, which is served at six-thirty. Dinner is at six. Meals are taken in mindful silence." Lawrence led Alexa on a tour of the humble, rustic and alarmingly run-down Hermitage buildings and grounds. "Visitors and resident monks alike spend the majority of their day in silent, individual meditation, either seated or walking the grounds. It's a pretty quiet place, overall."

More like silent. They'd been greeted by a monk in traditional saffron robes when they parked, and after a silent, smiled greeting, he handed Lawrence a small bundle of papers, bowed and walked away without a word. Lawrence had made her leave her phone and electronics locked in the trunk of his car.

"This place has been here a long time?" She asked.

"You mean, it looks a wreck?" His enigmatic smile flashed briefly. "Some of the buildings since the mid-sixties, but the Hermitage less than twenty years. It was created as a meditation retreat where western teachers could work with local people, share what they've learned, and pass it along. And the intention was always to maintain a special focus on environmental awareness and sustainability. The facilities are humble, to be sure. We've been intending to redevelop the main teaching and communal spaces for some time, expand the school."

"You have the funds?"

He nodded. "We have some donations set aside." Lawrence turned and pointed. "Check the sign on the main building for scheduled Dharma talks. I recommend at least one to get you started. There is also guided yoga, often midday. I'll meet individually with you each afternoon."

They continued to stroll the peaceful pathways that twined around the large rural property. "This will be your private *kuti*." He led her to the door of a rustic hut set in between tall trees, its door open. She could see a simple single cot inside, with fresh linens. A bright cushion on the wooden plank floor. "You may choose to spend your time in meditation here."

"It's perfect," she said, looking around at the simple, uncluttered interior, shards of sunlight leaking through gaps in the walls, painting lines on the floor. She set down her small bag.

"Usually guests check in at three and get started the next day after a bit of social time. Today you can sit in on a Dharma talk in about forty-five minutes with Lama Eran. It's not a beginner class, but you'll catch the drift, I'm sure." He said, his grand moustache lifting, his wise eyes crinkling with humour. "I've signed you up for dinner prep for your daily Karma yoga. So after we have our chat, at about four-thirty, you can take out your frustrations on the vegetables." And with that, he left her alone.

She changed into soft loose clothing, mindful of the resident monks by choosing full coverage, compensating for the summer heat with light fabrics, such as she had. She certainly hadn't envisioned herself at a four day Buddhist retreat when she set out for this holiday with Bruce and the kids. But here she was.

Plunking herself down cross-legged on her lime green and fuscia woven cushion, she set about trying to meditate. She had previous experience, and understood the basics, though she had never been any good at it. She wondered if Lama Eran was going to be able to teach her anything useful. Approximately three minutes later, she was fidgeting and readjusting her legs, which were cramping already. She huffed.

"Come on Jenner. You can do this. You need this."

How long had it been, after all, since she'd had the luxury of being alone with her thoughts? No interruptions, no deadlines. Those thoughts, however, were intrusive and jarring. One dark problem chasing another around and around in her head, no matter how many times she tried to quiet her mind.

Another ten minutes later, after repositioning herself to gaze at a multicoloured geometric Thai weaving on the wall, then again out her one small window, through which she could see an empty golden meadow, she rose with a sigh of frustration and strode out of her *kuti*. Perhaps a walking meditation was better suited to her temperament.

Once outside, she was calmer. She gave up trying to empty her mind, instead allowing it to meander as her body did, along the small pathways that wove around the simple wooden buildings arranged on the Hermitage site. Meadows stretched off in every direction, framed by evergreen forests. She'd always loved nature, its forms, and the many ways that humans shaped and inhabited space. There were patterns hidden in both, and she loved to immerse herself in the problem of teasing them out, and searching for hidden meanings. One of the reasons she loved architecture was that her mind had an insatiable appetite for problems and puzzles, both physical, social and symbolic.

Not clear whether she had meditated or not, she approached the main building when the time for the Dharma talk approached feeling calmer and more centred. In a modest classroom, bare except for a few desks pushed up against the window walls, five or six people in casual clothing, and a couple dressed in the maroon and saffron robes of a monk, sat cross-legged on cushions in a crescent around another monk in an armchair. No one spoke, though two or three glanced up curiously. She nodded at the teacher and silently took a spot at the rear.

"I am Lama Eran. Today's Dharma talk will explain the Five *Skandha*, or Aggregates."

Alexa knew she was jumping into the middle of Buddhist study without proper preparation, but Lawrence hadn't said it was a problem, so she settled into make as much sense as she could of the teachings.

"The five aggregates are Form, Feeling, Perception, Mental Constructs, or thinking, and Consciousness." He went on to define each term.

It turned out to be simple, logical, and easy to understand. At least the way Lama Eran told it. The utter silence and stillness at the Hermitage somehow made it easier to concentrate on what he was saying.

Form, essentially, is all matter, classified in the traditional sense of earth, water, wind and fire, taken in via the sense organs. These in turn cause feelings and sensations which are either pleasant, unpleasant or neutral. So far, so good. After that, it got a little more abstract.

The way she understood it, basically, who we think we are and what we want is an illusion based our previous experiences, associations, our wishes, wants and fears, and our state of mind, so that those feelings and sensations are never objective. Consequently how we react to stimulus and what thoughts we form about it is based upon those perceptions. How we perceive what is around us and what we think about it and do about it is highly subjective. Nothing, in the end, is real. Not even our concept of self.

After the class ended, and the other students left, she remained on her cushion, mulling what she'd been told. It felt like a war was being waged inside her head, new concepts clashing with old, her foundations pulled away, her bearings lost.

Since she'd arrived here with two questions in her mind: who am I? and what do I want? she came away feeling thoroughly stupid, shallow, and deluded. As though her questions were irrelevant. She began to question everything she was about. It made her angry and agitated, and she didn't know what to do about it.

Bruce lounged in a faded folding lawn chair nursing a tepid beer. He ought to finish it before it got any warmer, or get up and get a fresh one from the fridge. The effort required to do either seemed beyond him, so instead he continued his lacklustre observation of the kids helping his mother pick apples in the orchard, slowing filling buckets with their sweet flesh while a few plump chickens strutted among them, pecking. She bent her tall frame to the children's level, patiently showing them things and fielding Maddie's constant barrage of questions.

She was really good with them. A natural. And she seemed to enjoy the antics of small kids a lot. It was disorienting, this clash between how she loved kids, his early, joyful memories of her, and everything that came afterwards.

He couldn't make out her words exactly, but the familiar lilting singsong of her voice exhumed gut-deep memories of his own childhood, and all the time they'd spent together while his three older brothers roughhoused, played sports or chased girls.

He felt a twinge of old pain in his chest and absently rubbed it with the heel of his hand– recalling when he'd suffered the injury. He'd been eight. Not too long after Mom had left. He'd been playing in the playground at the big park down the street one evening before dinner, unsupervised, as usual. His friend Robbie, wild, wiry Robbie, flung himself around the climbing frame and challenged Bruce to do the same. Naturally, he missed and flipped off the monkey bars, landing badly on his shoulder, cracking his collar bone, as he later discovered. Much later.

He remembered the pain had been excruciating. Robbie had turned white and run off, Bruce believing he'd gone for help. But he didn't return, and nobody else came either. Later he found out that Robbie had fled in fright, then gotten home and been swept up in his own family's dinnertime drama and completely forgotten Bruce. By the time Bruce had gotten himself up and staggered home, he was probably in shock. Of course he was pretty much ignored amidst the noisy chaos of his brothers. Derek had come home from football practice pumped full of aggressive adrenaline and picked a fight with Luke. The eldest, Rick, tried to break it up, but not without first fanning the flames by insulting both of them. Once Dad got involved, it became a shouting match that ended in everyone storming off in all directions, doors slamming. When it was safe, Bruce crept through the house, grabbed something to eat from the kitchen, and retreated to his room to nurse his wounds.

It wasn't until two days later, when he returned to school Monday morning, that someone noticed that he was sweating and favouring one side, and took him to the nurse. When the doctor at the hospital gently reprimanded Dad for taking so long to bring Bruce in, he was yelled at in his turn. Bruce still remembered the look of sympathy the doctor gave him as he gently patched him up. Mostly what Bruce recalled was feeling lost, alone and abandoned. Why didn't his Mom come? Didn't she know he needed her? Where was she? The physical agony seemed like a small thing compared to the ache he felt inside. An almost welcome distraction.

Suddenly the cold beer he'd wanted appeared at his side, and he jerked and looked up.

"Thanks." He accepted the cold bottle from his mom. She sat down on a chair beside him, and they both gazed toward the children, who threaded their way in and out of the rows of vegetables, Markus trailing a black hen, chattering away.

"Penny for your thoughts."

He shook his head. "You don't want to know." He wasn't even sure if it was seeing his mother that brought up these feelings of self-pity, or if he was smarting from Alexa's sudden departure.

"You're missing Alexa, I'm guessing."

His head shot up, and their gazes met for a silent moment. "I guess that's true. But I was actually remembering the time I fell off the monkey bars at the park and cracked my collar bone."

She sucked her lips between her teeth and nodded. "I heard about that."

He turned his head to glare at her. *She knew? She knew and didn't come back for him? That did not help. He didn't need to know it and it certainly didn't make him feel any better.* "When?"

Her eyes filled with tears. "I wanted to be there for you, Bruce. I really did."

"But you knew what was going on with me. How?"

"I've always watched you from a distance and followed your accomplishments, sweetheart. Your football and science fair. Your computer work. Your girlfriends." She smiled sadly.

He scowled. He hadn't seen or heard anything more about *her* until he was out of university. It came as a shock to find out that his brothers had been seeing her. There were family gatherings, when his father was absent of course, where she's shown up, unannounced apparently. Or so he'd thought. His brothers seemed to take it in stride that she was back in their lives. Married by then, they had wanted their children to know their grandmother and didn't seem to have an issue with her reappearance.

Bruce had no such motivation. Derek was right when he'd accused Bruce of avoiding contact with her. If he found out she was going to be around, he couldn't get away fast enough. And so it had gone on for the past ten years.

"I'm truly proud of you and your success. I wanted to talk to you many times about all the things you've done and accomplished over the years. Ask you questions about your company and your work. Your life."

He grunted. Too little too late.

After a long pause, she said, in a tremulous voice. "It means so much to me that you finally came to visit and let me see you again. I don't know why it's taken us so long."

"Well, it worked out this time." Of course it was more than that. Why couldn't he say so? "I've been pretty busy the last few years," he mumbled. He stole a glance, but couldn't bear to see her sitting there, leaning in, her eyes wet with tears. Instead he took another swig of his beer and kept his eyes on the children in the garden. They were squatting now, examining something in the dirt.

There was so much... so much he'd kept bottled up inside all these years. Words he'd said in his head, alone at night, in bed. Questions. Recriminations. Vitriol. Heartache. Nothing came to him now. What was he afraid of? The worst had already happened long ago.

He'd shut it all down, packed it away.

"I'm glad we at least have a chance to get to know each other now. That's my dearest hope. That's why Lawrence urged me on, pushing Derek to talk to you. I know we can never get back the years that we lost, but I've missed you a great deal. I do love you, Brucey. I want to be part of your life again, and you of mine. I don't know how much time..."

His throat spasmed, and he tried to wash the burn away with another sip of beer. He clenched his fist and fought the heat that blasted through his head. He should ask about her health. Her heart. But he couldn't bring himself to do that either. He wasn't sure he actually wanted to know. What good would it do to discover now that she was already sick and dying. He swallowed hard.

She sniffed and dabbed her eyes with a tissue. "Won't you please talk to me?"

"Don't have much to say at the moment." His throat squeezed off any further words he might have said. Instead he thrust himself out of his chair and strode off into the woods. He needed to be alone.

When Alexa glanced up, no further ahead, she saw Lawrence standing in the open doorway of the classroom. He'd changed into monk's robes. He nodded and entered, first turning to the teacher, who'd remained in his chair, eyes closed.

"Phra Eran," Lawrence said softly.

Lama Eran opened his eyes and looked up. He grinned. "Phra Lawrence."

The two men bowed slightly with their hands together in front of their chests, something she'd seen pretty much everyone she'd met here do. A greeting, she supposed.

Lawrence stood with one arm extended toward her. "Alexa?" He addressed Lama Eran. "You haven't met our latest student, Phro. This is Alexa Jenner. She's staying at the house with Tina and I. Along with Tina's son Bruce, and the children of their friends. It's been a lively couple of days."

Alexa approached to have her hand taken between both of Lama Eran's, who, now that he was no longer in teaching mode, exuded an air of jolly good nature. As he smiled, his rosy cheeks plumped up like shiny tomatoes. "A pleasure to meet you, my dear."

"It's time for our *darshan*. Follow me." They bowed again to Lama Eran, Alexa mimicking Lawrence, and then she following him to a small meeting room, feeling inexplicably like she was being led to the principal's office to get her wrists slapped.

"What were you thinking so hard about when I came in?" Lawrence asked as he sat down at a narrow desk, and gestured to the simple wooden chair opposite.

She sat, frowning and pondering her answer for a few moments. It was difficult to sum up. "It would be very easy to dismiss all that as some arcane spiritual mumbo-jumbo. If it weren't so logical and obvious. But we're so subject to the distortions of our own mind we're not aware of it. Now that it's been so clearly pointed out to me, I can't un-know it. So now I have to…" she paused.

"Integrate it?" He suggested.

She shrugged. "I get it. All fear comes from losing something you think is important, from the avoidance of pain. All desire comes from wanting to repeat or preserve that which was experienced as pleasant. And it's not that I'm addicted to suffering or anything. It's just that it completely upends everything I've ever done, as well as the rationale for it. But…" She sliced the air with her hands. "That'll have to wait."

Lawrence tilted his head, listening without interrupting.

"Maybe I'm jumping ahead a bit, and obviously I need more instruction and guidance, but where my mind went with all this is, basically, that I'm an architect. Okay? Everything I do has to do with form." She met Lawrence's steady blue gaze with a question in her expression, as though he could see her dilemma as clearly as she could. But he just waited for her to explain.

"Is all that void?" She chuckled. "Not void. You know what I mean. Is it moot? Irrelevant?"

"Why would it be?"

"Well... because we're supposed to be able to see that it doesn't matter, I guess."

"Does it matter to you?"

"Of course it does. But should it? I mean, what am I supposed to be doing? If this thing that..." She pressed her fist against her gut, "This thing that burns in me. This thing I channel. It feels real, and it feels important. I don't know if I can reconcile a world where it's only illusion."

Lawrence sighed. "Understanding the five *Skandhas* doesn't negate the existence of the physical world, Alexa. It's meant to help us detach from it, so that we can be freed from suffering and pursue enlightenment without distraction."

"Yeah, but I spend my life trying to understand and manipulate the physical environment, not detach from it. To respect it and imbue it with purpose and meaning. But is it meaningful?"

"We're in pursuit of the spiritual world, but we live in the physical world. We live in our bodies, on the earth. Here at the Hermitage, we're committed to creating a place of peace and harmony, where all can come to meditate, practice the Dharma, and explore the self. We have a special commitment to minimize our carbon foot print and create a self-sustaining community. Does that sound like it doesn't matter?"

"No. It sounds like what I do at work, actually. I'm very committed to environmentally responsible, sustainable design and building, too."

Lawrence's bushy eyebrows inched up. "Tell me what it feels like when you're designing something."

She gazed at the floor for awhile, channeling the sensations. "There's a lot of technical knowledge that goes into it afterwards, obviously. It takes a whole team of skilled experts to turn an idea into a physical thing. To communicate intentions to the contractors. But at the beginning, it's far more abstract. After studying the site, the program, and absorbing all of that... I don't know. It gets pretty mysterious. Somehow, all my training and experience and all the relevant information, plus a spark of... of insight, come together and flow through me. Are transformed into something else. Something much greater than its parts." She looked up at him.

He nodded for her to continue.

"That's the way it feels for me, anyway. I'm not some kind of egotistical *prima donna* who thinks she's so clever. I recognize it as a blessing, a gift, that this happens for me. I've been given a special ability, and when I'm using it, I feel most whole, most at peace. That's why it's so important to me to follow this calling. I don't take it lightly."

"It sounds like a meditation."

She nodded. "I guess. It's almost an out of body thing. Or, not that. But I feel like I'm channelling something that's way bigger than me. I see the connections between things, their shape and feel like I'm part of them. I just don't understand a world that would give me this insight, and then throw obstacles in my path."

"You are naturally endowed with very high *Paramis*." At her scowl of confusion, he continued, "That's another Dharma talk you can go to. You already have much *merit* in the bank, so to speak. But perhaps these obstacles you refer to are your own creations."

She let that sink in. She understood that he was referencing the five *Skandhas* from today's Dharma lesson. What was he saying? That the problem wasn't with her work, but with her life? Or not even that, but in her head? That she made her own problems? That she suffered as the result of her perceptions and feelings about things that were, in fact, not real? That, she would have to meditate on.

His wide moustache tilted up at the corners, revealing a small triangle of white teeth beneath. He ran a long-fingered hand down his beard. "Have you seen our *stupa*?"

She shook her head, no.

"You know, there's a great tradition of sacred geometry in Buddhism. I want you to do a little homework before we meet tomorrow." He sat up and pointed out the door. "Down the corridor is our library. You'll find some information, and some drawings there, that will be of interest to you. "But first, you have some vegetables to chop."

CHAPTER 27

Bruce and Lawrence lounged in the living room after dinner. Bruce could hear his mom and the kids singing rhymes and laughing while the kids had a bath. He reflected again how good she was with them. How much she seemed to enjoy them.

Despite how long and hard he pondered what she'd said this afternoon, he couldn't understand how she could have abandoned him if she felt that way. He remembered how close they were, how attentive a mother she'd been, how much fun they'd had together. She always made things fun.

She'd always worked, he realized, to shield his innocent young self from the ugly truth of their lives.

And then in a flash she was gone and his life became brutal. But he supposed *her* life had been brutal. It's not that Bruce blamed her for leaving her nasty husband. Only for leaving her youngest son.

His heart sat in the soles of his feet tonight.

If Alexa were here, he could talk to her. She'd understand how low he was and find a way to comfort him. Maybe she could help him find a way to work past the giant blockage he felt in his chest, sitting like a boulder, choking him. She really had a magic nurturing touch, even though she seemed to have nothing but disdain for her caring abilities. Maybe it was all those years helping to raise her houseful of younger siblings, support her exhausted mother, and understand her broken father, but she'd developed a finely tuned empathy and ability to heal with the right word, the right touch.

Alexa.

An ache bloomed in his heart at the thought that he might never feel her soothing touch again. Nor gaze into her smoky green eyes and feel with certainty that he was understood. Nor feel her fiery, wild desire. He felt a stirring of longing in his groin, quickly followed by a surge of frustration.

What the hell is she doing over there, anyway?

He pulled out his phone, woke it up and scrolled to her number. There were no missed calls from her. Maybe she'd cooled down and wouldn't mind talking to him.

What the hell. He pressed her number, waiting for the ringtone, even though she hadn't left in any kind of tumult of feeling or irrational outburst. If there was anything Alexa was *not*, it was irrational or emotional.

It rang, and rang, and rang. No answer. Had he really expected her to pick up? Just hearing her velvety voice on voicemail caused his chest to tighten.

"Hey. It's just me. Checking in to see how you're doing over there. The kids are missing you. Give me a call."

Lawrence, who'd been reading quietly, his glasses pushed down his nose, glanced at Bruce over their rims and said, "No cell phones, or technology of any kind, for guests at the Hermitage. Alexa doesn't have access to her phone."

"Can you pass her a message?"

Lawrence gazed at him so long he knew the answer before it was spoken, and more than that, was made to feel as though he'd been on the receiving end of a tongue lashing. Or maybe that was his own guilty conscience talking.

"No. She needs her time alone."

Bruce stared back, silently fuming. "What if I *need* to reach her? To tell her something."

Lawrence smiled kindly. "People that choose to go on meditation retreats usually have a good reason. They need time. You have to respect that, even if it's inconvenient for you right now."

"Inconvenient?" He huffed. One inner voice said: *I should have known better than to let down my guard and open my heart to her. I've made myself vulnerable and now she's leaving. She'll crush me.* The other said: *You're being a selfish immature sonofabitch.*

"She'll be back soon."

"How do you know?" How did he know she wouldn't decide being with him was just one big deviation from normal and she needed to dump him and go back to her real life? Maybe even back to Krystof, that bottom-feeding dog-shark. He felt hysteria rising inside him like a storm gradually brewing at sea, the wake kicking up, slapping the hull, the sails fluttering and the sheets jerking with the mounting fury of the wind. He needed to calm down. A restless energy gusted in him and forced him from his chair, the desire to prowl too powerful to contain.

Lawrence tilted his head back. "She'll discover what is right for her if you give her the space and time to work it out. Be patient, son."

He clenched his jaw, scowling. "I'm not your son."

Lawrence blinked, sucked his teeth and returned to his reading. Bruce stomped up to the loft like the toddler he seemed to be channelling. He realized he was acting crazy and immature. He was sorry for the outburst, realized he was blaming Lawrence for his frustrations, but too embarrassed, and not calm enough, to go back down to talk with him anymore.

He lowered himself to the mattress and pulled out his phone again, absently stroking a coiled, sleeping Lucy.

"Hey, Al. It's me again," he said to her voicemail. "It's not just the kids who miss you." He sighed. "I know you said this time was for you, but I... I can't help feeling a bit cast off here. I don't want to put any pressure on you. Maybe I am extra baggage and I'm making your life more complicated. I just... " His throat tightened. What was the point of professing his love for her again and again. Masochistic idiot. "I'm thinking about you. That's all."

The next moment the stairs were alive with the cacophony of Maddie and Markus's stomping feet and high swirling voices. Lucy shot up and scooted away. Then they were there, throwing themselves on him, knocking him sweetly back onto the mattress with giggles and kisses and questions, soft and moist in their pyjamas, scented of bubble bath suds and young skin and mint. He felt his heavy heart lift a little in their embrace, and wrapped his arms around them, squeezing them and pressing his face into their damp hair with gratitude.

"Play with uth!" demanded Maddie. "Let'th play a game. Let'th wrestle." Her snake-like arms wrapped around his neck.

He shook his head, pushing them away. "Sorry Scallywag. Too tired."

"Awwww. You're boring."

"Just not in the mood tonight. You two need to go to sleep."

Markus sulked, his bottom lip beginning to quiver ominously. He stared at Bruce reproachfully, his big blue eyes glassy with threatened tears.

"You're mean," announced Maddie, her lips a thin line of judgement. "I misth Alexa and I'm thick of you."

That stopped him. "That's fine thanks for taking you swimming."

"When Daddy and Mommy come home I'm telling them you're mean to uth."

Remorse twisted his insides. "Come here, Scallywag. I'm sorry." He sighed. "I'm missing Alexa too and I'm just... grumpy."

"We're here. We can keep you company." She pulled back, her arms laced around his neck, and studied him with the wise eyes of an old soul. "Why did Auntie Al go away?"

He shrugged. "I wish I understood. Lawrence and Tina say she needs time alone to think."

"What about?"

He shook his head slowly from side to side. "She's got some big choices to make about her job. Her life. It's important to her. We need to respect that." He tried to soften his words with another hug, pulling them closer.

A moment or two of silence passed while they all pondered his words.

"Boos, read us a stowy. Like Awick," Markus said, grabbing Bruce's ears like handles, pressing his round forehead against Bruce's, peering seriously into his eyes.

"Okay." He set them down. A bedtime story would soothe his weary soul as well as theirs. "Which one–"

Before he could finish his question, Maddie leapt from the bed. "Oh, I know. I saw one Tina has up here. Look! It's cute." She handed a slim black and red volume to him with a Rapunzel-like character on the front.

He turned it over. "Ah. This isn't for kids, Scallywag." It was by Angela Carter.

"It ith!" she argued. "It's called The Booby Chance." She pointed at the fine script words on the cover. It's cartoon-like illustration could easily be mistaken. "Look. '...*familiar fairy tales and legends*– Red Riding Hood, Bluebeard... hey, Beauty and the Beatht! Read that one."

"It's The *Bloody Chamber*. And it's not–"

"Ple-ase!" came their combined chorus, and he realized he'd have to take a page from Alexa's book, and read them a slightly edited version of whatever dark feminist tale he found on these pages.

They settled into the big bed, one kid on either flank, Lucy and Oscar returning to settle at his feet. Alexa's absence echoed all around them like a zephyr. He began to read... *"My father lost me to The Beast..."* The language was rhythmic and lyrical, lulling the children toward slumber, and as he read, he realized the meaning of the story was so deeply symbolic, there was nothing he really had to couch from the children. By the fourth page, Markus began to fade, his eyelids falling, and Bruce heard one last sleepy giggle from him when he got to *"Yes, my Beauty! GOBBLE YOU UP!"*

Maddie's breathing slowed and deepened as he recounted Beauty's first days at the Beast's villa, when she still denied him his request to see her unclothed. Glancing down at Maddie's sleeping face, he continued reading aloud for a page or two, captivated by the language, and despite his audience drifting off, intrigued by this fresh version of the classic fairy tale. The role reversals, the way the beast was gentle and lonely and kind, and Beauty's beastliness of character, until she learned to see him as he truly was, intrigued him.

The rest of the story he read in silence, slowly, stopping to mull over such lines as "...denied me rationality..." and "...imitative life among men..." and pondered, astonished at Alexa's unconscious arrangement with her exploitative boss Krystof and, he supposed, perversely, father-figure. No matter what the choices were that she now faced, he was glad she was free of his hold over her, and prayed whatever decision she arrived at during her retreat, she had the self-awareness never to let another man trick and bind her as Krystof had.

His instinct was to protect her and keep her safe. But he also wanted her to be empowered and free.

In that context, Bruce realized, perhaps he had the insight to see why she needed to decide her future in isolation, away from the heat and intensity of their blossoming... romance? passion? love? Whatever it was, or might become, it was certainly colouring his own judgement, for better or worse. Maybe it confused her too.

He didn't want to be another one of those men, who tricked and cajoled a woman to serve his own needs at the expense of her own. Perhaps she would uncover her true nature at the retreat, and if he were a lucky man, she would discover that he was not a threat, and that it was in her interest to be with him. Neither as an exploiter nor a protector, but as a companion, an equal.

He understood that Alexa was a fiercely independent woman. He knew this about her. This is who she is, had always been. This was the woman he fell in love with. Why couldn't he give her this time she needed without behaving like a spoiled child? In truth, because he knew she didn't need him at all, crude un-evolved beast that he was. He had to prepare himself. He had to steel his heart to be abandoned again.

~

After nearly twenty-four hours of silent meditation, seated, walking and, perhaps not surprisingly, studying and tracing drawings in the library of the Hermitage, Alexa sat in her next *darshan* meeting with Lawrence. He wore his monk's robes again, and she was able to see him more as a teacher, and less as the man married to her lover's mother. That twisted scenario had been pushed out of her mind as she'd contemplated her own place in the universe.

"I hear you've been spending time in the library," Lawrence said.

She nodded, reluctant to disturb her silence.

"It's okay to talk now."

She nodded again, and swallowed. Lawrence poured a glass of water from a pitcher on his desk and handed it across to her. Gratefully, she took it and sipped.

"I'm sorry. I've been revelling in the silence. It almost hurts to break it," she said softly, her voice sounding odd in her own ears.

It was his turn to nod. "The more often you give yourself the gift of silence, the easier it is. But do not fear that you will lose the skill of it. There is plenty of silence, if you want it."

"I wonder," she said. "I've been studying the drawings in the library. Various Buddhist temples, monasteries. The plans for your stupa project. Re-drawing them and studying the geometry. I really had no idea that sacred geometry was such a big part of the philosophy."

Lawrence nodded. "I imagine as an architect you find that especially interesting."

MAKING ROOM FOR YOU

She felt her heartbeat race. "I feel as though I'm back at school, studying the Parthenon and da Vinci and Frank Lloyd Wright, Louis Khan and Le Corbusier, revisiting all the fundamental concepts that are gradually revealed to us through time and exemplars. Implicitly or explicitly, the study of these ancient geometric codes is very much embedded in the study of architecture. Whether we draw inspiration from nature, from history or cultural patterns, they all draw on this same system."

Lawrence's eyes widened slightly.

She leaned forward, energized by her topic, and enthusiastic about sharing her discovery. "We're taught that there is a relationship between all things, large and small, and a well-executed design concept applies equally to the site plan and the smallest details. I had one teacher who always spoke of the *essence* of a thing, a chair, a house or whatever, and the idea that the archetype for a chair exists within every manifestation, and that the potential for every chair exists within the archetype, too. Just like every crystal or snowflake or galaxy is unique, and yet part of a larger set of rules that permeate all of reality."

"I see you've found your voice," Lawrence said, chuckling. After a moment he sobered. "We're taught that the experience of Sacred Geometry is essential to the education of the soul. It provides a bridge to an intuitive way of understanding truth. I see you've been absorbing the teachings in your own way."

"Yes, I guess I have." She peered at him. "Is that okay? I haven't been talking to anyone, just soaking it up."

"Yes of course. Everyone finds their own path. You're familiar with Buddhist sand painting?"

"Heard of it, yeah. I can see how it's kind of the same. Another way to open the mind, right?"

He nodded. "These patterns and codes are symbolic of our own inner realm and echo the subtle structure of awareness. Our teachers tell us that there is a relationship between the sacred, our consciousness and the profound mystery of awareness... the ultimate sacred wonder. Sacred Geometry takes on another level of significance when grounded in the experience of self-awareness."

"So..." she continued, "...taking that idea to its limits, the geometry applies to, or underpins everything from the structure of a cell in an organic body, to the rules governing the cosmos, and even to the realms we can't see or touch. The unconscious, and the one universal mind."

Lawrence exhaled and leaned back, studying her acutely until she began to feel self-conscious. "You're a very quick study. So tell me then, Alexa. How is it you have such a deep understanding of all this, and yet you don't *believe* it. You don't live by it."

His words hit her like a blast of wind, hard, knocking her back. "What do you mean?"

"What are you most afraid of, Alexa? What do you most yearn for?"

She pondered his questions. That's what she came here to figure out. She knew what she wanted in the external world, her career success, the autonomy and recognition that it would– aha. "Validation? Respect?" she ventured.

He nodded slightly. "Okay. If you say so. And what do you most fear?"

She sighed, looking at the ceiling. "Being swallowed up. Not being free to pursue my passion."

"Passion for work, at the expense of anything else in life? Like love, or a family? Isn't that a bit greedy?"

"Greedy?" She was aware of her hackles rising in indignation, but she didn't allow herself to be distracted. This was too interesting. What was he getting at? "It's only that I can't imagine loving and being loved without self-sacrifice because that's always how I've been. That's what's been expected of me. I adore my family, but taking care of them drains me. I do yearn for love, like anyone does, but not at the expense of self. Does that make me greedy?"

"As though these things exist in isolation, and in discrete, limited quantities. The more you give, the less you have for yourself. The more you need, the less you can afford to give. Is that it?"

She hummed, tapping her fingers on her knees, feeling herself being backed into a metaphysical corner.

"You believe in scarcity– scarcity of time, energy, love, creativity? You're afraid of being used up, and having nothing left for your own journey of discovery and creativity. But how does that belief fit into the big picture we've been talking about?"

"Oh." Greedy. Now she could see what he meant.

"You know about Prana, or Chi, yes?"

"Yes, more or less. It's like energy, right?"

"The universe is made up of Prana, energy. Including we beings in our little physical bodies and our little miserable lives. It flows through us and through our world. And we can align with the path, or channel it, if you like, by being open. Or we can block it. You've heard of chakras, and mudras?"

"Mudras are the hand things?" She confirmed, demonstrating by making Buddha hands, thumbs touching forefingers, and holding them up.

He nodded and smiled. "It's wonderful how much our teachings have permeated general knowledge in recent decades."

"It's too bad so many people are more interested in expensive yoga gear than the actual dharma practice."

"Everyone has to start somewhere." He said. "So. Prana flows. And the more you can quiet the noise in your mind, and the distractions of the world, the more you can balance your Prana and allow it to flow through you."

"So cut to the chase, Lawrence. What am I missing here?"

"Things happen for a reason, and perhaps the unusual events of the summer were meant to provide you with just the lesson you need. You've been fighting, pushing, opposing forces rather than learning how to flow. The universe knows this."

"You're saying I've been making my life harder? Me?" Alexa thought of the Arts Centre, and all the hassles of settling down to doing the actual work. She thought of her relationship with Krystof, her animosity toward Nathan, her fear of being sidelined by the important clients and losing the recognition she so craved, how hard she held onto her wins. The way she weighted one job over another, attributing more clout to some, when she knew perfectly well that some designers excelled at turning every small project, however seemingly insignificant, into a headliner. Why? Because they undertook those projects with their whole heart. They, she supposed, in Lawrence-speak, allowed the energy of the universe to flow through them. And it showed.

And then there was Bruce. Her heart squeezed, reminding her not to forget him in this tangle of her life. What role was he meant to play. Why did the universe send him to her?

"So, in order to realize my full potential, I can't be fighting. I can't feel that I'm sacrificing part of myself, or feeling conflict. I can't be greedy, choosing to value one part of life over another. Because it's all the same. It's all equally important."

"You have to be one with the Prana. Studying and working with

Sacred Geometry can open you up. When you accept this, the obstacles will remove themselves."

Finally, she was coming to see that she didn't have to, shouldn't in fact, deny the feminine side of herself, or her loving, nurturing heart, in a painful effort to fit in or compete in a world that she perceived as masculine or hostile. She just needed to be herself. That's what made her unique, and gave her particular insight into the world and her work as a designer. It also allowed her to balance her desire for work and for love and family, if she chose to.

She still didn't know what to do about Krystof, exactly. Returning to her old job didn't feel like she'd be in the flow. So what was the solution?

Alexa was beginning to realize that she could both be a woman, and be powerful. Embrace her femininity and her strength. She could care for herself and for others. Even though it was frankly terrifying to realize that she neither had, nor needed, a mentor to show her how to be successful, how to forge her own path. If she took her dharma lessons and applied them, tried to take them into herself, it would require trust. A kind of trust she'd never felt before. Trust in the universe. There was something dark and scary about that kind of acceptance.

It was almost as though she had to return to a kind of primal way of being– something animalistic or child-like, with a total faith in the earth and the universe to take care of her and guide her. A full return to her instinctual animal self, at one with nature. She didn't have to emulate someone else to be a successful architect or woman any more than an African lioness needed to be shown how hunt, mate or raise her young. Her success didn't have to look like anyone else's success. As long as she was true to herself, and answered her own calling, and worked hard, she would be the best architect she was meant to be. Her own unique self. She would find and forge her own path. This was something with which she was familiar. This searching was how she always found the answers she sought. She simply hadn't looked at herself, her life and career as another project.

She was excited to share her revelation with Lawrence. She blinked and looked up, only to find his chair empty. How long had she been sitting here alone? She got up and went out to meditate and walk in the woods.

CHAPTER 28

The next morning, Lawrence rose from the table, wiping his moustache with a napkin. "Well, I have to go. I have a management meeting this morning, and I'm meeting with Alexa again afterwards."

Bruce sat with Maddie and Markus, the remains of their breakfast scattering the table like a battlefield, wondering what these meeting were about. His coffee was cooling, and he dreaded another day alone with his mother making no progress. He'd much rather take the kids to the lake for a swim, or out for a hike, but the sky had turned sullen, and a cool breeze whipped at the trees. A summer storm was brewing.

"I thought we'd have a couple more days together here before we have to go back to the city. Simon and Kate are due back soon. It's almost time to go back."

"Is she coming back today?" Tina asked Lawrence. "Maybe we should plan a nice celebration dinner."

Bruce grunted noncommittally. What would they be celebrating exactly?

Lawrence paused. "I'd better let you know, love. She might want another day. Let me call you a little later and tell you what she's decided."

Tina bent and squinted out the window. "Well, I'm going to harvest some vegetables just in case. It looks like it's going to rain."

Melancholy stole over Bruce. He wished they hadn't come. What had he accomplished? If anything, he was worse off than before.

Tina gazed at him sadly as they listened to Lawrence's tires crunch on his way out of the yard. "We can still have fun before you go." She swept her gaze around the table to take in the kids. "Maybe we should all make a project in the studio today."

Markus squeaked his delight at the suggestion. "Piggies!"

"I have to finish my teapot for Daddy," said Maddie.

"Right. We'll be sure to do that today, so it's ready to take home."

Bruce rose and cleared away the breakfast dishes, setting them in the kitchen sink. He wished Alexa would come back, and ease his misery. He wasn't making any progress with his mother, and he wasn't sure it was entirely his own fault. The divide they had to bridge was just too large. Maybe even, a voice in his head whispered, insurmountable. Too much time had passed.

∼

On Lawrence's advice, Alexa had pondered the hows. How she wanted her life to look. How she wanted to practice architecture. How she wanted to relate to the people she worked with, whether clients or staff. Instead of stewing over the dilemma she faced, which was getting her nowhere closer to a decision, she needed to work backwards from the experiential and qualitative. And so that's what she'd been doing.

Lawrence's office was empty when she arrived, so she loitered in the hallway waiting for him. It wasn't long before she saw him striding down the hall, his usual grin stretching his bushy moustache and curling up its ends.

"Thank you for waiting. I'm sorry to be late," he said as he strode past her and behind his desk. "Sit down, sit down."

She followed him in and closed the door behind her, but was too fired up to sit down.

Clasping his hands in front of him on the desk, he said, "Well!" and waited for her to talk.

She was well accustomed to this now.

"I've been deciding how I want to practice architecture, like you said. Not about where or the specifics of a project, but meditating on what it feels like if I'm in the perfect place, and have the ideal career."

"Very good. What did you discover?"

"Well, some of it's abstract, as you might expect. I want to practice with integrity." She started to pace back and forth in his tiny office. "I want to work for clients I respect, who respect me in return, who come to me because they believe in what I can do for them. I want to do work I believe in and can stand behind, and not be a pawn to corporate greed or a developer's ego, or get caught up in bureaucratic power struggles. I want to use my abilities to make better spaces for people to inhabit, and to make better cities, to leave a legacy of quality and value."

"Excellent," he murmured. "What does that look like?"

She took in a large breath and exhaled. "A team. It's not all about me. In fact I always have good people around me and I want to keep that. I love to collaborate with other smart people, and I want to nurture young professionals. I don't want to have the kind of practice that hires talent, exploits it and uses it up. I believe better quality work comes from teams that are empowered and appreciated, and on the same page. All I want in return is sharing their talent and skill. Starting with Peter and Stephanie. Then we'll see."

Lawrence cleared his throat. "Forgive me if I misunderstand, but it doesn't sound to me like you're choosing to return to your old position at… what was it called… Vision?" She'd given Lawrence a brief history back at the house, and was surprised he'd been paying that much attention.

"No." She sat a moment, and he waited patiently for her to order her thoughts and find the words. "I really want my project, but I can't go back there. I couldn't put myself back in that position knowing what I know now. I don't know. Maybe there's something we can work out. But if not, then…" she shrugged. "It wasn't meant to be. I just know I'm ready to launch my own firm, and direct my own future."

Finally she took her seat, and folded her hands in her lap. They looked at each other. She sat tall, and her gaze was steady.

"So."

"So." She nodded. She could feel it in her body. This was the right decision.

Lawrence took a deep breath and let it out, then began speaking in a conversational tone. "I had a management meeting this morning."

She tilted her head, a little confused at the turn in direction. Maybe it wasn't important to him what decision she'd arrived at, as long as she was happy with it. And she supposed, that was as it should be.

But then he went on. "Lama Eran Renpoche, Lama Pho Tenzin and Lama Greg Renpoche and I have been working on a project for some time." He paused, his gaze on her significant. "I mentioned when we arrived that we had received donations that would allow us to redevelop the school and temple."

She nodded. She assumed they'd been given a few thousand dollars. "I remember you said you were interested in sustainability."

"Yes. Our wish is to redevelop the site with intention, with care to the environment. To set an example, to respect and nurture the environment, but also to make changes in keeping with sacred geometry to the extent possible. We wish our home to maximize and channel spiritual power, to nurture the residents and students who come here and focus their work."

"Like with your stupa project," she said. She'd been studying the drawings and reading about the small sacred monument that was partially built in their yard.

"It's been our dream to redevelop the main teaching and communal spaces and expand it into a real school. Add more accommodations, and rebuild the kitchen and bath facilities. We would be able to host larger events and bring teachers from far away. We may not have enough money to do everything we want all at once, but the plan should be in place for future phases."

"I get it. You don't want to do the wrong thing. Put something in the wrong place, or…" She shrugged. If they had enough money to do a kitchen addition or a few classrooms, then they didn't want to waste it. "I'd be happy to talk to your board about general concepts, big picture stuff. Maybe a program and budget for your long term goals. You know, so you could decide on the little things."

"You're correct, we're concerned about how the development takes shape. That it be in keeping with our principles and beliefs, that it is very sensitive to the natural environment of the island."

"Do you have a budget for the site planning stage as well as whatever you want to build first? I don't mind donating some time, but now isn't really a great time for me, as you know. I'll have to focus on getting my business afloat."

"That's what we discussed this morning. It will take a sympathetic mind, and a delicate hand, to meet all our needs and wants. Our budget for master planning and the main building is about a million and a half."

She frowned, puzzled. "A million and a half... what?"

He mirrored her confusion. "Dollars? Is that not enough?"

Where were they going to get that kind of money? "When might this happen?"

"We'd like to start right away. We've been waiting for a sign. Worried about who we can entrust with this work. And then you arrived." His teeth flashed in his beard.

Alexa sat quietly, struggling to understand what he was saying. Her pulse fluttered behind her ribs like a bird struggling to take flight in the confines of her chest.

"What I conveyed to my brethren this morning is that I've got to know you rather well in the past week, and I have begun to see your talent and ability as an architect. Your sensitivity to the dharma teachings, and your interest in the importance of sacred geometry and sustainability and self-sufficiency for our community have convinced me that you are the person we've been waiting for. We are in agreement."

Alexa ignored the quiet flutter behind her ribs. She wouldn't let herself believe what she thought he was saying. "Let me understand you clearly. You're saying that, not only do you have a million and a half dollars to do the master plan and develop the new main school building, but that you want to do this right *now*?" She paused, eyeing him keenly, trying to determine if she was crazy, or he was pulling her leg. "And. You want *me* to do it?"

"His smile broadened further. "That's exactly what I'm saying."

"I don't believe it." The flutter flapped its wings a little harder.

"We'd like to be your very first clients."

"I'd be happy to put a proposal together for you to look at, but..." she laughed. "I'm not even set up yet. I have no office, no staff, very few resources."

Lawrence shrugged. "You'll do. I trust you, Alexa. I'm sure you'll figure it out."

The winged creature escaped and took wing.

∽

Bruce followed his mom and the kids into the pottery studio. Markus marched in as though he owned the place, and headed straight for the low bench where he'd been working with clay. Tina opened a barrel and pulled out lumps of fresh moist clay for them. With a sly smile, she set a lump of clay in the palm of Bruce's hand. He recognized the wet, dense weight of it. Maddie drew back a damp canvas rag to reveal a roundish bowl with dented sides, like a large apple that had seen better days.

"Look at my teapot Bruce."

He strolled over to take a closer look. "It's missing some parts, isn't it?"

"Today we're making the spout and handle. Tina says that's the hardest part."

"That's great Scallywag. Your Dad's going to love that for his tea."

"I know, right?" She set to work rolling out a lump of clay into a snake.

He chuckled, and after looking at Markus's latest clay piglet, at least that's what he'd been informed it was, he wandered around the studio peering at his mother's own works-in-progress. She had three wheels, one of which was larger than he'd ever seen, with it's base low to the floor and a little clay-splattered step stool next to it. He tried to imagine his mother throwing the huge urns in the yard.

"Do you have a kiln large enough for those big pots you do?" he asked.

She nodded, and gestured to a door at the back of the studio. This kind of equipment was expensive, and he wondered how much money they had, and where they'd got it from. He couldn't imagine surviving financially as a potter or a Buddhist teacher, but what did he know?

While he walked, he pinched and moulded his blob of clay between his fingers. The familiar soft silkiness of its texture, and the wet mineral scent that rose up to his nose opened a floodgate of memory. Images flashed in his mind's eye from when he'd been small. At that time, his mom's beginner studio occupied one end of the garage, and was a constant source of conflict between his parents. She was either taking up too much space, making too much mess, wasting money or spending too much time away from her wifely duties.

But when no one else was around, Mom's studio had been a wonderful, sacred space, where she sang while she worked, and he played alongside. In those moments, their peace and contentment was complete and made up most of his memories from those early days, one day flowing into another like water.

The rest came to him only in sharp fragments, as though illuminated by a strobe light. Bits and pieces. The expressions on his mother's face. His father shouting. Broken shards of pottery. A shoving match between Dad and Rick. Clinging to her with his young arms around her as she wept.

He shook away the dark shards of memory and gazed across the studio at her, bending over Maddie, explaining how the handle had to attach to the bowl to be strong. He'd been very close to Maddie's current age when she left. He tried to imagine how Maddie would feel if Simon, with whom she was so close, just disappeared one day and never came back.

His heart twisted and his throat tightened as his mouth flooded with salty saliva. It would devastate her. A tidal flow of sympathetic emotions swallowed him whole, like a tiny impotent ship in a cosmic sea of shock, confusion, anger and grief.

Loneliness washed over him in waves of remembered pain.

If she loved his like she said she did, how could she have done that? To him? She was his whole world. He was important to her, too, wasn't he?

He felt her beside him, leaning against a bench. "Why the big frown?"

He peered hard at her. He didn't wish to disturb the peace in the studio. Nor did it seem appropriate or kind to criticize her or chastise her in her own home. She'd been nothing but warm and generous and kind since they'd arrived, making them feel welcome. And he loathed bickering, criticism and raised voices because they'd made up the fabric of his home life growing up. He'd spent his adult life cultivating an air of lightness and good cheer to counteract just such behaviour. Yet the resentment and anger inside him refused to stay down.

"Why was it so important to talk Alexa into leaving?"

She straightened, lifting her strong chin with a frown. Her green eyes glinted with a sharp intelligence. "It's what she wanted."

He studied her unruly curling hair, dark brown like his own but generously seasoned with strands of grey, the arch of her brow, the precise curve of her cupid's bow, the exact whorls of her ear. Feminine versions of his own anatomy. It struck him how little he took after his father and how much after her. It puzzled him, that despite his being a large man, and she an older woman, he hardly recognized her. In his memory, she was shorter, slighter, a much less colourful woman, even though he'd been a small child at the time. How was that possible?

"And needed," she added, with an upward flick of her dark brows.

He almost hesitated, pulled back, but the resentment won out. "Who put the damned idea in her head?"

Her gaze sliced to the children, silently chastising him to watch his language, keep his voice down. "Oh, I don't remember. We were just talking." She wiped her hands with a dirty rag. "She's a woman with a very clear purpose, and yet she's full of doubt. Her choices so far haven't made her happy."

"Are you referring to me?"

Her lips pursed and she shook her head. "I don't think so."

"So, what, I'm insignificant in her life?"

A wry smile tugged at her mouth. "I didn't say that either, sweetheart. She just doesn't believe there's room in her life for you and her work."

"She won't choose me."

"She might."

"She won't!" Another surge of anger rose up inside him like a sudden spray of seawater crashing against the bow, blinding him. He lurched in response.

"You should have minded your own business!" The kids glanced up at the tone of his voice. He turned his back to them and dropped it to a hiss. "This is the first time in my entire life I've had a real meaningful relationship with a woman, someone I genuinely want to be with, and you're trying to mess it up before it gets started. Were you just trying to get her out of the way so you could... I don't know... assuage your guilt by pretending you wanted to spend time with me or something? How's that been going?" He swung an arm toward the children, as if to infer that alone time, and a serious conversation, were impossible anyhow.

"Bruce. This is not the time."

"There will never... never be a time to say or do whatever you think needs to be said. There's no going back. No fixing what you did."

She grabbed his arm and tugged him toward the door. "Come outside."

He glanced at the kids, whose wide eyes showed their concern. He flashed a fake, reassuring smile at them, and followed his mother out the door. A gust of summer wind pulled at his shirt, and lifted his hair. Her skirt ruffled with the breeze that carried on it the scent of dust and rain, and the cool green of the forest.

When they'd stepped around the corner, so they could watch the kids through a window, she said, "This isn't about Alexa at all, is it?"

He turned on her. "It is. You say you want to know me. What you don't understand is that I've never let anyone get that close to me. And just when things are starting to go my way, you and Lawrence convince Alexa that she needs to get away from me. As though I'm some kind of a problem for her. To figure out what she wants? What kind of mother does that? It's like you really don't want me to be happy, or to have any love or stability in my life at all!"

She remained silent, gazing up at him with eyes that shone with tears, her brow furrowed.

"I'm broken Mom, because of you. That's who I am. I'm a thirty-nine year old man and I've never been in a relationship before." He paused, fighting his own burning tears, and struggling to keep control of his wavering voice. "I really don't understand you. And I'm not sure I even want to." He turned his shoulder to her, staring at the kids in the studio, and made a sudden decision. "We're leaving."

He strode back to the doorway. "Hey kids. Change of plans. We're heading home."

Their confused voices rose up in protest.

Turning back to his mother, taking in her shocked expression, the pain in her eyes, he sneered and said, "This pretence has gone on long enough. I'm going to pack."

"Don't do it. We're finally talking. Why are you running away?"

He spun on his heel and faced her, all the pain of her abandonment surging through him, slicing at his heart anew. "Running away? Running away? How can *you* accuse me of that. You're the expert at running away from responsibilities and loved ones."

"I know you were hurt. I can see that. But we still have time to make up for the years we lost. I don't want to fight with you. I want you to be happy."

"I *was* happy, until you interfered with my life and sent Alexa away!"

"You really love her? If you're in love with her, you won't leave. You'll wait for her."

"No, I'm not. I don't love anyone. And no one loves me. I learned to live without love years ago. Alexa can do as she pleases, it doesn't matter to me. I'm done here."

Tina stared at him wide-eyed. Her shoulders hunched forward, looking like she'd been sucker-punched.

A twinge of guilt zinged up his ribs, across the back of his neck. He waited a second for her final volley, but she didn't speak.

"Don't get all melodramatic now. It's a bit too late to play that card."

Still nothing. He wasn't sure what he was waiting for her to say. What he was hoping for. Her lips moved, but it wasn't coming. She stood and stared.

He grunted and stormed away from the studio, heading to the house to pack their things. He glanced at his watch. If he hurried, they could be on the 2:40 ferry. Alexa could find her own way home. She was a big girl. He needed to get the hell away from here. What was the point of sticking around, buried by betrayal?

He longed for his boat, his house, his solitude. There was nothing wrong with his life. Why did he decide to come here? Nothing but lies.

In the living room, he began gathering the kids' stuff that was scattered around.

Suddenly, he heard a crash echo from outside. A muffled scream from Maddie. Then a piercing howl from Markus. The sound he made when he was really scared.

Bruce dropped what he was doing and rushed back to the studio, his heart hammering, picturing crushed fingers and blood and…

He burst through the door.

Tina sat crumpled on the floor, leaning against the workbench, clutching at her chest. She remained locked in an awkward, twisted position, her hand splayed across her chest, gasping. She looked like she was frozen in shock. Her lips were tinged blue and her eyes glazed with pain.

Her gaze spun toward him in the doorway, eyes wild and scared like a cornered animal. "Brucey. Bruce. Call Lawrence," she gasped as though she were holding her breath, "Please call Lawrence." Rigid, she slid slowly to her side onto the floor.

His heart thundered in his chest like a runaway train. His gut turned to stone, and his breath rushed out of his tight throat. "Mom? Mom?" This couldn't be happening. He fell to his knees beside her. Screw Lawrence. He pulled his cell phone from his pocket and dialled 911.

Alexa left Lawrence's office floating on cloud nine, convinced she was going to wake up and discover she'd dreamt the entire conversation. After a brief congratulations and handshake with the other monks on the executive of the Hermitage, they discussed whether it was time for her to go home. Lawrence said he was going to pop home to tell Tina and Bruce that she would be staying an additional day. Alexa returned to her kuti.

She took the time to meditate in her kuti, since it had started to drizzle, and then went to a yoga dharma practice. The whole while she forged a plan. The first thing she would do was take care of all the paperwork to set up her own practice. She'd tell Peter, but nobody else. Later when she was organized, she'd ask Stephanie if she'd join her. Then, well, she'd actually have to find a small workspace of her own to rent, and probably hire at least one, maybe two more people. Mentally she calculated costs against her savings. Her mind ran through various buildings where she might lease space, and a few technicians she knew. It would not be cool to poach more staff from Vision, however tempting.

The Hermitage redevelopment was like manna from heaven. Or some equivalent Buddhist analogy. Prana from heaven. How was that for mixing her ideologies? In any case, it was wonderful. Unexpected, but totally, completely wonderful. But it wasn't quite enough to get things off the ground. She had her savings, set aside for this very day, but if she were going to get a business start-up loan, she'd need to convince a bank that she was worth investing in. And in order to do that, she needed just one more thing to make it all work.

It would be very nice to have not just one but two projects starting out.

When she noticed Lawrence had returned, she went to talk to him. "Can I get my cell phone out of your car? I'd really like to make a couple of phone calls, to get things rolling, if that's okay."

He got her phone, but it was stone cold dead.

"Oh. I should have plugged it in, I guess."

"You can use the land line in my office," he said.

"But they'll be long distance."

He shrugged. "We'll deduct it from your bill." He chuckled and led the way.

"How are Bruce and Tina making out? Did you talk to them?"

Lawrence shook his head. "They were all in the studio. I could hear them talking. I didn't want to disturb them, so I left Tina a note and slipped in and out without letting them know I was there." He pursed his lips. "I got the sense they are finding their way at last. There was something in the tone of their conversation, though I didn't make out the words. Perhaps Bruce is feeling especially vulnerable right now."

"I can see that. Or… Is it because of me?"

"All the time you've been with us, Bruce was holding back. You made that possible for him, by mediating. I understand how hard this is for him. But, he's a grown man. If he wants to reconcile with Tina, he has to find the courage. When Tina and I talked this morning, she felt they were getting closer. He's confused, but he'll be alright."

Alexa reconsidered the wisdom of returning. "Maybe they just need more time alone. I should leave him here for a while longer and take the kids home by myself."

Lawrences made a non-committal face. Whether or not they'd had a breakthrough or were still limping along, she doubted Bruce would agree to that plan.

Lawrence left her in his office and closed the door. She plugged in her cell phone in to get a little juice while she made her calls. Calling the office, she asked for Pete first. When he picked up, all she said was, "Did you mean it? Are you coming with me?"

He laughed. "To the ends of the earth, girlfriend. What do you want me to do?"

She smiled. "Nothing right now, sweetie. Just be ready. I'll call you in a few days when I'm back in town with details."

"That's my girl. You sound like Alexa again."

"Pass me back to Leslie, would you?"

"It'd be my pleasure."

She waited for the transfer with a smile on her face. Leslie informed her that Krystof was on a conference call. She said she'd call back in a few minutes, and hung up to wait. But now that she faced talking to Krystof, she felt triggered, her body tensing and her jaw stiffening, recalling her last angry exchange with him. It brought with it memories of the past several years, and her entire relationship with him, intertwined with her development as a professional under his mentorship. It was a heady, emotional blend that sent adrenalin rushing through her blood, setting her pulse racing and her stomach swirling with stress.

She remembered her teachings and the calm perspective she'd gained over the past three days, and took a deep breath, centring herself, letting go of expectations and judgements.

Her cell phone came to life and issued a rapid sequence of ding-ding-dings, and at a glance she could see a string of voice and text messages coming in. Bruce-Bruce-Kate-Megan-Bruce-Kate-the office-Bruce-Bruce-Owen-the office again. Too many messages to take in at a glance. Wow, three days incommunicado and she felt overwhelmed by the attention, astonished at the number of people who seemed to need to be in touch with her. A moment later, her cell phone rang in her hand, startling her.

"Hello?"

"Jenner!"

Ah, Krystof. Sounding agitated. Interesting. That didn't take long. She steadied her breathing. Ok. Let's do this.

"Krystof."

"At last. I've been trying to reach you."

"You gave me a week."

"I know, but how long does it take? Everything here's on hold while we wait for your decision. There are a lot of people in limbo because of you."

She sighed. It wasn't a problem when he was the one delaying assigning the project architect role. "It's a big decision, Krystof. Not one to be made without some thought to my future."

"Jenner. Your future is here at Vision. It always has been. We're a team."

"I'm not convinced of that."

"What? What else would you do? It doesn't get better than this, believe me."

Still an arrogant bastard, even while he begged. She shook her head. He wanted this too. And he needed her. She had to remember that. "I have options. I've been mulling them over."

"You've got another job offer? From whom?"

"Don't sound so skeptical. And it's not your concern."

"What do you want? More money?"

"Have you conveniently forgotten our last conversation?"

She heard him breathing on the line. "I can do the partnership, but a junior share. That's all I could convince Biljiana to give up. Ten percent."

She laughed bitterly. "I don't want that anymore. And that wouldn't cut it anyway. I need control of the project."

"It would be yours. I promise."

"Your promises are worth nothing to me."

He remained silent on the other end of the line for a long time. "So this is it? You're going to let the project go. You're going to let your petty complaints determine the fate of the most important civic project either of us have ever had within our grasp? I'm disappointed in you Jenner. And, I have to say, surprised. I thought you were serious about your career."

Petty. What an asshole. "Oh, I'm serious, Krystof. Very serious. But it's not that simple."

"How do you mean?"

And she filled him in on her plan. By next week, she'd apply for a certificate of practice, and file papers of incorporation, and if he and the clients agreed, they would also file an application for a certificate of joint venture for the Arts Centre project, with *her* named as architect of record. She also told him she was taking Peter with her, just to be fair.

She would call the shots on the project, and he, as the larger firm, would provide production resources.

"Take it or leave it, Krys. I can always joint venture with someone else." There was no doubt in her mind what his answer would be.

Over time, she would build up a larger staff, but that couldn't be done overnight. It would be challenging enough with the Hermitage project going on at the same time. But it wouldn't be long before she wouldn't need help from Krystof, or anyone else.

CHAPTER 29

Bruce sat in a chair beside his mother's inert form, her cold, cold limp hand in his own. She lay on the sofa, where he'd carried her, her breath shallow and uneven, her blue eyelids fluttering. Suddenly she looked ancient, and he was filled with the most sublime regret. All those wasted years.

His chest was tight, his heart heavy, as he realized that she could have died a half hour ago. Could still die. She wasn't out of danger yet. Because of their remote location on the island, it would be a several more minutes for the ambulance to arrive, as it had to cross the ferry first. Fortunately, his mom was sufficiently with it to remember where her nitroglycerin tablets were located when the dispatcher asked. He'd been guided through the steps to make her comfortable and answered a dozen questions.

He'd tried repeatedly to call Lawrence, with no luck. He left an urgent message, but didn't want to give details that way. It would be too much of a shock. He'd even tried Alexa's cell phone again, though he knew from experience that she was not picking up.

The irony struck him now so poignantly. All this time, he could have, with a little effort, had his mother. Known her again. And now that he'd finally made the effort, she was, could be, leaving again. This time forever. If ever there was a time to atone, it was now. Now or never.

Maddie crouched at Tina's feet, her face tense and sad. He'd asked her to go upstairs and put all their clothes and things into their suitcases the best she could. He figured, it would take him less time to finish the job than to do all of it, and it kept her occupied. He'd explained that they'd probably have to spend tonight in a hotel room near the hospital.

"What about my teapot?" she demanded, her voice plaintive.

Tina's eyes cracked open. "You can come and visit me again, Madison, and make a new one. Or, if you like, I can finish it for you, bake it and send it to you so you can give it to your Dad."

Maddie's eyes widened at this idea. "You could?"

"Sure I could. As soon as I'm back home, I'll do that."

Bruce prayed that was true. That she'd truly be home again soon and able to get around and do her usual things.

"Tell me about the spout, and the glaze. What shape and colour do you see it in your head?"

They discussed the teapot quietly, as Bruce had taken the kids aside and explained what was going on in the simplest terms, and told them they had to stay calm and be quiet. Bruce turned his attention to Markus, who sat on the floor, leafing through a picture book. He looked like he was ready to drop from exhaustion.

"Hey, Markus. Do you need a little nap, buddy?"

Trancelike, Markus slowly lifted his head. His eyes were glazed and drooping, the muscles of his face lax. The poor kid, he was nearly asleep sitting up. He'd worn himself out earlier crying and screaming.

"Scallywag. Can you take Markus up to the loft and help him lie down until the ambulance comes? Maybe lie down with him to keep him calm?"

"I wanna thtay with Tina," Maddie whined.

"It's just for a while. Please. It'll help everyone out a lot. Be a big girl, okay?"

Maddie reluctantly slid off the sofa and took Markus by the hand, leading him upstairs.

"See if you can get the cats in their cages while you're up there."

He turned to his mom. "Do you need anything? A drink of water?"

Her head shook minutely. "I'm okay," she whispered. "Just sit with me."

He took her hand again, gazing down at it, running his thumb back and forth over the silky soft skin, the blue veins that bulged slightly. "Mom."

"Let me speak first," she rasped. "In case I run out of time."

He winced at her bluntness, and felt the same eagerness to express his feelings before he lost the chance. But he nodded.

"I know... you think I'm some kind of monster." She drew a ragged breath. "But I want... you to understand why I left."

"I understand why you left," he said. "Even though I was just a kid, I remember enough about how it was. How Dad was."

"Do you? I never knew what you understood at the time."

"I felt everything you felt. The persecution. The oppression. I clearly remember that last day, when he trashed your studio."

"That was it for me. He pushed me out that day."

"I really didn't understand, you know. Where you'd gone."

"Dad didn't explain?"

He glanced at her and rolled his eyes away.

"I know." She looked away. "I'll always be sorry, Brucey. I hope you know that. But at the time I didn't see that I had any other choice."

"How you could leave your own kid? Dad, yes. Of course. Even the other boys. I don't suppose they needed you much just then, being teenagers. But me?" He paused, turning his gaze out the window, steeling his nerve to ask the question he'd always wanted answered. He swallowed and stiffened his spine. Asked the question he'd always wanted to. "What I never understood was why you didn't take me with you." He'd planned for his voice to be stronger, not so strangled. He had to clear his throat. "I would have been happy anywhere, as long as I was with you."

It took her a long time to answer.

She released her breath on a long, sad sigh. "I wanted to. At first I thought, I'd just get settled somewhere, and then I'd send for you. But that didn't... that couldn't happen like I believed it would. I had no job, no money, no home to bring you to."

He peered at her with narrowed eyes. No home?

"I didn't know what I was doing. I just couldn't take it anymore, and I ran. That's all. I had no plan. Later... I was staying with a friend for the first while and I contacted Stan to ask about you. That's when I learned about your accident. It was months later, by then."

He took a slow breath and let it out, trying to keep it steady through the tightness and tremor in his chest.

"Didn't Dad have to support you?"

"I didn't know the law. And it was different back then. As far as anyone else was concerned, it was my choice. He didn't beat me." She shrugged. "I abandoned my family."

Bruce remembered how his parents were together. Maybe Dad didn't beat her, but in Bruce's heart he knew Dad might just as well have. He was abusive. He just used other, subtler weapons. Power. Control. Money. Hurtful words. Shame.

And threats of physical harm vicariously through the destruction of things she valued, breaking her spirit. Her dishes, clothes, heirlooms. Her pottery. Anything that was just hers was fair game. The ghostly image of shattered pots flashed again through his mind. He'd driven it away, along with all the memories of his mother. Buried it deep and built a fortress around it.

And Dad had manipulated the older boys by belittling her in front of them, so that by the time they were teenagers, they had figured she was fair game. Everyone's virtual punching bag.

"Why didn't you come back for me, then?"

"I was going to, like I said."

"What?"

"I couldn't take you at first. I had nothing. No plan. No money. No stability. Just a bag of clothing. It killed me to leave you, but I had no choice."

"And then...?"

"I didn't know it would take me so long to get settled. I didn't know where I was going. When I finally felt I had a situation I could bring you into... well two things happened. At first, your father wouldn't let me see you. I tried..."

"You tried to see me?"

She nodded. "A few times. Then... when I was able to see you from afar, you seemed to have adjusted. You were doing so well, you were so successful in school, in sports. You were popular and happy at your school. It didn't seem right to tear you away from all that." She paused. "That's what he told me, anyway."

"Dad said I was okay?"

"Whenever I begged to see you, he said... I'd made my choice. He made me believe I'd be doing you further harm by taking you away from your home. Your school. He convinced me that you'd suffer more. And he convinced me that you were angry with me, and didn't want to see me anyway. That you were happy and thriving–"

"That's bullshit," he murmured.

"He said it wasn't fair... to take you away from your brothers and friends." Feebly, she squeezed his hand. "He said I'd caused you enough pain. I believed him." She shook her head. "In those days I was emotionally very much under his thumb. So I believed him. I already felt guilty enough. I wanted what was best for you. You were better off without my coming and going, or the unsettled life with me that you might have had. Your life would have been upturned badly."

His breath rushed out of him in frustration. "My life was *already* upturned. And Dad lied. I was miserable. I acted out a lot. Sure, I worked hard in school, and played sports like a maniac. But it was because I needed some way to channel my anger. I had nobody." His voice broke. That was the truth of it. He'd been abandoned, yes. But he'd also been lonely. "I felt like a... a misfit. The other boys didn't understand. Nobody seemed to care."

"I cared. It hurt me so much to leave you. I just need you to understand that staying wasn't an option. I wasn't strong enough. And most of all... I didn't want you to grow up with a mother that was broken. It was either that or..." her glassy eyes turned toward him, her pain in remembering that time seared him to his soul.

He patted her hand. "It's okay now. Stay calm. Let's talk about other things."

"First..." She tightened her grip once then relaxed. "I want you to understand why I counselled Alexa as I did."

He was afraid to ask.

"She was already so apprehensive... She'd seen her mother's life crushed by family responsibilities. And she was at a crossroads. I advised her to take care of herself, and know herself, so that the choices she makes... she could live with." She met his gaze. "It was for you, Brucey. It won't work if she's not committed."

He got what she was saying. That she was trying to protect him from something worse. But it still felt like a betrayal. He wondered whether he really blamed his mom, or whether his complaint was with Alexa, for not feeling as deeply and sure as he did about their future. He took a deep breath and let it out, letting so much rubble fall away. He felt bruised and raw. But maybe, finally, able to begin again.

"I have a question for you."

By his change of tone, she seemed to know he'd dropped the serious talk. "Shoot."

"How old was I when I stopped wearing diapers?"

She smiled and huffed a little feeble laugh through her nose, then rolled her eyes to the ceiling, remembering. "I'd say... about two and a half. Maybe three."

He huffed. "That late, hey? And I was patting myself on the back for doing some brilliant work this summer, getting Markus potty trained. It was going to be this wonderful gift to Simon and Kate."

"I'm sure they'll be thrilled, no matter what. You are brilliant with him. I'd love to see you with children of your own."

"Yeah," he brushed aside the implied question. "Well, we'll see." The answer to that question depended on something ... no *someone*, outside of his control. He hoped the ambulance arrived soon.

When she left Lawrence's office, she'd asked him to pass a message to Bruce when he went home. If Bruce was finally in the middle of "the big talk" with Tina the last thing she wanted was to interrupt with a phone call. She was sorry to leave him alone, but she'd decided to find a ride back to the city on her own. He could handle the kids, and they were enjoying themselves. She'd get the house cleaned up and ready for Kate and Simon's return in a couple of days. Lawrence, his eyes somber, agreed.

Back in her kuti, alone with her plans, Alexa found herself ill at ease, filled with restless energy. Despite the sullen drizzle, she pulled on a hoody and set out for a walking meditation along the wooded trails, trying to let go of some of the tension today's big events had caused.

She should be more excited about her career, her future. So why did she feel so low? So sad? So bad? It didn't make sense. Instead of the elation she'd expected to feel on this day of new possibilities, she was swamped by a rising melancholy. She ought to be feeling ecstatically happy and optimistic about her deal with Krystof, the Arts Centre, the new Hermitage project, the fact that she was building a new firm with her friends at her side, striking out on a bold new path. Was she having reservations? Had she made a mistake? Overlooked an important detail? Or was it simply fear of the unknown? What was wrong with the picture?

It's true, she was wound tight with anxiety over the big leap she was taking, but also looking forward to the future. Even though the circumstances that brought it about were chaotic, and stemmed from mistakes and misunderstandings, she *was* ecstatic with the outcome. These next steps she was about to take, venturing out on her own, forming her own team, taking on ultimate responsibility for two large, fascinating projects, was her dream come true. That there had to be some pain and disruption to get from there to here, well, she supposed that was the way of the universe. Rebirth was always preceded by death and decay. There was always mess. One thing had to be torn down before another could be built. Existing patterns needed to be disrupted before new ones could emerge. She had to let go of her craving, her clinging, her fear in order to make space for clarity of thought, word, action and livelihood. It was the way of Prana. Disruption by design. She supposed she was only feeling the effects of this miasmic upheaval.

After a time, her mind finally calmed and she was able to lose herself in her footsteps, her heartbeat, her breathing. Her mind began to wander. The trees reminded her of the forest surrounding Bruce's house. Images of the summer began to replay in her mind. That first conversation she'd had with him about space and setting. She found herself reliving the evenings when she and Bruce had shared bath and story time with the kids before bed, and found herself laughing at the recollections. Her heart swelled with memories of moments of intense emotion, such as the shared fear and pain when they'd thought they'd lost Markus, the surprising feeling of camaraderie and solidarity at the birthday party. She remembered the sweet, easy sense of belonging and warmth during the special meals they'd shared. Her own sense of betrayal and loss over her job. His anxiety and determination to reconcile with his mother. And of course, the intense unguarded primal passion they'd shared, and the delicious sense of intimacy and belonging that followed as they set out on this trip. Had it only been five weeks? It seemed like they'd shared a lifetime.

It didn't seem right to abandon him in the midst of all they were going through now. He very likely needed her to lean on, regardless of how things had gone with Tina. It would be emotionally trying. She should be there for him. She found she *wanted* to be there for him.

And, in truth, she wanted to share her own epiphanies and victories with him more than anyone else. They would not be complete, somehow, until she shared them with him. She could almost see the expression on his handsome face, the sparkle in his dark eyes. He'd caress her, hold her... oh, wow. A shudder ran through her from nape to knees. She so needed to feel his arms around her, his powerful body touching hers.

She missed him so much, she lifted her phone and flicked to the messages he'd left over the past three days.

Hey. It's just me. Checking in to see how you're doing over there. The kids are missing you. Give me a call.

Hey, Al. It's me again, he'd said to her voicemail. *It's not just the kids who miss you.* A heavy sigh. *I know you said this time was for you, but I... I can't help feeling a bit cast off here. I don't want to put any pressure on you. Maybe I'm extra baggage and I'm making your life more complicated. I just...* A long pause. Just the sound of his breathing, making her feel closer to him. *I'm thinking about you. That's all.*

The sound of his voice did things to her insides, melting them and setting them aquiver with longing.

Feeling sentimental, she listened to a few of the messages from her sisters and brothers. Megan was mad at Bronwen because she refused to go out together with her and her new boyfriend. Bronwen was worried about Megan and her terrible choice in men. Her new boyfriend was a loser. She was so self-destructive. Dylan had left a mysterious message, saying he had big news. He sounded drunk. Owen was still agonizing over his course selection for the fall, now that he'd decided on a major, and now wanted her opinion on his dorm room as well. She laughed. It had always been like this. If she were in fact their mother, she was sure they wouldn't share every detail of their lives with her, asking for guidance. It's funny. She hadn't had the time or attention to balance her sacred career with the cares of a family.

But Tina was right. When had she ever stopped?

She hadn't. She just carried on juggling them both, because they both mattered. And that would never change. She would never abandon them. What would her life be like without them in it? Very hollow indeed. She loved them. And that never stood in the way her of achieving her goals.

Images of Bruce continue to flash in her mind. How small and broken he'd seemed when she left. Her heart squeezed with compassion for him, chased by a flurry of guilt. What had happened with Tina? Had they managed to talk? Alexa felt sure Tina would have forced the issue. Then again, maybe not. She wondered if Bruce had the courage to face his fears. She hoped he did. She wanted him to be free of the painful past that haunted him. She wanted him to be happy. Most of all she wanted him to understand how deserving he was of love. In fact how much Tina loved him, though he grew up believing it wasn't true. How much she, Alexa, loved him.

She stopped in her tracks.

She loved him. She loved Bruce.

She really did.

What did that mean?

How could she have missed this part? She reconsidered what she'd learned over the past four days. What Lawrence had taught her. How she'd been compensating for her mother's pain and lost dreams. She'd figured that had driven the decisions she'd made with her career, by overcompensating. But what else had she done? She'd hurt herself in the process by keeping love at bay. Thinking that loving someone could stop you from being yourself. From achieving your dreams. The truth was that her dreams included love. There was space for work and passion and love and caring. And family. Prana was infinite, if only you got out of the way. Lawrence and Tina had pointed out to her that she'd never stopped caring for her family, even though she single-mindedly pursued her career. The only thing that really got in her way had been her fears. And all that did was lead her to tell herself lies, and ultimately put her dreams at risk by allowing herself to be manipulated by someone as mercenary as Krystof.

Suddenly the most important thing was to see Bruce. To tell him all her news. But most of all to tell him that she loved him. She raced back to the Dharma building, praying Lawrence had not yet left.

CHAPTER 30

The ambulance arrived without a sign of Lawrence. Bruce could see the fear and disappointment in his mother's eyes. They both knew he had to stay with the children, and that meant she'd be riding alone.

"It's okay. I'll be fine."

"We'll take good care of her," the attendant said as they loaded her in. "It's going to take us a few minutes to get on the boat and then it won't leave right away. Don't worry. She's stable now."

"We'll be right behind you. I've left a detailed note, and if he's not here in five minutes, we're leaving for the ferry too. We'll be right there with you. I promise."

He met her gaze bravely, trying to look confident and assured, but it was a lie. His head felt hot, and his eyes and throat burned with the tears he couldn't show. He pinched the bridge of his nose to hold it together, but he was losing it. What if she died? What if he never saw her again, after finally reconnecting?

She pressed his fingers and nodded past the oxygen mask over her face. Then they closed the door and pulled away.

They'd taken her vitals and stabilized her, given her pain medication and and IV, assuring him she would be fine. Her vitals were good. If he missed the ferry, they'd all be reunited at the hospital in less than an hour, where she'd be run through tests and observed overnight.

"Okay kids. It's time to get in the car. We have to go now."

"What about Alexa?" Maddie cried.

"Alexa will..." he didn't even know how to answer. "She'll be along as soon as she can, Scallywag. We have to stay with Tina, now."

All he could do was hope that Lawrence showed up in time to make it to the ferry. Bruce knew even if they had to catch a later ferry, it wouldn't be that long, but that hour alone would be very hard on his mom. He had to stay close to her. He raced to finish packing and loaded the suitcases and the cats in his SUV. Then he tried one last time to reach Lawrence. Why wasn't he answering his phone, damn it?

Markus sat strapped in his seat, but Maddie still wandered around the house, rummaging under pillows and blankets, searching through drawers, mumbling a string of questions. "How long will it take to get there? Is she thcared by herthelf? What if the dies?"

He stood by the open door of the SUV. "Come on, Madison. Get in!"

"Quit yelling! I'm looking for thomething."

"It's too late. Whatever it is, it's not important."

"It ith important!" she screamed back at him. "You're mean." She glared at him with venom in her green eyes, her chin quivering, as tears gathered and spilled over onto her cheeks.

He couldn't take it. At the sight of her, his own tears forced their way out, and he stopped to press a hand against his face to block the sob that threatened to burst out. He couldn't show the kids how frightened he was. He shook it off and cleared his throat but he couldn't speak to ask her what she searched for.

Markus's hand stroked the side of his face, startling him.

Bruce turned to him, saw the worry and compassion in his sweet young face, and his tears kept flowing. "Oh, buddy. I'm sorry." He bent into the car to wrap his arms around the boy, pat him and stroke his silky baby hair. He murmured, "Don't be scared. I'm sad that Tina got sick, but she'll be okay. Let's go and see her, okay?

He stood upright to find Maddie standing beside him, clutching a book to her chest, a stern frown on her face. This time he saw past her prickly facade to the fear and the strength of character she hid, and a light went on in his head. "Hey Scallywag." He lifted her up and tucked her into the car, half-hugging her in the process. "Did you find what you were looking for?"

She nodded. "I needed tape. I want to fix Tina's book. Markus ripped it. I want to give it to her to read in the hospital."

He looked down. She held the Carter fairy tale book they read the other night. It was indeed ripped. She must have hidden it from him. And now she was concerned about Tina and wanted to repair it for her. Prickly was her way of hiding her fears, and of pushing past it. He realized he knew of another green-eyed girl who hid her feelings behind a prickly facade.

"You're a good, brave girl, Scallywag. We'll get some tape when we get there. Tina will really appreciate having something to read in the hospital. I know this has been a scary day, but Tina will be okay." He buckled her into the car. "The ambulance people know what they're doing. They're taking her to the hospital and there are really smart doctors there. We won't lose her."

Markus patted Maddie on the arm. "It's otay Maddie."

"Why do you call her Tina?" Maddie asked as she tucked the book in beside her. "She's your mom isn't she? Why don't you call her Mom?"

"Why didn't you call Kate Mom until this week?"

Maddie pondered this a few moments as he pulled out of the driveway and onto the main road to the ferry terminal. "I dunno. I didn't know her very well before. And I already have a mom."

"Did the fact that she got sick this summer make you realize that you didn't want to lose her? Because she's important to you and love her, right?"

She was silent. He caught her gaze in the rear view mirror, and she gave him a shy smile.

"We won't lose my mom. And your mom will be home in a couple of days, and you can see that she's okay too. We'll take care of them both and make sure of it. Right? Taking care of the people we love is the most important thing we can do."

As he drove to the ferry terminal, Bruce's mind drifted to the ways people protected themselves from the things they feared the most, and often hurt themselves in the process. Protected themselves by building defensive walls around their hearts. Walls of prickliness. Walls of resentment. Walls of isolation or indifference.

But loving and being loved meant you were vulnerable. That's just the way it was. You couldn't shut people out to avoid being hurt. You had to be strong and brave and just be there for them. You had to show up.

No matter what Alexa did, no matter what she wanted, he could support her and accommodate her just by showing up. And refusing to leave when her wants clashed with his own. He wouldn't let her defensive walls push him away. He loved her, and he didn't have to hide from that, or from her. He wasn't a child anymore. In order for her to abandon him, he'd have to let her do it. And he wasn't about to let that happen.

This time he'd choose love over fear.

∼

"Was that Bruce's car?" Alexa's pulse kicked up.

"I didn't see. Was it?" Lawrence kept his gaze firmly on the narrow country road.

"I don't know. I thought so. Where could he be going so fast?"

Lawrence shook his head.

Alexa hoped that it wasn't a sign that his heart-to-heart with Tina had gone badly and he was escaping.

They pulled into the driveway a couple of minutes later. There was no car parked there.

"I guess it was him," Alexa said, stepping out.

Lawrence stepped into the house, peering cautiously inside. Alexa stayed right behind him.

"Quiet in here. Maybe Tina's still busy in the studio with the kiddies." Lawrence walked through the kitchen to the side door to go and check. Alexa set her bag down in the entry foyer and looked around at the cluttered living room. It seemed as though she'd been gone a lot longer than three and a half days. She felt like a different person.

Why was it so messy in here? Tina usually kept the place clean and tidy, if casual. There were piles of cushions and blankets on the floor, books and magazines scattered around. Dirty breakfast dishes on the counter and in the sink, crumbs everywhere. This was weird.

She stepped to the kitchen bar and began picking up dishes. Then she saw the note. "Lawrence? Lawrence!" She'd only just begun to read it when he reappeared.

"Nobody out there. Do you suppose they all–" He saw the expression on her face. "What is it?"

Her voice shook as she read him the note. It was too long and detailed to take it all in. She met Lawrence's shocked gaze before she got to the end. A heart attack!

The colour had drained from his cheeks.

"Oh, my God! That's where Bruce was speeding off to. We just missed him!"

"Get in the car," Lawrence growled. "We can catch up."

Speeding to the ferry in silence, Alexa reread the quickly scrawled note. It was clear Bruce was agitated when he wrote it. It was hardly legible and barely made any sense. All she could infer was that he'd taken everything, just in case. She assumed he meant the kids, the cats and all their things.

"Did he have Tina with her?"

She scanned the note. "No. Ambulance. He followed with the kids. Couldn't reach you apparently."

"I left my phone in the car, and I wasn't in my office. Damn it!"

"Stay calm. At least she's in the ambulance. They'll know what to do." She said the words to reassure him. She'd never seen him lose his cool, ever. But his knuckles on the steering wheel were white, as were his lips.

"I've been trying to work less, be at home more, since she had her last tests. Her heart isn't in great shape. But I didn't think–" Lawrence's voice trembled.

"Just breath, Lawrence. We'll see for ourselves very soon. He says they were heading for the two-forty ferry."

"But once the ambulance is on board, they won't stay to schedule. They'll just leave."

"Well we'll be right behind them," she said as they careened around the corner by the general store and down the hill to the ferry terminal. There were a few cars lined up, so he pulled over into the oncoming lane, and honked to let people know he was coming through.

The ferry was still in dock!

A minute later, they jerked to a stop at the small terminal building near the ramp. They both jumped out and raced toward the ramp, which was already pulled up, though the ferry had not yet pulled away. The water churned as its engines revved. As they ran up to the rope, the attendant turned to them, her arm upraised.

"Whoa. You're too late for this one Lawrence. What's the rush?"

They peered across at the ferry. The ambulance was clearly visible.

"Tina's in that ambulance, Jan," he said to the ferry worker. I have to get over there."

"Hold on, let me radio the crew. It might be too late." Jan stepped away from them and bent her head to her radiophone.

Alexa stood, gripping the rope, peering past the elevated ramp. She could see Bruce's SUV parked askew with its door ajar, but no sign of Bruce. Had he gone into the ambulance?

Jan's radio squawked.

The back door of the ambulance swung open, and Bruce stepped down.

Her heart thumped. "Bruce!" She waved her arms in the air. "Bruce!"

~

Bruce couldn't believe they'd made it aboard just in time. They were pulling the rope across when he screeched to a halt and begged to be let through. After hearing his explanation, of course they obliged. He leapt out of the SUV to cross to the ambulance and let them know he'd made it. He wanted, most of all, to reassure his mother. He was still left with the problem of having to leave Mom alone in the ambulance while he drove with the kids. He felt terrible for her, and pretty lousy himself, for leaving Alexa behind.

The attendant had let him climb in to speak with his mom, and he could see the relief in her eyes when she saw him. He'd barely spoken to her when the driver said, "There's some commotion on the dock."

Tina's eyes lit up. Could it be Lawrence? Bruce sat up, releasing his mom's hand. "I'll find out."

The other attendant opened the door for him, and he stepped down from the ambulance, his gaze scanning the dock. It *was* them. He recognized Lawrence's bushy hair and beard, but he was deep in discussion with the ferry worker. Alexa stood a little ways to the right, her arms waving wildly overhead.

"Bruce!"

She came back. His heart swelled with the thrill of seeing her again. But what did it mean? He turned back. "It's them, Mom. They made it. But the ramp is up. I'm going to go see what I can do."

He strode to his SUV. "You kids alright in here? Stay put, okay? Maddie? Stay with your brother." He closed the door he'd left hanging open in his haste.

About three car lengths of empty deck separated him from the stern, the rear of the boat left empty. He closed the distance to the barrier in a few quick strides, resting both hands on the railing. Perhaps twenty-five or thirty feet separated them, but it might as well have been a hundred. Over the rumble of the engine, they couldn't hear each other. Alexa and Lawrence couldn't join them aboard unless the ferry captain agreed to re-dock and drop the ramp. Surely, under the circumstances, they wouldn't object.

He leaned out, cupping his hands around his mouth, and shouted, "Alexa! I thought you were staying longer!"

She shook her head, no. She shouted back, but he only caught a few words. *Change... News...* and *Sorry*. The rest were carried away on the wind, swallowed by the churn of the sea.

What was she sorry for? Mom's heart attack? Leaving him? What news? Damn it. He had to talk to her. He leaned over the railing, cupped his hands around his mouth and shouted again. "We need to talk!"

She shook her head and lifted her hands in confusion.

Damn it! He strode to a ferry worker beside him. "What's happening?"

The ferry worker held up a hand and scowled, listening to someone talking on his radio.

"What's the problem?"

"Excuse me, sir. " He walked away from Bruce, one hand over his headset. "What's that? Repeat that?"

Bruce followed. "You have to let them on."

The man spun on his heel. "We *have* to do nothing. We already stopped to let *you* on because you said your mother couldn't go to hospital alone. Now you're out here insisting we stop the ferry to let another of your party on, and delay the crossing again."

"But she needs him." He pointed to the shore. "And I need her."

"This ferry is not for your personal convenience, *sir*. You don't seem to be concerned that every delay stops the ambulance from actually getting your sick mother to the hospital."

"That's not the point. She's stable, but not having her husband with her is causing her stress. Stress she does not need right now." He pointed again, this time at his SUV. "And I can't actually ride along because I have the kids..." Unbelievable. He wasn't getting through.

The man shook his head slowly. "We are required to adjust our sailings to accommodate emergency vehicles. We are *not* required to adjust the schedule to accommodate their entourages!" He stalked away.

"Are you kidding me?" Bruce mumbled under his breath. This couldn't be happening. Bruce ran back to the stern barrier. The engine seemed to be revving faster causing the boat to rock side to side, as though the captain had his foot on the gas and the brake at the same time. The hull of the boat screamed as it ground against the rubber fenders lining the dock funnel. There was no way to communicate across this divide.

He shot another frustrated glance toward Alexa, then cast his gaze around and up to the captain's bridge. An old fashioned cabin sat high above the open car deck, a literal bridge spanning from side to side, with one hundred eighty degree windows, topped with a mast, various antennae, radar dishes, flags and other gear sticking up from its roof. He could see the shadowy outline of two or three uniformed men inside the tinted glass.

He had an idea. Without stopping to consider whether it was viable, or crazy, he ran toward another ferry worker, who stood at the foot of a narrow metal staircase that led up to the bridge. Avoiding eye contact, he dashed past the worker, past the 'crew only' sign and up the stairs three at a time, hauling himself up by the handrails.

The next moment, he barged into the narrow cramped cabin, ignoring the outraged barks of "Stop!" and "You can't be here, sir!"

He tried to explain, but they weren't listening, or maybe his explanation came out garbled. He looked like a maniac. One of the crew grabbed his arm, tried to turn him back toward the door. He saw the crewmember from below climbing the stairs, closing in on him. They'd drag him away. He had to do something to make them stop. He spun in the man's grasp, and then saw it.

The public announcement system.

He grabbed the mouthpiece and pushed the button on its side. It squawked, the sound amplified and reverberated through the air outside the cabin as well as within.

"Alexa!" he cried into the mic.

Strangely everyone was so shocked, they stopped cold. His heart pounded, but he couldn't stop now. He peered down to the dock, where Alexa and Lawrence still stood.

"Alexa if you can hear me, wave." Nothing happened for a moment or two while everyone searched around, puzzled. But then they were looking up toward the bridge. He held his breath. Her arm came up in a slow motion wave.

"Alexa, baby. I'm sorry about this." Ah, hell. His words reverberated, with a crackle and squawk, and with a half-second delay, he heard them twice. "I'm sorry about everything. I tried to get them to stop and let you on, but they won't." He slid a glance at the captain, who stood a few feet away, an expression of disbelief on his face. The guy beside him, co-pilot or first mate, looked quietly murderous. Bruce swallowed and kept the button pressed. Whatever they did to him up here was public record, with all the witnesses he'd attracted. He looked back to the dock. Alexa's arm slowly dropped.

Time seemed to stand still.

"Lawrence. Mom's all right. She's going to be okay. But, you know, tests and stuff. You should be here with us. Both of you. You're my family. I'm talking to you, Al. I want you to know... even though we're apart right now...I, uh..." He dropped his voice, as though whispering were possible in this situation. But he wanted, he imagined, that it was just the two of them, alone, and he could hold her close, and whisper in her ear. "I want to be with you, babe. No matter what. I can't live *without* you, Al."

He was suddenly acutely embarrassed. His entire head felt like it was on fire, and he was full-on sweating. There was so much he wanted to say. And not, my God, not like this. But he'd begun. And she needed to know what he'd come to realize, and what he felt.

"Alexa. I love you. Unconditionally. I'm sorry I was such a child. You were right about me. I was stuck, like Pet– like that guy you mentioned. I had some stuff to deal with. But... well, I did. And now I see how wrong I was. I get it."

"Aw, hell," muttered the captain, and made some adjustments on his control panel. Bruce felt the tenor and vibration of the engines change under his feet.

"I really get it. I want to help you, and support you with your career. I had my turn, and I don't really care about that anymore. But you do. I understand how important it is to you. And I know that means you'll need space, and time. And I... well whatever you need, I want to give it to you. All I need... all I need is *you*."

Bruce was vaguely aware that the ferry had nestled into the dock and the engines were quieting. Then the ramp was dropping, the stern gate was sliding open, the rope was pulled back, and he watched, disbelieving, as Alexa walked across while Lawrence hopped in his car and drove onto the ferry as they pulled back the chain. His heart was in his throat, he felt lightheaded, and his lips and fingertips tingled.

He took one quick look at the captain, who smiled wryly and shook his head, then dashed for the door, grinning.

"Careful on those stairs on the way down, son."

CHAPTER 31

Once Alexa stepped aboard, everything happened quickly. The ferry crew rapidly lifted the ramp and secured the stern of the boat behind Lawrence's car while the engines revved and churned wake again. The ambulance attendant exchanged a word with Lawrence, who climbed in and disappeared. Alexa strode toward Bruce as he leapt down the stairs and slowed at the bottom.

Their gazes met, and she felt an instant connection. How could she ever have doubted him?

Bruce's strong arms came around her, and he pressed his lips to her ear. "I love you. Please don't leave me, Alexa."

"I'm not going anywhere without you."

"I'm sorry—"

"No, I'm glad. I have so much to tell you."

With his arm securely around her, they walked together toward the ambulance, glanced inside the open door to see Lawrence holding Tina's hand, and she lying quietly.

Standing beside his SUV, Alexa filled Bruce in on her news, in the fewest words possible. That she'd decided to start her own firm, that she'd been awarded the Hermitage project, and perhaps most noteworthy of all, that she'd called the shots with Krystof, and got him to agree to a joint venture.

"Are you happy?"

She nodded. "Happy. Scared."

"You're going to be fantastic. I'm so proud of you. I'll leave you alone as much as you need. But please don't shut me out of your life." He cupped her face between his hands and kissed her forehead, her cheeks, her lips. "I want to help in any way I can. I'll lend you money, I'll buy you an office, be your IT guy, I'll take care of you, do housework. You won't have to do a thing. And I know this is crazy and hard for you, and maybe not the right time to say it, but I want to have a family with you, Alexa. I'd even have the kids for you if I could - or we can adopt if you'd rather, just please consider it. I'll make it easy for you. I'll make sure you never regret it. I promise."

"Bruce." She laughed. "I have so much more to tell you, too. Things I learned at the retreat. Things about me. Things about you. About architecture. About life! But right now, I just want you to shut up and kiss me!"

And he did.

∼

"They're gorgeous, Brucey."

Bruce grinned at his mother past the humongous bouquet of orange roses and pink hydrangeas and some other fragrant things he'd forgotten the name of, that Alexa had helped him order online, and had rush-delivered to the hospital. By helicopter probably.

He met Mom's gaze, and was relieved to see a sparkle in her green eyes, and some colour returned to her cheeks and lips. Despite the terrible scare, she was going to be fine. They'd run a dozen tests, kept her under observation overnight, and given her a bunch of new medications. She'd had a coronary artery spasm, not a full-on heart attack, but they were still checking for blockages to make sure it wasn't more serious than that.

Lawrence was reorganizing his small bag in anticipation of their imminent departure. "You're going to have to hold them on your lap all the way home!"

"I don't mind." Mom smiled again.

He knew it was a ridiculous bouquet. It had cost him over three hundred dollars. But he didn't care. He just wanted something extravagant to celebrate the fact that she was all right, to celebrate all that they'd been through and accomplished. To apologize for being an idiot and a jerk. And to mark the beginning of something new.

The night before they'd all spent hours and hours waiting around the hospital, for doctors to show up, and then for examinations and tests, until everyone was cranky, the kids were asleep and he and Alexa were just about there themselves. The nurses basically kicked them out by coming into Mom's room to set up a cot for Lawrence to sleep on. Then they'd checked into a nearby Best Western on the highway and collapsed in exhaustion.

"Well, if we're going to catch that ferry to Vancouver, we'd better head out," Alexa said, and approached Mom's bedside for a farewell hug. "Tina." She carefully leaned over the tubes and wires, and gently embraced her and kissed her cheek. "Thank you. For everything." Both Markus and Maddie had already been lifted up for their hugs and kisses, and were assured that Mom would be alright.

"Bye-bye Tina," Maddie said.

"Thank you for visiting me, Madison. Bye Markus." She waved.

Then Alexa hugged Lawrence, whose white teeth flashed as he said, "I expect we'll be seeing more of the both of you."

"You will. I promise. I'll be in touch next week, once I get settled."

"No rush, Alexa. We're a patient lot."

She laughed. "No reason to take advantage of you, Phra Lawrence." She touched her fingertips together and bowed.

"You bring my son with you when you visit the Hermitage."

"I will."

Bruce shook Lawrence's hand after kissing his mother on the forehead, and they were off down the corridor and out of the cardiology ward, each holding the hand of a child. Bruce's chest expanded with an unprecedented feeling of contentment and he grinned at Alexa.

"Please tell me you're going to take a few days off before you launch into a crazy work schedule," he said, pulling her close with an arm around her waist.

"Making demands already?" she teased.

"Yes. I am. After we hand these rascals back to their lucky parents, I want you all to myself for... oh, at least forty-eight hours." They stepped into the elevator, and as the doors drew closed, he dropped Markus's hand and pulled her in for a soul deep kiss with his hungry, searching tongue. There would be no mistaking what he wanted to spend forty-eight hours doing.

"Ew!" Maddie said. "Grosth."

"What, you've never seen your dad kiss Kate?" Bruce asked.

"They're more thivilized," she mumbled, rolling her eyes, and they laughed.

Driving to the ferry, and during the crossing, they talked about various details of their lives, but mostly Alexa shared with him her excitement about her projects and her new, about-to-be-minted architectural practice. They threw around a dozen clever names, and rejected them all in favour of *Alexa Jenner Architecture, Inc.*

She said she would work from home immediately until she found an office space, even though with two large projects she'd need a fairly big space to fit her new staff in.

"I've already told Pete. He's excited. But we talked about this for years. And Stephanie's a good bet but I haven't confirmed with her. Then I'll need to recruit an admin person and a couple of technicians, at least."

"I know you've saved some money for start-up, but I'd really like to help out by financing you to make the transition easy, to help you get launched in style. Let the world know you're a big deal. Furnishings and equipment, signs, stationery, whatever. You know I've got it."

"Thank you. But no. I really don't want a leg up from anyone. I'm going to do this myself."

"I'm not talking about charity. I want to invest in your business. What if I were a partner, a silent business partner. Then you'd have to be successful because I'd sue your ass if you lost my money."

She seemed to consider it. "It's better than a bank loan, in some ways. But then would the firm still be mine? I have to have controlling interest, since you're not an architect. Let me see."

"Alright. Hey, don't forget your firm has one more very important project to complete."

"No I don't. I'd remember that." She skewed her puzzled gaze at him.

"My... *our* house. The sooner it's done, the sooner we can move in, the sooner you can use your condo as an office."

She raised her brows. He knew he was pushing, and made a funny face to ease the pressure. They hadn't exactly discussed permanent cohabitation. She might need more time to think about that degree of commitment, but he didn't. He didn't want to lose a single opportunity to look at her gorgeous face, or kiss her, or hear her sexy voice, or hold her in his arms. "Interesting idea, but I'm pretty sure that's not an allowed use. I'll have to find another space, especially if I'm going to accommodate my people."

She'd neatly sidestepped the question, and he chuckled. "What's Kate doing with her old loft?"

"Hey, you're good with the bright ideas, Koz." She punched his bicep.

"See, you need to keep me around. I'm indispensable."

He leaned over and caressed the side of her face, planted a half dozen kisses on her, and gave her a discrete squeeze. He couldn't wait to get her alone. It was driving him insane. The chemistry between them bubbled as he drew out the kiss, until they both moaned softly under their breath, and he pulled away, their eyes locked and he caught his breath.

"Whew. What were we talking about?"

"I believe we were discussing how arrogant you are, Mister Indispensable. But… I can think of *one* thing you're good for."

He lowered his voice to a growl. "And what might that be?" He dipped his head and consumed her mouth again, until she gently pushed him away.

"You'll have to do the cooking."

He laughed. "For you, Al, my sweet, I'll become a five-star Michelin chef."

EPILOGUE

The day of Simon and Kate's return had finally arrived.

Alexa and Bruce and the kids drove to pick them up from the airport. To Alexa, it felt like a honeymoon, and she was almost surprised they had to stand around the arrivals lounge rather than board a plane for Hawaii or the south of France. It was just the bubble of elation that sat permanently in her chest. It made her giddy.

She and Bruce couldn't seem to stop talking. They, or maybe it was just she, was almost manic. But no, Bruce seemed very happy too. As if a huge weight had been lifted, they felt free to talk about anything. They shared stories from their childhood, and college days, they puzzled out a thousand practical details of their current lives, and they shared dreams of the future. Nothing was out of bounds.

"I'm very glad Daddy and Mommy are home," Madison sighed.

"Why's that Scallywag?" Bruce asked her, lifting her up and peering into her eyes.

"Becauth you guys are really boring now. You don't pay any attention to uth at all!"

"Alright then, let's see if they're here, hey?"

They shuffled through the crowd right up to the glass doors at international arrivals. Alexa held Markus up. He'd gotten so heavy over the past month he must have grown a lot. She hoped they arrive soon or her arms would give– oh! There was a beep-beep and crowd parted. There they were! "Look!" She pointed. Kate, looking more pregnant than ever, Simon, and his parents, and a tall stack of luggage were piled onto a club car, driven by an airport attendant. Simon's leg, in a cast, extended straight out on one open side, resting on the step. They wore grins from ear to ear.

"Daddy!" screeched Maddie.

"Mommy!" hollered Markus.

"Wow, she got huge!" said Bruce, and Alexa kicked his shin.

"She looks beautiful," Alexa countered. Though in truth, her best friend was pale, looked exhausted and seemed to have lost ten pounds, even though her pregnant belly was considerably more pronounced than when they left.

All at once they were there, climbing off the cart, and the six of them huddled together in a tangle as they pulled their children into their arms, kissed them, and attempted to hug and kiss Alexa and Bruce at the same time. Everyone spoke at once. They ended up laughing hysterically from the sheer silliness and joy of it.

After seeing Simon's parents into a taxicab, they, all squeezed into the SUV and drove back to the house. Alexa asked questions about Kate's health and pregnancy, which she tried to answer over the hubbub of both kids making noise and the men having a conversation of their own about their respective experiences. It wasn't more than ten minutes before either Alexa or Bruce had said something, she wasn't sure what, that gave away their new status. Conversation halted and the car fell silent.

"What's going on here?" Kate said.

"What?"

"Are you two together?" Simon asked, his tone implying nothing short of incredulity.

"It's true, Dad. All they do is kith, now." Maddie volunteered with a sneer.

"Are you kidding me?" Simon said and punched Bruce in the arm.

"Hey! I'm driving."

Then the excitement of their news and ensuing questions and answers filled the SUV the rest of the way home.

After unloading passengers and suitcases and cats and loading up the remainder of their own things, Alexa and Bruce prepared to take their leave so their friends could rest and enjoy their reunion with their children.

"Where are you going?" Kate asked at the door.

Alexa looked at Bruce with a question. "Um. My condo?"

He grinned. "Sounds like a plan. At least until the house is habitable. I'd rather stay with you than on my boat. And if I work hard, we can move in by the spring.

They turned to Madison and Markus, and a melancholy air overtook them both.

"I'm going to miss you guys so much," Alexa said, crouching to take Madison in her arms for a tight hug. Her throat and eyes were suddenly flooded with tears, and her face crumpled. "We had some adventures, didn't we?"

"I'll miss you, Auntie Al. Will you come and visit soon?"

"Of course I will, honey. I need to catch up with your mom, too, don't I?

"Booos!" Markus wailed, suddenly catching on that his beloved caregivers were leaving. He leaned out of Simon's arms and threw himself at Bruce, who lifted him into a full body embrace, wrapping his arms tightly around him.

Bruce buried his face in Markus's neck, sniffling. He mumbled, "You know I love you, don't you, little buddy?"

Seeing them made Alexa's tears flow more freely. Then Kate was crying too, and pulled Alexa into a hug, bumping her with her bulge.

Finally, they calmed a little and pulled away, setting the kids down.

"What about me?" Maddie whined.

Bruce rested his hand on her head and ruffled her messy brown curls. "I love you too, Scallywag. I'm going to miss you like crazy."

Madison said, "Are you guys gonna have your own kids so we can play together?"

Aware of Simon and Kate's stunned expressions, Alexa kept her mouth shut and lifted her brows. Bruce laughed and kissed her, then grinned at Maddie, saying, "Don't rush me, Scallywag. I'm working on it."

∼

WANT TO READ THE PREQUEL IN THE HAVING IT ALL SERIES?
BUY EBOOK ON AMAZON

WANT TO CONNECT WITH ME?

maryann (at) maryannclarkescott (dot) com
maryannclarkescott (dot) com

THANK YOU!

Want to read the FIRST Book in the Having it All Series?
Buy Ebook On Amazon

Want to connect with me?
maryann (at) maryannclarkescott (dot) com
maryannclarkescott (dot) com

If you enjoyed reading this book, please rate it and leave a review wherever you purchased the book. Your opinion can make or break an author's success, and it means the world to me.

Thank you to my writing colleagues and friends, who make the journey not only possible but fun. Thanks especially to those who helped nurture this book into existence, including beta readers, critique partners and editors Susan Lyons, The Mavens Joanna Drake, Donna Barker and Michele Fogal, Heather Toews and John Scott.

As always, thanks to my family for your unfailing support while I toil away and neglect your needs for attention, nutritious meals and a clean house. Thanks for being troopers.

Finally, thank you to my readers. Without you, this is just one very laborious and expensive hobby. Thanks for buying and reading books, and for your enthusiastic support through reviews and social media. I love to hear from you so keep it up! You make it all worthwhile.

XO, MaryAnn

BOOK CLUB DISCUSSION QUESTIONS

1. Alexa is initially portrayed as an unsympathetic, hard career-focused women. Do you think it necessary for an ambitious career woman to make sacrifices to their personal lives or do you think this is a myth? Can you Lean In and Have it All at the same time?
2. Do you think some women project a harder image in order to compete in their professional environments or is it that serious ambitious women are perceived as bitches? Is this fair?
3. What is your opinion of office romances? Do you think Alexa and Krystof crossed a taboo line when they had an affair? Do you think Krystof exploited his position of power?
4. How would you have dealt with the client lunch where Alexa was sidelined by the old-boys club?
5. Do you think Bruce's career burn-out is a common experience for successful men? Do you think more would quit if they had the money to do so?
6. Alexa reconnects with her passion for design while at a retreat at the Buddhist monastery. Do you think her decision to venture out on her own instead of fighting to succeed at an established larger firm was a career cop-out? Do you think self-employment for women is a good way to deal with sexism in the workplace?

ALSO BY MARYANN CLARKE

Be Mine This Time
Book 1 in the Having it All series

ALSO BY MARYANN CLARKE

The Art of Enchantment

A Forged Affair

Books 1 & 2 in the Life is a Journey series

SAMPLE CHAPTER OF BEFORE YOU KNEW ME

Never one to shirk her duty, or shy away from a task, however unpleasant, if it served her purpose or was the right thing to do, Sharon was back in the office and sitting in front of Meacham's desk five minutes before the new client was due. In truth she was hoping if she sat there staring at the old man, he'd give her a clue as to the nature of the project before they walked in the door, so she could mentally prepare herself.

Clearly he had other ideas. He also had no problem sitting stoically examine briefs while she sat across from him trying not to squirm. Thankfully, the receptionist knocked and showed them in right on time.

A middle-aged woman entered, and Sharon stood to greet her while her mind quickly took in pertinent details. As it was a *pro-bono* case, she hadn't been expecting a corporate fancy. But this woman was extremely down-to-earth, in an inexpensive sweater tunic over black leggings and practical grey running shoes. Her salt-and-pepper hair was cut short like a man's, her smooth square brown face unadorned by makeup, though she wore a pair of wire-rimmed glasses over her sharp black eyes that gave her a professorial air. Crinkled corners belied her serious manner in the moment. This was a woman with wisdom and heart.

Meacham stood as well, and his stern old face lit up with a rare genuine smile. Obviously the woman was an old friend and that's why he'd taken on her case.

"Christine, come in!" he boomed, clasping her hand between his. "Sit down. It's good to see you."

"Hello, Arthur," she said. "It's you who's being good, as ever. Thanks for doing this."

"Anything for you, my dear. Anything to help you in your ambitious work."

"Sharon this is my old friend Christine Watts, with the Pathway Society."

Sharon's curiosity piqued, she offered her hand to the interesting woman and introduced herself.

"I'm giving you Sharon Beckett for the duration, and I know she'll do right by you and your organization, Christine. She'll leave no stone unturned. I trust her completely, and so can you."

That was news to Sharon, but she kept her editorial thoughts to herself.

Christine murmured as she sat down, "I hope it doesn't require too much of your valuable time, Sharon," without meeting Sharon's gaze, and a tiny red flag went up. This was supposed to be a quick and simple favour, *wasn't it*?

Sharon was about to take her seat again as Christine sat when she noticed a tall young urban lumberjack in a hoody step silently in behind her.

She flinched and caught her breath. "Oh! Hello!"

"This is Kent Sawyer," Christine said. "He works for me, and he's been spearheading the project, so Sharon will work extensively with him when I'm busy with the kids, which is most of the time. I haven't the time to devote to the project that I would wish and still keep the operation running. But Kent is on top of everything."

Sharon stepped behind Christine's chair and offered her hand to shake, looking up, way up at his lean, broad-shouldered form, kicking the part of her sex-starved brain that heckled, *everything?* The sullen man merely inclined his head with a jerk of his chin and a bare grunt of acknowledgement, not even removing the hands thrust into the front pockets of his wrinkled tan chinos. She frowned in confusion and withdrew her hand. She'd be liaising with him?

He didn't look old enough to have a position of responsibility, never mind run a project. Was he some kind of student trainee? His hood shadowed his eyes, so all she could really see was his scowling mouth and scruffy brown beard. For whatever reason, he was profoundly unhappy to be here. Irritation radiated off of him in waves.

Sharon cleared her throat and slipped past him to drag a third chair over from the side of Meacham's expansive office, turning it and offering it to him. Kent. Kent Sawyer.

He mumbled his thanks, grabbing the chair from her to adjust its position before sitting, his long-fingers momentarily brushing hers before she could withdraw them from the chair's back.

His fleeting touch sent a jolt of electricity shooting up her arm, and she jerked her hand back, glowering at her knuckles in confusion, as though she'd been burnt. The jolt had not been mere static electricity, but something organic, cosmic and far more powerful, zinging through her nervous system and shaking her down to the soles of her feet.

She glanced up, curious, to catch his sharp amber eyes flickering to her face. His eyes flashed in recognition of the moment. He'd felt it too.

Her breath came fast and shallow. Her pulse raced. Her thoughts scattered.

She dropped her gaze, taking in his long legs to see that he wore an extremely beat-up pair of brown leather Blundstone boots. They looked like he'd worn them every day for a hundred years.

How could the mere touch of a man, an inappropriate, unattractive man at that, stir such violent excitement in her, instantly liquifying all her lady parts? He wasn't in any way the kind of man she was attracted to. He wasn't wearing a designer suit, for one. In fact he was poorly groomed. Maybe even unclean by the look of him. He had horrible manners and no discernible communication skills. And as if all that wasn't enough, he was probably a decade younger than her. She hadn't even got a good look at his face. She'd admired many a man in her day, crushed on a few, but never had she encountered one that rendered her speechless with pure unadulterated lust.

No. Just no!

She had standards, for one thing. And he didn't even come close.

Blinking, she stole another glance at his face to find his angry gaze still riveted on her face, staring back at her. Their eyes met, his intense golden brown eyes radiating both maturity and intelligence, as well as confusion and curiosity that matched her own, for a split second his angry scowl gone. This time the zing of connection hit her through their linked gazes sending alarm signals through her nervous system, triggering small explosions in her throat, chest and core. In that suspended moment, Sharon thought she knew him from somewhere, he felt so familiar. But instantly the scowl returned, his Adam's apple bobbed, he nodded curtly and turned away to sit down.

Well, at least he wasn't quite as young or as dull-witted as she'd originally thought. But who or what was he, exactly?

She sat, mentally shaking herself to bring her focus back to the meeting. Christine was already talking to Meacham and Sharon couldn't afford to miss a single nuanced detail if she was going to do this right.

Even if she had to work with *him*!

Alright kid. You might not think you need me, but I need to know that you haven't fucked this up.

Kent Sawyer grabbed his leather jacket as he raced out the door, almost crashing into his coworker Sofia and knocking her over. They steadied each other with a half hug. "Hey Sofia, have you seen Harley?"

"Oh hi, Kent, no I haven't today. Do you have time for coffee?"

"Thanks, maybe later. I just wanna make sure he's OK before I start my day." He strode down the empty sidewalk along East Hastings Street, carefully examining the filthy piles of clothing and mounded tarps that kept some of the six thousand local residents warm overnight.

Where the hell was he? It had been two days already. Something churned in his stomach as the possible explanations spun through his mind like a flickering slide show. In the Downtown Eastside of Vancouver where he worked, none of them were good. That's why he insisted Harley check in with him at least once a day. That way, no matter what he got up to, Kent could keep him from the worst trouble.

He stopped once to peer behind a fully loaded shopping cart into the shadowy alley beyond to make sure Harley hadn't curled up with old Carl again, but the old man was already up and out, probably scouring the bins for recyclables before anyone else could strip them of his day's wages.

Not everyone slept on the street, but there were enough of them that it made it darned hard to track people down sometimes. Moreso if they didn't care to be found.

SAMPLE CHAPTER OF BEFORE YOU KNEW ME

Kent turned down Dunlevy Street and passed Oppenheimer Park, continuing to scan the streets without luck. His long legs took him quickly along Cordova, until he arrived at the door of the safe injection site on Hastings where he knew his mother would have hot coffee brewing for her clients.

Sure enough the door was open and already she had customers, though at this time of day they were probably here for the coffee. As he turned in he met a tall hunched youth who went by the name of the Fiddle for some reason he hadn't yet figured out.

"Morning, Fiddle. Did you see Harley last night?"

Instead of replying, Fiddle's eyes widened and his gaze darted out the door. He sped up, scuttling away from Kent. That was as good as a maybe as far as Kent was concerned, although if he just shot up, he may not have even registered the question. Which worried him, because he didn't like the company that Fiddle kept, and that could mean that Harley was hanging out with the wrong crowd again, too.

"Good morning darling," his mother called from behind her desk at the front of the spartan interior. "Were you up all night?"

He moved toward her, bent and kissed her cheek. "No, Mom. Just getting an early start. Did you happen to see Harley on your way in?" He walked to the coffee pot to one side of the waiting area and pour himself a cup. He was going to need it today.

"Don't you have some paperwork to do?" she said, giving him the side eye.

"Always." He filled his lungs and let out a long exasperated sigh, letting go of some of the tension that rode his shoulders night and day. "You know I just need to know he's OK."

"I know, Sweetheart, but he's not your responsibility anymore. If you wanted to do casework, you should've stayed with the ministry."

"You know I couldn't stand all the bureaucracy, and speaking of paperwork..."

He rolled his eyes, knowing there was no need to reiterate his gripes. His mother knew what he was talking about, as he well knew. Nurses had as much bureaucratic bullshit to deal with as social workers, as the pile of folders on his mother's desk attested.

"However," he added, "it turns out that project development brings its own host of administrative hassles. Thankfully Christine is happy to handle most of that."

"So what's your job then?"

"Looks like I'm spearheading approvals, lobbying. Community liaison. Getting the development permits is turning out to be more complicated than we realized when we started this project."

Mom looked up, a question in her eyes.

"Yeah, seems that another group has applied to the city to develop the same site. So now we're in competition and have to justify our existence." Just saying the words made his blood boil. The fact that a nonprofit group had to take the lead on a shelter for vulnerable street kids because the government wouldn't do anything was a major burr in his side. Now this.

A cluster of hungry-looking clients clambered noisily into his Mom's tiny clinic, suddenly making conversation impossible. She was intent on feeding them muffins and coffee as much as making safe injection available and her attention was torn.

Leaving her to do her own good work, he waved goodbye and slipped out to continue his search for Harley before meeting Christine at the godforsaken lawyers' office.

It was bad enough having to coordinate this project, work with designers, and raise the money. Now they had to fight for the right to do so.

End of sample - Before you knew me will be released early in 2020.

ABOUT THE AUTHOR

MaryAnn Clarke is a Chatelaine Grand Prize winner and Next Generation Indie Book Award finalist for The Art of Enchantment, first in the Life is a Journey series about young women on journeys abroad who discover themselves and fall in love while getting embroiled in someone else's problems. Her Having it All series is about professional women struggling to balance the challenge and fulfillment of their careers with their search for identity, love, family and home.

Always eager to fill blank pages and empty canvases with ideas swirling in her head, MaryAnn set out to write emotionally engaging stories that walk a tight rope between intelligent Women's Fiction and heart-warming Romance.

A polymath who studied Fine Arts, Urbanism, Architecture and Gerontology at university on both coasts of Canada, she turned to her first love, writing stories, when she realized she could have more fun with fewer rules to follow as an author, than working in an office as an architect, or in a university as a researcher. When not writing, she meditates while hiking wooded mountain trails, does yoga and Pilates to fend off decrepitude, reads eclectically, contemplates wormholes, experiments with painting abstract expressionism, kills plants and tries not to burn dinner while solving her next plot problem. Now that her chick has flown the coop, Clarke lives on beautiful Vancouver Island, Canada with her husband and cats. Although she knows she lives in Paradise, she still loves traveling the world in search of romance, art, good food and new story ideas.

Stay in touch to hear book news, special deals and updates about her next release- Before You Knew Me, Book 3 in the Having it All Series. You can always reach MaryAnn at maryann (at) maryannclarkescott (dot) com

WANT TO READ THE LATEST BOOK IN THE LIFE IS A JOURNEY SERIES?

BUY A FORGED AFFAIR : mybook (dot) to/Forged

WANT TO CONNECT WITH ME?
maryann (at) maryannclarkescott (dot) com
maryannclarkescott (dot) com

If you enjoy reading this book, please rate it and leave a review on Amazon or wherever you purchased the book. Your opinion can make or break an author's success, and it means the world to me.

Subscribe & Follow MaryAnn!
maryannclarkescott (dot) com
Question? Fan mail? Sure, you can find me here.

www.ingramcontent.com/pod-product-compliance
Lightning Source LLC
Chambersburg PA
CBHW020513080526
44583CB00013B/580